Kupilikula

Kupilikula

Governance and the Invisible Realm in Mozambique

Harry G. West

Based on research conducted in collaboration with
Marcos Agostinho Mandumbwe

and with assistance from
Eusébio Tissa Kairo *and* Felista Elias Mkaima

The University of Chicago Press
Chicago and London

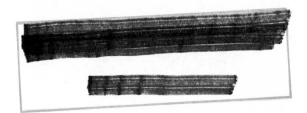

Harry G. West is lecturer in social anthropology in the School of Oriental and African Studies, University of London. He is the author of numerous articles and book chapters, and editor or coeditor of two previous volumes, including *Transparency and Conspiracy: Ethnographies of Suspicion in the New World Order.*

The University of Chicago Press, Chicago 60637
The University of Chicago Press, Ltd., London
© 2005 by The University of Chicago
All rights reserved. Published 2005
Printed in the United States of America
14 13 12 11 10 09 08 07 06 05   5 4 3 2 1

ISBN (cloth): 0-226-89404-5
ISBN (paper): 0-226-89405-3

Library of Congress Cataloging-in-Publication Data

West, Harry G.
    Kupilikula : governance and the invisible realm in Mozambique / Harry G. West ; based on research conducted in collaboration with Marcos Agostinho Mandumbwe and with assistance from Eusébio Tissa Kairo and Felista Elias Mkaima.
        p.   cm.
    Includes bibliographical references and index.
    ISBN 0-226-89404-5 (cloth : alk. paper) — ISBN 0-226-89405-3 (pbk : alk. paper)
    1. Makonde (African people)—Rites and ceremonies.   2. Makonde (African people)—Religion.   3. Makonde (African people)—Politics and government. 4. Witchcraft—Mozambique—Mueda District.   5. Magic—Mozambique—Mueda District.   6. Mueda District (Mozambique)—Social conditions.   7. Mueda District (Mozambique)—Politics and government.   I. Title.
    DT3328.M35W47   2005
    305.896′397—dc22

                                                                2004030815

Dedicated to the memory of
Maria Consolata Agostinho Mandumbwe

Contents

Acknowledgments

This book brings to fruition a project that has occupied me for more than a decade, and it has been my enormous good fortune over this time to labor in the company of so many talented and generous people. Indeed, taking stock of the many individuals and institutions that have rendered me assistance in this project is a truly humbling experience.

The Land Tenure Center at the University of Wisconsin–Madison provided me with opportunities and financial resources as I completed my graduate studies and undertook preliminary field research in Mozambique. My dissertation research was funded by the Fulbright-Hays Doctoral Dissertation Research Abroad Fellowship Program, the United States Institute of Peace Jennings Randolph Peace Scholar Dissertation Fellowship Program, and the Wenner-Gren Foundation for Anthropological Research Inc. Dissertation Fieldwork Grants Program. A grant from the Calouste Gulbenkian Foundation funded archival research in Lisbon. I received additional support in the form of a Charlotte W. Newcombe Doctoral Dissertation Fellowship (administered by the Woodrow Wilson National Fellowship Foundation) and a grant from the Institute for the Study of World Politics while writing my dissertation as an affiliate of the Carter G. Woodson Institute at the University of Virginia. Further field research on the Mueda plateau was funded by the Economic and Social Research Council (United Kingdom) and by the British Academy. An American Council of Learned Societies/Social Science Research Council/National Endowment for the Humanities International and Area Studies Fellowship, along with a Postdoctoral Fellowship from the Program in Agrarian Studies at Yale University, created both the financial conditions and the intellectual environment in which to produce the manuscript. The

School of Oriental and African Studies (University of London) provided assistance toward the production of the final manuscript.

As a Fulbright-Hays Fellow, I was assisted in Mozambique by the Maputo
office of the United States Information Service. The Land Tenure Center also
provided continuing logistical support. The Departments of Anthropology
and History at Universidade Eduardo Mondlane served as my institutional
host in Mozambique. The Pemba offices of the Arquivos do Património Cultural and the Associação dos Combatentes da Luta de Libertação Nacional facilitated my work in Cabo Delgado by identifying within their ranks key
people with whom I was able to collaborate. On the Mueda plateau, I was
aided not only by the offices of District Administration and the FRELIMO
Party in Mueda, Muidumbe, and Nangade Districts but also by the United Nations Mission to Mozambique (ONUMOZ), the Cabo Delgado Oxfam UK
project, the directors of the Mueda SIL International project, and the Catholic
mission at Nang'ololo.

Although the individuals who have assisted me are innumerable, I wish to
recognize those whose contributions to my project have been greatest: Joce-
lyn Alexander, Maria José Artur, João Baptista Cosme, Aleixo Batime, Teresa
Berry, João Paulo Borges Coelho, Margaret Bothwell, David Brent, John Bruce,
Father João Brunninks, Pamela Bruton, José Luís Cabaço, João Carrilho, Is-
abel Casimiro, Sven Cawley, Sister Rosa Carla Cazzaninga, Arlindo Chilundo,
Amanda Coleman, Chris Colvin, John Comaroff, Rafael da Conceição, Margot
Dias, Nuno Domingos, Elizabeth Branch Dyson, Matthew Engelke, Angelo
Fernandes, Richard Flores, Peter Geschiere, Carol Greenhouse, Patty Grubb,
David Hedges, Lorraine Herbst, Alcinda Honwana, Sharon Hutchinson, José
Kathupa, Shelley Khadem, Scott Kloeck-Jenson, Catherine Lawrence, Benjie
and Rhoda Leach, Óscar Limbombo, Marcelino Liphola, Ana Loforte, Nicole
Lorenzini, Tracy Luedke, Luís Madureira, Adriano Malache, Kay Mansfield,
Boaventura Massiette, Aguiar Mazula, Asubugy Meagy, Ratna Menon, Lázaro
Mmala, Rafael Mpachoka, Estêvão Mpalume, Father Elias Pedro Mwakala,
Rafael Pedro Mwakala, Father Amaro Mwitu, Gregory Myers, António Nativi-
dade, Maria Luísa Natividade, Sister Ângela Lucas Ng'avanga, Severino
Ngole, Fernando Nhantumbo, Raimundo Pachinuapa, Deborah Poole, Ro-
drigues Quicho, Rayna Rapp, Glenn Ratcliffe, Camilla Roman, Todd Sanders,
Michael Schatzberg, Lee Schoen, Jim Scott, David Smith, Lois Woestman, Eric
Worby, and two anonymous readers.

The contributions made to this work by Marcos Agostinho Mandumbwe,
Eusébio Tissa Kairo, and Felista Elias Mkaima are too great to be recognized
only here; their appearances within the pages of this book, and on the title
page, speak for themselves. They not only guided me on the path toward

completion of this project but also embraced it as their own. Moreover, they shared with me the joys, aspirations, and sorrows that defined their lives and partook of those that defined mine. Their families have become mine, and mine theirs, giving rise to an ever-increasing number of namesakes among the most recent generation. Among my fondest memories are times spent sharing food and conversation with them at the end of a day "in the field." I thank them for their fellowship during the many years we have worked together.

The families who hosted us in the many plateau villages in which we conducted research, and the people with whom we spoke and otherwise interacted, are too numerous to be named here; a great many of them appear by name in the text. In any case, I thank them all for allowing me to spend time with them and learn from them.

Lastly, I wish to thank my own *likola*—Mom, Dad, Aunt Lois, Anita, Denny, Paul, Amy, and Mark—for their many expressions of pride and confidence in me; and my partner, Catherine, for her enduring and empowering patience, encouragement, and affection.

⚏

Earlier versions of a number of passages in this book have appeared in the following articles: "A Piece of Land in a Land of Peace? State Farm Divestiture in Mozambique," *Journal of Modern African Studies* 34, no. 1 (1996): 27–51, coauthored with Gregory W. Myers; "Creative Destruction and Sorcery of Construction: Power, Hope, and Suspicion in Post-war Mozambique," *Cahiers d'Études Africaines* 37, no. 147 (1997): 675–698; "'This Neighbor Is Not My Uncle!' Changing Relations of Power and Authority on the Mueda Plateau," *Journal of Southern African Studies* 24, no. 1 (1998): 141–160; "Betwixt and Between: 'Traditional Authority' and Democratic Decentralization in Post-war Mozambique," *African Affairs* 98, no. 393 (1999): 455–484, coauthored with Scott Kloeck-Jenson, reprinted by permission of Oxford University Press; "Girls with Guns: Narrating the Experience of War of FRELIMO's 'Female Detachment,'" *Anthropological Quarterly* 73, no. 4 (2000): 180–194; "Sorcery of Construction and Socialist Modernization: Ways of Understanding Power in Post-colonial Mozambique," *American Ethnologist* 28, no. 1 (2001): 119–150, © The American Anthropological Association, reprinted by permission of the University of California Press; "Voices Twice Silenced: Betrayal and Mourning at Colonialism's End in Mozambique," *Anthropological Theory* 3, no. 3 (2003): 339–361, reprinted by permission of Sage Publications Ltd; "Power Revealed and Concealed in the New World Order," coauthored with Todd Sanders, and "Tax Receipts, Virgin Mary Medallions, and Party

Membership Cards: (In)visible Tokens of Power on the Mueda Plateau," both in *Transparency and Conspiracy: Ethnographies of Suspicion in the New World Order,* ed. Harry G. West and Todd Sanders (Durham, NC: Duke University Press, 2003); "Inverting the Camel's Hump: Jorge Dias, His Wife, Their Interpreter, and I," in *Significant Others: Interpersonal and Professional Commitments in Anthropology,* edited by R. Handler (Madison, 2004), reprinted by permission of The University of Wisconsin Press; "Villains, Victims, or Makonde in the Making? Reading the Explorer, Henry O'Neill, and Listening to the Headman, Lishehe," *Ethnohistory* 51, no. 1 (2004): 1–43.

Prologue

Immaterial Evidence

"We looked everywhere in the man's house," Simão said, "but we never did find the materials that he used to make them." He forced a smile. "The guy was clever, you know."

"But he *had* made them?" asked Marcos.

"Everyone knew that he had made them," Simão replied. "*Vantumi va ku mwitu* [bush lions] don't behave the way those lions did. Those were *vantumi va kuvapika* [fabricated lions]!"

Marcos and I were sharing an afternoon meal of butter beans and *ugwali* (porridge) with Simão Benjamim, the locality president in Miula. As Marcos later observed, Simão was rather young to hold such a position of authority. Marcos had in fact informed me when Simão and I were first introduced that Simão had been a primary school student under Marcos's charge in one of the bush schools in the liberated zones during the war for Mozambican independence (1964–1974). The young Simão, however, was a man of considerable self-assurance. The "I Love Vegemite" T-shirt that he wore was a bright, clean white. His smile was broad, and his posture relaxed. While Simão treated us, his guests, with respect, he also sought to be treated by us as a fellow man of learning. He had continued studying after the war. He had taught elementary school for a time but eventually underwent training for a career in state administration.

"It's a good career," he told us, "but it's difficult living out here all the time."

He looked each of us in the eye and then gazed out over the village square beyond the yard of his house. Women, dressed in faded *capulanas*,[1] queued by the standpipe with twenty-liter tin buckets. Men in tattered T-shirts and frayed trousers clustered around a wooden table awaiting cash from a representative of one of the shops in Mueda town for the fifty-kilo sacks of maize that they had brought to market.

"There's a lot of ignorance in these villages," Simão said. "No one is interested in learning. It's rare that I get the chance to have an intelligent conversation with people like you."

Notwithstanding his mild condescension, Simão, we discovered, was well liked by the villagers under his jurisdiction. He governed with diplomatic finesse and good humor. He also conversed with great skill, endearing him to villagers and visitors alike.

As Simão's wife deposited two plates on the ground before us, I asked him how he had ended up in Miula. His arrival, he explained, was intertwined with strange events in one of the villages under his charge.

"I was posted here just this year [1999], near the end of the rains in April." He leaned forward in his seat and pushed the plates closer to his guests' feet. "My predecessor had failed to resolve a delicate situation in the village of Kilimani. I was told to make it my first priority."

"Tell us about it," Marcos responded, digging his fingers into the common plate of *ugwali* sitting on the ground before us, molding a ball of porridge in his hand, and dipping it in the plate of beans.

Simão followed suit, placing a moistened ball of *ugwali* in his mouth before responding. "The problem first came to our attention when the people of Kilimani sent a letter to the district administrator reporting the appearance in the village of several lions."

"What kind of lions?" Marcos asked, knowing that the story depended upon the answer to this question.

"That's just it," Simão replied. "The villagers accused a fellow resident of making the lions and of using them to threaten his neighbors."

"What did the district administrator do?" I asked Simão as I dabbed the bean plate with a ball of *ugwali*.

"He sent word to the village, by way of my predecessor, that the villagers would have to resolve the situation among themselves."

"And did they?" I asked.

"No," Simão said, as if such an outcome were not likely. "It only got worse. The lions continued to appear, and the villagers became more and more upset."

"What happened then?" I asked.

"My predecessor instructed the villagers to cease their hostilities, but they continued. That's when I was sent to replace him."

Marcos and I sat, transfixed, waiting for Simão to continue his account. He just laughed, nervously, until Marcos blurted out, "So what did you do?!"

We all leaned in over the half-eaten plates of food, as if conspiring together.

"I went and talked with the villagers to try to figure out what was going on. I realized that the situation was very grave. So I summoned a council of elders from the village to hear the case. I also asked a few elders from outside the village to attend: the village presidents of Miula and Chicalanga, and the elder Shindambwanda."

"Shindambwanda, the *nkulaula* [healer]?" Marcos asked, with irrepressible glee. We had worked closely with Shindambwanda in recent days, learning from this respected healer what we could about *uwavi* (sorcery) and learning from others that Shindambwanda was himself suspected of being a powerful *mwavi* (sorcerer).

"Yes," Simão replied matter-of-factly. He paused for a moment, perhaps to compose his narrative, perhaps for dramatic effect. He continued: "Many people testified that the lions that were menacing the village had been made by the accused man, but no one could produce any material evidence."

"What kind of evidence were you looking for?" I asked.

"They say that to make such lions, you need certain things . . . certain kinds of *mitela* [medicinal substances] . . ."

"*Dimika?*" I said.

"Eeh-hee," Simão said in confirmation, "but no one ever found anything."

We finished the food before us. Marcos found the bowl of water that Simão's wife had quietly place behind us as we had been eating and held it for me until I had rinsed my hands. I then took the bowl and held it for him. Simão took his turn washing his hands while measuring his words. He then said, solemnly: "There was no evidence, but the elders were certain that the man was guilty. I knew that if I did not intervene, someone would die. In these kinds of situations, villagers take justice into their own hands. So, I facilitated a settlement."

"What kind of settlement?" I asked.

"The accused man was fined and transferred to Chicalanga."

"Did that resolve the problem?" Marcos asked.

"Yes," Simão answered with only partial satisfaction. "The lions have disappeared from Kilimani."

"And the man who was moved to Chicalanga?" I asked.

"He's not causing problems for anyone there," Simão answered, simply.

***

The events that brought Simão Benjamim to Kilimani at the end of the rainy season in 1999 were not without precedent on the Mueda plateau. During time spent in the Mueda plateau region (between 1993 and 2004) conducting ethnographic field research, I heard hundreds of accounts of lions made by sorcerers or of sorcerers who transformed themselves into lions. I huddled around cooking fires at night as Muedans speculated on the identities of the sorcerers behind such beasts and on the identities of their intended victims. I passed time with medicinal specialists who told me what they knew of the methods used by sorcerers to accomplish these feats and who shared with me what they were willing of the techniques that they used to render these lions vulnerable to hunters' arrows or bullets.

Indeed, the residents of the Mueda plateau, who mostly identify themselves ethnically as Makonde, have known of *vantumi va kuvapika* (fabricated lions) for as long as the living can remember.[2] The accounts of sorcery that Muedans have provided to me in recent years reinforce what I have read in the literature about the Muedan past. António Jorge Dias and Margot Schmidt Dias—anthropologists working among the Makonde of Mueda in the late 1950s—reported that their informants spoke to them of sorcerers' lions, which could not be distinguished from ordinary lions except by a few specialists in possession of the medicinal substances and the knowledge needed to detect and overcome such beasts (Dias and Dias 1970: 363). Dias and Dias also reported being told on one occasion that the mauled remains of a lion's victim, discovered in a plateau village while they were conducting their research, were illusory; the victim's true body, they were told, was being held in the home of the sorcerer who produced the lion and would be eaten by this man in due course (1970: 369).

To fully appreciate the significance of the Kilimani case, however, one must consider it within its immediate sociohistorical context. Only a few years earlier, the villagers of Kilimani would not have dared to send a letter to the district administrator accusing one in their midst of sorcery. From the beginning of its guerrilla campaign to liberate Mozambique from Portuguese colonial rule, the leadership of the Mozambican Liberation Front (Frente de Libertação de Moçambique, or FRELIMO) vigorously condemned what it categorized as "obscurantist" beliefs and practices, including those associated with sorcery. Both during the war and after—when FRELIMO rose to power over the newly independent Mozambique in 1975—FRELIMO leaders enforced policies that banned divination (to determine the identity of sorcerers), sorcery trials, and countersorcery prophylaxis and healing. FRELIMO leaders considered each of these practices to be counterrevolutionary forms of "false consciousness." Those who persisted in speaking openly about sorcery or who engaged in sorcery or countersorcery practices were punished by the state, at times with extreme severity.

What is more, a few years earlier, a FRELIMO locality president such as Simão would not have allowed a village-level council of elders to play so central a role in the resolution of a conflict like the one he encountered in his first days on the job in Miula. These elders derived power from their positions atop political institutions organized according to the principles of kinship. From its inception, FRELIMO looked upon such authority figures with deep suspicion. The Portuguese colonial policy of using local "chiefs" as administrative intermediaries rendered these institutions corrupt and illegitimate, according to FRELIMO pronouncements. Throughout the independence war, FRELIMO excluded holders of these titles—at least as such—from formal positions of authority in the guerrilla command structure. Upon independence, the FRELIMO government banned the chieftaincy altogether, establishing local organs of state intended to supplant chiefs' authority on matters such as land distribution and the settlement of intra- and interfamily disputes. FRELIMO also banned rites of initiation and ancestral supplication and the control of sorcery/witchcraft, ritual practices through which the authority of chiefs had been consolidated.

When I first began research on the Mueda plateau, Muedans hesitated to speak openly about sorcery-related topics, in no small measure because local officials had prohibited them from doing so for more than twenty-five years. Immediately before I went to Mueda, I was told by Isabel Casimiro, a Mozambican researcher at the African Studies Center (Centro de Estudos Africanos, or CEA) at the Eduardo Mondlane University (Universidade Eduardo Mondlane, or UEM), that a recent CEA research project had tried to investigate the significance of "phantom lions" in Mueda but had failed in its attempts to get people to talk about the phenomenon. All this was to change, however, as the historical events that defined Mozambique while I was in the field made it possible for Muedans once more to speak candidly among themselves, and with others, about sorcery.

After sixteen years of devastating civil war (1977–1992) following independence, the FRELIMO government and the leadership of the Mozambican National Resistance (Resistência Nacional Moçambicana, or RENAMO) reached an accord in October of 1992. As I began fieldwork on the Mueda plateau in early 1994, Mozambicans prepared for the first multiparty elections in the nation's history. RENAMO had few supporters in Mueda—a region sometimes called the cradle of the FRELIMO revolution because FRELIMO had maintained its central base there during the independence campaign and because so many Muedans had fought for FRELIMO against the Portuguese. Even so, the civil war contributed substantially to the collapse of FRELIMO's program for "socialist modernization" in Mueda, as elsewhere in Mozambique.

As the warring parties approached a settlement, FRELIMO had abandoned its commitment to Marxism-Leninism, adopted economic austerity measures that would eventually meet with the acceptance of the International Monetary Fund (IMF), and amended the constitution to permit the formation of multiple political parties. With the end of the Cold War and with the disappearance of Soviet and Eastern-bloc assistance, Mozambique had quickly became reliant upon Western donor nations and international relief and development agencies to facilitate the peace process and to help rebuild the nation's damaged infrastructure. Now, while donors pressed the Mozambican government toward "democratic decentralization," development practitioners sought to reinvigorate Mozambican "civil society." In rural Mozambique, where the post-independence socialist state had either co-opted or repressed many of the institutions that Western donors might have considered elements of civil society, officials and development workers alike began to entertain the idea that "traditional authorities" might indeed constitute a Mozambican form of civil society.

Researchers working for a donor-funded project housed within the walls of the Mozambican Ministry of State Administration suggested that "traditional authorities" potentially embodied a distinctive sort of African democracy, allowing for local-level governance through culturally sanctioned consensual processes. As such, it was argued, they might readily serve the nation as means for the expression of "the will of the people" in rural areas. Because the RENAMO insurgency had resuscitated "traditional authority" in the areas of the country that it came to control during the war—albeit often by appointing as "chiefs" local individuals of their confidence who may or may not have had historical or hereditary claims to the position—and because RENAMO had used these authorities effectively as administrative intermediaries, some in the ruling FRELIMO party began to consider politically expedient cultivation of the support of this influential constituency in the new democratic era.

Simultaneously, officials in the Ministry of Health, in conversation with development consultants and practitioners, began to entertain the notion that "traditional healers" might be able to play a role in the reconstruction of rural health care networks that had been almost completely destroyed during the war. Along with democratic decentralization, Western donors celebrated local initiative and autonomy wherever it might be found. Traditional healers, many argued, had survived years of government repression and had filled the gaps in rural health care created by wartime shortages of trained medical personnel and medical supplies. They were, many suggested, the respected bearers of a detailed knowledge of the local pharmacopoeia, and with proper training they might serve to extend the reach of "modern" health care further into rural communities than otherwise possible.

It was, then, with these ongoing changes as background that Simão Benjamim convened the Kilimani council of elders.

⁂

Only days after Marcos and I heard from Simão about events in Kilimani, we had the opportunity to speak with Simão's superior, Mueda District Administrator Ambrósio Vicente Bulasi. Ambrósio, as everyone in Mueda called him, was only a few years older than Simão, but he fashioned himself as far more cosmopolitan.[3] The sleepy little town of Mueda moved at great speed in his immediate environs. When we approached him in the administration building, he suggested that we meet in the evening at his home, where things were calmer. When we arrived, he was powering up the generator in his yard—one of only two in the town of Mueda. He invited us to sit on the verandah while he attended to several individuals who, having failed to gain an audience with him at his office, now waited in ambush for him at his home.

After instructing a young woman inside the house to bring beer for us, he finally joined us. We shouted back and forth under dim lights as the generator roared. Ambrósio apologized because the beer—having sat all day in a refrigerator without power—was warm.

After discussing other topics, I mentioned Kilimani to Ambrósio and asked him if it was difficult to handle such situations. He laughed and waved his hand dismissively.

"Let me tell you something," he said. "These kinds of things happen all the time."

He raised his glass, said, "*Saúde*" (To your health), and continued. "Only today, I received a letter from villagers in Chappa telling me that a chick with four feet had hatched. The villagers were convinced that it was because of sorcery. The letter ended, 'We await your instructions.'"

He laughed, as did we.

"The trick to governing in a place like this is knowing how to dress for each occasion," he said, as he unconsciously slipped his hand between the buttons of his dusty silk shirt and readjusted the way it hung over his shoulders. "You don't put on your Sunday clothes to go work in your *machamba* [fields], do you? You put on your work clothes."

I looked at him inquisitively.

"It's essential, here, to find a balance between *scientific governance* and *local tradition*," he responded.

Only when Ambrósio arose did I notice the man standing behind us in the yard. Ambrósio excused himself for several minutes before returning.

"I have persuaded the director of the roads project working on the route to Nangade that he should make use of the equipment, while it is in the district, to resurface the road through Mueda town," he proudly informed us, looking in the direction of the man now walking away. In the weeks to follow, we would indeed witness excavators and graders digging up what was left of the pothole-riven street that connected one end of Mueda town to the other. Town residents, accustomed to slow-moving vehicles on these streets, would soon be sent scrambling for their lives as the few vehicles in Mueda traversed the road at breakneck speed.

We returned to our conversation.

"A while back, villagers in Namaua sent word to me that they needed arms to kill several lions that were menacing the population. I arranged a few arms for them, but when they tracked the lions, they came to a point where the lions' prints turned into human prints. They asked *me* what to do." Ambrósio sipped his beer.

"What did you tell them?" I asked.

"I said, 'You asked for arms to kill lions; if you can't find the lions, that's your problem, not mine.'" He threw up his hands. "What *could* I do?"

In years past, administrators would have intervened forcefully in such cases, reprimanding or otherwise disciplining villagers who spoke of such things as purveyors of "obscurantism." Now, the state acted with great caution.

Ambrósio looked me in the eye. "Of course people cannot make lions and send them to attack other people. These things arise out of conflicts between families. Tensions lead to accusations of sorcery." He finished his beer and called to the young woman inside the house to bring three more, despite the fact that neither Marcos nor I were even halfway finished with ours.

He turned his attention back to us: "It is essential not to get drawn into such matters. If you try to adjudicate, you wind up taking sides. It is better to have them reach a resolution on their own. I tell them that they must sort these things out for themselves."

To be sure, Ambrósio's administrative technique might have been interpreted as a mode of "democratic decentralization." As we carried on conversing, however, it became clear to me that Ambrósio's strategy derived from other motives as well. In the atmosphere of multiparty politics, Ambrósio and his FRELIMO party were wary of alienating voters. "Democracy," Ambrósio told me, "means that each one has the right to believe what he believes." If villagers believed that their fellows made lions that threatened to kill them, who was Ambrósio, in the new democratic Mozambique, to tell them that they were wrong?

Ironically, the elders of Kilimani, like many Muedans, interpreted Ambrósio's "liberal" approach to sorcery rather differently than he intended. Fundamental to what they "believed" and, now, freely expressed about sorcery was that good governance entailed not only the administration of mundane affairs in a world visible to all but also the exercise of power over dangerous agents—sorcerers—who operated in an invisible realm. In the days before FRELIMO gathered Muedans into "communal villages," these elders, like most Muedans of their generation, inhabited dispersed settlements. It was incumbent upon those who exercised authority in these settlements to monitor and structure both the visible and the invisible realms that constituted their respective jurisdictions. Indeed, they challenged destructive forms of sorcery in their settlements through the enactment of their own kind of sorcery. Elders referred to this as *uwavi wa kudenga* (a sorcery of construction). When the occurrence of sorcery in a settlement reached intolerable limits, elders frequently told me, the settlement head would go out into the settlement center in the middle of the night and call out for all to hear: "I see you! I know who you are, you sorcerers who are killing people in my settlement! If you do not cease, I will deal with you myself! I see you! I know who you are!"

The elders of Kilimani sent their letter to Ambrósio already knowing that he would not punish them for identifying the sorcerer in their midst. They followed political developments in Mozambique on the radio every evening. They knew that FRELIMO socialism was a thing of the past—that democracy had arrived in Mozambique. They knew that their rights of free expression were protected—that they could now speak openly about sorcery. They even heard accounts of sorcery-related incidents in news broadcasts on Radio Moçambique's local service out of Pemba.

What they asked of Ambrósio was not that he "respect their beliefs," as he put it. Rather, they demanded that he deal appropriately with the sorcerer they had identified. Ambrósio's party had built the villages in which Muedans lived and continued to appoint those who administered these villages. Therefore, the elders reasoned, it fell upon this FRELIMO representative to do what responsible elders had done in the settlements of old, namely, to police the invisible realm and quash the nefarious activities of sorcerers therein. "Those who govern the lives of people," Muedan elders often told me, "must themselves be sorcerers."

In the end, it seems, Ambrósio was not as adept as he thought at dressing appropriately for each activity required by his job. The directives he habitually issued in response to petitions for his intervention in sorcery cases were read by many Muedans not as tolerance for "local tradition" but, instead, as a refusal to practice countersorcery against the destructive sorcerers who proliferated in postsocialist Mueda. If a man of Ambrósio's station did not practice sorcery of construction, they wondered, what kind of sorcery *did* he practice? Perhaps, they sometimes hinted, his fine clothes and other objects of personal wealth were the products of his own predatory activities in the invisible realm.

Simão, too, was a man of authority, even if of lower rank than Ambrósio. He, too, was widely believed to be capable of acts of sorcery, for how else could a man so young have risen to such a position of power? He, however, heard the grievances of Kilimani's residents. He, ultimately, enforced discipline on the accused sorcerer. The admiration and respect shown him by most of those he governed were inseparable from the decisions he took in cases such as the lion incident at Kilimani.

As Simão shared his account with us, however, I wondered what the accused might have thought of all of this. Only a few days later, Marcos and I traveled to Kilimani to see if we could paint for ourselves a fuller picture of what had happened there.

The road to Kilimani included patches of deep sand, Simão had warned us, so we would not be able to travel there in the low, two-wheel-drive pickup truck that we had borrowed for our research from Marcos's nephew, Nelito; we would have to journey several kilometers by foot from a lumber camp just off the Mueda–Ng'apa road. Because of this, and because Marcos knew no one in Kilimani and hesitated to appear there and begin asking sensitive questions without any introduction, we had accepted Simão's offer to escort us.

As we drew near the village, Marcos put his hand on his former student's shoulder and said, "Simão, when we do this kind of work, it is usually best for us to work alone." Simão, who had clearly been looking forward to being a member of our research team, appeared betrayed.

Marcos reinforced our solidarity with Simão, albeit at the villagers' expense: "You know how people are. They sometimes get overwhelmed if there are too many 'big people' around. They sometimes try to say what they think they are supposed to say, rather than just telling their stories and answering the questions."

Simão agreed.

When we entered the village, Simão introduced us to Silvestre Vintani, a man in his late forties or early fifties, I guessed, whom we were told was the village court's presiding judge. We were seated in front of Silvestre's house, and a few villagers gathered around. Simão excused himself "to attend to other affairs," but as the village comprised only eight or ten houses, and as most of its residents were at work in their fields, there was little for him to do and nowhere to which he might easily disappear. He lingered beneath a shade tree, in sight but out of earshot.

Marcos and I conversed with Silvestre for a while about the history of the village, which we discovered had been founded only in the late 1980s. Kilimani clung to the plateau's descending southwest margin near the site of a pumping station that pulled water from lowland sources for delivery to plateau villages. When the pumping station was threatened by RENAMO during the civil war, the government agreed to allow those with land in the vicinity to leave their communal village (called Lunango) some two hours' walk away and to form a small village of their own. The villagers would be protected by government militiamen guarding the pumping station, whom they would help to feed.

In time, I shifted the topic of conversation. "We have heard reports that you had trouble with lions here recently."

"It is true," Silvestre told us. "They began to appear at the beginning of last year. They came from the lowlands around Nambali," he said, pointing over his shoulder.

"Is that an area with a lot of animals?" I asked.

"Monkeys, but not much else. A few gazelle."

"Aren't there normally lions and leopards there too?" I asked, drawing on what I knew of the region from previous conversations with Muedan hunters.

"Leopards sometimes get caught in the traps that we set for bushpigs."

"So there are bushpigs there?"

"A lot of them. They ruin our fields, so we set traps for them."

I thought of what hunters often said: "Where there is meat, there are meateaters."

"So," I said, "lions were first seen last year . . ."

"Lions and hyenas. They came from the direction of Lunango. These animals threatened us. They came right into the village, right up to our houses, right up to our doors. We fought to chase them away. It was a serious struggle, I tell you. The village president went around at night telling people: 'I don't want these beasts here! If these beasts kill someone, then I will kill that person!'"

Silvestre's account of the village president's proclamation constituted an unmistakable description of *uwavi wa kudenga* (sorcery of construction).

With my next question, I made it clear to Silvestre that I had understood this: "Did the village president know who the sorcerer was?" I asked.

"It's possible," Silvestre answered. "I don't know. I don't know who was making them. Maybe the village president from that time knows, but he has retired, and he is away from the village now."

I was surprised. "Wasn't there a trial here?" I asked.

Silvestre looked straight ahead. "Because no one was identified, there could be no trial."

I sat back in my chair, not knowing how to proceed. We had come to talk about the trial, but the village judge was now telling us that no trial had been held. Marcos returned my bewildered glance with his own expression of confusion and frustration and then reposed the question, but Silvestre again pleaded ignorance.

I had forgotten completely about Simão, who now suddenly appeared in our midst. I wondered for a moment if his presence was the cause of the elder's reticence, but with Simão in our circle, Silvestre began to speak with confidence again.

"My house was surrounded by four lions," he said. "Several elders in the village determined that this was the work of a certain suspected man who lived among us. This man was confronted and, soon after, he left the village."

Marcos nodded in affirmation to Simão, who now sat with us. With this, I realized how complex and sensitive the case remained to the residents of Kilimani even in this, the democratic era. I now wondered if Silvestre spoke because he feared Simão or, perhaps, Simão's superiors. If so, did he fear one or the other of these men as government officials or as sorcerers? Or could such a distinction even be made? On the other hand, I thought, perhaps he feared Marcos and I. Perhaps he feared *for* Simão. Perhaps he suspected our inquiry might lead to a reversal of the decision in which he and Simão together had been involved.

As these thoughts raced through my mind, I became aware of another figure approaching. I looked up to see an old man with white hair and a scruffy white beard, walking stiffly, glowering intensely. He cradled a gun loosely in his right arm, the long barrel pointing at me. A boy who was sitting on a log that he had dragged into our circle abandoned his seat, and the old man inhabited it, facing me.

Marcos reached out, placed his hand on the man's leg, and asked him his name. He was Francisco Shityatya Namalakola Ndomana Muendanene, he told us; and then, somehow knowing the topic of our conversation, he began to speak.

"Lions came to the village three times. The first time, one lion came and stole pigs from the village. It left the pigs' feet behind, and it left the pigs' intestines close by. This made us suspicious. What kind of lion does this? A normal lion will eat everything when it kills a pig, but this lion left the feet because they had *matakenya* [fleas]."

The barrel of Shityatya's gun drooped as he became engrossed in telling his story. "The second time, four lions surrounded this one's *cabana*,"[4] Shityatya said, pointing to Silvestre. "This happened in the afternoon, out by his field."

"The third time, a lion came into the village, but it didn't take any animals. It only grabbed a pair of pants that were hanging on a cord to dry in the sun. Outside the village, it tore up the pants and then ran away."

Shityatya shook his head. "Only an *ntumi kulambidyanga* [false lion] would do these things."

"Did you ever figure out who was doing all of this?" I asked Shityatya.

He looked at me hard, massaging the barrel of his gun.

"Why don't you tell us?" he said.

He looked at my camera, which sat on top of my field bag.

"Why don't you use your *science*? Look into that machine of yours and tell us who the lion is. Here, we know when someone dies, and we know who those are that kill. You try to match these things up. We don't do that."

I was taken aback. Here I was, trying to make the links that I expected Muedans to make while they denied what they must have expected me to deny.

"Didn't someone perform *yangele* [divination]?" I asked.

"No," he answered firmly. "*Yangele* sometimes lies."

Shityatya's face remained hard. Our questioning was leading nowhere. The barrel of the old man's gun was once more pointed at me. I wondered if it was loaded. I wondered if ammunition could still be purchased for such a gun.

Marcos perceived my growing anxiety and seized the moment to disarm Shityatya—in more ways than one. He reached out and put his hand on the barrel of the gun as if to identify it as the subject of his speech while, subtly, directing it away from me.

"*Espera-pouco*," he announced.

The broken Portuguese phrase literally means "wait-little-bit," but Marcos now told me what I had already learned in other conversations with other elders. *Espera-pouco* was the nickname Muedans gave to the muzzle-loaders many had acquired in the era of the slave trade. Reloading these arms with shot and powder after each discharge proved inexpedient in the heat of battle. Muedans joked that combatants were compelled to call out to their enemies, "*Espera-pouco!*" after each firing as they scrambled to prepare for the next.

The phrase-turned-name invariably brought laughter when uttered in conversation among elders. Upon hearing it, the people assembled around us laughed, predictably.

Shityatya looked at Marcos. "Ehhh," he said, in affirmation.

Marcos now said, "It looks like you've been waiting a long time, *nang'olo* [elder]."

Again, the small crowd around us laughed, this time at the aged Shityatya.

Shityatya glared at Marcos, who grinned back at him triumphantly. The elder then said: "I've heard nothing more from my enemy since he told me to wait. It seems he ran away in fear. But I still wait!" The audience laughed *with* the elder now, at Marcos's expense.

Even so, the tenor of our encounter was transformed, as Marcos had intended. The rivals had earned one another's respect in their brief duel of words. Shityatya's face softened into a smile, as he allowed Marcos to examine his gun. As I, too, looked over the weapon, I realized that Shityatya was addressing us once more.

"Yes, there was a trial here last year because of these lions."

He spoke, suddenly, with candor and with ease as he filled in the details. "It resulted in a man being expelled from the village. He had recently come here from Chicalanga to tend his father's sugarcane fields. His father was Assani Kuva, of the Malavoni *likola* [matrilineage], just like Silvestre. This land is Malavoni land. Assani Kuva had land here, but he was forced to move to Lunango with everyone else at independence. He was one of the group who negotiated with the government to allow us to return here to this land, but he died before we moved. His brother, Mashalubu Kuva, informed Assani's son, Sefu Assani Kuva, that his father had died. Sefu was in Chicalanga with his mother then, but Mashalubu invited him to take his father's fields here in Kilimani. The fields are large, and very rich. So he came."

"Was he a good farmer?" I asked.

"He was," Shityatya said, begrudgingly. "He had a large sugarcane plot. He also had banana trees. People came from Mueda to buy his sugarcane and bananas, and the *lipa* [liquor] that he made. His father's land was very good land."

"What was his behavior?" I asked.

"He drank a lot, and when he was drunk, he used to say, 'Don't mess with me! If I want to, I can make a lion and kill you!' Everyone with plots around his land abandoned them because they feared him."

"So he made good on his threats?" I queried.

"When these lions started showing up, people went to the village president, who was also an *nkulaula* [healer]. I don't know if he divined or not, but he summoned all the village elders to meet with him in the lowlands, and they identified the culprit."

"What happened to him?" I asked.

"He was beaten six times with a *chamboco*[5] and his land was taken from him. He went back to Chicalanga."

Days later, Marcos and I tried to find Sefu Assani Kuva in Chicalanga but were told that he was away from the village, in Nampula. He was not expected back anytime soon.

When Marcos and I parted ways with Simão after our trip to Kilimani and returned to Mueda town at the end of the day, we found a beer stall on the edge of the market and ordered two bottles.

"So, what do you think?" I finally asked him. "Did this Sefu Assani Kuva make lions?"

"You heard the old man," Marcos responded with a playfulness matching mine.

I took a long drink. I sensed that the young woman attending the stall was listening in on our conversation; when I glanced at her, she quickly turned her head away.

"I'm not convinced," I told Marcos.

He asserted his position: "Those lions walked into the village like they were looking for someone. They lingered around houses. Bush lions don't do that. They left parts of the pig in the village because they didn't want to eat fleas. Bush lions don't do that. They took a pair of pants off the line and tore them up. Have you ever heard of a bush lion doing that!?"

"True," I admitted. "Those are strange things for a bush lion to do."

"You know what proves it, though?" Marcos asked me.

"No, what?"

"The guy said he knew how to make lions. He told them that he was going to do it! That guy's a sorcerer for sure."

I sat quietly for a moment, preparing my words. Finally, I said: "Here's a guy who lives with his mother's matrilineage in Chicalanga. One day, he is told that his father is dead but that the elder has left him lots of very rich land. He moves to Kilimani and starts farming. But there, he lives among people of a different matrilineage, many of whom are upset that this rich land has gone to someone who is not one of them—not Malavoni."

"Ehhh." Marcos nursed his beer.

"This guy is insulted and mistreated from the day he arrives. Maybe he's a good guy, and maybe he's a nasty drunkard, but he's among rivals, and he has to defend himself all the time. Maybe people threaten him. Maybe they say things to him that he understands as threats—as sorcerers' words."

"So he answers their threats with his own?" Marcos said, in anticipation of my argument.

"Yes." I paused for a moment to sip my beer. "It's a fine line between defending yourself and threatening someone—between courage and provocation. Who knows what this guy said? But whatever he said, if he remained there in the midst of all that hostility, they were going to worry about his courage—worry about *what he knew*."

The phrase "to know something" serves in the Shimakonde language as a euphemism for sorcery. Sorcerers, Muedans often say, fear little because they "know something" that protects them.

"What about the lions?" Marcos asked.

"You know as well as I do that there are lions down there. Hunters tell us all the time that there are lions—bush lions, that is—in those lowlands. It was the rainy season, when lions like to move up out of the lowlands. The Malavoni *took advantage of* the lions to get rid of this guy."

Marcos sat quietly for a moment. He then said, "You're right. These things need to be studied *scientifically*."

I now sat quietly, satisfied that Marcos had come to see sense in my interpretation of the case.

"You know what they say," Marcos added, in time. "Where there is lightning, sorcerers use it. Where there is war, sorcerers use it. Where there is illness, sorcerers use it. *These Malavoni used lions*."

Seeing that we were nearly finished with our beers, the attendant rose from her stool and pulled two more from the refrigerator. She wiped the condensation off the bottles with her *capulana*, opened them, and put them on the low table between us.

I remembered that I did not really know what Marcos meant when he suggested—as he often did—the need to study sorcery "scientifically."

"Maybe they were just bush lions," I suggested, sensing my interpretative triumph slipping away.

"*Mano* [brother]," Marcos said, with a hint of exasperation. "They took clothes off the clothesline. They left the pigs' feet. *Someone* made those lions!"

Introduction

In the conduct of anthropological field research between 1993 and 2004 among the residents of the Mueda plateau, I frequently witnessed, and often participated in, conversations centered on the topic of sorcery. Such dialogues are the source and the substance of this book.

When I took part in these conversations, I sometimes spoke the lines of the skeptic—but not always. At times, Muedans themselves challenged the ideas put forth by fellow Muedans who suggested, for example, that people among them could make or transform themselves into lions, could make others into zombie slaves, or could sabotage cars, trucks, and helicopters by inserting within them the invisible crania of infant children whose flesh they had devoured.

"Is it true?" I heard Muedans ask.

"Impossible!" I sometimes heard others exclaim.

"I know a woman who saw it herself!" others might respond.

Or, occasionally, "I have seen it with my own eyes!"

Such exchanges often spawned other questions—sometimes openly articulated and sometimes implied in the expressions and subsequent actions of parties to the conversation: Who is the sorcerer in our midst? Why has this particular victim been chosen? What can be done to eliminate or to restrain these sorcerers or, at least, to protect ourselves from them? How might we recognize the effects of sorcerers' attacks before it is too late? What can be done to reverse the afflictions these sorcerers cause us?

In moments of reflection, these questions begat broader ones: What world have we made for ourselves with all of this sorcery? If not for our envy and our fears—if not for our suspicions and our recriminations—might we eliminate sorcery from our world?

The debates Muedans waged, and continue to wage, about sorcery ripple well beyond the edges of the plateau. However, when such topics have been taken up in government circles in, for example, the Mozambican capital, Maputo, different questions have been asked. Whereas some Mozambican policymakers have wondered if greater official tolerance for "local beliefs and practices" might not ease tensions between the state and rural communities, others have asked whether such beliefs and practices might not provide fertile ground for opportunism and charlatanism as well as potentially impeding economic development by fostering fears of supernatural leveling forces. Even as some have suggested that "traditional authorities" might serve as vehicles for the public expression of the "will of the people" in rural areas, others have warned that vesting power in institutions such as these might undermine the rule of law and jeopardize the individual rights enshrined in the new Mozambican constitution.

Much is at stake in these debates, not only for Mozambican democracy but also for myriad flesh-and-blood people like Mueda District Administrator Ambrósio Vicente Bulasi, Miula locality president Simão Benjamim, Kilim1ani village court judge Silvestre Vintani, and alleged sorcerer Sefu Assani Kuva. As Mozambicans seek to consolidate the peace and find prosperity in the post–civil war era, state officials and subjects alike have looked for ways to ensure popular participation in the processes of governance and economic development. The lives, careers, material possessions, and human dignity of Mozambicans of various categories all lie in the balance.

The Cameroonian historian Achille Mbembe has argued that the project of democratization in contemporary Africa depends not upon the application of a Western model of power to African realities but, instead, upon the cultivation within Africa of "other languages of power" that express emergent African political ethics. These languages, Mbembe asserts, "must emerge from the daily life of the people, [and] address everyday fears and nightmares, and the images with which people express or dream them" (quoted in Geschiere 1997: 7).[1]

Following Mbembe, I take Muedan sorcery discourse to be one such "language of power." With this book, I seek to contribute to a fuller appreciation among policymakers, analysts, scholarly commentators, and students of African affairs more generally of the importance of *uwavi* (sorcery) to the conception and operation of power on the Mueda plateau and, by extension, of the political salience of such languages of power elsewhere in contemporary

Africa and beyond. If Mbembe is right—as I believe he is—the objective is one of urgent consequence. So long as policymakers and citizens speak mutually unintelligible languages of power, the project of democracy is impossible. To this end, I hope that the volume will inform, and even challenge, the views of policymakers (whether in government, international agencies, or nongovernmental organizations) working toward the political and economic liberalization of Mozambique—not to mention their counterparts involved in regime transition elsewhere in the world.

Where the difference in perspective between rulers and ruled derives not merely from misunderstanding but also from a divergence of interest, it is also my hope that a deeper understanding of the languages of power through which ordinary people express their fears and dreams—to paraphrase Mbembe— will better equip policy analysts and scholarly commentators to formulate their own critical perspectives on neoliberal reform in Mozambique and elsewhere. To this end, I intend the book to contribute to academic debates concerning culture, power, and governance in contemporary Africa and other postcolonial and postsocialist contexts. It is my hope that the volume will contribute to the emergence of a new field of inquiry: namely, the comparative study of neoliberalism and the political cosmologies that find continued expression in the wake of the former's global spread.

Beyond this, it is my hope that the volume renders immediate and accessible to students issues and debates that have long animated the disciplines of anthropology and comparative political philosophy. In the exploration of Muedan sorcery discourse, I hope to illustrate not only Muedans' cultural distinctiveness but also their shared humanity in a profoundly complex and interconnected contemporary world.

Ironically, the interconnectedness of our world renders more challenging Mbembe's mandate to identify, and "cultivate," other languages of power, for, as we shall see, many Muedans are conversant in multiple languages of power, having gained various degrees of fluency in the languages introduced to them over the years by *their Others,* including the language of the slave trade, the language of Portuguese colonialism, the language of revolutionary nationalism, the language of scientific socialism, and, finally, the language of neoliberal democracy.

Muedans are not by any means alone in speaking the languages of Others. Indeed, as the Russian linguist Mikhail Bakhtin has argued, the words that any individual speaks are always already someone else's and are always destined to become someone else's still (Todorov 1984: x): "No member of a verbal community can ever find words in the language that are neutral, exempt from the aspirations and evaluations of the other, uninhabited by the other's voice. On the contrary, he receives the word by the other's voice and it remains filled with that voice. He intervenes in his own context from another context, already penetrated by the other's intentions. His own intention finds a world already lived in" (quoted in Todorov 1984: 48).[2] According to Bakhtin, not only is every utterance formed dialogically, intersubjectively, but so too are languages. Correspondingly, the linguistic universe as Bakhtin conceives it comprises "a multiplicity of tongues, mutually animating each other" (Todorov 1984: 15).

Though the boundaries delineating various languages, as well as the communities of those who speak them, may be tenuous social imaginings, the use (not to mention the study) of language nonetheless requires that one imagine such boundaries—requires that one assume a "we" among whom experience and meaning are shared (Voloshinov in Todorov 1984: 42)[3] and that one generally use language *as if* it were a stable system.[4] According to Bakhtin, such imaginings give rise to "spheres of language" comprising "*relatively stable types* of utterances," which he categorizes as "discursive genres" (Todorov 1984: 82). "Each genre," Medvedev writes, "has its methods, its ways of seeing and understanding reality, and these methods are its exclusive characteristic" (Todorov 1984: 83).[5] In seeking to fulfill Mbembe's mandate, I focus in this book upon the discursive genre of *uwavi,* or sorcery discourse.[6]

I translate *uwavi* as "sorcery" but also use this Shimakonde term throughout the text to remind my readers of the distinctiveness of *uwavi*'s "ways of seeing and understanding the world."[7] By "distinctive," I do *not* mean "exclusive." Discourses of the occult are widespread not only in Africa but also elsewhere in the world; notwithstanding Medvedev's idea that discursive genres possess "exclusive characteristics," discourses of the occult *share* a great many traits.[8] It follows that, by "distinctive," I do not mean unintelligible to others. Through dialogical engagement, I argue, discursive genres such as *uwavi* may be learned; indeed, I argue, one may approximate *uwavi*'s ways of seeing and understanding the world in another language, although something is inevitably lost in translation.[9] As Muedans engage with their world through multiple languages, however, so must those seeking to learn something of their distinctive perspectives and experiences. Accordingly, Mbembe does not call for us merely to *translate* or *explain* African languages of power for non-African audiences; rather, he challenges us to engage *through* these languages with African realities from which these languages can scarcely be disentangled. I therefore ask my readers to engage, along with me, in this dialogue with Muedan *uwavi* by learning a few terms in Shimakonde—to participate in the project of developing a broader, shared lexicon through which they might learn more about Muedan realities, not to mention a reality shared with Muedans—even as I limit the number of Shimakonde words in the text to ensure readability.[10]

As I approach *uwavi* discourse in these pages through multiple languages of power, I present readers with questions that Muedans would recognize as their own, and with others that they would not. Among the questions I ask in the discursive genre of sociocultural anthropology are the following: In what cultural and historical contexts has Muedan *uwavi* emerged and flourished? To what extent does *uwavi* discourse constitute a distinctive form of "local knowledge" about the operation of power in Mueda, and to what extent is it the product of Muedan participation in the "modern world"? How do Muedan conceptions of power as expressed through *uwavi* discourse differ from and/or resemble conceptions of power as expressed in the global discourses presently animating democratic reform and economic liberalization in Mozambique? Do Muedan pronouncements in the discursive genre of *uwavi* shed light on these contemporary events and processes? Or do Muedans confound themselves through their "belief" in *uwavi*? And, finally, what are the implications of *uwavi* discourse for the ongoing project of economic and political reform in Mozambique?

As I recount conversations in which I participated about people who become animals, who fly invisibly through the night, and who devour the flesh of their neighbors and kin, I also re-present questions Muedans posed in the discursive genre of *uwavi*—questions that may be uniquely inflected but that should nonetheless be comprehensible to readers. In the language of sorcery, Muedans ponder the nature of the reality in which they are suspended, asking if it is possible that a select few among them somehow enjoy privileged access to, and control over, that reality. They wonder whether, and how, some people are able to garner and deploy exclusive—even undetectable—forms of power, while others are not. As they discuss the potential identities, motives, and means of sorcerers, they scrutinize the institutions and norms that govern the world they inhabit. They ask who infringes these norms and who pays the consequences of such infringements. They wonder aloud if existing, or proposed, political institutions and arrangements are sufficient to protect the common good—indeed, if such institutions and arrangements are even designed to do so.

Because *uwavi* discourse constitutes a social dialogue situated in space and time, its distinctiveness is bound up with the particular social history of those who have produced and sustained it. Following Bakhtin, who tells us that "discursive genres . . . are the transmission belts between social history and linguistic history" (Todorov 1984: 81), and Medvedev, who asserts that "the true poetics of genre can only be a sociology of genre" (Todorov 1984: 80), my study of *uwavi* discourse is necessarily a historical sociology of those who have participated in the conversation that is *uwavi*. In these pages, I tell the story of a Muedan social world made and remade by the historical forces of the slave trade, colonial conquest and administration, revolutionary nationalism, socialist modernization, and postsocialist neoliberalization. I also tell the story of Muedans' dialectical engagement with this changing world—the story of how, through the reproduction of *uwavi* discourse, they have reproduced their world. In the process, *uwavi* discourse has itself been transformed in the interface with other languages of power gaining currency on the Mueda plateau. Indeed, many of the Muedans whose stories I tell demonstrate fluency in other languages of power in addition to *uwavi*, invoking multiple interpretive logics in the midst of concrete historical experiences.[11] My account of the historical dynamics of sorcery discourse constitutes, I believe, one of the volume's principal contributions to the literature on occult cosmologies in Africa and elsewhere.

Ultimately, I conclude with Bakhtin that although "genre lives in the present . . . it always remembers the past . . . guaranteeing the unity and continuity of [the evolution of creative memory]" (Todorov 1984: 84). Thus, as Muedans have reproduced the discursive genre of *uwavi*, they have sustained distinctive sensibilities about the workings of power in the world they inhabit. They have interpreted and engaged with their world through a dynamic but enduring cultural schema (Ortner 1990) historically sustained within the discursive genre of *uwavi*. According to this schema, power is by definition the exceptional ability to transcend the world most people know in order to gain leverage on the world to extraordinary ends. Sorcerers move in a realm beyond the visible world. From this privileged vantage point, they envision the world differently than ordinary people do and bring their visions to fruition, generally in the service of their own selfish interests and to the detriment of neighbors and kin. While power indeed produces visible disparities in wealth and well-being, according to this schema the explicit mechanisms and dynamics of power remain concealed from ordinary people, who are by definition relatively powerless.

According to this cultural schema, however, not all power is destructive. Indeed, power is essential to the production and maintenance of social wellbeing. Power finds beneficent manifestation in the acts of responsible authority figures who—like maleficent sorcerers—possess the ability to enter into the invisible realm to elaborate and realize transformative visions of the world. The exercise of beneficent power in fact entails transcendence of the world produced by maleficent sorcerers and the undoing of their destructive acts of power. Thus, power is an unending series of transcendent and transformative maneuvers, each one moving beyond, countering, inverting, overturning, and/or reversing the one preceding it. Power, indeed, is synonymous with such maneuvers: the (albeit temporarily) decisive unmaking and remaking of another's exercise of power, referred to in *uwavi* discourse as *kupilikula*.

Even as Muedans have been exposed to and, in some cases, gained competence in other languages of power, then, the cultural schema of *uwavi* has animated Muedan understandings of and engagements with a changing world. In fact, Muedans have generally conceived of the speakers of unfamiliar languages of power *as sorcerers* proclaiming transcendent visions of a world transformed. Such has been the case, as we shall see, in relation to colonial administrators, Catholic missionaries, nationalist guerrillas, and socialist planners.

Ironically, in conceiving of these powerful figures as sorcerers, Muedans have articulated their own visions of the world—visions fixing these powerful figures in *their* sights. They have, tentatively, cautiously, participated in the dialogues conducted in their midst, countering, inverting, overturning, and/or reversing many of the assertions made by more vocal and more powerful interlocutors. They have, themselves, unassumingly undertaken their own countermaneuvers (*kupilikula*), even while denying—just like sorcerers and countersorcerers—the power to do so.

In the postsocialist period, during which I conducted my field research, Muedans were introduced to yet another language of power: the discourse of neoliberal reform. Those who spoke this language suggested that, after years of debilitating civil war and deepening corruption, power in Mozambique might be rationalized through the opening of markets, the staging of multiparty elections, and the constitutional consolidation of citizens' rights. Neoliberal reformers, like those preceding them—whether colonial administrators, Catholic missionaries, nationalist guerrillas, or socialist planners—pronounced their vision of a world transformed. Unlike their predecessors, these reformers suggested that the world they envisioned afforded space for the visions—the "traditions"—of those they governed. Indeed, these reformers suggested that, with the establishment of democracy, Mozambicans could effectively govern themselves in accordance with their own views of their world (so long as they viewed the world as reformers expected them to). Despite such pronouncements, however, Muedans detected troubling dynamics in the emergent political order. The withdrawal of the state from various spheres of Muedan life did not empower Muedans as citizens so much as leave them vulnerable to the unrestrained exercise of power by self-serving individuals of both local and foreign origin. In the "spaces" afforded by a more "tolerant" regime, Muedans observed the powerful feeding their own appetites at the expense of others. They understood the assertion of such maleficent power to be bound up with the refusal of regnant authorities to monitor and control power's unseen dynamics and to enact power on behalf of all. Indeed, Muedans saw in the processes of neoliberal reform the transformation of beneficent authorities into maleficent actors. Whereas reformers asserted in the discursive genre of neoliberalism a vision of the world wherein the operation of power was rendered transparent and, thus, susceptible to popular control, Muedans expressed enduring suspicion of and deep ambivalence toward power through the discursive genre of *uwavi*. Even as reformers tried (or claimed to be trying) to eliminate "endemic conflicts," "abuses of power"— even "politics" itself—from the realm of governance, Muedans preserved through *uwavi* discourse their understanding that social life is inescapably an endless struggle between competing, potentially dangerous forces.

In countering the language of neoliberal reform with suspicions expressed in the distinctive language of *uwavi*, Muedans, as I have suggested, scarcely revealed themselves as *uniquely* suspicious. Nor did they demonstrate *uwavi* discourse as a language predisposing its speakers to look upon power with *exceptional* ambivalence. According to my argument, neither Muedans nor *uwavi* discourse even *resisted* the ordering gazes of power— whether in the colonial era, in the socialist period, or in the contemporary moment of neoliberal reform. Rather, I argue, *uwavi* discourse provided Muedans with a sensory organ (Cassirer 1946: 8) through which to perceive profound contradictions in the emerging neoliberal order. Through *uwavi* discourse, Muedans (re)made their world, although not at their whim. They envisioned a world within the bounds of the historically conceivable. Indeed, they articulated visions of a world they perceived to be decidedly *not* of their own making, even as they looked upon this world with dissatisfaction and alarm. In so doing, they continued to turn over (*kupilikula*) the powers they encountered—to peek at power's dangerous underside to see, if only vaguely, if only momentarily, what they were up against.

⬛

What I know of *uwavi* derives, as I have said, from my own dialogical engagement in *uwavi* discourse—from myriad conversations that I have attended since initiating fieldwork in Mueda in 1993. So closely interwoven with these conversations is my understanding of *uwavi* that I have chosen to use exemplary dialogues as the building blocks for this volume. Rather than advancing my arguments in the form of several article-length chapters, I instead present my readers with shorter chapters, each one framed by excerpted accounts of one or more particularly provocative conversations in which I have participated. From these vignettes arise issues that become the substance of my argument.

Of course, knowledge of sorcery cannot be gained merely through talk about sorcery. While talk about sorcery may inevitably situate one within the field of sorcery (Favret-Saada 1980), sorcery is subjectively experienced by different categories of actors in vastly different registers and through various senses (Stoller 1995). As evidenced in these vignettes, my "dialogue" with Muedans comprised various kinds of verbal and nonverbal interactions and exchanges, including participation in various socially meaningful practices that afforded *me* various kinds of subjective experiences.

Many who have conducted anthropological research on sorcery have apprenticed themselves to sorcerers or to countersorcery healers (Castenada 1968; Stoller and Olkes 1987; Stoller 1989; Plotkin 1993; Prechtel 1999).[12] The ethnomusicologist John Chernoff has argued that apprenticeship allows the researcher to "bring something of a different order into [his or her] own world of understanding [while] at the same time recogniz[ing] and appreciat[ing] it on its own terms" (1979: 3). However, as virtually no one in Mueda professes to be a sorcerer, apprenticing with one would have been impossible. In times past, countersorcery healers were generally trained and inducted by masters, but countersorcery apprenticeship is giving way, in Mueda, to self-taught healers. Nearly all Muedans "learn a little healing" in their lifetimes, and I did just this in the presence of both ordinary Muedans and healing specialists. While it might be argued that my extensive, and in some cases intensive, inquiries concerning sorcery constituted an apprenticeship of sorts, neither I nor my interlocutors generally understood me to be training as a countersorcery healer, even if more than one healer eventually came to consider me as a "colleague" in countersorcery knowledge.

Like many scholars of sorcery, I place myself in my narrative, producing what James Clifford—drawing on Bakhtin—has referred to as "dialogical ethnography" (Clifford 1988: 41–44). However, whereas other scholars of sorcery have made the story of their apprenticeship the central thread of their narrative—often in the form of accounts of personal journey from incomprehension to understanding—I have rejected this narrative trope. My reasons for doing so derive from the awkward tension I discovered to exist between my experience of studying *uwavi* in the field and the understanding of *uwavi*

I developed over the years both in the field and "back home." In the field, the study of *uwavi* was oftentimes profoundly disorienting. Knowledge gained one day was lost the next as I gathered contradictory evidence or became aware of disparate perspectives. Not only was my journey nonlinear, but it seemingly led to no final destination. The more I studied *uwavi*, the less I seemed to *know*. Muedans with whom I worked—including renowned countersorcery healers—often told me that they themselves did not know the path to understanding *uwavi*. What *uwavi* discourse told Muedans was that the world is made, unmade, and remade in a hidden realm. What most Muedans knew about *uwavi* was that they *didn't* know *uwavi*. This state of affairs— not to mention my experience of it as an anthropologist—may be commonplace (Taussig 1987; Stoller and Olkes 1987; Stoller 1989). Through the trope of apprenticeship, however, anthropologists have often given a rather different impression.[13]

In the construction of an ethnographic account, one can scarcely avoid making some kind of sense of the topic at hand. Indeed, as one can scarcely live in a world without seeking to understand it, I have, like the Muedans with whom I conversed, sought to see the unseeable, to know the unknowable, to make sense of the senseless. It is quite another thing, however, to suggest that this sense revealed itself, as such, over the course of the journey of fieldwork. My struggle to make sense of *uwavi* was not confined to my time in the field. My understanding of *uwavi* was continually transformed in various contexts outside the field—in the library, in the seminar room, and in front of the computer screen. This book conveys my understanding of *uwavi* at the time of its writing. Although it comprises accounts of events and conversations that occurred in the conduct of field research, the chronology of these encounters has yielded in my narrative to another order of presentation, for each of its constituent episodes has come to coexist with the others in my memory, each one interrogating the others across boundaries of space and time, each one shedding light or imparting confusion upon the others. The narrative not only follows strands of Muedan history but also threads through the logics of *uwavi* as I eventually came to conceive of them, all the while ferrying back and forth between simplicity and complexity, clarity and ambiguity, certainty and doubt.

The book is arranged in three parts. The chapters in part 1 provide readers with a thumbnail sketch of the logics that have generally pertained in the realm of *uwavi*, as well as how *uwavi* has reflected and refracted social relations. Part 2 tells the story of *uwavi*'s transformations within the context of a Muedan world subjected to Portuguese colonialism and Christian evangelization, followed by revolutionary nationalism and socialist modernization.

Part 3 returns to the present-day dilemmas introduced in the prologue, dilemmas produced by neoliberal reform of the Mozambican economy and polity. Each of the three parts is preceded by a brief summary of the ground to be covered and the conclusions to be drawn from the chapters within it. Readers wishing to have, in advance, a more detailed outline of the volume should read these summaries in succession now, before proceeding.

⬛

My understanding of Muedan *uwavi* has been productively informed and rigorously challenged by those who assisted me in the conduct of field research and participated most intensively with me in dialogue about power and its operation in Mueda. When, in 1993, I informed Estêvão Mpalume—director of the Cabo Delgado nucleus of the Cultural Heritage Archives (Arquivos do Património Cultural, or ARPAC), which served as my host institution while I was in the field—that I wished to work with two research assistants, one male and one female, he first introduced me to Felista Elias Mkaima. Felista was in her early twenties at the time. She was married to a provincial government officer and had two young children. Since finishing school, she had not had work, but Mpalume promised that once she had gained research experience working with me, she would be hired by ARPAC-Pemba, which had no women in its employ at the time.[14] During the period of my dissertation research (1993–1995), I paid Felista a daily wage, which she sometimes used to augment household income and sometimes passed on to her father, a retired military official. Felista acted as my principal field assistant when I was in Pemba, the provincial capital of Cabo Delgado Province, making contacts on my behalf, scheduling interviews, gathering data, and copying documents. She often accompanied me when I traveled to the Mueda plateau. Tentative at first, Felista quickly learned how to conduct field research. She eventually became adept at conducting interviews and at getting the small groups of women with whom we often worked to talk about their lives in the presence of a white male stranger—no mean feat in rural Mozambique.

To round out my research team, Mpalume allowed one of his staff researchers, Eusébio Tissa Kairo, to work with me in the field for extended periods. When I arrived in Cabo Delgado Province, Tissa was in his early twenties and was studying to complete his high school degree in hopes of gaining entry to university. He was enthusiastic about working with an "American professor" with whom he might speak a bit of English from time to time. Tissa used the wages that I paid him to meet school fees and to provide for his wife and children. In the field, Tissa demonstrated an abiding curiosity in the culture and history of northern Mozambique. After participating with me in structured interviews, he generally shared with me related stories and information that he had garnered in his previous research or that he had simply picked up in informal conversation with other Muedans.

Unexpectedly, I developed a collaborative relationship with a third Mozambican, who, ultimately, made profound contributions to my research. When, at Mpalume's suggestion, I entered the Pemba headquarters of the Association of Veterans of the War of National Liberation (Associação dos Combatentes da Luta de Libertação Nacional, or ACLLN) to seek out potential interviewees, I encountered Marcos Agostinho Mandumbwe, a man in his midforties with a full beard and a charming smile. Mandumbwe, I quickly discovered, was awaiting my arrival, having heard about me and my project from his superiors in the provincial political hierarchy. His post at the ACLLN mandated him to collect historical data on the Mozambican war for independence. The ACLLN, however, had been crippled by budget cuts in the wake of structural adjustment in the late 1980s. Mandumbwe—a man supporting a wife and seven children—received a small monthly salary, but he was provided with none of the equipment, supplies, or travel funds necessary to do his job. After we shared brief outlines of our research projects with one another and discovered that we shared many interests, Mandumbwe proposed that we collaborate in our work. He would draw upon his knowledge of Muedan history and culture to steer me to the right places and people. I would use my resources to meet our financial and logistical needs. He would interpret for me as I learned Shimakonde.[15] I would ensure that we both retained copies of the tapes, transcripts, photos, and other materials that our work produced.

I deliberated for several days over Mandumbwe's offer. I was wary about the effects that collaboration with a party/state functionary might have on my research interactions with Muedans of all categories, but I knew that "FRELIMO" was a historical identity that most Muedans enthusiastically embraced. Any attempt on my part to refuse all association with FRELIMO would, I knew, shut me out of Muedan life completely. On the positive side, working with a man of Mandumbwe's qualifications and experience would undoubtedly facilitate my entrée into the field and might possibly make me a more efficient and more effective field-worker. I accepted Mandumbwe's offer on a provisional basis after warning him that I would, at times, question FRELIMO's motives and methods in my research. Although, because of his standing as a party employee, I did not initially pay him as a "field assistant," I found other ways to compensate him for his contributions to my work—for example, by donating household provisions to his family before taking him away from them on research trips, thereby effectively augmenting his income.

Marcos (Mandumbwe and I soon came to be on a first-name basis) quickly proved himself to be an ideal research collaborator. In the field, he drew on a variety of valuable life experiences. He had, it turned out, worked for several years as an ARPAC researcher before taking up his post at the ACLLN. Prior to that, during the Mozambican war for independence, he had served FRELIMO as a district-level primary school superintendent in the Cabo Delgado "liberated zones." His years of work with communities in the midst of war had taught him how to establish rapport with strangers. These same experiences had broadened his social networks throughout the plateau region. I quickly noticed and appreciated his uncanny ability to work the links of kinship and camaraderie to find connections and commonalties with the people we encountered in the field. He was dynamic and persuasive when speaking, attentive and compassionate when listening. He demonstrated keen interest in the nuances of Muedan history and shared with me his deep insights about the workings of Muedan society.

From the very beginning, Marcos put his stamp on my program of research in Mueda. As I prepared to embark upon my first extended stint of fieldwork with him, I asked him to assist me in locating a place where I might establish a semipermanent residence either in Mueda town or in Mwambula (the seat of Muidumbe District, located on the southeastern corner of the plateau). Marcos advised me against pinning myself down in one place, particularly in one of the larger towns where one could rent accommodation. He told me that I would want to have easier conviviality with the Muedans who lived outside the district seats, in the plateau's hundreds of villages. When I asked him where I would live, then, he told me, "You have family all over the plateau." Indeed, although he, Tissa, and Felista each lived in the coastal town of Pemba when I met them, they were each born and raised on the Mueda plateau and had extended family networks that reached into dozens of plateau villages. Marcos advised me to make these networks my own and to stay with these families when working in their villages, which I did.

In the conduct of the research upon which this book is based, I worked in nearly a hundred villages, returning frequently to a half dozen and making one in particular (Matambalale) my principal research site. After an initial eleven months in the field in 1994, I returned to Cabo Delgado Province during academic holidays in 1996, 1997, 1999, 2001, and 2004 for shorter stints. I generally worked in the company of one or more of my research companions. I did indeed find "family" everywhere that I worked in Mueda.

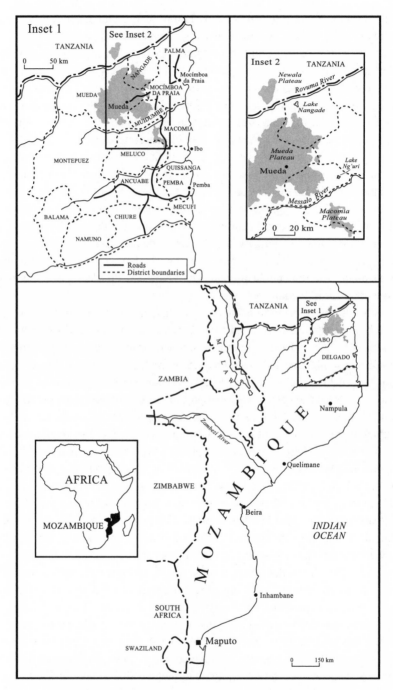

Map 1. The Mueda Plateau, Cabo Delgado Province, Mozambique (ca. 1994)

Frequently, my hosts were the biological kin of those with whom I traveled, but not always. During the independence war, many Muedans found adoptive kin in the midst of turmoil and tragedy, giving rise to intricate and lasting networks among plateau residents. I was woven into these networks. Even unescorted, I was warmly welcomed into my hosts' homes when I returned. Indeed, I was chastised when I failed to visit my "families" when passing through their respective villages or when I stayed away too long: "Andiliki," my adoptive kin would say (calling me by my Shimakonde name),[16] "you've gone missing!"

I worried, when I first began staying in Muedan homes, that my presence created undue strain on my hosts. Because there are no natural sources of water on the plateau, and because the piped-water system rarely functioned, women often walked for more than an hour each morning to the base of the plateau to fetch water in twenty-liter buckets. My daily bath—which I quickly discovered could not be refused without insulting my hosts—seemed an extravagance to me, even after I learned to bathe with only a couple of liters of water. I was eventually taught not to feel the guilt of a guest but, rather, to behave as a genuine son by finding ways to show my respect and to provide, as able, for the needs of my family. In sharing meals with my host families, I contributed sources of protein to meager diets otherwise limited to cornmeal or manioc porridge and dried fish. I sometimes bought a chicken, a goat, or a pig in the local market, making possible a rare feast for many of the families with whom I stayed. I purchased pots, pans, knives, agricultural tools, blankets, and shoes and other articles of clothing in Pemba and offered these goods to members of the families with whom I stayed.

During my 1994 research stint, I made use of a two-wheel-drive diesel pickup truck, equipped with a cap over the bed, that I purchased in Pretoria, South Africa, and drove to Cabo Delgado via Malawi. Because this vehicle sat low to the ground and frequently got stuck in the sandy plateau roadways, Marcos dubbed it *a tartaruga* ("the turtle" in Portuguese). Our turtle served us well as a mobile field office, tape and photo archive, food storehouse, and (when not broken down) means of transportation. The bench I had installed in the back to carry passengers also provided extra bunk space when needed. I sold the truck when I finished dissertation research, and in subsequent years I borrowed an even smaller pickup from Marcos's nephew, Nelito, while using a two-person tent as a mobile field office, storehouse, and bunkroom.

Marcos's influence on my methodology ran far deeper than mere logistical advice, however. Marcos taught me, as Charles Briggs has simply phrased it, "how to ask" (Briggs 1986). As I observed Marcos work in the first weeks of our collaborative research, I discovered the effectiveness of his approach of

"These things need to be studied *scientifically,*" asserted Marcos Agostinho Mandumbwe.

working outward from the thumbnail life histories he delighted in collecting. Over subsequent years, Marcos, Tissa, and Felista identified Muedans with whom I could converse whose personal narratives encompassed a tremendous variety of life experiences and perspectives. Following Marcos's example, I came to know these Muedans first by asking them to tell me about their ancestors, their parents, their childhoods, their marriages, the work they had done, the journeys they had taken, and the children they had borne and raised. I came to know Mueda's larger stories—those of war and social conflict, colonialism and liberation, religious conversion, and modernization/development—in large measure through listening to the stories of individual Muedans and piecing together a composite picture.

I also witnessed in Marcos an extraordinary capacity to ease tensions, to allay suspicions, and to make people comfortable with the ethnographic encounter. From the very first moments in which I worked with him and through

"Are you sure that our little car will get us there?" Tissa sometimes asked me before we set out on a journey from one village to another. "Ahhh, sure it will," Felista usually answered before me. "It's a car, isn't it?"

subsequent stints in the field, Marcos rescued me when I strayed into trouble spots in the unending and sometimes perilous dialogue of fieldwork, finding spaces for laughter within the most serious nooks and crannies of life. In significant ways, I modeled myself as a field researcher after Marcos, who taught me how to dance around delicate topics without abandoning them, how to assert myself in the face of hostility, and how to preempt tension with good humor.

Once we had been working together for some time, Marcos confided in me that his life's dream was to publish a book on the history and culture of the Makonde people that he might present to his children as his legacy. Over the course of his career as a researcher, he had gathered a wealth of material, he told me, but he had found himself unable to write such a book. Neither Marcos nor Tissa nor Felista participated in the writing of this book;[17] the text conveys ideas and opinions with which they may disagree and for which they should not be held accountable. Even so, the vision of Muedan society that I articulate in this book was shaped in substantial ways in dialogue with these three Muedans. Their names appear on the title page in recognition of the contributions they made to this work as dedicated and skillful researchers and as incisive and imaginative interlocutors.

1

Part 1 of this volume offers readers a thumbnail sketch of the operation of power as Muedans with whom we worked conceived (of) it through *uwavi* discourse. Whereas Muedans used the language of *uwavi* as if *uwavi* (and by extension *uwavi* discourse) were a stable system, they paradoxically recognized *uwavi*'s logics to be grounded in a historical past that differed in substantial ways from the present in which they lived. Truly, for them, *uwavi* both lived in the present *and* remembered the past (Bakhtin in Todorov 1984: 84)—a past that receded over the horizon of direct experience for even the most aged among them. When they spoke of *uwavi*, their words simultaneously divided them from *and* connected them to their forebears. Indeed, although *uwavi* discourse constituted a marker of Makonde identity, it remembered a past that predated the human settlement of the Mueda plateau and the emergence of the Makonde ethnic group, thus linking contemporary Muedans with, as much as distinguishing them from, present-day residents of neighboring regions and members of other ethnic groups.

To a significant extent, *uwavi* discourse bears evidence of continuity through more than a century of turbulent change. According to Muedans with whom we worked, power in contemporary Mueda shared fundamental commonalties with power in the precolonial era insofar as it operated in two realms—one visible, the other invisible. Where contemporary *uwavi* discourse bore evidence of the historical transformation of power's forms and functionings in the visible realm, in the invisible realm, or in both, it often (re)produced the past as a more orderly universe against which present-day happenings might be judged aberrant and condemned, as we shall see in parts 2 and 3 of this work. In any case, in exploring the logics of power as contemporary Muedans conceived (of) them through *uwavi* discourse, part 1 also presents readers with an account of power's workings in a past that serves Muedans today as an enduring point of reference—a past that will also serve as a baseline in the analysis of the historical dynamics of *uwavi* discourse in part 2.

The precolonial era provided Muedans with a rich vocabulary with which to speak about power, both past and present. Prior to Portuguese conquest of the region in the early twentieth century, residents of the Mueda plateau lived in matrilineal settlements whose affairs were administered by settlement heads. The successful settlement head was said not only to satisfy his own expansive appetite but also to feed his people by balancing the needs and desires of settlement residents through the appropriation, management, and redistribution of goods produced by his subordinates and acquired in trade. In a region wracked by drought, famine, interethnic conflict, and slave raiding, he not only organized the defense of the settlement against predatory neighbors but also prepared raids to prey upon other settlements, thereby capturing more wealth and augmenting the settlement's numbers with captives, who were eventually adopted into the matrilineage. The most powerful settlement heads were said to swallow local counterparts into their own settlements, making political subordinates of them and their people. The ambivalence with which Muedans spoke of past and present forms of power in conversation with us echoed that of their ancestors, who passed on to them this political language of predation and consumption.

Indeed, contemporary Muedans used this language to speak of the exercise of power in the invisible realm, too, just as, they told us, their ancestors had done. In precolonial days, as in the present, powerful individuals in possession of exotic substances and knowledge of how to use them were said to gain access to an invisible realm wherein they not only developed unique perspectives on the visible realm they left behind but also derived from their extraordinary vision a capacity to alter the visible world. Some were said to use this power to satisfy boundless cravings, feeding upon the well-being of rivals, neighbors, or kin through invisibly enslaving them and/or consuming their very flesh, producing in their victims visible misfortunes, illnesses, or death. In moments of crisis brought on by suspicion of attack, the vulnerable turned to specialists—diviners, healers, and figures of political authority, including settlement heads—whom they hoped and expected to be also capable of entering into the invisible realm. Whereas ruinous sorcerers escaped the bounds of the world known to ordinary Muedans, the specialists to whom Muedans turned were thought to move even farther beyond these predators. Such (counter-)sorcerers inverted or reversed the invisible acts of their predecessors and thereby remade the world. According to those with whom we worked, this transcendent maneuver, called *kupilikula*, defined power, in the past as in the present.

Along with a world divided into visible and invisible realms, precolonial Muedans bequeathed to their descendants a compulsion and a means to monitor the visible world for signs of power's invisible and capricious workings, as well as a propensity and a method to perpetually judge the motives and actions of the powerful. The portrait Muedans painted of their present-day world owed its subtle shades of gray—as we shall see not only in part 1 but throughout this volume—to an enduring suspicion of power conveyed through time by the language of *uwavi* they professed to have learned from their forebears.

1

The Settlement of the Mueda Plateau and the Making of Makonde

"There are lots of bandits in the villages these days."

Maunda[1] raised his head and looked beyond his compound toward the center of Mueda town, directing our thoughts to the marketplace, where idle young men passed their days.

"They would have been sold into slavery in the past," he concluded, with a hint of nostalgia.

Maunda Ng'upula was a valued historical source not only to us but also to Muedans. It was often said that he knew more than any other Muedan about precolonial times. Nearly every elder with whom we worked told us, at one point or another, that we should speak with Maunda. These men—many quite aged themselves—often asserted that, when they were boys, Maunda was already an old man. "He looked as old then as he does now," they often said, prompting me to consider the adage that the elderly had more time to learn sorcery's secrets; age apparently empowered Maunda and, in turn, his power manifested itself in prolonged life.

As we sat with Maunda on this cool, misty morning, I was struck by the fact that his words resonated with accounts of the earliest European travelers to the region. Until Henry E. O'Neill—then British consul to Mozambique— ascended the not-yet-named plateau south of the Rovuma River in 1882, the plateau's inhabitants appeared in the historical record only as the objects of rumor and speculation. Following their African guides, European travelers referred to these people as "Mavia," meaning "fierce" (Liebenow 1971: 30). The British geologist and explorer Joseph Thomson surveyed the Rovuma River region only a few months before O'Neill's journey and wrote of these "Mavia": "They are noted as the most exclusive tribe in East Africa, as even the Arabs have as yet been unable to penetrate beyond the outskirts of the country. . . . They are said to live apart from each other, not forming villages. There are few roads, and these hardly passable. They are described as being very treacherous, and difficult to deal with" (1882: 79).

O'Neill, however, succeeded where his predecessors had failed and traveled inland along the southern bank of the Rovuma some 60 miles and ascended the 3,000-foot-high plateau in the company of a headman named Lishehe who had heard of O'Neill's arrival in a lowland village at the plateau base and had come to see for himself this strange white-skinned visitor (see map 2, in chapter 9). O'Neill described Lishehe's settlement as follows: "A circular belt of about 60 or 80 feet in width was thickly planted with trees and thorny underbrush, every crevice in which appeared to be filled up so carefully that it became an utter impossibility for man, or beast of any size, to penetrate it. At two or three points a narrow path was left for entrance and exit, which is strongly guarded by double or treble gates. . . . During my stay at Lishehe every gate was carefully closed at sunset" (1883: 399).

The defenses O'Neill described were intended to protect Lishehe's settlement, which was in the midst of a turbulent region that for centuries had been beleaguered by raiding and slave trading (Alpers 1975). Indeed, O'Neill traveled the area in order to gather evidence of the continuing trade in slaves despite Portuguese assent to the trade's abolition in 1842. Whereas O'Neill's predecessors vilified the Mavia as a hostile tribe in a perilous region, O'Neill portrayed them as the quarry of predatory slave dealers, who gave them good reason to mistrust visitors. He further cast them as people who might benefit from—even embrace—British overrule in this unruly corner of southern Africa.[2]

The picture of these times painted by living descendants of the plateau inhabitants who so fascinated O'Neill and his contemporaries suggests that raiding and slave trading shaped social life on the plateau in myriad ways. Unlike these European travelers, however, present-day Muedans, including Maunda, generally spoke of their forebears neither as treacherous villains nor as innocent victims but rather as complex historical subjects living and acting in a turbulent environment.

When we asked Maunda to tell us about the time before the arrival of the Portuguese, he said:

[In that time], there were many slaves [in the settlements on the plateau]. People would come wandering through the region, and they would come to the settlement of the *nang'olo mwene kaja* [settlement head] Maunda.[3] There, people would give them food, but the hosts would mix *ntela* [a drug] into the *ugwali* [porridge] that they offered. After leaving the settlement, these wander-

Maunda was perpetually in motion when we visited him. He sometimes swept his dirt yard as we conversed, requiring that we follow in his dusty wake to learn what he knew.

ers would lose their sense of direction because of the drug. They could be captured then. If it was known where they were from, the settlement could demand a ransom for their return. The captors would play a drum to signal to the surrounding settlements that someone was captured and that if they wanted the captive back they would have to bring a musket or some cloth. If those captured were not ransomed, they could be adopted into the *likola* [matrilineage] of their captors, or they could be taken to the coast and traded. If the captors wanted to trade the captive at the coast, they might not even play the drums. They might just take [the captive] and sell [him or her]. . . . Some of those sold at the coast were taken from within the settlement, but these people were normally tricked by family members. A man would pretend to be going to the coast, or to another settlement, to trade, and he would ask a nephew to go with him. Then, he would sell the boy there. This would happen if the settlement needed arms. They would choose a youth who wasn't worth much—one who behaved badly.

The acts Maunda described to us contrasted only in their subtlety with the more aggressive tactics that other elders told us were used to take captives on and around the plateau in this period. Herman Nkumi, an elder in the village of Nanenda, told us of the time of his mother's youth:

> Even to go to the fields, women needed an armed escort. The young men would go out ahead of them, yelling all the while, "We see you!" even if they saw no one. They did this to scare away attackers. Then, all the women would work fields in the same area while the men guarded them. It was worse when the women went to the water sources at the base of the plateau. This was a favorite place for bands of raiders to take captives.

In any case, according to oral accounts in general, no settlement was impervious to the slave trade, whether as victims or as perpetrators. Indeed, in a dangerous environment, each settlement sought to defend itself from predation by augmenting its numbers through preying on (generally weaker) neighbors and absorbing captives into its ranks. The same elders often told me how their forebears both guarded the women of their own settlement when fetching water and, on other occasions, lay in wait at water sources to capture the women of other *makola* (matrilineages).[4]

As a result of these practices, most settlements comprised persons of diverse origins, including, sometimes, people taken captive in the lowlands surrounding the plateau. Marcos told me that his Makonde matrilineage, Vamilange, was (and is) called Amiransi in the Makua-speaking region where they originated. After his "mother"[5] was captured by the Makonde Vaivava matrilineage, she was "eaten" by them—that is, adopted as a Vaivava woman. Later generations questioned why her offspring descended from Vaivava on both sides only to find that they did not—that they were *vana va mulidodo* (leg children), meaning descendants of slaves (cf. Gengenbach 2000: 530). Marcos told me: "There are many, many *makola* on the plateau who are 'leg children.' Each one shares its history—its origin myths—with a matrilineage somewhere off the plateau, some among Makua, others among Yao, Angoni, or other groups."

While many contemporary plateau residents descended from peoples who were captured in the precolonial period by plateau dwellers, others descended from peoples who took refuge on the plateau from raiders and slave traders in the same period.

"We came to the plateau from Mataka's country, fleeing Angoni," an elder told me in Mwambula.[6] "We were once Yao."

Our host when in the village of Matambalale, Augusta Bento—known to us as Binti Bento (daughter of Bento)—was a skilled potter. Although contemporary plateau residents could purchase lightweight tin water buckets in the marketplace, many continued to store water in their homes in clay vessels such as the ones she made, which kept their contents cool throughout the day.

"We are really Makua," said another. "We took refuge here from the slave caravans."

As the historian Malyn Newitt has written, with reference specifically to Mozambique:

[T]he slave trade was not simply an export trade. Slaves were sold internally in Africa and accumulated in the hands of chiefs and warlords, and many of them were used to build up private armies, to increase the number of productive women in a community, or to support the status of chiefs and other leading males within matrilineal societies. . . . [T]he slave trade led to the emergence of large protected settlements, militarised societies and large-scale political organization, particularly among the matrilineal peoples north of the Zambesi. The losers were the small, scattered disorganized communities which often had to abandon whole areas of countryside and gather under the protection of some warlord or retreat into more easily defended regions. The depopulation created a vacuum and encouraged migration, so that whole chieftaincies relocated in the early nineteenth century. (Newitt 1995: 253)

The oral testimony of Muedan elders with whom we worked generally suggested that migrants to the plateau south of the Rovuma were none other than the "losers" described by Newitt—"small, scattered disorganized communities" who fled to "more easily defended regions." The plateau—previously unsettled owing to its porous soil and, hence, total absence of sources of water—served these peoples-in-flight as a more defensible home.

According to oral testimony, the plateau's first settlers referred to themselves by the names of the elders who led them to their new homes and founded the settlements in which they lived. Those led by Lishehe, for example, called themselves Valishehe (or Vanalishehe) and called their settlement Lishehe. Although these migrants undoubtedly sought *likonde* (fertile land) that would allow them to grow the crops they needed to sustain themselves—and found that land beneath the dense bush growing on the high plain—they would come to call themselves Makonde, said by some (e.g., Dias 1964: 64) to mean "people in search of *likonde*," only with the passage of time.

Even as these settlers reconstituted their social, economic, and political institutions and thus gave birth to a new collective identity, however, they spoke of power, according to their descendants, in the language of sorcery. In their struggles for survival, the clever sought competitive advantage against rivals through the use of medicinal substances such as the *ntela* that Maunda told us the people of his settlement used against strangers. In a world whose every crevice potentially concealed peril, the powerful persuasively boasted of their abilities to see enemies not only lying in ambush at the water source but also, as we shall see, in an invisible realm.

2

Provocation and Authority, Schism and Solidarity

"As a young man, I had a reputation for provoking fights," Mandia told us.

We sat together on the verandah of the elder's home in Nimu, the village where Tissa had grown up and where his father and younger brother still lived. The reverence Tissa exhibited for Mandia surpassed ordinary respect for one's elders. But then, Mandia was no ordinary elder. He was, Tissa told me with pride, one of only three *vahumu* still living among the Makonde of the plateau region.

"When we went to dance *mapiko* in neighboring settlements," the *humu* continued, "I was always insulting people."

He spoke softly, holding his arms and hands still and close to his body rather than gesticulating as most Muedan men did when speaking.

"If someone insulted my *likola*, I was off to war."

So gentle was the *humu*'s demeanor, I found his words difficult to believe. He addressed this contradiction directly when he next spoke: "Eventually, those in my *likola* became tired of it—tired of participating in the fights that I had started—and so they decided to make me *humu*. That way, they reasoned, I would have to behave more responsibly and be finished with this thing of going around provoking fights all the time."

Mandia's career embodied the paradoxes that defined power on the Mueda plateau in generations past. The acts of *ushaka* (provocation) through which he demonstrated his courage and audacity, and through which he won respect as an *nkukamalanga* (provider), sometimes gave rise to tensions within his matrilineage. Mandia sometimes bit off more than he—or his Vashi-tunguli brethren—could chew. The Vashitunguli digested the young Mandia's energies by making him *humu*—charging him with balancing the appetites of his peers and serving the matrilineage as diplomat.

Although *vahumu* were never used by the Portuguese as native intermediaries—and therefore were not subject to the post-independence FRELIMO ban on the chieftaincy—the institution fell out of favor in the years following independence. When we met with the *humu* Mandia in 1994, he had not performed the *humu*'s distinctive ritual dance in many years. Because he had no one to drum for him, Marcos stood in, attempting as best he could to produce the high-pitched frenetic beat he remembered from dances he had witnessed as a boy. The aged Mandia tired quickly. So happy was he at having performed, however, tears welled up in his eyes and ran down his cheeks.

As he explained to us: "In times past, the *humu* acted as counselor. When others in the *likola* were unable to resolve a dispute, the *humu* intervened. In wars between matrilineages, *vahumu* were not touched by anyone on either side."

Vahumu, however, were not the principal figures of authority among plateau populations of the precolonial period. Their existence was in fact necessitated by complex dynamics between plateau settlements and the authority figures who governed them: *vanang'olo vene kaja* ("settlement heads"; literally, "elders-stewards-of-settlement": *vanang'olo* meaning "elders"; *vene* meaning "chiefs," "heads," "stewards," or "lords"; and *kaja* meaning "settlement"). Settlement heads traced their authority to the ancestor-founders of the settlements they governed, inheriting from these matrilateral kinsmen not only titles but, often, also names. Deceased settlement heads were remembered by their successors in rites of ancestral supplication, called *kulipudya*, during which requests were made for the beneficent intervention of the departed in the affairs of the living.

Some settlement heads enjoyed greater prestige than others. If a *nang'olo mwene kaja* (s.) claimed descent from a founder who had settled virgin lands, he inherited from this founder status as a *nang'olo mwene shilambo* ("land chief"; literally, "elder-steward-of-lands": *shilambo* meaning "lands"). Descendants of migrants who had requested land and amicable relations with the existing occupants of the regions they settled—as many were forced to do with increasing population density on the plateau over the course of the nineteenth century—recognized their hosts as land chiefs, expressing their dependence and gratitude in perpetuity by participating in the *kulipudya* ceremonies of their hosts.[1]

The continuity of a settlement was by no means assured in the midst of the chaotic and dangerous environment of precolonial northern Mozambique—shaped, as it was, by episodic drought and famine, as well as by endemic raiding and slave trading. Among those that perished, for example, was Lishehe's village. When in 1999 I sought to identify his descendants so that I might discover whether accounts of O'Neill's visit had been passed down to the present day, I found that his name was still uttered in rites of ancestral remembrance in the region, but that Lishehe and his people had fallen prey to more powerful matrilineages and disappeared completely.

In attempts to forestall such catastrophe, settlement heads (whether founders or latecomers) and their populations (whether large or small) stood to gain much in the precolonial period by forging alliances with others. By the time of Portuguese conquest (ca. 1917), plateau populations had begun to form concentrated alliances, comprising as many as ten or twelve matrilineages, under the leadership of powerful warlords (sometimes land chiefs and sometimes not) capable of organizing and protecting caravans to trade India rubber, gum copal, beeswax, and sesame at the coast for cloth, iron, and, most importantly, arms, ammunition, and powder.[2]

The elder Lyulagwe, in the village of Litembo, provided us with an excellent description of the settlement in which he grew up. The *nang'olo mwene kaja*, Malapende, was widely feared in the southern central region of the plateau, Lyulagwe remembered, and other settlement heads in the vicinity were forced either to forge an alliance with him or to contend with him as an enemy. Malapende, Lyulagwe told us, integrated into his defenses the settlements of less powerful *vanang'olo* who requested Malapende's protection. Other elders shared similar descriptions with us of the settlements of powerful warlords in the regions with which they were familiar. As we shall see, the power of such warlords was inseparable from their reputations as capable sorcerers.

Despite alliances and residential conglomerations, however, *likola* identity remained the foundation of social organization among plateau residents into the twentieth century (Dias and Dias 1970: 11–116). Daughters of the matrilineage might never live in its settlement, being born in their fathers' settlements and moving to their husbands' upon marriage. Perpetually in dispersion among other matrilineages, women nonetheless enacted their *likola* identity by feeding the settlements of their matrilineages with their sons, who, upon coming of age, would take up residence adjacent to an *njomba* (matrilineal uncle), who provided them with the means to marry and establish a household.

As ranking elder, the *nang'olo mwene kaja* was considered *njomba* to the entire settlement. The successful settlement head played many roles. If he and his settlement were capable, he organized caravans to trade at the coast and, in some cases, led them personally. He was both entitled to the goods procured in trade and responsible for distributing them among his followers as necessary. The settlement depended upon arms for self-defense but also used them, in combination with other goods, as bridewealth to consolidate the marriages of the young men who would take up residence in the settlement. Thus, to ensure the strength of the matrilineage, the settlement head sought to strike a balance between the settlement's simultaneous needs for guns and for the young men who would bear them. Power relations within and between matrilineages took shape as arms passed from one hand to the next. Powerful settlement heads sat atop an arms-trade hierarchy that subjugated youths to their matrilineal uncles, and women to the men who negotiated their marriages. The relatively younger and less powerful had little choice but to allow the relatively older and more powerful to appropriate, and to redistribute, the wealth that they produced in their fields, gathered in the hunt, and procured on their trading trips to the coast.

Notwithstanding client relations with more powerful neighbors, even weaker matrilineages enjoyed a substantial degree of autonomy over their internal affairs, exercising the right, for example, to pass on the most basic of resources—land—to junior affiliates of the *likola*. This was true even when lands had been originally acquired by a settlement founder from a land chief belonging to another *likola*. Consequently, all settlement heads played a role in land distribution. Their role, however, was often subtle. Land claims were nested, meaning that an individual granting land to another maintained a residual claim on that land indefinitely, even if the receiving individual granted it to someone else. This principle applied to land granted by a settlement head to fellow members of the matrilineage, to land granted by an adult male to a nephew, to land granted by a man to his wife, or to land granted by a woman to her children, just as the principle applied to land granted by a land chief to incoming migrants. In any of these contexts, however, granted land was rarely reclaimed as long as social relations were sustained between grantor and grantee. Land transactions or transferals thus took place most often at the lowest levels in a hierarchy of claims, meaning that a *likola* member could give land to his nephew, or a man to his wife, without the direct involvement of the settlement head. Nonetheless, the settlement head played an important role in the resolution of disputes over land arising between residents of the settlement. In concert with other elders—whose council was called *kupakanila*—he bore witness to and preserved historical memory of land transactions and claims.

The role that the settlement head played as social arbitrator was as complex and as essential as any. The perilous environment in which the *likola* sustained itself ensured that a high value was placed upon daring and bravery. Young men gained reputations for themselves through committing acts of provocation (*ushaka*), such as raiding a neighboring settlement and taking a captive bride without giving up a weapon as bride-price. Aggression sometimes turned inward, however, spawning conflict between members of the same *likola* or, even, affronts on the part of the "ambitious" (*washojo*) to the authority of the settlement head. Such occurrences could lead to the emergence of factions and prompt a group to abandon the settlement to establish its own at a distance.[3] Splintering of the *likola* in this way weakened it vis-à-vis other matrilineages and posed a serious threat to the security of all its members.

So difficult was it to manage intra-*likola* tensions that, by the turn of the century, many Makonde matrilineages had established a new political institution to cope with the consequences of splintering. Whether living in the same settlement or not, members of such matrilineages nominated a *humu*, who subsequently "belonged to" no specific settlement but, rather, commanded respect from members of the *likola* resident in any of its settlements.[4]

The *humu* Mandia described the role of the *humu* to us in language that emphasized its establishment among plateau Makonde as a means of suppressing excessive, predatory appetites: "War did not satiate us; this thing of constantly fighting would have no end, so we needed a person to quench it from time to time. That is what the *humu* did."

In material affairs, the *humu* enjoyed less privilege than the *nang'olo mwene kaja*. He was restricted from travel beyond *likola* territory, was barred from working his own fields, and was not permitted to accumulate personal wealth. He was made to remain still and quiet, for the most part, in one of the settlements of his *likola*. Although his basic physical needs were provided for by the *likola*, his station was that of service, and his living conditions were no more comfortable—and probably less so—than those of his fellow *likola* members. The *humu*, however, was considered to embody *likola* solidarity. Through swallowing obscure medicinal substances in the course of his ritual investiture, the *humu* internalized powers greater than any individual member of the *likola* and held them secure within his body—within the *likola*'s body. His counsel was never challenged by *likola* members. Indeed, members of other matrilineages also fell silent before *vahumu*, who frequently also intervened in inter-*likola* disputes (see also Dias and Dias 1970: 318–319).[5]

Vanang'olo vene kaja and *vahumu* worked together to prevent the fracturing of the *likola* and the dissipation of its strength. As we shall see, however, there was more to this endeavor than first meets the eye.

3

Meat, Power, and the Feeding of Appetites

"It is only the rare person who eats the meat of a lion," Kalamatatu said.

As well as I had come to know the elder, I couldn't be certain whether he was on the verge of grinning widely or, instead, just squinting to see through the cataracts that clouded his vision.

"*Kushulula*," he added.

I had never heard the verb before. I turned to Marcos, who sat beside me. *His* smile was unmistakable.

"*Kushulula* is a very special word," Marcos said. He put his hand on my thigh as a friendly, apologetic gesture before continuing. "You *vajungu* ["foreigners" or "white people"] eat meat every day but, among us, that is considered a defect."

"So what does *kushulula* mean?" I asked.

"It depends upon how the word is used," Marcos responded. He reflected on the question for a moment.

"When the tap on the standpipe does not shut off completely and water drips from it, that is *kushulula*." His hand moved rhythmically, closing at the top of its motion and opening at the bottom to mimic dripping water splashing on the ground.

"The same thing happens when an animal smells food. Saliva drips from its mouth—*kushulula*." He now made a similar gesture in front of his own face.

He paused for a moment, then added: "When the word is used to speak of a person, it refers to an insatiable appetite."[1]

Suspended as I was between Shimakonde (in which we spoke with Kalamatatu), Portuguese (in which Marcos spoke to me), and English (in which I sometimes spoke to myself), I scrawled field notes in whatever language came to me. Words blended into one another as I attempted to surround the new word—to define it more by association than by translation. "*Kushulula*," I wrote; then "avarice," followed by "voracious" and, finally, the Portuguese word *vício*—which translates into English as "vice."

I heard Kalamatatu say, "Ehhh heee," in response to Marcos's explanation. It now seemed to me that the elder was laughing, ever so slightly.

Kalamatatu, Marcos, and I had come to the question of people eating lion meat by way of a conversation about wildlife and hunting in the plateau region. Kalamatatu, I knew from previous conversations, had been a skilled hunter in his younger days. He told me that he had great experience in hunting bushpig, impala, and even buffalo. When I had asked about hippo and elephant, he had told me that he had tasted their meat on many occasions, but that he had never killed these animals himself.

I knew that, in his role as a *muntela* (medicinal specialist), Kalamatatu had been summoned on many occasions to accompany hunters in pursuit of lions that prowled in the environs around plateau villages. He once told me: "When a lion is seen in the bush nearby, I prepare a pumpkin gourd with *ntela* [the generic term for any medicinal substance]. Then I go to the place where the lion was seen, and I set fire to the bush. The fire [burns] to where the lion is hiding. People follow the fire, discover the lion there, and kill it. The *ntela* prevents the lion from harming anyone."[2]

I knew that Kalamatatu had killed many lions, for which he had gained tremendous renown across the plateau. Some of these, he had told me, proved to be ordinary bush lions. Others, however, turned out to be *vantumi va vanu*, "lion-people." Kalamatatu had proved this by conducting autopsies and discovering *shidudu* (ground cassava leaves, eaten by Muedans as a relish) in the guts of these animals.

I knew that the meat of lion-people was not eaten, for to do so would be tantamount to cannibalism. I wondered, however, what became of the flesh of ordinary bush lions, and whether these animals were ever hunted for their meat. On his way to telling me that the consumption of lion meat was an audacious act, undertaken only by a "fearless" man (*munu akajopa sinu*), Kalamatatu continued criticizing the defect that he called *kushulula:* "If you eat meat every day, you will finish off your livestock in no time. It is imprudent." He sat on the slab of tree bark that he carried from his house and placed on the ground each time we came to visit him. As he spoke, he rocked forward on his feet, his bottom now and then lifting slightly from his seat. "You end up isolating yourself from others by eating more than they do. Others will be reluctant to share a plate with you for fear that you will eat everything."

I readied myself for a lengthy lecture from the elder on the immorality of greed. Kalamatatu's denunciation of *kushulula*, however, was suddenly cut short. His wife, who knelt on a reed mat on the ground close by, winnowing manioc flour, had been listening attentively.

She now chimed in, irreverently: "*Kushulula*?! Ahhhh! I would never turn down such a man!"

We turned our heads in time to see her broad smile as she exclaimed, "I love to eat meat!"

When I turned my attention back to Kalamatatu, his head was bowed. I thought for a moment that he was ashamed of his wife's remark, but I soon realized that he was hiding a mischievous smile. Quietly, but forcefully, the elder responded to what his wife had said by telling us: "*That* is why I learned to hunt."

Muedans have long expressed ambivalence toward power in the idiom of consumption. In conversation with us, they acrimoniously described the powerful in their midst, simply, as "those who eat well" or "those who eat everything." Powerful Muedans, for their part, often bemoaned the endless demands placed upon them—as well as the expressions of envy directed at them—by poorer, less powerful Muedans by saying, "They want to eat me." Those who had acquired wealth elsewhere were often reluctant to return to the plateau, where they risked "being devoured."[3]

Muedans of all social categories condemned *wakwaukanga*—"those who eat alone." Kalamatatu told us that, as a boy, he was horrified of being labeled an *nkwaukanga* (one who eats alone). He described such people to us not only as greedy but even as ugly. As a youngster, he watched and emulated older boys who butchered and shared out the meat of the animals they had taken from the forest. Accordingly, he learned to give the most prestigious parts to his settlement head and other choice cuts to his *likola* elders and respected women in his immediate family; for himself, he kept mere morsels. Through this process, he and fellow youths learned to measure their own appetites against the appetites of others as they both submitted to and reproduced the social hierarchy of the settlement.[4]

At the same time, hunting provided young men like Kalamatatu with opportunities to develop and to realize their ambition (*shojo*). Like other elders with whom we talked, Kalamatatu expressed great pride in having "fed" the residents of his settlement as a young man, whether through hunting, working the fields, or earning wages. "Providers" (*wakukamalanga*) such as these men accrued unto themselves reserves of social capital that they could later

Marcos was not with me when I first met Kalamatatu, nor had he ever before encountered the elder. When I introduced the two of them on my second visit to the elder's home in Matambalale, Kalamatatu was astonished that I had remembered his name. He nudged Marcos and said, "Did you hear that?! He said my name!" He then reached out to clasp my hand and said to me, "From now on, you too are `Kalamatatu'!" His wife, who sat close by, held her belly and laughed. "Tell them what it means," she said to her husband. The elder informed us, "*Tatu* means three, of course. *Kalamatatu* means a three days' journey away from home. When I was a younger man, I liked to travel a lot." His wife cried out, "You liked to visit women!" Kalamatatu smiled impishly: "Yes, I had many women in those days. So my wife would tell me, 'Three days is enough to conduct business; the fourth day you will have to account for!' As I would leave, she would call out behind me, '*Kalamatatu*'! Eventually, it became a name."

convert into other forms of power and/or wealth. Muedans may have condemned avarice (as Kalamatatu did in his conversation with Marcos and me), but they as easily admitted to—even celebrated—strong appetites (as Kalamatatu's wife did with us). In the very act of criticizing the appetites of others, Muedans inescapably highlighted their own longings to taste the fruits of power and privilege.

Prescient Muedans such as Kalamatatu indeed realized that the power to feed others and the power to feed oneself were bound together in complex ways. The powerful, they realized, needed not themselves hunt meat. Instead, the powerful hunted subordinates, the fruits of whose labor they appropriated and redistributed. Warlords like Malapende were said by Muedans to "eat" not only their rivals but also their subordinates. But such powerful figures also "fed" the very people they "ate." The satisfaction of their appetites sustained those who constituted a part of their expansive bodies. Indeed, insofar as they came to embody the unity of the social group, they ate on behalf of all (such as the *humu* Mandia was expected to do upon accepting his title, as discussed in chapter 2).

Muedans not only exhorted the powerful among them to share the bounty of their plates but assessed the legitimacy of such individuals as authority figures in accordance with whether or not they fed others. The power of self-serving individuals was thus undermined.

The idiom of consumption through which Muedans assessed the legitimacy of power referenced not only the social distribution of meat and other material goods. It referred also to a parallel world of predation—the domain of sorcery. Those who *fed on* people rather than *feeding* people,[5] those who fed only themselves, those who "ate alone," were indeed suspected to be bearers of extraordinary, horrific powers.[6]

4

The Invisible Realm

"Seven helicopters lifted off to attack this house," the elder Komesa Baina told us. "One from the village of Lutete, one from Miteda, one from Wavi, one from Matambalale, one from Nampanha, one from Namacule, and one from Muatide."

Komesa sat rigidly in his seat in the shade beneath the eaves of his home. He did not look at Marcos or me but, instead, stared straight ahead into his yard.

"The one from Lutete burst into flames as it took off," he informed us matter-of-factly. "The other six burned here, in Namande." Emphatically, he pointed to the ground, beneath his feet.

I struggled to make sense of what we were being told. Only moments earlier, Komesa had been telling us that there had been a *kolela* (cholera) outbreak in the village of Namande in which he lived. He had then added, "It wasn't really *kolela*," and before I knew what had happened, he was talking about helicopters.

It was August 1999. The last time helicopters had flown Muedan skies, to my knowledge, had been during the 1994 United Nations–led campaign to demobilize FRELIMO and RENAMO soldiers in the months preceding the nation's first multiparty elections. The last time helicopters might have actually attacked anyone in the plateau region, I had assumed, was during the war for Mozambican independence, which had ended more than twenty-five years earlier. The communal villages Komesa named did not yet exist then.

Marcos, apparently, did not share my confusion. "So you were their target!" he said to Komesa excitedly. "I heard about these helicopters!"

Although Komesa knew that Marcos was born and raised in one of the settlements whose residents now lived in Namande, and that he kept up with events in the village via family networks, the elder's expression—reinforced by momentary silence—betrayed a certain pride that people living far from Namande knew of the incident. He continued his story.

"After the attack of these helicopters, people in the seven villages that I named came down with a strange form of diarrhea. The health officials who came called it *kolela*. But as I said, it wasn't *kolela*." Komesa looked low in the sky, just over the bamboo fence that demarcated his yard, before adding, "It was *uwavi*."[1]

He then looked at Marcos and me briefly as he clinched his case. "My uncle, Shitutu, died of this *kolela*. Soon after he died, someone walked the village at night. They called out, 'Shitutu died in Komesa's house!'" (meaning that he died trying to kill Komesa by means of sorcery).[2]

After pausing, Komesa punctuated his story by saying, "That's all I know."

I pressed Komesa, nonetheless, to explain these occurrences to us further. He added, simply, that the helicopter that burned in Lutete may have accidentally struck an antisorcery mine there but that he was protected from the other six by his own defenses, which not only caused the helicopters to crash and burn but also "turned the attacker's *uwavi* around" (*kupilikula*).

"The people who died from this diarrhea all died trying to kill me," he said stoically.

Marcos asked Komesa if we might be able to see where the helicopters had crashed.

Komesa's gentle laugh melted into a faint smirk. "You can go there, but you won't see anything. Those who told me about the helicopters could see them, but they are *vakulaula vavi* [sorcerer-healers]."

Marcos smiled and turned to me, saying playfully, "*Vakulaula vavi* are the 'black boxes' for these crashes!"

Komesa rose and headed for the gate at the side of his house. We followed, uncertain how far we would be traveling. Only ten or fifteen meters in front of Komesa's house, we stopped. The row of houses in which Komesa's was situated opened onto the village center, where a few children sat under a mango tree watching us attentively. Komesa directed our gaze back toward his house. At the front right corner stood a cashew tree, no more than five meters high, to which he pointed.

"That's were they went down," Komesa told us.

For a moment, I failed to notice the strange, pale-brown shade of the bark. I then realized that the tree was dead.[3]

"I don't know why people are envious of me," Komesa Baina said when I asked him why he was attacked by sorcerers. "I don't provoke anyone. I stay at home and don't bother anyone. I'm just an old man." In fact, Komesa was a man of relatively great power and wealth in the village of Namande. He had held positions of authority in local government, his house was covered with a zinc roof, and he dressed well. "It must be part of a larger project to destroy me," he said. He looked at each of us directly before adding, "Your having visited today means that surely I will be attacked tonight."

ıllı

When Muedans spoke with me or in my presence about sorcery, they often punctuated their accounts as Komesa did, saying, "That's all I know." Indeed, Muedans frequently told of what they knew in the voices of others who, they said, had seen and reported sorcery's strange happenings. On occasion, Muedans spoke of specific occurrences of sorcery, naming assailants and/or victims (sometimes themselves). More often, however, they spoke in vague terms about the patterns of sorcery's occurrence. In such accounts, passed along the grapevine and down the generations, the present was informed by the past, and the past was animated by the present.

Not until the colonial era had Muedans heard of "*kolela.*" Helicopters were unknown to Muedans until the independence war. Even so, Komesa Baina saw in the attacks upon his home and in the outbreak of disease in the surrounding villages something that would have been recognizable to generations of his forebears. "It was *uwavi*," he told us.

Like Muedans of the precolonial period, Komesa saw evidence in his world of the existence of hidden, often menacing forces. Indeed, Muedans have long understood their world to comprise obverse and reverse sides: one, the visible realm of mundane affairs; the other, the invisible realm of phenomena both fantastic and terrifying.[4] The invisible realm, as we shall see, simultaneously mirrors and negates the visible. It exists as a realm apart—in imitation of, contradiction with, and opposition to the visible—but also exists within the visible, as well as subsuming the visible within itself.[5]

According to Muedans, the keys to passage between the two realms making up their world were *mitela* (s., *ntela*), physical substances available in the visible realm but used to gain entrance to and operate in the invisible realm to astonishing ends. While the category of *mitela* has expanded in recent years to include such exotic materials as Orange Fanta and the acid of disposable batteries,[6] Muedans of the precolonial period generally harvested their *mitela* from the flora and fauna of the plateau region. Even as we worked in Mueda, many of the most widely known and used *mitela* derived from the roots, bark, and leaves of trees and shrubs found growing wild in the bush.[7] The antlers, horns and tusks of local wildlife also continued to serve Muedans as *mitela*.

Muedans often told us that, like their ancestors, they (or at least others among them) knew how to do great things with *mitela*. *Mitela* could be used to prolong lives, to enhance physical strength, to ensure successful harvests, hunts, and travels, and to protect people from illness and misfortune. On the other hand, *mitela* could be used to other, more sinister ends—for example, to steal from one's neighbors or kin or to do others harm by causing them misfortune, including sending illness or death to visit them or members of their families.

While specific purposes might be achieved only with specific forms of *mitela*, Muedans told us that many forms of *mitela* served multiple ends. A single form of *ntela* might be used in the commission of either socially sanctioned or socially reprehensible acts. In other words, Muedans conceived of *mitela*, categorically, as morally neutral sources of power that could be used to create or to destroy, to protect or to attack, to cure or to kill.[8] According to Mueda's colonial-era anthropologists António Jorge Dias and Margot Schmidt

Dias: "*Ntela,* as a magic drug, has the power to fortify the vital force of men, to diminish it, or to steal it completely" (1970: 367, my translation). They further conclude: "Man increases his powers or loses them according to his use of beneficial *ntela;* or others use *ntela* against him. It is *ntela* that explains why some live many years and remain healthy while others grow weak and die; it is all a question of *ntela*" (367, my translation).

In precolonial days, as now, the most powerful form of *ntela* known was *shikupi.* This obscure substance allowed its bearers to render themselves and their acts invisible to ordinary people. As the elder Mushimbalyulo Naku-lungene explained to us when we spoke with him in the village of Magaia: "*Shikupi* permits someone to do something without anyone seeing it, without anyone realizing it."[9] Users of *shikupi* were able not only to render themselves invisible but also to *see* extraordinary things, including one another and the acts that their colleagues committed under *shikupi*'s veil.[10] Through the use of *shikupi,* then, its bearers effectively produced and sustained an invisible realm in which they moved and acted "outside" or "beyond" the world as ordinary people experienced it, free of the strictures and constraints of the mundane visible realm.[11] Muedans quite simply referred to this transcendent act, and to the invisible acts that this transcendence made possible, as *uwavi,* while referring to those who commit such acts as *vavi,* "sorcerers" (s., *mwavi*).[12]

According to what Muedans such as Komesa Baina told us, as sorcerers created and inhabited the invisible realm of *uwavi,* they not only doubled the world in which they lived but also doubled themselves.[13] Even as sorcerers moved about invisibly at night, their bodies remained visible to ordinary people, who might find them innocently sleeping in their beds. In their doubled world, these doubled Muedans mimicked ordinary social life, bonding together to sustain and reproduce themselves by dancing together in the wee hours of the morning in the center of the village (or, in the days before independence, in the center of the settlement). Sorcery, Muedans often told me, had to be danced.[14] Through dancing sorcery (*kuvina uwavi*), however, sorcerers also inverted social norms.[15] They danced naked, without shame—usually in the presence of family members of the opposite sex—demonstrating through their boundless conviviality their absolute disrespect.

Sorcerers, of course, not only crossed over into the realm of the invisible but also crossed back again—while still themselves invisible—making manifest the invisible realm within the visible. Through ghastly forays into the visible realm, they invisibly circumscribed and controlled it.[16] Their extraordinary vision allowed them not only to see one another and the invisible realm in which they moved but also to see from a unique perspective the visible realm and its inhabitants. Sorcerers thus formulated novel visions of the world.[17] Their hidden vantage points served them as points of unusual leverage on the world, revealing to them the world's operative logics and allowing them to manipulate these logics to accomplish fantastic feats.[18]

The elder Mushimbalyulo told us: "With *shikupi*, one can mount an attack, and no one notices." To this end, sorcerers have long used other medicinal substances in conjunction with *shikupi*. Sorcerers, for example, sometimes surreptitiously deposited a substance called *shongo* in an unsuspecting victim's food or drink, producing illness.[19] They also buried *mitela*-treated objects called *mashesho* beneath the pathways over which their victims walked. *Mashesho* exploded like bombs, producing pains in their victims' legs and backs.[20]

The *effects* of such attacks *were* noticeable. When confronted with misfortune, Muedans generally suspected someone in their midst of practicing *uwavi* to malicious ends—*uwavi wa kujoa* ("sorcery of danger" or "dangerous sorcery"), as they called it, or *uwavi wa kunyata* ("dirty sorcery," "ugly sorcery," or "bad sorcery"). When a person's goods or property were discovered to be damaged, or when his or her good fortune suddenly diminished, they suspected *uwavi wa lwanongo* ("sorcery of ruin" or "sorcery of destruction"). When someone fell ill or died, Muedans suspected *uwavi wa kubyaa* or *uwavi wa kulogwa* ("sorcery of killing/murder").

Sorcerers, Muedans averred, did not merely sabotage, destroy, and kill. They sustained themselves on the declining fortunes of those they attacked. In some instances, sorcerers harnessed the labor power of their victims. In others, they made of them their prey, invisibly feeding on their flesh as they withered and died.[21] Indeed, visible signs of suffering, fatigue, and illness were often interpreted by Muedans as the effects of a person being forced to labor at night for a sorcerer-master or as the effects of a sorcerer's consuming the person's flesh. Sorcerers, Muedans told me, were capable not only of concealing themselves but also of hiding their victims—replacing their bodies, as needed, with banana trees made to look like them. Indeed, the corpses Muedans buried were said sometimes not to be corpses at all but, instead, banana trees; the dead, in such cases, were said to live on as *mandandosha* (slave laborers)[22] or to have been eaten entirely by their invisible assailants.

For as long as living Muedans can remember, sorcerers have also masked their actions by transforming themselves into animals or by making animals to do their bidding (see also Dias and Dias 1970: 369).[23] Muedans told me that these animals sometimes operated in subtle ways. Sorcery owls, for example, gathered information or stole objects from the homes of those they visited. More dramatic cases involved dangerous and/or predatory animals, such as snakes, leopards, and lions that killed and sometimes ate their victims. These attacks could take place behind the veil of *shikupi;* mauled by an invisible lion, for example, a person would appear, in the visible realm, to be wasting away with illness. Other times, people actually witnessed the attacks of such animals or, at least, saw the victim's mauled remains.[24]

When I asked them why anyone would perform the dreadful deeds of which sorcerers have long been accused, Muedans often claimed ignorance. "How should I know?!" Kalamatatu often said to me. "I've never done these things!"[25] While the question truly vexes Muedans, when pressed, many divulged their ideas about what motivates sorcerers. The most common explanation offered was envy (*ing'ou*). The envy of sorcerers might have been provoked by almost anything. In precolonial days, a woman might have been envious of a neighbor's harvest, of a co-wife's many healthy children, or of a daughter's youthful beauty.[26] Among contemporary Muedans, she might have coveted her neighbor's clothes or shoes or her store-bought cooking utensils. In the past, a man might have envied an uncle's authority. In present-day Mueda, he might have coveted a son's education or a neighbor's cash-paying job. The targets of envy and, thus, of sorcery might have been anyone, but the intense interactions and ample opportunities afforded by the ties of kinship have long ensured that sorcery often struck within the family.

Others explained sorcery differently to me. "Sorcerers love human flesh," Marcos often told me. "That's reason enough for them to kill." Some suggested to me that the taste of human flesh cultivated an insatiable, addictive appetite. Children, some told me, were made into sorcerers by being given a piece of human flesh or by being allowed to find a piece of human flesh lying on the ground near them. Once a child ingested such flesh, he or she hungered for more and, eventually, discovered how to feed this craving. An appetite for human flesh was similarly cultivated in adults. Sorcerers recruiting people to join them, many said, provided a feast of human flesh, not only fostering addiction but also creating debt.[27]

According to many with whom we spoke, sorcery recruitment sustained a parallel invisible economy whose idiom was human meat and in which debts had to be repaid in kind. The elder Libata Nandenga once explained to me the rules of exchange in this flesh economy: "Money or other goods will not do; only human flesh. If someone has eaten the flesh of a young girl, then that person must repay the debt with the flesh of a young girl; if they have eaten the flesh of another kind of person, they must give back meat from whatever kind of person it was. They must kill someone from their own family, and if they fail to do so, those they owe may eventually kill them."[28]

Libata's daughter, Mbegweka, once told us that the vicious circle of flesh debts was what kept sorcery going, drawing new recruits into the circle of sorcerers and amplifying sorcery's destructive force in Muedan society, now as in the past.[29]

5

Healing Visions

"The guy was going mad!" Marcos said. "He said he had pains in his chest. He tore off his shirt. He was in a real panic—saying that he was going to die."

"So you were in a serious predicament, then," I said.

"I sure was," Marcos answered, understatedly.

As the story had begun, Marcos was traveling with a friend of his—a soldier on leave—in a motor convoy during the civil war.

"In those days, you couldn't travel alone," Marcos had said. "RENAMO would ambush you. So everything moved in convoys, with military escorts. We were in one of those convoys."

It was when the convoy paused in one of the villages along the route that Marcos's friend had become agitated.

"The problem was that the convoy was stopping only for a few minutes to let passengers off and take others on. If we weren't ready to travel when the leader gave the signal, we would be left behind. It might have been ten days, or two weeks, before another convoy came through. The village wasn't the safest place to be. And if I didn't get home, who would make sure there was something for the kids to eat?"

"So you had to be in that convoy when it pulled out," I said by way of confirmation.

"Exactly. But I couldn't leave my comrade. And he couldn't continue in the state he was in. He was carrying on and yelling. He would have attracted attention."

"It would have been dangerous," I said, demonstrating my understanding of the dilemma Marcos faced.

"Right," Marcos answered. He paused briefly, as if gathering his composure in the moment of which he spoke. He then continued:

"So I thought, 'I'm going to take care of this guy.' I went off to the side of the road and found a tree with green leaves. I don't even know what kind they were. I ripped off a few leaves, I shredded them, I mashed them, and I mixed them with water to make a paste." As he spoke, he simulated the acts he described.

"I put that paste on the guy's chest and I started to call on my ancestors." The voice of the storyteller now became that of the man reverently summoning the spirits of his forebears. "'Shonde,' I said." A smile brought Marcos's reverence to a quick end as he added, "and all the rest."

He continued, smiling but still serious: "I called the names of all the ancestors I knew. Especially Ndikutwala. Ndikutwala. Ndikutwala. Ndikutwala."

"Your mother's mother," I said.

"That's the one."

"So, what happened?" I asked, after Marcos had remained quiet for a time.

"When the guy heard this, he thought, 'This guy's a healer,' and he calmed down. I got him back on the convoy, and we made it to Mocímboa."

"Was he alright?" I asked.

"He was fine," Marcos said, with a grin. "I *healed* him."[1]

                        ᴫ

In his classic work on shamanism in the Americas, Mircea Eliade wrote that "the difference between layman and shaman is quantitative. . . . we could almost say that every Indian 'shamanizes,' even if he does not wish to become a shaman" (1964: 315). Much the same might be said of Muedans and healing. Marcos often told me, playfully, "I'm no healer, but sometimes I know how to heal!"

Marcos was, in fact, fascinated by Muedan healers' homes. When we sat together with a healer, as we often did during the conduct of our research, Marcos became engrossed in the environment. He gazed at the assorted containers that invariably cluttered healing spaces, trying to discern their contents. When given one to examine by its owner, he studied it—even fondled it—as he asked questions about the substance it contained.

Most Muedans, like Marcos, sought to know at least "a little something" about *mitela,* for knowledge of these substances could fortify one's life, and ignorance of them might prove disastrous. Notwithstanding near universal curiosity about *mitela,* however, not all Muedans enjoyed equal opportunity to learn about *mitela.* The greater range of movement enjoyed by men—in the present day and, even more so, in the past—afforded them better chances than women to broaden their knowledge of *mitela.* Elders had an advantage over their juniors; the longer one lived, the more chances one had to learn about the various forms and uses of *mitela*.[2]

Even elder Muedan men encountered moments when they considered their knowledge of *mitela* insufficient to ensure their own well-being in the face of menacing and invisible forces, however. When confronted with misfortunes and afflictions, nearly all Muedans turned for assistance to specialists whose knowledge of *mitela* exceeded their own.

Muedans consulting specialists initially sought to understand the nature of their affliction. This required divination (*yangele*). In the Mueda region, there existed a vast array of divination techniques. By way of example, Salapina Atalambwele, a resident of the village of Nandimba, showed us how she divined by setting a stoppered wine bottle filled with water on the ground and then posing questions about her patient's illness.[3] After each question, she propped an ebony-wood staff against the side of the bottle. If the answer to her question was affirmative, the staff remained upright. If negative, the staff slipped and fell to the ground.[4]

In the precolonial period, Muedans were sometimes told by diviners that the cause of their troubles was the spirit of a forgotten ancestor, and that by propitiating the spirit through performing a rite called *kulipudya* (which involved pouring out libations around the grave of this ancestor and calling upon him or her to restore the health or good fortune of his or her descendant), such problems could be resolved. Contemporary afflictions were less often attributed through divination to forgotten ancestors. In the wake of Catholic evangelization on the Mueda plateau (beginning in 1924), a new category of illness emerged, namely, "God's illnesses"—a category that somewhat eclipsed the category of ancestral discontent, as we shall see in part 2.[5] Muedans with whom we worked generally resigned themselves to the misfortunes that diviners attributed to God. They sometimes spoke of such plights as their destiny or as fate. More importantly, Muedans treated "God's illnesses" as ones innocent of foul play.[6]

Alternatively, diviners might indicate foul play, meaning *uwavi*. Contemporary diviners in fact attributed a great proportion of misfortune, illness, and death to sorcery. While many asserted that they were able not only to discern whether an illness was caused by sorcery but, if so, also to identify the sorcerer (and if they were healers—as many diviners were—to treat the illness), most with whom we spoke did not, as a matter of policy, inform their clients of the identity of their assailants.[7] Diviners often reminded us that sorcerers moved imperceptibly among us, overhearing our words, particularly when we spoke of them; offending such people by talking about them would have been imprudent.[8] While diviners and other specialists claimed not to fear sorcerers as ordinary Muedans did, they generally considered it poor strategy to taunt and unnecessarily antagonize those with whom they did battle. More importantly, perhaps, when diviners identified assailants to their victims (as they did more frequently in the past), violent confrontation could arise. When Dias and Dias conducted their research in the late colonial period, they found that, generally, the perpetrators of sorcery remained, to those who consulted diviners, the unidentified agents of suffering, destruction, and death. Occasionally, however, sorcerers were identified. In such cases, if the accused was a resident of the same village, he or she might have been subjected to an ordeal (the details of which Dias and Dias do not describe) and might have lost his or her life in the process (Dias and Dias 1970: 370). If he or she lived in another settlement, the accusation might have been sufficient cause for hostilities between settlements (371–372).[9]

In the past, as more recently, diviners openly identifying sorcerers to Muedans were generally foreigners who suddenly appeared from parts unknown and pursued for a time their declared objective of ridding the communities they visited of the scourge of witchcraft and/or sorcery before disappearing again. The name by which Muedans have long referred to such diviners—*waing'anga* (s., *ing'anga*)—indeed resonates with the terms by which many peoples south of the Zambezi River refer to their own healers and/or witch doctors, perhaps betraying links (whether by descent or by association of some other kind) between early Muedan *waing'anga* and Nguni invaders. Makudo Shalaga Ntumi Ngole, a diviner living in the village of Nshongwe, described for us a ritual that he witnessed long ago wherein the men, women, and children accused of sorcery by a visiting *ing'anga* were seized, shaven, and made to drink substances which, they were told, would burst inside them like a bomb if ever they practiced *uwavi* again. Makudo concluded that *waing'anga* could get away with openly accusing *vavi* (sorcerers) because they were, themselves, "dangerous." What is more, as "outsiders" they were not bound by intimate ties. When their acts provoked problems within a settlement or in the broader region, they could easily depart.[10]

As local diviners have generally forgone openly identifying sorcerers, and as *waing'anga* have, for as long as living Muedans can remember, been few and far between, Muedans have long relied on others to combat sorcery. Principal among these were the category of persons Muedans referred to as *vamitela* ("medicine people"; s., *muntela*)—medicinal specialists who used their stocks and knowledge of *mitela* to a variety of ends, including combat against sorcery. Many, although not all, diviners were *vamitela*; and many, although again not all, *vamitela* were diviners.

Muedans with whom we worked glossed (in Shimakonde) an entire complex of antisorcery activity as *kuvatela vavi* (defense against sorcery). To begin with, through a vast array of practices, *vamitela* fortified people and their environments against attack. These medicinal specialists and their clients conspired to armor and adorn human bodies, material possessions, livestock, houses, fields, and villages with *mitela* to protect against predatory sorcerers. Wherever and however possible, they inserted *mitela* within or mixed it with the animate and inanimate objects they wished to defend. Indeed, through such means, Muedans filled virtually every crevice of their world with *mitela*.

Essential to such antisorcery practices was a category of *mitela* Muedans called *mashishi*. Medicinal specialists generally said that the *mitela* that made up this category were no different from the *mitela* that sorcerers used in their predatory activities. What made these substances *mashishi*, however, was their use for defensive purposes.

Kabaka Nanume Kapembe, a *muntela* living in the village of Nshongwe, informed us that the term *mashishi* derived from the verb *kushishila*, meaning "to hesitate." He explained, "When a sorcerer encounters *mashishi*, he or she hesitates while trying to figure out which ones to deal with, and how to deal with them. Hesitation brings fear, and fear brings respect."

There were, Kabaka informed us, many different kinds of *mashishi*, used in differing ways to defend different things. As he conversed with us, he pulled from his goatskin bag a small cloth sack, no bigger than a chicken's egg. He told us that it was called *ilishi* and that it was to be hung on a cord around a person's neck to protect his or her body from sorcerers' predation. I most often saw *dilishi* (pl.) tied around the naked waists of infant children. Adults wore them too, although—unless they were *vamitela*—generally concealing them beneath their clothing.[11]

Medicinal specialists also used other means to protect human bodies against sorcerers. The *humu* Mandia (like most *vahumu*, a *muntela* of great renown) explained to us that a newly installed *humu* went from home to home, treating those who fell under his protective jurisdiction with a medicinal substance called *ing'opedi*. Mandia demonstrated the practice as he treated Marcos and me. He placed his right thumb over the opening of a small bottle containing an ivory-white powder and turned it upside down. He then pressed his thumb gently to Marcos's forehead, painting first a vertical line and then a horizontal one; he "treated" me similarly. He explained to us that the substance was made of sorghum flour mixed with certain kinds of *mitela*.[12] The marks on our foreheads would soon disappear, he told us, but the protection they afforded us would linger. For some time, sorcerers would see the marks and know that, should they attack us, they would have to contend with Mandia.

I first met Kabaka Nanume Kapembe at his home in Nshongwe. Tissa and I sat conversing quietly with the elder for hours, asking about his healing knowledge. Following structural adjustment and the rise to prominence in Mozambique of Western aid agencies, most of the clothing available to Muedans came from the United States via Goodwill donation and was referred to as "*roupa* Reagan" ("Reagan's clothes" in Portuguese). The rich floral-print ladies blazer that Kabaka generally wore, unbuttoned, somehow accentuated his gentle dignity. On other occasions, his aged body came to life. As a *nalombo* (master of initiation rites), the white markings that adorned his bare trunk would flash brilliantly as he danced with great energy and agility.

Vamitela used *mitela* not only to protect individual bodies but also to protect social bodies and the built environments in which people lived. Many *vamitela* were specialists in *kushindika ing'ande,* or *kukandyanga ing'ande* ("treating the home/hearth"). Such practices served as well as any means to protect a home and its inhabitants, we were told by Pikashi Lindalandolo, who practiced in the village of Nshongwe. The principal object used in so defending the hearth was a *lipande* (pl., *mapande*), a sort of antisorcery bomb (see also Dias and Dias 1970: 370).

"In olden days, we dug holes in the ground inside the house and buried a clay pot filled with certain kinds of *mitela,*" Kabaka told us, "but later, when other vessels, like glass bottles, became available, we started using them."

Luís Avalimuka, who lived in the town of Mueda, showed us how he made these antisorcery bombs. He smashed a stone into small pieces and put the pieces in a conch shell. He then added the ashes of burned roots, leaves, and bark—*mitela* whose sources he did not specify. To this, he added ground pieces of wood that came from a tree that had been struck by lightning. Next, he added chopped-up pieces of a wood called *ntameka,* along with bits of other kinds of wood. On top of this, he added smaller crushed stones that appeared to me to be quartz. These stones, he told us, acted as a fuse. Finally, he mixed in a handful of black-spotted red seeds—no bigger than snow peas— that he called *dinumbinumbi.*

"To set this, I will dig a hole in the ground and bury it," he told us. "When a sorcerer comes to attack that house, it will go off like a bomb. It will explode and injure the sorcerer. It might kill him but, normally, it will just injure him and drive him away."

I asked Avalimuka if the *lipande* might injure anyone else in the yard— for example, someone living in the house.

"Only if he or she is a sorcerer," he responded.

"Would an ordinary person—say, the owner of the house—see that the *lipande* had gone off when they passed through the yard in the morning?" Marcos asked.

"No," Avalimuka answered. "After the sorcerer is wounded and driven away, the *lipande* goes back into the ground. It doesn't need to be reset. It will work again when the sorcerer returns, or when another sorcerer comes."[13]

In preindependence days, when Muedans lived in small, dispersed settlements, medicinal specialists used other techniques "to defend the [entire] settlement"—*kushililidya ikaja.* Many settlement heads were themselves competent *vamitela.* If they were not, they relied upon such specialists to supply them with the *mitela* necessary to fortify their respective domains. Stakes treated with appropriate medicinal substances were driven into the earth beneath the pathways leading into the settlement. Should sorcerers tread on these, they would be injured.

Just as important to the practice of defending the settlement, Kabaka told us, was *imale,* a substance that was scattered throughout the settlement to render it invisible to potential enemies.[14] The *vamitela* that we interviewed also told us about other substances that have long been used to hide material possessions. Objects treated with these forms of *mitela* would disappear when approached by sorcerers. Tissa, who knew of this phenomenon from his many previous interviews with Muedan *vamitela,* marveled: "A sorcerer can stand in front of a thing and see it. When he steps forward, it disappears. When he steps back, it reappears. Imagine that! Imagine how it must frustrate him!"

Notwithstanding the many lines of defense against sorcery laid down by medicinal specialists, sorcerers still sometimes succeeded in reaching their intended targets, producing misfortunes and afflictions of various kinds. In such instances, Muedans again relied on specialists practiced in the art of healing (*kulaula*). Indeed, many—although not all—*vamitela* (medicinal specialists) were also *vakulaula* (healers).[15] Some *vakulaula* used their knowledge of *mitela* only to treat mundane afflictions. Many, however, also treated afflictions they deemed to be caused by the predatory attacks of sorcerers.

Healers, Muedans said, cured sorcery's ills by "annulling sorcery," by "overturning sorcery," or by "turning sorcery around" on its sender, each expressed in the phrase *kupilikula*.[16] Healers were capable of such feats because they were able to see sorcerers and the heinous acts they committed. Some *vakulaula* openly claimed to have, and to use, *shikupi*—the medicinal substance that allowed sorcerers to render themselves invisible; in any case, Muedans assumed that all healers who practiced *kupilikula* knew *shikupi*. Through using it, Muedans generally agreed, healers themselves entered into the invisible realm where sorcery was practiced and therein practiced their countersorcery.[17] Following the sorcerers with whom they contended, *vakulaula* moved "beyond," or "outside," the world as most Muedans experienced it.[18]

Whereas Muedan sorcerers used the hidden realm as a platform from which to formulate novel visions of the world and to bring these destructive visions to fruition, healers did much the same—albeit to decidedly different ends—(re)modeling the world in accordance with their healing visions. Where sorcerers distorted and subverted the social order through their *excursions of imagination*,[19] healers, through their own *flights of invention*,[20] monitored sorcerers' behavior and the disorder it produced, thereby producing/restoring a beneficial order to the world.[21]

To achieve their healing ends, *vakulaula* transcended not only the world as known to ordinary Muedans but also the world as known by the sorcerers who menaced them. They knew stronger forms of *mitela*, and better methods of using what forms they knew, than did sorcerers. They moved farther "beyond" or "outside" the constraints of the visible realm than did sorcerers. They fixed sorcerers in their gaze, just as sorcerers fixed the Muedans that *they* attacked in *their* gaze. In so doing, *vakulaula* not only "cognize[d] the world"—as James Fernandez has phrased it (1991: 220)—but also persuaded their patients through the "imaginative assertiveness" of their healing practices (219) that they exercised superiority in a world beyond their patients' view. Whether through words or deeds, *vakulaula* achieved this through articulating the visions they formulated, from the platform of the invisible realm, of the visible world and its workings.

Healers not only painted a picture for their patients of the forces that attacked them but also portrayed to them a world in which these forces were undone. They told their patients, through word and deed, that their sufferings were mere sorcerers' imaginings—that they were "made up" and that they could consequently be "unmade." Garro and Mattingly have suggested that the "imaginative journey" of healing is often achieved through the telling of a "compelling story" (2000: 11; see also Lattas 1993: 68); Muedan healers embraced this mandate by undertaking the transcendent maneuver called *kupilikula*, by narrating, as we shall see, a world in which sorcerers' powers were inverted, negated, and/or annulled. Calling upon his ancestor Ndikutwala to soothe his comrade as their convoy prepared to pull out, Marcos—the healing nonhealer—himself undertook such a maneuver.

6

Victims or Perpetrators?

"Why would sorcerers come to you?!" I asked Shindambwanda, greatly surprised.

The healer busied himself with the task at hand—an extended answer, by means of a demonstration, to my question as to how he knew if the patients who came to him suffered from sorcerers' attacks. Marcos—his model client—sat patiently on a reed mat on the ground with his legs extended in front of him. Shindambwanda sat behind Marcos on an *igoli*.[1]

"Many of those who come to see me are not the victims of sorcery," Shindambwanda had said as he tugged at Marcos's shirt, prompting Marcos to remove it.

I had expected the healer to tell me that the others he treated suffered from "God's illnesses." Instead, he told me, "Many of them are sorcerers."

Shindambwanda held in his hand a recycled perfume bottle that was filled with a deep-blue liquid and stoppered with cork. He directed Marcos to straighten his back and to lean forward slightly.

In response to my expression of surprise, he said: "Sorcerers make trouble for themselves."

"What do you mean?" I asked.

Shindambwanda used a piece of cloth to polish the bottle's surfaces. "The things that sorcerers attack are often protected against sorcery. If sorcerers trip the defenses placed around their targets, they can be wounded."[2]

Shindambwanda now placed the bottle on Marcos's back, gingerly, and held it there. He spoke, but his words were inaudible to me.

Marcos, whose ears were only a few centimeters from the elder's mouth, served as an amplifier for me, simultaneously translating the elder's words into Portuguese as if he were hiding them from their speaker. "He's saying that if I am the victim of sorcery, the bottle will fall to the ground, but that if I have wounded myself attacking someone else, the bottle will stick to me where it is."[3]

Shindambwanda slowly removed his hands from the bottle. I watched in suspense. The bottle clung to Marcos's skin. As the moments passed, in silence, Marcos grew tense. Shindambwanda sat motionless, gazing at the bottle. Finally, he removed it.

Neither man spoke. Through my anxiety, I managed to ask, with forced levity, "So, what does that mean?"

"You'll have to ask the elder," Marcos said.[4]

I looked at Shindambwanda.

"This one is not ill," he said, referring to his mock patient, "so this *yangele* [divination] is not true."

In spite of his words, Shindambwanda busied himself with continued intensity. His narrative explication of the acts he performed ceased, leading me to wonder if what he did now was still for my benefit or not. He wiped the perspiration from Marcos's back and adjusted the angle at which Marcos sat. He blew on the bottle and polished it. Then he repeated the divining exercise. Once more, the bottle hung suspended against Marcos's back.

This time, not even I spoke.

After the procedure was repeated a third time with the same result, Shindambwanda reached for Marcos's shirt and placed it over his shoulder. Marcos arose without a word, dressed himself, and sat beside me. Shindambwanda eventually began to speak.

"This is what I do to distinguish between those who have been wounded by sorcerers and those who have wounded themselves."

As he spoke, he looked at me rather than at Marcos. With his words, he both addressed what had transpired before my eyes and ignored it.

"If a person denies being a sorcerer, I cannot heal him, but if he confesses, I can work with him."

Shindambwanda was not alone among healers in suspecting those who came to him for treatment of being sorcerers. "Most people who go to healers are not *vakulogweka* [victims of sorcery]," the healer Boaventura Makuka, of Matambalale, once told us. "Most are *vakulibyaa* [those who have injured themselves undertaking sorcery]."

Makuka's assessment was shared by many Muedan *vamitela*. After all, as

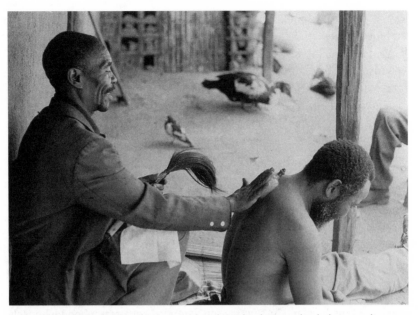

Baptized Tomás Jakobo Almeida, Shindambwanda took a Makonde name when he began work as a healer in 1976. His father, Jakobo, and his father's father, Almeida, were healers before him. Because of this, Shindambwanda was said to possess some of the most powerful forms of *mitela* in the Mueda region.

medicinal specialists they knew well that most every object and/or person that sorcerers might target was protected by antisorcery *mitela* that would harm attacking *vavi*. Most any victim of a successful attack would seek the aid of a healer, who would turn sorcery's effects back upon its sender. With so much sorcery ricocheting around, there were bound to be many who injured themselves in thwarted attacks.

Healers focused great attention on determining whether their patients were sorcerers' victims or wounded sorcerers, for wounded sorcerers who failed to confess their crimes, they said, did not respond to treatment.[5] "Wounded sorcerers are the easiest patients to heal," Renata Damião told us, "but they rot quickly if they don't confess."[6]

Some healers asked their patients if they were wounded sorcerers. Nantulima Lipatu, in Miula, told us, "I can usually tell when someone is a wounded sorcerer. The most common ailment that they suffer is back pain. But they usually tell me, also, that they are *vakulibyaa.*"

Shindambwanda had less confidence in his patients to confess when they were wounded sorcerers, prompting him to divine (as he demonstrated upon Marcos) to determine if his patients were sorcerers' victims or wounded sorcerers. "I can't heal them if they don't confess," Shindambwanda told us. "I send them away. I tell them to find another healer."

Vantila Shingini, of Namande, approached the problem differently: "Any time treatment doesn't work on a patient, I begin to suspect that the patient has wounded himself/herself."[7]

Limitedi Untonji, the blind healer of Nandimba, took the same approach: "When a wounded sorcerer doesn't confess, ordinary treatments won't work, so if my patient doesn't respond to treatment, I suspect him/her. In these cases, I will try a treatment that is appropriate to wounded sorcerers. If it begins to work, I will try to get him/her to admit to sorcery so that I can finish the job."[8]

Not all healers treated wounded sorcerers. Some said that they did not know how to treat such wounds. Those who did treat them justified their work in varied ways. Sinema Kakoli, of Mwambula, told us simply that wounded sorcerers paid well to be healed. By contrast, Limitedi told us that they sometimes did not pay at all. He treated them in any case, just as he treated sorcerers' victims. "The law of medicine is to treat all who are ill," he told us.

Atanásio Herneo, of Matambalale, also adopted this policy. When Tissa asked him how he could justify treating wounded sorcerers when he himself also set traps to wound sorcerers, he answered: "They are people too. Sometimes, parents bring their children to me. These children have injured themselves trying to kill their parents. But their parents want them to be healed."

Marcos once argued with Limitedi on this point: "If I were a healer, I'd never treat wounded sorcerers. I'd let them die. That way, they could be eliminated." Limitedi responded to Marcos by saying: "That's impossible. New sorcerers would always appear. Sorcery can never be eliminated."

Most healers agreed with Limitedi that, despite their work, sorcery could never be eliminated. The perpetual threat of sorcery produced certain anxieties with which Muedans had to cope by taking the necessary precautions against sorcery's occurrence and by seeking the aid of specialists in extraordinary circumstances.

Ironically, consultation with a healer—who was as likely to accuse those who visited him of sorcery as to consider them victims of unprovoked attack (especially if their illness persisted)[9]—often served to deepen anxieties and to produce even greater uncertainties. In the days following our session with Shindambwanda, the normally loquacious Marcos said nothing about the incident. His silence pronounced his lingering angst.

7

Complicated Careers

"Now here is a *mwavi!*" Marcos said, placing his hand on Shindambwanda's knee as he shifted from Shimakonde to Portuguese. I looked Marcos directly in the eye. Although we sat in the shade, his face glistened with perspiration. His tone was playful but, nonetheless, sincere. I was reluctant to speak. Although I had never heard Shindambwanda speak Portuguese, I felt sure that he understood enough to know that Marcos now accused him of being a sorcerer.

This day's conversation with the *nkulaula* had begun with a question posed by Marcos. "*Nang'olo* [elder]," Marcos had said. "Can you tell us something about sorcerers who make lions?"

"*Uwavi wa kupika,*" Shindambwanda had responded, naming this category of *uwavi* as "sorcery of making," or "sorcery of fabrication." The elder continued: "There is a thing called *imika* that is essential for sorcery of fabrication. *Dimika* [pl.] are pieces of wood that have been treated with *mitela.*"

He held up his hand, showing us a string of wooden pieces that he wore as a bracelet around his wrist. "These are *dimika,*" he said. He paused, as if conjuring up a vision. "There are other kinds of *dimika* that are used to make animals."

He drew close to a small wooden stool on the ground before him. "A sorcerer lays a piece of *imika* on the ground," he said, tapping the surface of the stool as if it were the earth. "Then, he says, 'Tomorrow, I want to find a snake here.' In the morning, when he returns, he tests the *imika* by taking it to a tree and saying, 'Now, I want you to bite.' When he says this, it will bite the tree. Then he knows that it is ready. He can then tell it to go and bite the person that he indicates."[1]

Marcos watched Shindambwanda as if he were witnessing the scene that the elder described. Shindambwanda played to his audience, measuring the dramatic effect of his words carefully. He continued: "When you talk to a lion, you tap it with a staff." He mimed the motion, drumming on the stool before him. "To prepare it to kill, you dig three small holes in the ground and fill them with water. You tell the lion to drink from one pool, and then the next, and then the last. Each time, you tap it on the head with the staff." Shindambwanda also feigned each of these acts for us. "With each pool of water, the lion becomes more aggressive."

Like children listening to a storyteller, Marcos and I watched Shindambwanda. I felt a chill as I imagined the scene.

"After the lion has killed, you make it drink from the pools of water in reverse order. The beast will cool down with each drink."

Shindambwanda smiled and let out a snort of laughter. "It is very risky," he said. "After a lion has eaten its victim, you may have trouble calming it. If you fail to do so—if you run away—the lion may go wild and kill anyone.[2] That's when you need to call a good *muntela* who knows how to take care of such things."

The three of us, nearly in unison, uttered the name "Kalamatatu." Our laughter broke the tension that had enveloped us, and the conversation turned to other matters.

Before we departed, however, I sat quietly writing a few observations in my notebook. Shindambwanda and Marcos conversed. Suddenly, in the presence of the elder—even if in Portuguese—Marcos was telling me that Shindambwanda was a sorcerer. The elder remained nonplussed, but I became nervous. Finally, I responded to Marcos with a question: "What makes you say so?"

Marcos smiled and leaned forward. "How do you think he knows all of that?! You saw him! He sat there and showed us how to make a lion. You can't know all of that unless you have done it!"[3]

"But he has to know how they're made in order to unmake them, doesn't he?" I protested.

"Sure," Marcos agreed, "but what I'm saying is that he knows how to make them because he has done it! He practically made one right here in front of us!"

I reached for Marcos's hand and clasped it, uncertain as to how he would respond to what I intended to say. "He also once divined right here in front of us that you were a sorcerer."

Marcos looked at me with a faint expression of betrayal—even exasperation. "That was just a demonstration."

"So was his description of how to make a lion," I said.

Marcos looked at me hard: "The elder's demonstration of *yangele* showed that he can do true *yangele* when the circumstances call for it."

He sat, waiting for me to follow his unspoken argument that the elder could truly perform *uwavi wa kupika* when the circumstances called for it—that his demonstration of his knowledge of how to make a lion was a declaration of his ability to do so.

"And now that we have seen the elder make a lion, I suppose that we can make lions, too," I said, jokingly.

"Maybe we can," answered Marcos, with continued sincerity.

ᴵᴵᴵ

When speaking with us of sorcerers, Muedans often shrouded their commentary in euphemism. Tellingly, Muedans often spoke of healers in the same euphemistic language.[4] It was often said of a healer—as it was said of a suspected sorcerer—that he or she was "complicated" (*andikamadyanga*). Kalamatatu, for example, was often described to me by others as "a complicated man." Muedans also spoke of healers and sorcerers alike as "fearless" (*kujoa*, which can also be translated as "dangerous"). Healers, like sorcerers, were said to be fearless because they "knew a little something" (*andimanya shinu shoeshoe*, "he/she knows a little something") that ordinary people did not know, allowing them to act with decisive force in the hidden realm.

It was often said that in days of old healers came to possess the knowledge that empowered them by apprenticing with a master healer. Libata Nandenga spoke explicitly about the master-apprentice relationship when we conversed with him at his home in Mueda. He told us: "I started to learn *mitela* from my father when I was just a boy. I was already a *muntela* before I underwent *likumbi* [boys' initiation rites]. In those days, healers learned from elder healers."

I asked him if it was sufficient to learn about *mitela* in order to become a healer.

"No," he answered. "To be a healer, in those days, you had to be installed by your mentor in a ceremony called *shipito*. If your mentor taught you his *mitela* but died before he installed you, you couldn't practice. *Shipito* activated your knowledge of *mitela*. If your mentor didn't organize *shipito* for you, your *mitela* could be easily overturned [*kupilikula*]. All along, as your master taught you *mitela*, he might overturn you himself. He might be envious of you or just be playing with you. He could make you forget your *mitela* or make your efforts backfire on you or even make you go mad or die. Once you passed through *shipito*, he could no longer do this. He could no longer

Libata Nandenga took his name from the term by which Muedans referred to a duck (the Portuguese word *pato* transliterated into Shimakonde). Whereas his name provoked laughter, his scowling demeanor provoked fear and respect.

overturn your *mitela*.[5] My father organized my *shipito* just after I returned from rites of initiation. Nowadays, healers come about their knowledge in different ways."

Libata's brother's daughter, Terezinha António, afforded an excellent example of this. Terezinha was born in 1949 in Palma. Her parents, who had migrated to Palma from Mueda town, baptized her when she was born. "I was never given a Makonde name," she told us, matter-of-factly, "but the name I use in my healing practice is Mbegweka."

Her parents both died while she was young—of what, she did not tell us. She passed the independence war years in the Imbuho lowlands in a zone controlled by FRELIMO. At independence, rather than returning to the Palma region where she had no one, she moved to Mueda town. Around this time, she became ill. She was taken to a healer who tried to heal her, but her illness persisted. Eventually she was told that she was possessed by a spirit.

Mbegweka explained to us: "In the past, this kind of affliction—being possessed by spirits—was called *mangonde*. But in my case it was something special. I went to see my father's elder brother [Libata], who was also a healer. He told me that the spirit possessing me was my mother's father, Ndonagwamba Shing'oma, who had been a powerful diviner. These kinds of spirits—the spirits of ancestors—are called *vanungu*. In the past, when a person was possessed by this kind of spirit, she would get fevers and begin to tremble. Then, the ancestor would ask her to perform a ceremony. Once she did this, it was finished. Nowadays, it's different. These spirits stay with you. They return again and again. Ndonagwamba left no successor when he died, so he was calling me to follow him. I started treating patients around 1978 or 1979. I learned my *mitela* from my uncle."

Mbegweka was guided in how to use her *mitela* by the spirit of Ndonagwamba that possessed her. In time, other ancestors on her mother's side, and on her father's, possessed her as well, helping her to determine what afflicted the patients who came to see her.

Many of the Muedan healers with whom we worked passed through illness on the way to becoming healers.[6] Shapatintwa Shikumula Shitwanga, a healer living in the village of Miula, learned to cure headaches from the *nkulaula* who cured her of the headaches that she suffered. In the same village, Nantulima Lipatu told us that he turned to a career as a healer after he was cured of tuberculosis, aching bones, and "weakness" by a man named Lingala. Verónica Romão, in Matambalale, told us that she became blind in 1988 after a year of worsening problems with her eyes. Once the healer Tomás Nido, of Nampanha, had healed her, she started treating others. Komesa Baina, of Namande, began to treat people with the same *mitela* that Armando Mwikumba had used to heal him of stomachaches. Renata Damião's healer, possessed by a spirit named Fatuma, told her that she would recover from the illness that had plagued her for six years only if she learned to heal others; this she did, thereby curing herself.

So common in the Mueda plateau region was the scenario of healers learning to heal by being healed themselves that Marcos once suggested to me: "You can't treat something unless you have suffered it and been treated. What I mean is, for example, you can't treat a snake bite unless you've been bitten." In spite of Marcos's words, however, not all Muedan healers traced their careers to a moment in which they overcame illness. And certainly, many healers treated illnesses from which they had never themselves suffered.

Many contemporary Muedan healers with whom we worked also drew inspiration from spirits such as those that possessed Mbegweka. Renata Damião, like Mbegweka, had a grandfather who had been a healer when he was alive. He had died before Renata was born. When working, Renata would call his name and he would possess her, telling her whether or not, and how, she should treat a patient. As Marcos and I sat talking with her about her life as a healer one afternoon, her grandfather's spirit was with her. Marcos told me he knew this from the deep belches that rose from within her several times a minute.

Verónica Romão told us that she, too, worked with spirits—particularly with the spirit of her uncle. "They tell me who the sorcerers are that are causing people problems," she explained.[7]

Luís Avalimuka, a healer living and working in Mueda town, came about his healing knowledge in yet another way. "No one taught me how to heal," he told Marcos and me. "What I know, I learned from dreams." When Luis was forty-five years old, he heard a voice in his dreams telling him that there was an ancestor, from a place called Shipishi, who regularly visited his house and went away hungry and thirsty. Luís wondered who it might be and asked a family elder named Likanganyanga. The elder told him that the ancestor must be Nunduma, a man Luís had never known. As the dreams continued, Luís became restless. He asked Likanganyanga to take him to Nunduma's gravesite, but the elder refused. After this, Luís dreamed of a woman and a small boy who took him to Nunduma's land, where he introduced himself and explained why he was there. When Luís awoke, he traveled to the place where he was taken in his dream, near the Shipishi River. There, he asked for members of his matrilineage, who dispatched a boy to take him to Nunduma's grave. He cleared the gravesite and erected a thatched-roof covering over it. When he next visited the grave, the covering had burned down, so he built a larger one. After this, he dreamed from time to time of the gravesite and, along with it, of certain roots and leaves and tree bark that he should harvest. Not knowing what use they might have, he began to collect these things. At night, he dreamed of elders who told him how to use these forms of *mitela*. According to these elders' instructions, Luís burned these materials, pulverized them, and mixed them with castor oil. He told us that he had used these substances to cure patients for many years, inspired all along by his dreams.

In the days of Libata's youth, healers dealing with complex cases sometimes summoned assistance from their ancestors by performing rites of ancestral supplication (*kulipudya*). However, like many healers of his generation, Libata considered the pronounced reliance of younger healers on dreams and

Carmelita Milonge and her late husband together specialized in the practice of a healing technique called *takatuka*. Long ago, practitioners of *takatuka wanalyuva* (*wanalyuva* derives from the verb *kulyuva*, "to shed," as in a snake shedding its skin) were summoned to the scene of serious injuries such as broken bones and deep puncture wounds, where, we were told, they transferred the patient's wounds to the limb of a tree, which dried up and died, leaving the patient with a small wound elsewhere on the body. Through *takatuka*, the precolonial Makonde warlord Mbavala was said to have grafted the heads of slave captives onto the bodies of his mortally wounded warriors, giving them new life. When I asked Carmelita about such cases, she replied: "Mbavala's sister died in 1998 with such a head. Her original head was beautiful, but she was killed in a war and the head she was given to bring her back to life was that of an ugly slave woman." Carmelita told us that such dramatic cures are no longer undertaken, for there are no longer slaves whose bodies may be used in this way.

possessing spirits to constitute a departure from the ways of the past, when the reputation of a healer derived solely from the fact that he or she had inherited powerful *mitela*, and the knowledge of how to use them, from an elder mentor.

The aged Carmelita Milonge, a healer in the village of Nandimba, concluded that most contemporary healers were in fact sorcerers. "Where have they *learned*? From *whom* have they learned?" she asked us rhetorically. "They just set themselves up one day as *vakulaula*. Where does this knowledge come from?" Kalamatatu's son, Lipapa, once told us that healers who inherited their *mitela*, as he did, were not sorcerers, but that those who invented their own *mitela*—"founders," he called them—were sorcerers.

Those with whom we worked, however, generally suggested that most *vakulaula* fell into the category of those who were, indeed, sorcerers. At the same time, nearly all asserted that they were not, themselves, sorcerers. Kalamatatu, for example, told us that he came by the knowledge that he used to heal through "unique circumstances." The story he told us of his learning to cure from the man who treated him when he was afflicted was commonplace among healers.[8]

Healers sometimes embraced the euphemistic descriptions made of them. Many boasted to me, as they did to their clients, that they "feared no one."[9] Just as often, however, healers dodged these innuendos. When I asked Kalamatatu why sorcerers transformed into lions and devoured their neighbors and kin, remember, he answered me first by saying, "How should I know?! I've never done it!" Only then did he speculate that sorcerers were motivated by envy. Healers rarely spoke openly and/or in detail about "what they knew."[10] Verónica Romão, for example, dissociated herself from the knowledge by which she healed: "Those who possess me were sorcerers themselves, so they can recognize other sorcerers. That's the only way that I can know what the problem is and how to treat it. I can't see these things myself." Verónica's stance was common among healers. By contrast, Shindambwanda's demonstration of how sorcerers make lions was a rare performance, indeed—one that, it must be remembered, invited Marcos to accuse him of sorcery.

Marcos's "scientific" approach to sorcery had him asking, constantly, if healers were in fact sorcerers. He suspected that they were. He reasoned, at least, that if it was true that a healer could only heal those afflictions from which he or she had personally suffered, then only those who had wounded themselves in the act of sorcery could heal wounded sorcerers.

We sat one day with Mbegweka. Marcos asked her how she was able to see the sorcerers whose destructive acts she worked to undo (*kupilikula*). She explained to him that the spirits possessing her told her who the attacking sorcerers were and how to overcome their *mitela*.

"So," Marcos asked, bluntly, "are you a sorcerer?"

Mbegweka hesitated a moment. She then said, cautiously, "If my father [referring to her father's brother—her mentor—Libata] left me with *uwavi*, then I am." She paused, before adding, "But I'm not. I work with the aid of spirits. I work against sorcery."

After meeting with Verónica Romão for the first time, I commented to Tissa on how young she was. "Can such a young woman possibly know as much about *mitela* as some of these older men and women with whom we have worked?" I asked. He let out a quick burst of laughter at my naiveté. "You can be sure that she knows something!" he said. "For such a young woman to work as an *nkulaula*?! . . . You can be sure that she knows a great deal!"

Marcos followed up. "So, there are healers who are sorcerers, and there are healers who are not sorcerers?"

"That's right," Mbegweka answered. She quickly added, however, "But generally, all healers are sorcerers."

"But you aren't?" I asked.

"No, I'm not," she said, this time with greater confidence.

"And your uncle Libata isn't?" Marcos asked.

"Libata? Well . . . ," Mbegweka smiled.

"He told us he wasn't," Marcos quickly added.

"Libata!" Mbegweka was scandalized. "Libata told you that?!"

"Is it not true?" Marcos and I asked, in unison.

"Well, I don't know if it's true or if it isn't," Mbegweka said. After a short pause, she added, with certainty, "But Libata is a sorcerer."

"This is the problem," Marcos said to me, with apparent frustration, soon after we left Mbegweka's compound. "Every healer with whom we speak tells us that healers are sorcerers—that's the rule, they say. But when we ask them if they are sorcerers, they always say, '*Nangu? Mene!*' ['Me? No!']."

Marcos's observation was accurate. No healer with whom we spoke admitted to being a sorcerer, yet each of them asserted that other healers— sometimes *all* others—were sorcerers.[11] So often did we hear this that Marcos began to tease those we interviewed. "*Nangu? Mene!*" he would say, throwing up his hands when they told us how they had become healers without being sorcerers. Almost without exception, these healers would smile with a certain finality that brought to a close Marcos's line of inquiry.

Ordinary Muedans looked upon healers with ambivalence.[12] Libata, for example, bore quite a reputation in Mueda town. He was aged and fond of *lipa* (cashew liquor). Because of his sour disposition, Muedans sometimes laughed at his expense. Even so, they were careful not to offend the old man. Marcos's brother-in-law, Joseph Mery, once warned me: "That guy can do horrible things." When I asked him to give details of these horrible things, Mery laughed nervously and replied, "Ahh, *cunhado* ["brother-in-law" in Portuguese], you don't want to know!"

In contrast with her uncle, Mbegweka was a graceful, kind-spirited woman, but she too was looked upon with deep ambivalence. As Mbegweka grew closer to the spirits that possessed her, her living family pushed her away.

"The name I go by as an *nkulaula*, 'Mbegweka,' means 'I am alone; I have no mother, no father; I have no one.'"

She further explained to us the troubles she encountered upon becoming a healer: "My family wanted to kill me. . . . They thought I was a sorcerer. When my brother died in a car accident, they blamed me."

Muedans generally assumed that the healers to whom they went for expert knowledge and beneficent intervention in the invisible realm were sorcerers. "How else would they recognize *vavi*?!" Muedans often asked, rhetorically.[13] "How else would they know the *mitela* that *vavi* use?!"

The view once expressed in conversation with me by Eusébio Matias Mandumbwe (Marcos's cousin) conveys the understanding of a great many Muedans. Eusébio had referred to a prominent healer on the plateau, in Portuguese, as "the king of all *feitiçeiros* [sorcerers]."

"He's an *nkulaula*," I said. "Isn't there a difference between an *nkulaula* and a *mwavi*?"

"Yes, and no," Eusébio said, "yes, and no."[14]

Still, when Muedans believed themselves to be under attack by sorcerers, they sought out the assistance of healers. Despite the fact that they suspected these specialists of having tasted human flesh—despite suspecting that they may have been practiced killers—ordinary Muedans felt they had no choice but to engage healers on their side in the life-and-death struggles that shaped their world.

"*Uwavi* is war," Eusébio told me. "Only a warrior can deal with matters of war. Only a soldier can fight other soldiers."[15]

To comfort themselves in the midst of encounters such as these, which accentuated their vulnerability, Muedans often told themselves that the healers to whom they turned had abandoned their predilection for human flesh—that they were "reformed" or "retired" sorcerers who used their knowledge to do battle with their former colleagues (see also Dias and Dias 1970: 360).[16] It was an idea, however, of which they remained only partially persuaded and from which they derived only a tenuous sense of security.

8

Sorcery of Construction

"I see you! I know who you are! You are killing us, the people of this settle-ment! You are killing us with your *uwavi!*"

The elder Vicente Anawena sat on the ground, his knees bent close to his chest. So quiet was his voice, so tightly contained his posture, that I found it difficult to imagine him standing at night beside the *shitala* (the men's meet-ing pavilion in the center of the settlement) admonishing sorcerers, as he was telling us he had done before the independence war, when Muedans lived in dispersed settlements. Anawena, however, had been head of his settlement (*nang'olo mwene kaja*); it had fallen upon him, as he told us it did all settle-ment heads, to police both the visible and the invisible realms that consti-tuted his settlement.

"We don't want your *uwavi* here!" the elder continued. "If you do not stop, I will drive you from this settlement! If someone dies because of your *uwavi,* I will kill you! I see you! I know who you are!"

Anawena now lowered his head and contextualized his oratory reen-actment, saying, "When *uwavi* reached intolerable limits, that is what we would do."

In the settlements to which Anawena referred, the encounter between Muedans and the specialists to whom they turned when suffering affliction was, as we have seen, saturated with ambivalence and mutual suspicion. The constant occurrence of illness and misfortune, and of divining and healing, was bound up with the endless promulgation of rumor and innuendo, accu-sation and denial. In this atmosphere, Muedans sometimes sought to put dis-tance between themselves and those with whom relations had become strained. Groups of varying sizes sometimes abandoned the settlement, tak-ing up residence at a distance, beyond sorcery's reach.[1] Such schisms, how-

When in the village of Matambalale, I visited Vicente Anawena frequently. He treated me as one of his own family, and I did my best to provide for his needs as a wage-earning young man such as I was expected to do. He made certain, however, not to let the gifts I brought him—a new pair of trousers, a shirt, or a pair of shoes—define our relationship. When we sat together, he always asked me for news of my family. When his vision began to fail him and he could no longer see the photos of my relatives that I carried with me, I painted pictures for him with words, telling stories that brought a smile to his gentle face.

ever, brought potentially disastrous consequences for the matrilineage, rendering it—in the precolonial era, at least—vulnerable to hostile neighbors.

With so much at stake, settlement heads could ill-afford to sit idly by while others waged war in the invisible realm of sorcery. To avert crisis, settlement heads themselves intervened in the invisible realm in a variety of ways. Although these elders often acted with the aid of trusted *vamitela* living in their settlements, settlement heads bore ultimate responsibility for defending the settlement (*kushililidya ikaja*) by mining the pathways leading into it with antisorcery devices and by spreading *imale* through it to render it invisible to would-be attackers, as mentioned in chapter 5.

The antisorcery interventions of settlement heads were not, however, limited to preventative measures. In moments of crisis—generally marked by the occurrence of illness or death in the settlement—the settlement head asserted himself with vigor. As Anawena told us: "The *nang'olo mwene kaja* would go out into the *shitala* in the wee hours of the morning, just before sunrise, and he would stand and speak out loud at the top of his voice: I see you! I know who you are!'" He "counseled" the sorcerers afflicting his people to desist and warned them of dire consequences should they continue their destructive acts.[2]

The ability of settlement heads of old to fix sorcerers (and the destructive acts they perpetrated) in their gaze was inseparably linked to these elders' capacities to—like sorcerers and like healers—transcend the visible realm and enter into the invisible. Settlement heads were assumed capable of moving even farther than ordinary healers beyond, or outside, the world most Muedans knew, and certainly farther than simple sorcerers.

Indeed, Muedans assumed that settlement heads were sorcerers.[3] As with healers, they reasoned, "How else could *vanang'olo vene kaja* 'see' *vavi?*"

When Tissa asked Anawena how a settlement head could monitor the movements and activities of sorcerers in his settlement, Anawena (who had himself been one) responded (in the third person): "He was a *mwavi*. He had to be in order to know who the others were—in order to . . . control them. All *vanang'olo vene kaja* were *vavi*. This ensured that the *uwavi* practiced in the settlement was *uwavi wa ishima* [sorcery of respect], in which limits were observed."

The term Anawena used on this day to categorize the settlement head's intervention in the realm of sorcery was revealing. He called the act *uwavi wa kudenga*—literally, "sorcery of construction" (also, translatable as "sorcery of edification").[4]

Sorcery of construction was a term with broad currency among the Muedans with whom we worked, but other terms were also used to describe socially beneficial forms of sorcery. The healer Libata referred to the practice of sorcery in protection of the settlement's interests as *uwavi ndenga kaja*, "settlement-building sorcery." Others used the Shimakonde words for "monitoring," "controlling," "advising," "recommending," "calling attention," "criticizing," and "ensuring respect" as adjectives to describe sorcery practiced by responsible authority figures. Regardless of which term was used, the idea was the same: through his own practice of sorcery, the successful settlement head delimited and defined the realm of invisible power, quashing within that realm the acts of others that could be categorized as "ugly," "dirty," or "bad" (*uwavi wa kunyata*), as "dangerous" (*uwavi wa kujoa*), or as "ruinous" (*uwavi wa lwanongo*).

Readers familiar with the literature on African witchcraft and sorcery may find unusual the many adjectives used by Muedans to characterize *uwavi*, but they may recognize within this Muedan practice a familiar theme. Just as Muedans considered *mitela* neutral sources of power, they also considered morally neutral the power to which these substances gave rise.[5] According to those with whom we worked, Muedan sorcerers—like the medicinal substances they used—could either protect or harm, cure or kill, feed or devour, construct or destroy.

In any case, the respected settlement head not only used his distinctive vantage point in the invisible realm to discern the world's operative logics but also elaborated his distinctive, critical vision of the world's (dis)order. He brought to fruition this transcendent vision of the world as he stood alone at night beside the men's meeting pavilion, articulating his vision for all to hear—(re)ordering the world in accordance with his words. The tremendous power that he wielded through the practice of *uwavi wa kudenga* was, to use the words of Arens and Karp, "an artifact of the creative faculty of [his] moral imagination" (1989: xxv). As such, it constituted an assertion not only of his superior "semantic creativity" (Parkin 1982: xlvi) but also of the material force of his creative imagination. The successful settlement head (re)constructed the world as he envisioned it, negating and/or overturning (*kupilikula*) those within his realm who had acted to destroy his world.

Like healers, settlement heads invariably denied that they were sorcerers, granting themselves exemption from an association between authority and sorcery that they generally considered valid in relation to other settlement heads. Many asserted, for example, that they worked with the aid of medicinal specialists who were sorcerers. Such assertions were, however, rarely (if ever) believed, for Muedans looked upon settlement heads with deep ambivalence, just as they did healers and other medicinal specialists.[6]

Vahumu (matrilineage counselors) were also assumed to be powerful sorcerers. Although they commanded none of the material resources that settlement heads did, *vahumu* were treated with even greater respect and fear, for it was generally assumed that they were without peers in the invisible realm. The elder Francisco Ming'ondo Ntumbati remembered in conversation with us how he and his age-mates behaved as boys in the presence of his matrilineage's (Vaivava) *humu*, Ntumbati: "His entrance into the *shitala*, even in the daytime, brought silence. We sat on the ground when he was there." Ntumbati—like many *vahumu* and like some settlement heads—was also a healer. What is more, he was also head of his settlement—rare among *va-humu*. His many titles undoubtedly reinforced his social standing, but the respect and fear afforded him by Ming'ondo and his age-mates ran deeper than this. Ming'ondo explained it to us by saying, simply, "*Vahumu* are *vavi*."

Ntumbati, like all *vahumu*, had undergone the requisite rites of investiture, supervised by other *vahumu*. The *humu* Windu once described these ceremonies to us using the words *kunyata* ("dirty," "ugly," and/or "bad") and *kujoa* ("dangerous"), the same words Muedans often appended to the maleficent and destructive acts of common sorcerers. This was not to imply that *vahumu* acted with malice in the invisible realm; rather, it bore evidence that, in the moment of investiture, *vahumu* engaged with the same forms of power as all sorcerers. Upon becoming *vahumu*, these men learned cult secrets about the uses of the most powerful forms of *mitela* known and obtained the ability to act *decisively* in the invisible realm.

More tellingly, among the substances that *vahumu* ingested in the course of investiture was *lukalongo*—the throat meat of a slain lion. The *humu* Mandia explained to us that, having done this, a *humu* could speak with the lion's voice, allowing him to command the respect and deference of members of his own matrilineage, not to mention other matrilineages.[7] So close was the *humu*'s association with the lion that, in the words of Mandia, lions would "recognize" him in the bush and, even, yield the path to him. Once he had ingested *lukalongo*, a *humu* was prohibited from hunting lions or eating their meat because, as Mandia phrased it, "the *humu* has no contradictions with the lion."[8]

As we have seen, the most lethal of sorcerers in the Mueda region were closely associated with lions, either making such beasts or transforming into them. Beyond this, as Kalamatatu intimated, those who consumed lion meat were rare, and fearless, individuals—traits often invoked, euphemistically, in reference to sorcerers. The *humu*'s association with the lion was different from that of the common sorcerer, however. In the visible realm, the *humu* was barred from benefiting materially by his station. Indeed, he committed himself to a life of service, living in relative poverty. In the invisible realm, too, the *humu* was supposed to act in the interests of the matrilineage rather than in his own interest. By ingesting the lion's meat, the *humu*, whose body symbolized the matrilineage itself, swallowed this dangerous power and metabolized it for the good of the entire matrilineage.[9]

Even so, the association of the *humu* with the lion betrays the profound ambivalence with which Muedans looked upon power. Revealingly, the *humu*'s hold over the violent power of the beast within him was tenuous: upon his death, the *humu*'s body required elaborate treatment by other *vahumu*, who cut his hair and nails and carried these exuviae far into the bush lest the dangerous predators they spawned turn upon the *humu*'s own matrilineage.[10] Even though *vahumu,* like settlement heads, were considered to be "sorcerers of construction"—who monitored the realm of the invisible and quashed the urges of predatory sorcerers therein—they were, quite simply, also feared *as sorcerers.*

▩

Uwavi, as Muedans conceived of it, could be practiced to socially constructive or socially destructive ends. Our understanding of Muedan sorcery would be impoverished, however, if we concluded that Muedans conceived of *uwavi wa kudenga* (sorcery of construction) as "good sorcery" and *uwavi wa lwanongo* (sorcery of ruin) as "bad sorcery," or that respected settlement heads and trusted healers were "good sorcerers" and that those they battled were "bad sorcerers."[11] Muedan ambivalence about sorcery ran deeper than such simple dichotomies. As we shall see in part 2, the categories with which Muedans have spoken of sorcery have changed and proliferated over time as Muedans have debated and contested the morality of specific people and particular acts. Interpreted from one perspective, certain people and acts may have been conceived of as constructive while, from another, destructive. Even individual judgments have been subject to change over time, shifting to and fro with altering social contexts. Simply put, the lines dividing categories of sorcery among Muedans have often been blurred, if not indistinguishable.[12] Unlike Evans-Pritchard's world of distinct categories of "black magic" and "white magic," the Muedan world of sorcery has been filled with shades of gray whose textures and contrasts derive—as Bakhtin would appreciate— from the overlay of myriad Muedans' voices, perspectives, and judgments.

Muedan ambivalence about power as expressed through sorcery discourse has been accentuated by the fact that, in times of vulnerability and crisis, Muedans have turned to precisely those figures whom they most deeply suspect as sorcerers. In comparison with Azande, as described by Evans-Pritchard, Muedans have relied much more heavily upon specialists and figures of authority to protect them from the unseen forces of sorcery. Where those with whom Evans-Pritchard worked turned to their own oracles (Evans-Pritchard [1937] 1976: 41),[13] Muedans have visited diviners. Where Azande were told by their oracles who afflicted them and confirmed through their oracles when their vengeance magic hit its target, Muedans have generally had to trust that sorcery directed at them was successfully turned around (*kupilikula*) by healers and that the figures of authority who policed the hidden realm acted in their interest.[14] Sorcery has swirled around Muedans, coming and going according to the whims and appetites of sorcerers who have long remained unidentified and have rarely been slain.[15]

Jorge Dias and Margot Dias called attention in their work to the strong links between sorcery, fear, and respect for authority among Muedans: "Respect for the *vanang'olo* is effective because everyone believes that [*vanang'olo*] have more powerful *ntela* as well as recourse to sorcery. . . . It is in this play of sorcery and countersorcery that . . . lies hidden one of the important sources of Makonde social control before the organization introduced by the Portuguese administration" (1970: 372, my translation).[16] Dias and Dias further suggested that the "order" and "equilibrium" produced by fear functioned as an "effective limit to . . . cravings to satisfy desires and appetites" that, if left unchecked, might lead to "chaos" (372).[17]

The conclusion drawn by Dias and Dias that "the dominant emotion among the Makonde in general is more fear than piety or love" (1970: 352, my translation) is rash, for one emotional disposition does not preclude others. Their observation should not be dismissed, however. Fear has long been woven into the tapestry of Muedan life. In the dangerous northern Mozambican environment of precolonial times, as we have seen, residents of the plateau region lived with the constant threat of attack by hostile neighbors and with the possibility of capture and enslavement. In the colonial period, during which Dias and Dias worked among them, Muedans lived under the endless specter of state-sponsored violence and coercion, as we shall see in part 2. As we shall also see, the war for Mozambican independence, the post-independence campaign for "socialist modernization," and the Mozambican civil war introduced Muedans, in succession, to new risks and perils.

Just as most Muedans have long experienced power in the visible realm in the form of menacing and invasive forces deployed by others, they have generally understood power in the invisible realm to operate capriciously. In Muedan experience, these visible and invisible realms have resonated one with the other, each shaping the other, in dialectical fashion. The power exercised in the visible realm by authority figures has been inseparable from the power attributed to these figures to act decisively in the invisible realm. What is more, as Muedans have turned to specialists and authority figures for protection against invisible dangers, they have *reinforced* the power that these figures have exercised in the visible realm.

As Muedans have scrutinized sorcery in changing historical contexts, however, they have also subjected to perpetual judgment the very powers— both visible and invisible—that have shaped and reshaped their world, deploying what Mariane Ferme has referred to as "a hermeneutic of suspicion"

(2001: 7). Like Vicente Anawena and his fellow *vanang'olo vene kaja*, ordinary Muedans have themselves monitored the world for signs of dangerous and/or destructive power. Even if, like most medicinal specialists, they have generally denied their abilities to do so, Muedans have, as we shall see in part 2, sometimes transcended the world in which they have lived, sometimes succeeded in quashing (*kupilikula*) potentially menacing forces, and sometimes (re)constructed their world—at least in part—through their contributions to *uwavi* discourse.

II

Part 2 of this volume chronicles how Muedans have interpreted and engaged with the forces shaping their world over the past century through *uwavi* discourse, as well as how *uwavi* has itself been transformed in the Muedan encounter with institutions, practices, and ideas of foreign provenance. Indeed, where exogenous powers have sought to remake the Muedan world and to eliminate from it sorcery-related beliefs and practices, Muedans have conceived of these interventions *as novel forms of uwavi* and, through their conceptions, have reproduced and transformed *uwavi*.

Whereas Robin Horton suggested in his classic essay "African Traditional Thought and Western Science" ([1967] 1970) that belief in witchcraft, sorcery, possessing spirits, and the like was possible only in "closed" societies—where alternative ways of seeing the world were nonexistent and where internal contradictions and empirical shortcomings were ignored because "any challenge to established tenets" constituted "a threat of chaos, [a threat] of the cosmic abyss" (154)—historians have since argued that Africans have, for centuries, sustained multifaceted intra- and intercontinental relations with varied Others who have seen the world differently.[1] What is more, peoples throughout the continent have elaborated and sustained occult cosmologies in the midst of dramatic social transformations brought on by encounters with their Others.[2]

Muedans, as we shall see in part 2, have for centuries lived within a vortex of cultural encounter and transformation, notwithstanding their depiction as an isolated people of timeless tradition by, among others, their colonial-era ethnographers, Jorge Dias and Margot Dias (see West 2004a). Indeed, it might easily be argued that Muedans (and colonial subjects like them elsewhere) have undergone more profound and concentrated changes in recent centuries than have the peoples who colonized them. In any case, Muedans have been presented constantly with alternatives to their ways of thinking and doing and have even had alternatives imposed upon them.

Far from being a discrete people, with a "discrete system" of beliefs and practices (Jean Comaroff and John Comaroff 1991: 249), the Makonde and their "traditions" have emerged and congealed at interfaces with historically constructed Others who have themselves been engaged in simultaneous pro-cesses of formation and reproduction (Jean Comaroff and John Comaroff 1991: 212). Makonde identity and Makonde "tradition" have been configured and reconfigured in historical moments of interaction and juxtaposition with Other identities and traditions—whether Makua, Yao, or Nguni, whether Arab, Portuguese, or Dutch, whether Christian or Muslim, whether socialist or democratic.

Marshall Sahlins has concluded that, in refitting culture to changing his-torical circumstances, people do not lose their distinct identities but, rather, become "more like themselves" (1993: 17). While Sahlins's assertion pro-vides a necessary corrective to arguments that Western imperialism, whether colonial or postcolonial, obliterates cultural difference, it greatly oversimpli-fies the complex global dynamic between cultural homogenization and het-erogenization played out in places like the Mueda plateau. In their multifar-ious historical encounters with exogenous actors and institutions, Muedans have sometimes become more like their Others—indeed, sometimes em-bracing various Other identities so as to become, in their own view, less like themselves. In other instances, they have aspired to and/or succeeded in dif-ferentiating themselves from various Others while, in the process, losing something of their distinctive senses of self. While some Muedan Others have sought to differentiate themselves from Muedans, others have sought to make Muedans in some respects more like them—on occasion, seeking to make themselves, in other ways, more like Muedans in order to facilitate the pro-cess. The strategies of various Muedans and their various Others have vari-ously succeeded and failed, producing multiple new divisions and alliances among Muedans themselves. As a consequence, Muedans have become more like some of their fellow Muedans and less like others. One might further complicate the picture, but hopefully the point has been made.[3]

All the while, Muedans and their Others have debated the efficacy of *uwavi* as a means through which to interpret and engage with the world. These debates have introduced within Muedan society new lines dividing those who see the world in one way from those who see it in another. In other words, as Muedan identities have proliferated, so too have perspectives on *uwavi* and—some would say—forms of *uwavi* and the identities of those who practice it. According to those claiming to see into the invisible realm, not only have Muedans and their ever-changing forms of *uwavi* contributed to the transformation of the Muedan world, but so too have Muedans' Others and *their* novel forms of *uwavi*.

With the conquest of the plateau by the Portuguese military circa 1917, colonial governance produced tensions between ordinary Muedans and elders whom the concessionary Nyassa Company and, later, the Portuguese administration used as native intermediaries in the collection of taxes and the recruitment of corvée labor. Colonial rule further alienated plateau youths from the heads of their settlements by driving them into the wage economy—often across the border in British colonial Tanganyika—and thereby decreasing their dependence upon family networks for access to land and bridewealth. In the early 1960s, plateau youths joined the nascent Mozambican Liberation Front (FRELIMO) en masse and supported its guerrilla campaign (based on the Mueda plateau) not only to end colonial rule but also to purge Mozambican society itself of exploitative political hierarchies. In postindependence Mozambique, the revolutionary socialist FRELIMO party attempted to supplant all forms of kin-based authority with its own political institutions.

Simultaneous with these dramatic transformations, the novel powers to which Muedans were exposed in the twentieth century sought to disabuse them of their beliefs in sorcery. Christian missionaries at first dismissed *uwavi* as the stuff of superstition and, later, classified it as "the work of the devil," all the while seeking to persuade Muedans that Christ alone provided "the way, the truth, and the light." FRELIMO socialists cast sorcery beliefs as "false-consciousness," asserting that Mozambicans could liberate themselves from those who fed off of their suffering only by cultivating revolutionary class consciousness and embracing scientific socialism. In the historical interface with agents of colonialism and Christianity, and then with agents of Mozambican nationalism and revolutionary socialism, Makonde "tradition" was defined even as it was transformed. What is more, Muedan traditions proliferated along with Muedan subjectivities as plateau residents experienced the differential effects of evangelization, literacy, vocational education, wage labor, political mobilization, and socialist modernization. As Makonde "tradition" was defined in relation to various "modernizing" processes, "traditional authorities" and "traditional healers" alike were relegated to the margins of Muedan society.

Through it all, however, *uwavi* remained familiar to most Muedans. The complex of discursive and material practices through which Muedans have engaged with the invisible realm of *uwavi* has sustained among them a dis-

tinctive cultural schema concerning the workings of power—a schema drawing form from past Muedan experience while giving form to Muedan involvement in, and understanding of, ongoing historical events and processes.
Even if, through *uwavi* discourse, Muedans have conceived of *uwavi* as an
enduring, albeit regrettable, Makonde "tradition," as they have invoked this
schema within the context of the transformative events and processes in
which they have participated, this schema has itself been transformed in the
moments of its reproduction.[4]

Muedans with whom we worked themselves spoke of the dialectic between *uwavi* and history, albeit in different ways. They asserted that their ancestors, like themselves, lived in a world shaped by *uwavi*'s existence while
also suggesting that *uwavi*'s present-day forms and effects differed in many
ways from those of the past. *Uwavi*, Muedans averred, has a history, bound
up with the history of the people who have known it. In some respects, they
said, *uwavi* has remained constant—a fundamental aspect of human existence. Because *uwavi* is linked profoundly to institutions of political authority that have suffered dramatic transformation over the past century, however, Muedans also recognized that *uwavi* itself has undergone substantial
change. In the words of the *humu* Mandia: "*Vavi* are always studying to improve their techniques—to advance their *science*."[5] Hence, according to the
healer Luís Avalimuka, where sorcerers have long communicated with one
another over vast distances, the state of the art in *vavi* communication today
is radio transmission; others told us that any self-respecting sorcerer these
days communicated only by cell phone. Where sorcerers once rode on the
backs of hyenas and other animals, they now pilot helicopters and jet planes.

By Muedan accounts, not only has *uwavi* survived exposure to Other
ways of thinking and doing, but its forms have proliferated and flourished in
the ever-shifting interstices between Muedans and their Others (both Muedan
and non-Muedan),[6] as have the categories of Muedans who practice *uwavi*.[7]
Muedans told the story of their defeat at the hands of the Portuguese military
as a battle fought to decision in the invisible realm of *uwavi* between rival
Makonde warlords—some of whom resisted the Portuguese and others of
whom joined with them. In the colonial period, plateau dwellers accused labor migrants returning home with unprecedented riches of using sorcery to
feed themselves to the exclusion, and at the expense, of others, while these
returnees suspected folks back home of using sorcery to consume or destroy
them and their hard-earned objects of wealth. Christians attracted the envy
and suspicion of non-Christians, and accusations of sorcery passed in both
directions. Muedans then interpreted the hide-and-seek maneuvers of guerrilla warfare in the familiar language of *uwavi*, blaming lethal attacks on Por-

tuguese forms of sorcery and/or on the collaboration with the Portuguese of maleficent Muedan sorcerers living in their midst. When FRELIMO settled Muedans in communal villages after the war, Muedans read the initiative as an attempt to consolidate state power through creating conditions for closer surveillance of both visible and invisible realms.

Ultimately, Muedans heard something familiar in the visions of the world's workings articulated by historical actors such as Catholic missionaries and FRELIMO revolutionaries, each of whom claimed that their truths nullified the validity of *uwavi* beliefs and practices. Muedans interpreted these truth claims as proclamations of the ability to transcend the world that ordinary people knew and, even, the world known by Muedan sorcerers—in other words, as enactments of even more powerful forms of sorcery, that is, as transcendent, transformative maneuvers (*kupilikula*). Where Muedans benefited from the power of these new figures of authority, they generally judged them to be sorcerers of construction in the tradition of responsible Muedan elders. Such was increasingly the case with regard to Catholic missionaries, whose many initiatives enriched and/or empowered church adherents and whose increasingly liberal approach to Makonde tradition allowed Muedans to embrace Christianity without ceasing to be Makonde. FRELIMO leaders, too, sometimes encouraged Muedans to conceive of them as powerful sorcerers by conversing—even consulting—with Muedan medicinal specialists during the independence war. Insofar as Muedans experienced FRELIMO power as a means to achieve liberation from Portuguese rule, they judged FRELIMO leaders to be sorcerers of construction. As FRELIMO's campaign for socialist modernization stalled during the postindependence Mozambican civil war, however, FRELIMO authorities were seen by most Muedans to exercise power increasingly to their own exclusive benefit, "eating everything" and, many surmised, "everyone." As Muedans thus scrutinized power in their changing world through the discursive genre of *uwavi*, they sometimes themselves succeeded in inverting, annulling, or transforming (*kupilikula*) its dynamics.

9

Imagined Conquerors

"That's him," Marcos said, assuredly.

"How do you know?" I asked, with surprise. "You told me you had never met him."

Marcos ignored my question. Staring in front of us, he simply repeated, "That's him."

As we pulled closer, mirth-filled laughter briefly bubbled up from within Marcos's chest. I looked at him to discern the source of his amusement, but I quickly realized that his was not a laughter meant to draw me in or to share humor with me. Marcos, it seemed, was suspended in another place or time, absorbed with the object of his laughter—the object of his trancelike gaze.

As Marcos had introduced me to Mueda and to Muedans during the early months of my first research stint on the plateau in 1994, he had suggested that we focus our attention on historical issues about which we might converse without striking the nerves of contemporary politics. Muedan elders, I soon discovered, greatly enjoyed talking with us about events such as the Portuguese conquest of the plateau. Several elders provided us with vivid accounts of the heroic resistance put up by their forebears. Legendary among the *vanang'olo* (elders) who fought against the Portuguese was Malapende. We were informed by many with whom we spoke that, if we truly wanted to know Malapende's story, we had to travel to the village of Litembo and speak with Lyulagwe, a nephew of the great warlord. Marcos had never met nor heard of Lyulagwe. What is more, although he had family in the cluster of villages to the east of Litembo, and also in the cluster to the west, Marcos knew no one who lived in or came from Litembo. We thus delayed seeking out this nephew of Malapende until it became clear to us that this heir was widely considered to be the bearer of Malapende's history.

On a clear July morning, we had driven our "turtle" into Litembo. As we passed between rows of houses, headed for the village center, where we might report to village authorities and ask them to direct us to Lyulagwe, Marcos spotted an aged man in front of a house on the side of the road. He pointed to the elder, who stood as still as a woodcarving, and pronounced him the man we sought.

After receiving no explanation from my research companion, I stopped our vehicle about twenty-five meters from the statuesque elder. Marcos climbed out, leaving the door hanging open, and approached the elder with measured, determined steps. The old man remained rigid, staring hard at Marcos, saying nothing. A sense of impending calamity passed over me. Although I could not fathom why, it seemed to me that the two men were preparing to fight, so hard were their stares at one another, so strikingly odd the silence between them.

Marcos positioned himself in front of the elder, awkwardly—aggressively—close. The elder stood his ground. Their eyes burned one another. Finally, with firm resolve, Marcos said, simply, "We have need of Malapende."

Moments passed. Then, the statue moved as if life had been breathed into it by the wind. The elder slowly raised his hand to his beard. His eyes drifted downward. He studied the ground for some time before looking up and meeting Marcos's eyes with a fiery glance. "*Tuke!*" (Let's go!), the elder said, and he turned and started for the yard behind his house.

What had moments earlier seemed to me madness on the part of my research companion now revealed itself as brilliance. Marcos had chosen to approach the elder, not as Lyulagwe, but instead as the living embodiment of Malapende, the most feared warrior in Makonde history. In the face of Marcos's challenge, Lyulagwe was filled with the fire of his ancestor, ultimately finding common cause in Marcos's bold sense of purpose.

Indeed, it now seemed that the elder had for years been awaiting our visit. Without noticeable word or gesture, he summoned another elder sitting in the adjacent yard. A youngster emerged, unbeckoned, from Lyulagwe's house carrying two chairs for Marcos and me and, then, a log upon which the elder and his neighbor sat. Two or three people approached the yard and seated themselves on the ground, eyeing us.

As I began my formulaic self-introduction and description of our research project, I opened my field bag and fumbled for my notebook and pen. I continued speaking as I located my tape recorder, pulled the plastic off a new cassette tape, and placed the cassette in the recorder. Only a couple of minutes into my remarks—which normally took fifteen minutes or more—as I was still fiddling with my gear, the elder interrupted with a snort of disapproval.

I looked up, startled. The elder's burning eyes were now fixed on me, producing within me abstract, but undeniable, fear.

"Do you want to talk about yourselves," he asked, "or Malapende?!"

I looked to Marcos, who now grinned mischievously.

"*Mano*," he said to me, gently, as if offstage, "he wants to begin."

By his voice, I could tell that Marcos anticipated an enchanted encounter and that, in the space of this historical reenactment, he and I would have to play our minimal parts with precise understatement, lest Malapende deem us unworthy of his story and abandon us in disgust. I looked at the elder and nodded, respectfully. His eyes flashed, and he began.

The elder informed us that the name on his official documents was Américo Nkangusha Nkunama, but that the name given him by his parents was Lyulagwe (meaning, in Shimakonde, "anvil"). His father, Nkangusha Nkunama, was from the matrilineage Vamilange.

Beside me, Marcos repressed his delight while responding, flatly, that he, too, was Vamilange.

Lyulagwe continued, telling us that his mother, Nembo Namajele, was from the Vanashilonda matrilineage. She was the youngest sister of the *nang'olo mwene kaja* Malapende, Lyulagwe told us proudly.

Like a praise poem, the name Malapende rolled off Lyulagwe's lips and settled into the crevices between the two dozen people who now surrounded us.

Even before the Portuguese assault on the plateau, Lyulagwe told us, Malapende was a warrior of great renown. Not only did he have many allies—several of whom built their settlements around his and incorporated their defenses with his (see chapter 2)—he also had many enemies. These varied relationships, Lyulagwe explained, were the result of an atmosphere shaped by slave raiding and trading between matrilineages. He illustrated this by telling us of one specific incident in which a young man from another settlement (Shindende's) took captive a woman from Malapende's settlement. "Malapende did not know how to send people to do his work," Lyulagwe told us proudly, before finishing the story with his account of Malapende leading his matrilineage's warriors into battle and forcing the return of the woman.

Lyulagwe now paused as we waited in silence. I thought that, perhaps, the elder was resting to gather his strength, until I noticed his eyes quickly surveying the crowd of thirty or forty people now gathered around us. I wondered when the elder had last had this kind of audience.

"When the *dyomba* [fish][1] came, Malapende was their greatest foe," Lyulagwe now said in a resonant voice. "They tried three times to mount the plateau. The first time, Malapende gathered his warriors together and he went to the lowlands near the Nakatulu River, below Nanenda. He fought there for two days and, on the third day, the Portuguese went away."

As he told the story of the battle in detail, Lyulagwe punctuated the volleys and countervolleys of firearms by extending one arm in front of him like the barrel of a gun and pulling its trigger with his other hand. Great phlegm-filled barking noises emanated from the elder's chest and rushed through his throat as he commemorated shots fired. With each volley, the children gathered around him fell backward in panicked fright.

Lyulagwe continued his account:

> [After the first battle], an enemy of Malapende's from the region between [what is now] the town of Mueda and [what is now] the village of Nandimba—a *nang'olo* named Mbavala—went to Mocímboa da Praia and presented himself to the Portuguese, saying: "This person that you are after, I know him. His name is Malapende, and I know where his settlement is found." A neighboring *nang'olo* named Namashakole discovered Mbavala's intentions, however, and went to warn Malapende. Malapende and Namashakole then formed an alliance at Ntoli [the site of Malapende's settlement]. The second time the Portuguese came, Mbavala accompanied them, and Malapende and Namashakole together fought them for a week until they retreated.

In subsequent conversations with other Muedan elders, Marcos and I would hear more about the complex relations between Malapende, Namashakole, and Mbavala. Maunda Ng'upula, the ageless elder with whom Marcos and I often spoke in the town of Mueda, was the son of a Vanashilonda father (Malapende's matrilineage) and a Vashitunguli mother (Namashakole's matrilineage). He told Marcos and me that Namashakole was the name of the settlement head Maunda's war chief[2] and confirmed for us that Namashakole and Malapende were allies. He explained:

> Shilavi, a Vamwanga, and Mbavala, a Vamwilu, were allies, but they had no other friends on the plateau. They fought with Malapende and Maunda. Many people died in these wars, but afterward there were treaties, and payments were made by the guilty. These payments were made in cloth or *espera-pouco* [firearms]. Once, however, people from Malapende's and Maunda's settlements came to Mbavala's settlement and beheaded Mbavala and roasted his head. Mbavala[3] had heard of the Portuguese at the coast, so he went to them to ask for their help in burning Malapende's and Maunda's settlements. On his way to the coast, he met the Portuguese coming to the plateau. The Portuguese were led by some Makonde who had gone to the coast to trade. The Por-

tuguese thought Mbavala was with the Germans[4] and tied him up, but then he persuaded them of his earnestness, so they released the other Makonde and kept Mbavala with them. These other Makonde returned to the plateau, where they warned people of the coming attack. Malapende and Namashakole prepared an ambush at Nanenda. There, two sentinels were posted in trees, and when the Portuguese arrived, these sentinels informed Malapende and Namashakole that Mbavala was in front but that he was bound. The Makonde opened fire. The Portuguese retreated.

In Mueda town, Eugénio Nanyunga Ndupa, a Vamwilu descendant of Mbavala, told us a different story. According to his account:

> Before the Portuguese arrived, Mbavala and Namashakole were friends. They were both sons of Vamwanga[5] and lived close together. Malapende and Maunda were also friends. When the Portuguese came the first time, everyone fought against them together, and the Portuguese failed to take the plateau. So, the Portuguese knew they needed help from someone on the plateau. Mbavala, like many at the time, would go to the coast to gather salt at the beach and to trade for cloth. When he went this time, an Indian trader informed the Portuguese. They tied him up and made him pay a tax. Then they forced him to go to the plateau with them.

When, and with what intentions, Mbavala went to Mocímboa da Praia are questions that remained hotly contested among Muedans with whom we spoke, including those unrelated to the principal protagonists. Some asserted that Mbavala went to the coast prior to the commencement of the Portuguese assault and that his offer to betray other Makonde headmen made that assault possible. Some agreed that he went at this time but insisted that he was captured and made to serve against his will as a guide to the Portuguese. Other accounts had Mbavala going to the coast after the first of several (usually three) Portuguese attacks at Nanenda, either to betray his rivals or to sue for peace. Some accounts even placed his trip to the coast after the successful Portuguese invasion of the plateau, describing it as an attempt to either secure for himself a position in the Portuguese administration or to negotiate a lower tax for plateau residents in exchange for the cessation of postconquest uprisings. In any case, all of those with whom we spoke recognized the eventual enmity between Mbavala, on the one hand, and Malapende and Namashakole, on the other, as well as the importance of this enmity in the Portuguese conquest of the plateau.

After telling us of the second assault of the Portuguese, Lyulagwe paused again for dramatic effect. I stole a glance at the crowd, which now numbered more than a hundred. Their bodies amplified the sound of Lyulagwe's breathing and, then, the rolling thunder of his voice:

> After this, all the Makonde on the plateau united behind Malapende near the Litembo River. The Portuguese came the third time on horseback, opening a road in front of them. The Makonde went to Kavanga, but the Portuguese were many, and Malapende and Namashakole failed to stop them, so they returned to Ntoli. Now, the Portuguese . . . led by a soldier called Nakashi . . . advanced toward Ntoli in order to burn Malapende's settlement. Before arriving at Malapende's, they built a camp at Ming'anga. Then they went to Malapende's settlement but failed to burn it. Malapende had built trenches all along the path leading to the entryway and had lined the path with walls of bamboo. The path was so narrow that the Portuguese had to move through it sideways. They could not fire. And while they advanced, Malapende's warriors—who had secretly come in behind the walls of bamboo—poked spears through the walls and killed their attackers. They speared them one by one in the stomach.

Lyulagwe now acted out the thrusting of spears, making a deep swooshing, gurgling noise at the end of each movement when his imaginary weapon had plunged into the flesh of its victim. A few children laughed. Lyulagwe shot them a scowling glance, sending at least two running from the circle in shrieks of fright. Lyulagwe played on the moment: "While his soldiers were doing this, Malapende himself sang, 'Malapende! Malapende!'"

Malapende's real name, Lyulagwe explained, was Nkaloma Mavinga, but he was better known by his war name. "Malapende," he informed us, was a taunting chant sung by dancing children after catching a cockroach, pulling its legs off, and placing it on the ground to wriggle and squirm.

Lyulagwe himself now chanted the name: "Malapende! Malapende!"

The combination of his childlike cadence and his elderly voice produced a strange, sinister effect as one imagined Malapende's impaled victims wriggling and squirming.

Lyulagwe returned to the thread of his narrative. He spoke softly now, and his ever-larger audience, now numbering nearly two hundred, leaned closer to hear his words: "The Portuguese tried for three days without success to burn Malapende's settlement, but in the end it burned by itself." The elder looked at me and smirked. "Malapende said, 'These people exist only because someone imagined them.' Such people, he said, could not burn his settlement. And so he ordered his own people to set the settlement on fire." The elder continued:

As Lyulagwe spoke, I imagined a time when Muedan young people cherished the stories told by elders such as him. With his words, Lyulagwe briefly realized this imagined past. Later, Marcos—a historian by trade—would refer to Lyulagwe's performance as "the greatest oral history" that he had ever heard told. "It's a good thing we recorded it," Marcos said, before listening to the tape and realizing that we had not—indeed, could not have—preserved the enchanted moment of its telling.

Malapende moved his people and built a new settlement near the Litembo River. He called this place Shendushendu and said that the name Malapende should no longer be used. But the Portuguese tried to burn this one, too. So he set it alight and moved again to a place nearby. There he surrendered to the Portuguese. But he sent his brother, Shikaulika, in his stead because he still didn't want to have anything to do with surrendering. He wanted to attack the Portuguese once again, but Shikaulika said, "This way, you will finish us all off." Shikaulika took a spear and a shotgun and gave these things to the Portuguese.

The elder was now deflated. He finished his account lifelessly as his audience began to disperse:

The Portuguese forced the Makonde to help them build the road that they were making. The Makonde had to dig by hand, piling red earth on the roadway and beating it down to make a hardened surface. This, Malapende could not stand. He could not watch his people work as servants. So, he moved with his people to build a new settlement far away, near Mtamba. Malapende never returned. He died there, after eventually being named a *capitão-mor* [a "chief" account-able to the colonial administration] by the Portuguese.

▥

The Mueda plateau was among the last areas in Mozambique to be "pacified" by the Portuguese. Due to a lack of investment capital, Portugal had in 1891 granted charter over the northern region of the colony, including the plateau, to a concessionary group called the Nyassa Company. In the ensuing years, the group struggled to raise sufficient capital to invest in the territory and proved unable to exercise "administrative control" over the region's inhabitants (Vail 1976; Neil-Tomlinson 1977). At the onset of World War I, the Portuguese sought to secure the Rovuma River border against German-held Tanganyika but first had to "subdue" the plateau region and link defenses on the southern bank of the Rovuma to the coastal towns of Porto Amélia (today Pemba) and Mocímboa da Praia (Pélissier 1994). To accomplish this, a company of Portuguese troops under the command of Captain Neutel de Abreu was dispatched from Mocímboa. They ascended the plateau on its eastern edge, near Nanenda, on 17 May 1917 and reached Chomba, on the plateau's western edge, on 14 June.[6]

Neutel de Abreu's biographer, Manuel Ferreira, provides a few details about the brief campaign (Ferreira 1946: 93–107). The column, he tells us, battled not only plateau inhabitants but also the forest through which it passed. Water was scarce, and giant boa constrictors and black cobras with deadly venom posed a constant threat (97, 99).

"The Makonde"—as the Portuguese, at least, now called plateau inhabitants—lay in deadly ambush, but the column moved with the guidance of "a Makonde chief" in its employ (da Ponte 1940–1941: 441). Portuguese accounts do not mention Mbavala by name but tell us that this chief's "sole worry consisted of beating some enemy chiefs" and report that he therefore "took the direction that best served the realization of his desires" (441).

The battle at Namashakole's settlement, "Mahunda" (the settlement in which our interviewee Maunda Ng'upula was then living), lasted from 11 to 17 July, we are told (Ferreira 1946: 98). Siege was laid to "Malupendo's" settlement on 13 July. The only detail reported for this day—on which Portuguese troops also attacked "Pananebane's" settlement—is that, in the midst of the battle, Portuguese troops were attacked by a swarm of bees (Ferreira 1946: 104).

On their passage through the plateau, the Portuguese column reportedly torched more than 150 settlements. Many of the names of these settlements

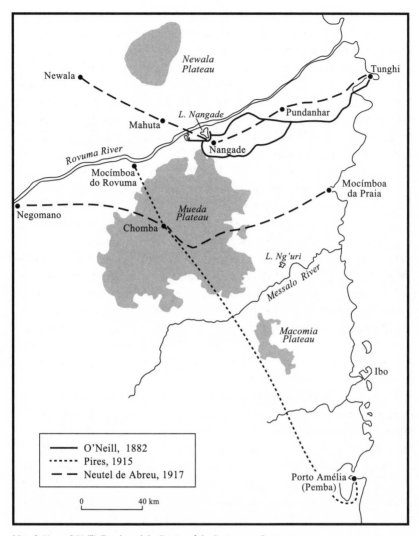

Map 2. Henry O'Neill's Travels and the Routes of the Portuguese Conquest

were recorded and, in some cases, inventory was taken of the number of huts burned: as many as 156 in Namamidia and 197 in Colinga; as few as 13 in Nindimpira and in Pachalampa.

We are told that Portuguese troops camped for the night beside the settlement of "Nacume" as it burned on 17 May 1917 (Ferreira 1946: 102). Herman Nkumi—who took his name from the eponymous *nang'olo mwene kaja* of this settlement—never knew the date, but when he talked with us in 1994, he remembered the day well, despite the passage of seventy-seven years. He and his family slept in the bush that night. In the days—and years—to follow, they asked themselves how it was possible that the medicinal substances used by Makonde settlement heads had failed to protect them from these attackers.

The Portuguese military officers who led the campaign to "pacify" the plateau south of the Rovuma attributed their triumphant campaign to superior weaponry. In their reports on the campaign, they seldom considered it relevant to name the *vanang'olo* they vanquished, but they documented for posterity the arms that they and their 2,000 "Makua auxiliaries" carried with them: 929 Snyder shotguns, 267 Kropatchek shotguns, and 37 Kropatchek rifles (Ferreira 1946: 99–100).

There may have been a time when the Makonde of northern Mozambique thought of firearms as instruments of *uwavi*—strange and terrible devices that allowed one to kill another human being at great distances. However, although Neutel de Abreu's troops carried with them weapons more sophisticated than any the residents of the plateau had yet seen, by the time of the conquest most adult male Makonde had considerable experience with firearms of one sort or another. For centuries, arms-bearing slave dealers—mostly Arab—had prowled the northern Mozambican interior and traded weapons with the Africans who served them as intermediaries in the commerce of human cargo. In time, Makonde blacksmiths learned to repair firearms and, even, to produce spare parts for them, making this once-astonishing technology increasingly mundane.

In present-day oral accounts of the conquest, Muedans recognized Portuguese firearms as dangerous but did not portray them as decisive instruments in the encounter between Portuguese and Makonde fighters. In fact, the Makonde were portrayed as using firearms as well as, or better than, the Portuguese and their mercenary forces—until their supply of powder ran out.

According to Maunda Ng'upula, after the Portuguese strayed into the ambush set by Malapende and Namashakole, Mbavala said to the Portuguese, "I told you they were mean!" As Maunda tells the story: "[T]he Portuguese responded by saying, 'That must have been the Germans!' The Portuguese went back to Mocímboa da Praia and returned three weeks later. The same thing happened again. They were ambushed and retreated. But this time the Portuguese believed Mbavala, who told them that it was Malapende and Namashakole, and not the Germans, who had attacked them."

Maunda continued his story: "Eight months later, the Portuguese returned and fell into an ambush. This time Makonde and Portuguese died. The Portuguese went back to Mocímboa da Praia. The Makonde had run out of powder and went back to get more."

When the Portuguese returned, the Makonde again ran out of powder, according to Maunda Ng'upula. Soon after, they set fire to Maunda's settlement and retreated to Malapende's, leaving the Portuguese to set up their "administration" in the ruins of Maunda's settlement.[7]

The most telling moments, in both Lyulagwe's and Maunda Ng'upula's accounts, however, come in the interlude between the exhaustion of Makonde supplies of powder and their eventual "surrender." In this interregnum, the "superior firepower" of the Portuguese is thoroughly neutralized by the clever stratagems of Makonde *vanang'olo*. In Lyulagwe's account, as we have heard, Malapende draws the Portuguese and their allies into narrow passageways where they are speared to death. In Maunda Ng'upula's, the tactic is even more incredible: "Then Namashakole said to Malapende, 'Let's sculpt a statue that looks like you and put it in a trench with a firearm in its hands.' This they did. When the Portuguese came, Mbavala saw the statue and the Portuguese opened fire on it until it fell. Then they came to capture Malapende's body, but they fell into the trench. The Makonde jumped on them and began to cut their heads off. . . . The rest of the Portuguese retreated, but later returned. When they returned, the same thing happened again!"

Muedans attributed these amazing events in part to the ignorance of the Portuguese but, more importantly, to Malapende's and Namashakole's capabilities as powerful *vamitela*. In their battles with one another, the most feared *vanang'olo* of the day, including not only Malapende and Namashakole but also Mbavala, had all developed great reputations as *vamitela*. For instance, according to Magwali Shakoma in Mpeme: "Namashakole had antibullet *ntela*. He couldn't be shot. Bullets would fall to the ground, and he would just pick them up."[8] Manuel Shindolo Nkapunda told us: "Malapende had *ntela* that allowed him to disappear. When he was caught, he would disappear. When he was shot at, he would disappear and reappear somewhere else. He would only get mad and then dance in anger."[9] Mbavala was said by many to have been capable of performing *takatuka*—grafting the heads and other body parts of slave captives upon the injured or deceased members of his own matrilineage in order to give them new life (see also Dias and Dias 1970: 364).

Just as the struggles between these powerful elders were said to have been played out in the realm defined by medicinal substances and by astonishing acts of sorcery, so too were their battles against the foreign aggressors they encountered in the early twentieth century. Until the moment of their defeat, Malapende and Namashakole proved more adept than the Portuguese in *seeing* their enemies, in *recognizing* the nature of their power, and in *turning it around* (*kupilikula*) on them. The medicinal substances that these *vanang'olo* deployed allowed them to undertake decisive maneuvers that

their enemies could not see. They used their relative superiority in the knowledge of *mitela* to draw their enemies into simple traps and to confuse them,
repeatedly, into mistaking simple decoys for human targets.

Why, then, did these powerful *vamitela* eventually succumb to the Portuguese? The answer, according to the accounts of most Muedan elders today,
lay not in the superiority of Portuguese weaponry or military strategy but, instead, in the realm of the invisible. This was not to suggest that the Portuguese, in the end, proved themselves more powerful *vamitela* than Makonde
elders—quite the contrary. Listen closely to Malapende's words, as spoken
by Lyulagwe: "Malapende said, '*These people exist only because someone
imagined them.*'" According to these words, the Portuguese were not themselves powerful sorcerers; they were, instead, the product of the maleficent
imagination of a malicious Makonde sorcerer—presumably Mbavala.[10] As
such, the Portuguese both constituted a novel danger *and* represented a familiar evil. They were understood both as an astonishing phenomenon *and*
as a menace that could be dealt with in conventional ways.

Malapende's statement, in fact, constituted an attempt to treat the crisis
brought on by the Portuguese invasion through familiar countersorcery measures. His bold declaration was performed in the discursive genre of countersorcery, echoing the words of a healer identifying a patient's afflictions as the
product of a sorcerer's malicious imaginings and echoing the cries at night of
a settlement head performing sorcery of construction in the settlement center: "I see you! I know who you are! I know what you're up to!"

Such maneuvers might have allowed Malapende and Namashakole to
emerge victorious over the Portuguese, most Muedans told us, were it not for
the fact that Mbavala, who stood behind (and, in this case, also in front of)
the Portuguese, was such an accomplished *muntela* in his own right.[11] Mbavala outmaneuvered (*kupilikula*) Malapende and Namashakole as they attempted to treat the dangerous effects of the menace that he had conjured.

"Mbavala knew Malapende's *mitela*," Manuel Shindolo Nkapunda told
us. "*That*," he assured us, "is how Malapende was beaten."

10

Consuming Labor and Its Products

"The *regulado*[1] was born with taxation," our aged interviewee told us. "Before the Portuguese came, there was no taxation, and before taxation, there were no *régulos*[2]—only settlement heads."

"Didn't the settlement head also take a portion of the wealth of his people?" I asked.

"That was different," he responded. "The settlement head redistributed goods among his people. He looked out for their well-being. The *régulo* ate people. And the Portuguese ate the *régulo*."

What made the elder's words remarkable was that *he* himself had served as *régulo* in the late colonial period.

"I was the fourth Régulo Ndyankali," he had told us. "The first was the son of Makapela."

"How was he chosen?" I had asked.

"After the Makonde were defeated at Nanenda, the Portuguese came to each zone on the plateau and asked, 'Who is chief here?' In this zone, Ndyankali descended from the original founder. He was *nang'olo mwene shilambo*. The land belonged to his ancestors, so he was identified. He was given a flag to fly in his compound. Other *vanang'olo vene kaja* in the zone—who until then paid respect to the *nang'olo mwene shilambo* and his ancestors—now took orders from him, and he took orders from the Portuguese. He was required to collect taxes and give the money to the Portuguese."

"You collected these taxes, too?" I asked.

"I had no choice. If I hadn't, I would have been sent to São Tomé to work in the sugar fields."

We sat quietly for some time before Ndyankali added: "I was *régulo* until

I bought a membership card from FRELIMO. I was told that if I did not have a card, I would be killed by FRELIMO after they freed us from the Portuguese. But when the Portuguese discovered that I had the card, they imprisoned me. I spent ten years in prison. I was beaten so hard, I went blind."

I looked with sympathy upon the frail, sightless Ndyankali, who could not return my gaze. In that moment, this object of Muedan history's scorn seemed more its victim to me.

"The Portuguese did eat you, didn't they?" Marcos said.

"You know who really ate us?" he responded.

Marcos and I awaited his answer.

"All those young men who worked for money on the plantations on the coast and in Tanganyika—the ones who eventually joined FRELIMO. They fed only themselves. They forgot their elders."

The story Ndyankali told us about his predecessor's selection as *régulo* was but one of many stories told to us of the aftermath of Portuguese conquest. As the Portuguese military demanded that each settlement identify a "chief," Makonde settlement heads and their respective populations deployed variable strategies vis-à-vis their new overlords. Many settlement heads simply presented themselves to the Portuguese command. Others refused to meet with their conquerors. Obstinate elders sometimes sent delegated juniors in their stead. In some cases, rival elders or ambitious juniors took the initiative to meet with the Portuguese upon realizing that the refusal of their *vanang'olo* to capitulate brought upon them the continuing wrath of the conquerors. In some instances, rivals or juniors who might never have been chosen as successors or delegates took advantage of the moment to usurp power from their elders. In still other instances, as backhanded gestures of capitulation, settlement heads sent "village idiots" to be recognized by the Portuguese.

As Herman Nkumi and other elders told us, once a "chief" presented himself to the Portuguese command and complied in placing a Portuguese flag in the center of his compound, the people of his area were permitted to rebuild their homes. This chief was then required to provide people from his settlement to serve the Portuguese column as it constructed the military supply road traversing the plateau.

When World War I ended and the Portuguese military withdrew to its barracks, jurisdiction over the region reverted back to the Nyassa Company, which, for the first time, effectively occupied the plateau.[3] At each of the several Nyassa Company posts built on the plateau after the war, post commanders worked with those chiefs already identified by the Portuguese military. Because settlement heads were too numerous to be dealt with directly, the company required populations in areas of a given dimension to name one "chief" to represent them all. Areas delimited by the company did not correspond with a settlement's territory, nor even, in most cases, with the territory associated with a particular *nang'olo mwene shilambo*. Because there were no "chiefs" who exercised dominion on the geographical scale that suited the Nyassa Company, such chieftaincies had to be invented to meet company demands.

The company granted the title of *capitão-mor*[4] to each of the "chiefs" elevated to positions of authority over their peers, and it required these figures to assist the company in the collection of hut taxes and in the recruitment of corvée labor (called *chibalo* in Mozambique). Beneath each *capitão-mor* in the company "administrative" hierarchy, the company recognized several *wajiri*.[5] In most cases, settlement heads (or their delegates or those who had usurped their positions) became *wajiri*. As such, these figures acted as deputies to their respective *capitães-mor* (pl.), giving the Nyassa Company an administrative structure that reached into every settlement and allowing the company to extract revenue and labor power from every household on the plateau. Elders often told us that, by means of this hierarchy, "the Nyassa Company *ate* the Makonde."

The Nyassa Company passed through the hands of several holding companies during the tenure of its charter but never marshaled sufficient financial resources to invest in the infrastructural development of the region. Instead, it fed off of the region's inhabitants (Vail 1976; Neil-Tomlinson 1977). One British visitor to the region concluded of company methods through which the hut tax and *chibalo* labor were extracted: "so far as the natives are concerned, this is a land of blood and tears, where the most brutal ill-treatment is no crime and murder merely a slight indiscretion" (in Vail 1976: 401).

When the Nyassa Company lease expired in 1929, the Portuguese colonial administration took over direct control of company territories, including the plateau. Continuity was observed at the local level, as company posts were transformed into colonial administrative posts, and many company officials stayed on as state officials.[6] Like their company predecessors, state officials continued to use local chiefs to assist them as administrative intermediaries, now calling these figures *autoridades gentílicas*.[7] The hierarchy established by the administration, however, was made to conform to the model for native authorities in other areas of the colony (Alves 1995); *capitães-mor* were thus grouped together and subordinated to one drawn from among their ranks, creating a third administrative level of "chiefs" called *régulos*.[8] Thirty-one *regulados* (i.e., areas controlled by individual *régulos*) were created in the plateau region (see map 3, in chapter 11).

While this three-tiered political hierarchy was clearly a colonial invention, it reflected preconquest relations in subtle ways, as Ndyankali's story indicated. A *régulo* was often the *nang'olo mwene shilambo* of his zone or a powerful preconquest warlord (or a recognized nominee or successor to one of these positions or even a usurper understood to have seized the position of such a figure). *Capitães-mor* were generally *vanang'olo vene kaja* (or nominees or usurpers) of settlements that were either relatively large in their own right or that had been founded relatively early in the history of the region. Simple *wajiri* were normally heads (or nominees or usurpers) of settlements that were relatively small or that had been formed as a consequence of a recent schism in a larger settlement.[9]

In the management of "indigenous affairs," Portuguese administrators gave *autoridades gentílicas* and their subordinates a relatively free hand in the exercise of authority over "*indígenas*," who had no status as citizens and were therefore neither subject to nor protected by the law. Not only did these authorities continue to oversee social relations in the visible realm—validating land transactions, arranging marriages, settling disputes, and so on—but they also continued to oversee relations in the invisible realm. Whereas the British and French generally enforced a ban on sorcery/witchcraft accusations, trials, and ordeals in their African territories (Mair 1969: 170; Chavunduka 1978: 14; Fisiy and Rowlands 1989; Mesaki 1994; Mombeshora 1994; Fields 1997: 75–76), the Portuguese demonstrated relatively greater "tolerance" for, and reliance upon, indigenous institutions and practices.[10] The colonial administration in Mozambique did advise administrators to limit the influence of *curandeiros*[11] and passed laws limiting the legal practice of medicine to licensed practitioners[12] and mandating *autoridades gentílicas* "to oppose the practices of *bruxarias* [witchcraft] and divination, especially those that represent violence against people"[13] (E. Green 1996: 50; Fry 2000: 126; Honwana 2002: 129). In the 1920s and 1930s, administrators in some parts of Mozambique reportedly punished practitioners of *feitiçaria* and/or *curandeirismo* with forced labor, imprisonment, or even deportation to the West African islands of São Tomé and Príncipe (Honwana 2002: 122–130; Meneses n.d.: 15), but such measures were not widely adopted.[14] Administrators generally permitted "indigenous practices" such as these, so long as they neither produced violence nor disrupted the colonial agenda (Fry 2000: 126; Gulube 2003: 101).[15] "Transforming the religious behavior of the indigenous population" was, as we shall see in chapter 11, ultimately left to the Catholic Church (Fry 2000: 126; Honwana 2002: 129).

Although many *autoridades gentílicas* were in fact also heads of their respective settlements, and although they continued to exercise authority in many familiar ways, the administrative hierarchies imposed by the company and, later, by the colonial administration slowly transformed the roles these elders played within their own matrilineages. The government, like the company before it, extracted *chibalo* labor via *autoridades gentílicas,* generally putting recruits in the Mueda region to work building roadways, a task referred to locally as *mwangani.* To provide an attractive labor climate for colonial enterprises large and small, the administration resorted to the familiar strategy of the hut tax and used *autoridades gentílicas* as tax collectors. In order to pay the tax, families were forced to cultivate cash crops such as peanuts, sesame, cashews, castor oil, or rice for sale to local merchants (Isaacman 1996) or to enter into contract labor arrangements with colonial interests. *Régulos* and their subordinates received a commission for every laborer they "provided" to local private settler farms and regional plantations (Adam and Gentili 1983: 44; Meneses et al. 2003: 345).

While the Portuguese consolidated the authority of *régulos* and their deputies, Muedans knew that these figures had been "eaten" by the colonizer, who used indirect rule to "feed on" the entire plateau population. As Ndyankali told us, each *régulo*—dressed in a uniform provided to him by the colonial administration—received orders from the Portuguese post administrator and passed these orders along to his *capitães-mor,* who, in turn, passed instructions on to their *wajiri.* If the orders given by *autoridades gentílicas* were resisted, these authorities dispatched native police (called *cipais*) to enforce compliance. If a *régulo* himself proved uncooperative or incompetent, he was liable to being publicly beaten, exiled to the plantations of São Tomé, or killed by the Portuguese.

While those who collaborated with the colonial regime and with local enterprises in the collection of taxes and in the provision of labor "ate well," most Muedans under their administrative control "went hungry" according to oral testimony. With so much at stake, legitimation crises festered among *autoridades gentílicas* throughout the colonial period as rivals contested one another's claims and competence.[16] Portuguese post administrators were sometimes dragged into these conflicts and, more often than not, were inclined to resolve them by selecting the contestant who promised to be most compliant with administrative demands. Thus, *autoridades gentílicas* themselves occupied tenuous positions betwixt and between a population they ostensibly represented and an administration that simultaneously "authenticated" their "legitimacy" (through the issuance of uniforms) and demanded that they act contrary to the interests of those "for whom they spoke."[17] Tensions and animosities were underscored by the fact that *régulos* and *capitães-mor* exercised authority over populations inhabiting settlements that had enjoyed autonomy prior to colonial conquest.[18]

Beyond this, the *pax lusitana* had other, even more profound, effects on social structure and the institutions of authority within Makonde matrilineages. As Ndyankali hinted in conversation with us, Portuguese rule, in a variety of ways, loosened the strands of *likola* solidarity that bound youths to their matrilineal elders. To begin with, the colonial administration enforced a ban in the region on commerce in firearms, the currency with which matrilineages had long brokered both marriages and intergenerational relations. Simultaneously, Portuguese rule eliminated warfare between matrilineages and, with it, the dynamics that had made weapons essential to the defense and reproduction of the settlement, thereby eradicating the dangers that had previously discouraged subordinates from breaking with the authority of a settlement head and moving off to found a new settlement (see also Dias and Dias 1970: 308).

What is more, even though young men remained beholden to their elders for access to land, the colonial era presented them with opportunities to earn for themselves the goods necessary to pay bridewealth and to establish independent households. Young men discovered these opportunities despite an unfavorable Portuguese colonial labor regime. Indeed, the prospects for earning wages in Mozambique were generally abysmal. The handful of colonial settlers operating in the plateau region hired fewer than fifty workers each (Adam and Gentili 1983: 45). Vieira e Baptista, who managed the German-owned Mocímboa Sisal Syndicate near the plateau (referred to by Makonde as Mpanga) hired substantial numbers of workers but paid a pittance.[19]

Plateau residents, however, pursued other options by fleeing across the Rovuma River border into the now-British colony of Tanganyika, where labor relations were considerably more favorable. Large numbers of Muedan migrants found employment on sisal plantations (which paid as much as sixty times the wage paid to workers on Mozambican sisal plantations; West 1997b: 106) and elsewhere in Tanganyika (Egerö 1974; Alpers 1984). A 1948 census (cited in Alpers 1984: 375) counted 27,489 "Mawia" (Mozambican Makonde) over the age of sixteen in the British territory—a substantial number considering that the 1950 Mozambican census placed the total number of Mozambican Makonde at 136,079 and the number living on the Mueda plateau at only 48,120 (cited in Dias 1964: 16–17).

Material conditions were so much better in Tanganyika that many Muedan migrants remained there. Taking up permanent residence away from the plateau, however, meant giving up the secure rights to land that derived from living among kin in one's area of origin. Resettlement also denied one access to familiar social networks that provided fellowship in the course of events ranging from the initiation of youths to marriages, festivities (such as playing music and dancing), and simple day-to-day conversation, not to mention mutual aid in times of crisis (e.g., loans or assistance with funeral expenses for a deceased family member). While a sizable minority of migrants remained indefinitely in Tanganyika, the majority returned, in time, to the Mueda plateau—some after a labor stint of less than a year and others after more than a decade or two. Young single men frequently returned home after a few years, carrying with them the wealth they needed to marry and to establish a household.[20] Many crossed and recrossed the border repeatedly, alternating between stints of work and extended "visits" with family. Eventually, as we shall see in chapter 13, young Muedans also found gainful employment at home on the plateau with the Catholic missions that were established there in the colonial era.

The wealth of Muedans coming of age in the colonial period took novel forms, as many remembered when speaking with us decades later. Migrant workers in Tanganyika used the wages they earned to purchase goods that were unavailable in Mozambique. Included among the most sought-after items were sewing machines, bicycles, radios, shoes, specific types of cloth and clothing, and firearms.[21] According to ex-migrant laborers and ex–shop attendants with whom we spoke, even basic goods (including cloth, tools, plates, cooking pots, soap, sugar, and salt) that had long been available to Muedans either on the coast (via preconquest trade caravans) or on the plateau (once coastal-based Indian merchants had opened shops there) were less expensive, and of higher quality, in Tanganyika. Muedan migrants learned to compare brand names, whether for bicycles, radios, penknives, or cooking pots, and invariably found better deals on the northern side of the Rovuma River.

According to oral testimony, migrants returning to the Mueda plateau often brought with them bicycles that could be used for travel between settlements to visit family members or to strengthen the bonds of commerce. They often brought radios, too, allowing them to follow events in Tanganyika (and elsewhere in Africa) via Swahili-language news broadcasts. Sometimes they returned with sewing machines, with which they could set themselves up as tailors back home and generate cash income. Invariably, returning migrants brought with them large sacks of fine new clothes, purchased with their savings from plantation wages. Muedans who had worked at the Catholic missions in the plateau region told us years later that they followed the lead of returning labor migrants, crossing the border, when they could, to purchase these sought-after goods with their wages.

Some of these young Muedans disposed of the objects of their wealth as their elders had disposed of the firearms, iron, and cloth that they had procured in caravan trade at the coast in their youth, namely, by handing them over to their settlement heads or to their *vanjomba* (matrilineal uncles). "Young men would squander such wealth," we were often told by elders reflecting on these days in which they had been young; "the settlement head knew how to use it properly."

Of course, settlement heads rarely "saved" what was given to them either. Even as these elders "ate" the riches of returning migrants, however, they used these riches to "feed" their populations. In doing so, they augmented their symbolic capital and consolidated their influence over the matrilineage. The young people who provided their elders with these goods were considered with respect as *wakukamalanga* (providers), just as successful hunters had long been. Remembering his return to the plateau with riches that he gave to his settlement head, one man with whom we spoke commented, "We were treated as 'saviors' of the settlement." Such acts eventually returned tangible benefits: elders marked off plots of their own land for these young men and saw to it that their bridewealth was paid.

This scenario was neither universal nor historically durable, however. Many of the goods that returning migrants brought with them were not easily shared. Bicycles, for example, could not be divided; they could only be loaned. Only the person with some training could use a sewing machine to productive ends, and the cash that one might earn with such a machine was easily hidden. Even bags of clothing frequently eluded the redistributive grasp of the settlement head. Patterns varied from settlement to settlement, as well as over time, but as the practice of repatriating wealth to the plateau became more familiar, it took on a logic of its own, according to those who remembered these times. Youths themselves took to redistributing the goods they carried with them, offering simple gifts to their closest kin and to others whose favor they wished to curry. The lion's share, they began to keep. Some even began conducting small trade—buying goods in Tanganyika and reselling them in Mozambique—to multiply their wealth.

Because young men now had direct access to the goods necessary to pay bridewealth and to set up a household, they became relatively less concerned with putting "meat" on the plates of their elders. Although *likola* elders maintained control over land, many young men could satisfy a greater proportion of their needs through other activities in the cash economy. What is more, for the first time, land could be secured on the Mueda plateau through paying "rent" to unrelated landholders. Returning labor migrants and mission employees alike thus proved capable of "feeding themselves" in greater numbers and at younger ages than their elders had. When they did feed others, they cultivated their own clients rather than currying favor with their elders.

A Muedan by the name of Lázaro Nkavandame epitomized this new generation of enterprising young men. The son of a *capitão-mor* named Nkavandame from Ndyankali's *regulado,* Lázaro worked for many years as a labor overseer on Tanganyikan plantations before taking up cross-border trade on a significant scale. In the late 1950s, Lázaro established several agricultural "cooperatives" in the Mueda region whose members the Portuguese recognized as exempt from other forms of labor recruitment. The success of Lázaro's cooperatives, both in terms of profitability and in terms of expanding membership, challenged *autoridades gentílicas'* monopoly role as brokers in the local supply of labor (Isaacman 1982; Adam and Gentili 1983; West 1997b: 128–137). Not surprisingly, the behavior of such youths was often cast by these elders as a form of "provocation" (*ushaka*) and/or "ambition" (*shojo*) that challenged legitimate authority.

Not only were the enterprising young men of Lázaro's generation often accused of "eating alone," but sorcery was said to circulate wildly around these youngsters of voracious appetite, as well as around the objects of their unprecedented wealth. Most Muedans considered the novel forms of wealth that appeared with increasing regularity in their midst to be neutral objects, much as they had long thought of medicinal substances (*mitela*). Nonetheless, these objects were the focus of concentrated social concern. These new artifacts of power—whether bicycles or sewing machines purchased abroad or trade tools or books received at the Catholic missions—were recognized as potentially enriching to the community and, even, necessary to its social reproduction in a changing world. At the same time, they were also understood to be potentially dangerous if used to self-serving ends.

In any case, as Muedans deployed the interpretative schema of *uwavi* to decipher how power worked through these novel forms of wealth and within the historical moments that produced them, the schema of *uwavi* was transformed along with the social contexts in which it was invoked. As loci of power proliferated in the visible realm, so too did loci of power in the invisible realm. Muedans observed in their midst new forms of sorcery and attributed these to new kinds of sorcerers.[22]

Muedans wondered and debated among themselves whether power in the invisible realm reflected or refracted power in the visible realm as measured by these new forms of wealth—whether it was generally the haves or the have-nots who perpetrated *uwavi*. When returning labor migrants met with misfortune in the form of illness or dissipating wealth, they generally suspected and accused envious neighbors and kin, who had never traveled beyond the plateau, of attacking them to destroy their "progressive" projects of individual advancement—of seeking to "devour them." On the other hand, residents of the settlement generally suspected that, during their time abroad, migrants had acquired insatiable appetites that could be fed back home only by consuming the flesh of their families and/or neighbors, and that these returnees had learned exotic forms of *mitela* from the strangers among whom they had worked which now enabled them to protect themselves and their possessions—in other words, to "eat alone."

11

Christianity and Makonde Tradition

"When my father heard that the *padres* were teaching people to read and write, he traveled to Nang'ololo to study with them," Luís Gabriel Mbula told us. "Many people were interested in learning to read and write, but very few were enthusiastic about Catholicism."

Mbula grinned as he appeared to be overtaken by memories.

"People used to say that those who accepted the *padres* wound up 'pulling the sun.'"

I looked at Mbula inquisitively.

"Makonde used to believe that the rays of the sun were cords. Those who lived badly were condemned each night to pull the sun by these cords from one side of the world to the other. No one wanted to be a Christian!"

Luís Gabriel Mbula was born in 1924. In the same year, Fathers Alain Lebreton and Emile Martin arrived on the Mueda plateau, having departed a mission station founded only two years earlier by their Montfort order among Makua in Namuno.[1] According to Lebreton, the Portuguese at the time sought to "counterbalance [the] influence" of British Protestant missions already established in the Lake Nyassa region and were interested, specifically, in seeing a mission built among the "newly subjected" Makonde, who remained "restive toward civilization" (Lebreton and Vloet n.d.: 1). Just as the capital-poor Portuguese nation was compelled to turn to foreign concessionaires to invest in its colonial territories, however, it was also forced—due to the widespread poverty and illiteracy of its own largely Catholic population—to seek the aid of foreign-based Catholic orders to meet its evangelical objectives in these same territories. Like the founder of their order, Lebreton and Martin were French.

With the assistance of a Nyassa Company post official, these two Montfortians selected a site near the present-day village of Lutete and, on 24 November 1924, founded the mission Sagrado Coração do Jesus dos Macondes (Sacred Heart of Jesus of the Makonde). As the water source near the mission site proved unacceptable, a few months later the missionaries requested permission to move the mission to a site high above, but within walking distance of, the clean waters of the Ng'undi River. At the instruction of the post administrator, Shiebu, the local *nang'olo mwene shilambo*, identified a 2,000-hectare tract of land for the mission to use (Lebreton and Vloet n.d.: 25). In time, the missionaries would discover that the place that they inhabited was called "Nang'ololo" after its residents, "those who like to eat bush fowl."

Company officials instructed the *capitães-mor* in the immediate environs of the mission to provide the Montfortians with able bodies to assist them in putting a roof over their heads and food in their stomachs. The missionaries paid to the company each worker's hut taxes, thereby acquiring "rights" to their labor (Cazzaninga 1994: 37). The missionaries also paid wages to those who worked for them: 20 escudos a month to each man, 12 escudos to each woman, and eight escudos to each child (Lebreton and Vloet n.d.: 5). Notwithstanding these wages, local residents apparently felt much the same about working for the missionaries as they did about working for the Nyassa Company or the sisal plantation owners, who normally commanded their labor power. Lebreton would admit in his journal: "Seeing them at work, one would say they were prisoners of war" (Lebreton and Vloet n.d.: 3).

During their first months on the plateau, the Montfort Fathers attempted to begin the work of education and evangelization with their labor recruits, but with little result. Lebreton remarked that what little interest these workers showed in his lessons was "to avoid work" (Lebreton and Vloet n.d.: 3). To attract youngsters to the mission to study with them, the missionaries offered various gifts, including cups of grain and, later, cloth. Attendance rose and fell with the mission's stock of gifts (6). The missionaries were frustrated, however, in their attempts to teach prayers and hymns across a seemingly insurmountable language barrier (7).

Relations between the mission and the surrounding population remained tense. The missionaries interpreted recurrent theft from mission storehouses and the mysterious deaths of animals in mission livestock pens as signals of local hostility. Most settlement heads, Lebreton reported, encouraged the members of their matrilineages to stay away from the mission, whether as laborers or as students.

On their journey to the Mueda plateau, the Montfort Fathers had been accompanied by two Nyanga Christians, Alfredo and Carlos, drawn from a Montfort congregation in Nyassaland (Cazzaninga 1994: 19). These men possessed only rudimentary knowledge of Emakua[2] and none of Shima-konde. Nonetheless, they were given the task of aiding the missionaries as interpreters.

Nearly two years after the missionaries' arrival on the plateau, the Mont-fort Fathers adopted a new tactic in their evangelical campaign, dispatching Alfredo to Shiebu's settlement to organize an open-air catechism for young men (Lebreton and Vloet n.d.: 28). The initiative was a moderate success, at-tracting an average of fifteen students. Among Alfredo's students was the fa-ther of our interviewee (Luís), Gabriel Mbula.

In the following years, the Montfortians summoned several more African catechists from Namuno to Nang'ololo, scattering them in the settlements surrounding the mission. In some cases, settlement heads supported these initiatives, sometimes attending classes themselves. In some settlements, at-tendance rose and fell with the agricultural seasons. In others, initial interest was followed by a total collapse of attendance, reflecting the rising and falling tide of opinion among residents over whether or not to permit the classes to be held.

While settlement residents demonstrated scattered and sporadic interest in the catechism, they generally held the mission itself at arm's length. Atten-dance at "school" at the mission fluctuated but time and again bottomed out at one or two students. The missionaries also struggled perpetually to recruit and sustain labor for the ongoing work of mission construction and agricul-tural production.

Where preaching and teaching failed to pull Muedans into the mission, however, the harsh colonial labor regime eventually pushed plateau residents closer to the church. In 1928, the colonial government issued a new labor law that prohibited the use of *chibalo* labor on private concerns but required all Africans either to cultivate a cash crop on one hectare of their land or to com-plete a three-month labor contract. By comparison with roadwork or contract labor with the Mocímboa Sisal Syndicate, work at the mission was attractive. Not only did the mission offer far better working conditions, but it offered higher pay as well. Like all contract labor, work at the mission also exempted a worker from taxation (whereas cash-crop cultivation did not). In the wake of the new law, the labor force at the mission stabilized, making possible the work of building and sustaining the mission while also giving the missionar-ies a captive audience for evangelization.

In May of 1928, the mission baptized its first two "converts": "Pedro" Mwa-kala (from the settlement of Shiebu) and "Paulo" Nciune (from the lowland settlement of Mwoho).[3] Attendance at the mission school remained in the single digits, however, with most students dropping out after less than a year.

While many plateau residents had come to accept the missionaries' presence among them, and while some availed themselves of the benefits of working for the missionaries, few were yet ready to embrace "the way, the truth, and the life" of which the *padres* spoke.

In their account of nineteenth-century Christian evangelization among the Tswana of South Africa, John and Jean Comaroff (1997: 198–251) suggest that, due to a relativist disposition that admitted for the possibility of many ways and many truths, the Tswana were inclined to contemplate the novel ideas and practices to which missionaries exposed them just as they had long considered, and sometimes adopted, the ideas and practices of their African neighbors. Indeed, before the encounter with European missionaries, the lines that divided the Tswana from their neighbors, the Comaroffs suggest, were relatively fluid. Christian missionaries to the Tswana, however, manifested the conviction "that they had brought the exclusive truths of civilization to the natives, truths that could not but displace existing heathen customs" (225). In the face of this cosmological inflexibility, the ideas and practices of the Christian missionaries' Others congealed into distinct "traditions" which the missionaries considered as obstacles to be overcome—differences to be obliterated—in the campaign to "convert" and, hence, save Tswana heathens (244–245).

Similar perspectives and dispositions animated the encounter at Nang'ololo between Makonde and Montfortian. The unwavering certainty of the missionaries in "the one true way" not only threw "Makonde tradition" into starker relief than ever before experienced by plateau residents but simultaneously identified that tradition as errant.[4] Plateau residents who endeavored to become Christians were expected by the missionaries to observe strict prohibitions on a variety of Makonde "traditions." To no insignificant degree, they were expected to cease being Makonde. It was a choice of which few were able to conceive, and to which still fewer were prepared to commit.

Reflecting on these times—times when he had not yet become a Christian—the elder Emiliano Simão Ncimi told us: "The problem was polygamy. Men didn't want to be baptized because they didn't want to give up the opportunity to have more than one wife. The *padres* made Christian men give up their second wives. They could only have one wife." Countless other elderly men, Christian and non-Christian alike, told us that the missionaries' condemnation of polygamy was among the greatest impediments to becoming a Christian.

Polygamy was not, however, the only Makonde tradition condemned by the missionaries—not the only impediment to "conversion." The missionaries also preached against *likumbi* and *ing'oma* (male and female initiation rites, respectively) and against *mapiko* (the dances usually held to celebrate passage through initiation rites but also staged in other festive contexts).

Luís Gabriel Mbula, who was to become one of the first Muedans baptized at the mission, told us that he went to the mission school without undergoing initiation.

"It was enormously difficult for us, and it was a great obstacle to evangelization for the church."

Mbula clutched his Bible as he spoke with us.

"At that time, people who had not undergone initiation were not considered adults—they were not yet fully human. An uninitiated man was called an *ncungu*, and an uninitiated woman a *namako*. If such people married, they were broadly condemned."

Mbula looked away from us now. In his disgust, he somehow partook of the sentiments that his words criticized.

"If a *namako* gave birth to a child," Mbula continued, "it was considered a horrific event."

Mbula went on to tell us that most of the mission's early converts had already undergone initiation when they began preparation for baptism by the church. The first to forgo these rites before being baptized, in accordance with mission directives, were a young man named Ludovico Mitema and a young woman named Bendita Mpalume. These two young Muedans, Mbula told us, became the objects of great social hostility. Some threatened their lives, while others simply treated them as children in perpetuity.

Ludovico, Mbula told us, was excluded from the knowledge of manhood that one typically gained in initiation rites—knowledge that included the secret that *mapiko* dancers were not spirits but rather mere men in disguise. For his "ignorance," Ludovico was then ridiculed. Bendita, Mbula recounted, was denied the counsel of elder women regarding her sexual maturation. When she became pregnant by her husband, Mateus Mwani, she was told that her child would be a *shitumbili* (referring to the bulging growth of the trunk of a wild banana plant) and that she would be left to give birth alone, in the forest, where she and her baby would die.

According to others with whom we spoke, Muedans of any age who accepted baptism faced other problems as well. The church barred members of its congregation from attending *matanga* (ceremonies marking the anniversary of the death of a family member) and from practicing *kulipudya* (ancestral supplication)—both rituals essential to the maintenance of relations with ancestors, who brought good fortune if remembered and misery if ignored. As Kalamatatu told us, Muedans addressed their ancestors directly: "'*Shonde*,' we would say, to ask for an ancestor's attention. '*Njomba* [uncle], assist me, help me. When I succeed, I will bring thanks to you.' And we would. When we gained that which we had asked for, we would cook *ugwali* and call upon our ancestor to share it with us. '*Sadaka*,' we called it, to thank them." As Emiliano Simão Ncimi informed us, the church called this into question: "The *padres* asked us, 'Didn't God make us all? How can God's children pray to one another, ask one another for these things? We must each ask God directly. Only he can answer our prayers.'" Muedans who complied with church prohibitions on *kulipudya* and *matanga* met with vigorous social condemnation. Word spread on the plateau, among Christians and non-Christians alike, that the ancestors of Christians sometimes appeared, wandering on the edges of their descendants' settlements and carrying enormous burdens on their heads. The reprimand to Christians was clear.

In time, however, the tone of the encounter between Makonde and Montfortian would subtly change. Again, colonial policy produced unintended effects. Amid rising Portuguese anxiety over French interests in Portugal's African colonies, the colonial administration in Mozambique manifested increasing hostility toward the French nationals staffing missions such as Nang'ololo. By 1928, the French Montfortians in Mozambique had been replaced by Dutch missionaries of the same order. The first Dutch Montfortian at Nang'ololo, Father Piet Kok, adopted a more liberal attitude than his French predecessors toward Makonde tradition. Within months of his arrival, Kok had produced a Shimakonde-Portuguese dictionary and a Shimakonde-language catechism (Lebreton and Vloet n.d.: 50; Cazzaninga 1994: 41). Delighted by Kok's work, the Portuguese administration assisted the church in printing copies of these texts for use at the mission. Father Kok's interest in the Shimakonde language was but one manifestation of his broader interest in Makonde culture and society. Kok, and many of the Dutch missionaries who followed him to the plateau, initiated a more open "conversation" (Jean Comaroff and John Comaroff 1991: 198–251) with plateau residents about the meanings of their respective traditions.

Augusto Shilavi, a devout Catholic from the Mueda plateau, told us what his elders had told him: "At first, the *padres* didn't understand our culture. Initiation rites, *mapiko* dances, mortuary rites—they condemned these things and barred Christians from taking part in them. Later, they reflected on these issues in a better way."

Another devout Muedan Catholic, the elder Lucas Ng'avanga, remembered: "The *padres* weren't getting anywhere with us Makonde. We didn't accept all these prohibitions. So they studied these things and consulted with the pope. The pope told them that some of it was all right. Then we came to a mutual understanding."

Lucas Ng'avanga was among the first Muedans I came to know. I met with him in his home in Pemba, where he had moved to be close to family, including his daughter, Ângela, a sister in the Catholic Church. Ng'avanga was a respected elder in the Makonde community in Pemba. Marcos urged me to visit with him often, even when I "had no agenda." I was at first reluctant to spend too much time with any one person, feeling the need to get as many perspectives as possible on the many issues that interested me in my research. Eventually, I came to understand that regular visitation of elders such as Ng'avanga was an essential means of demonstrating respect. As my relationship with Ng'avanga matured, I discovered great comfort in sharing time with him, allowing our conversations to wander where they would.

Whether or not the church's reflections on "Makonde tradition" reached the level of the Vatican, the changing church perspective was apparent to anyone living in the environs of the Nang'ololo mission. Perhaps the most striking signal of a reformed church was the decision undertaken by the mission to organize and stage its own "rites of initiation."

Luís Gabriel Mbula told us: "Fathers Wevers and Gebhard called all the Christians of Nang'ololo together and asked us why we were so few. We responded that it was because of the issue of initiation rites." Mbula tapped insistently on the table in front of us as he remembered the effect of his words and those of his fellow Makonde Christians on the missionaries: "They said, 'If we don't change, Makonde won't come into the church.' So, that year, the church decided to hold its own rites. When people found out about this, they were pleased."

The mission initiated thirty-three boys and three girls in the first year; among the initiates were Ludovico Mitema, Bendita Mpalume, and Luís Gabriel Mbula himself. In preparation for these ceremonies, Mbula told us, the missionaries consulted with Muedan *vanalombo* (initiation specialists), culling practices from the "traditional" ritual complexes that they deemed incompatible with church doctrine.[5] Mbula told us: "Normally, initiation rites included songs about sexual relations—songs that are insulting and obscene. Some of these songs were eliminated. Also, initiates were normally given food that had *malumyo*—certain kinds of medicinal substances—in it to protect them, but this, too, was eliminated because it was considered 'dirty.' Boys normally practiced the sex act on an overly ripened *lipudi* fruit, but not in the church's rites." We learned elsewhere that the traditional practice of ritual defloration of female initiates was also eliminated from church rites. Even if they incorporated church doctrine on coming of age, marriage, and raising children into the lessons traditionally provided during this period of seclusion, the missionaries, nonetheless, behaved in many respects just as Makonde masters of the rites would have, visiting the initiates in the bush, where they remained isolated during the longest phase of the rites (Cazzaninga 1994: 131).[6]

The *padres* also adopted a new position on *mapiko* dancing and allowed *mapiko* to be danced on church grounds, but they informed those who watched the dance of its secret. "Father Guillaume Meels took to delivering the *mapiko* dancer to the ceremony on the back of his motorcycle," Luís Gabriel Mbula told us. "On occasion, he even played the drums for the dance"; Mbula laughed before adding, "not very well!"[7] According to Marcos, who was a student at the mission in the early 1960s, Father Meels displayed a *mapiko* mask in his office for all who entered—men or women, elders or youths—to see as evidence that *mapiko* were mere masked men.

The missionaries also staged mortuary rites—ceremonies of remembrance for the dead that came to be called *matanga do cristão* or *ipesta* (a Shimakonde transliteration of the Portuguese *festa*).

Just as important as the church's concessions on initiation rites, *mapiko* dancing, and mortuary rites were its subtly changed positions on rites of ancestral supplication (*kulipudya*). Simoni Matola told us on another occasion: "We used to believe that when people died, they did not finish. They lived on, on the other side. We called them *mahoka*. When the *padres* asked us what it is that leaves the body when a person dies, we told them this: *lyoka* [s.].[8] So they said, 'Okay, that's your soul.'"

Augusto Shilavi told us: "Formerly, we believed that the spirits of the dead lingered about the settlement for a time. That was why we needed to appease them. The *padres* simply explained to us that this lingering was called purgatory."

The missionaries similarly "translated" the Makonde concept of *nungu*, a distant and vaguely perceived creator (see Dias and Dias 1970: 384), into a monotheistic deity. The *padres* eventually encouraged Muedans to think of their ancestors as being "close to Nungu." When Muedans addressed the departed, they took to referring to them in just this way. "We said, 'You who are close to God,' and then we spoke as we would have before," Matola told us.

In time, Muedans and Montfortians alike came to speak of Muedan ancestors much like saints, who might intercede with the Almighty on behalf of those who invoked their names (see also Dias and Dias 1970: 356).[9] Apparently, on occasion, the missionaries went even further than this. Shilavi told me that when water began to seep into the foundations of a mission building under construction, the missionaries called the elder Shiebu and asked him to request the blessing of his ancestor—the spiritual steward of the land— upon the project. Once Shiebu had done so, Shilavi told us, the problem was resolved.

In the years after the mission adopted this more liberal stance toward "Makonde tradition," a small but stable community of Christians arose, eventually forming their own settlement adjacent to the mission. In lieu of a *likola* identity, they were referred to, locally, as Vamissau (mission people) (Cazzaninga 1994: 150).

Houses were also built on mission grounds in which catechumens lived during the time of their training (which could last as long as ten years). The number of catechism graduates rose slowly to a dozen or so per year. Pedro Mwakala and Paulo Nciune, who were baptized in 1928, and the flock of ten baptized on 22 December 1932 formed the first "twelve disciples" of Nang'ololo. On their own initiative, these twelve had been "recruiting" people to the church since the days of the French Montfortians, hoping that by stimulating interest they could keep the *padres* from abandoning the feeble mission (Cazzaninga 1994: 158). Once baptized, they fanned out into the settlements as catechists, with Pedro Mwakala serving as their "inspector."[10]

Students of these catechists (and others who soon joined their ranks) learned to speak a little Portuguese and could exchange greetings with local administrators (to the latter's delight) in the colonial language. Catechists

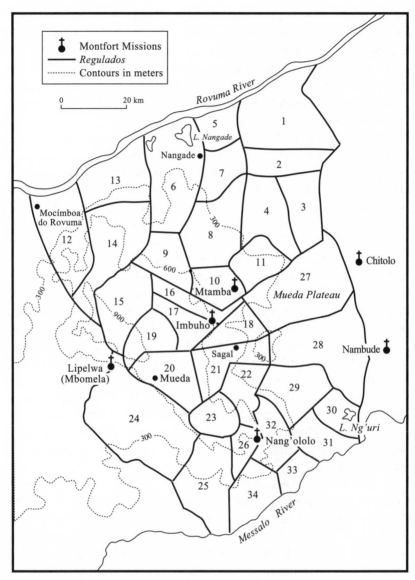

Map 3. Colonial-Era *Regulados* and Montfort Missions

1. Namunda	8. Shikadera	15. Mbomela	22. Nkapoka	29. Kavanga
2. Kitama	9. Nyanyangala	16. Shipungu	23. Naengo	30. Nekeuti
3. Nkonga	10. Shirumu	17. Masangano	24. Likomantili	31. Ng'ondo
4. Lingo	11. Mtamba	18. Lidimu	25. Mahomwe	32. Nkwemba
5. Shikungu	12. Kuitema	19. Mbavala	26. Ncingama	33. Liguili
6. Nangade	13. Metutuma	20. Shilavi	27. Shombo	34. Napula
7. Shikali	14. Mbalale	21. Ndyankali	28. Namakoma	

found that they had little trouble with the normally menacing *cipais* that policed the plateau on behalf of colonial *autoridades gentílicas*. Catechumens discovered that the Virgin Mary medallions that the church issued them protected them against the abuse of tax collectors and labor recruiters, who treated Makonde "pagans" as if *chibalo* labor conscription were still legal.

With the passage of the 1938 cotton law, which required plateau residents to cultivate cotton and to market their harvest to colonial concerns (Isaacman 1996), attendance in settlement schools rose sharply as Muedans sought to avoid mandatory cultivation requirements. In ever-greater ways, association with the church proved useful in keeping colonial agents at bay.

By the late 1930s, the mission claimed approximately 100 "converts" (Cazzaninga 1994: 157). Beyond this, the Legião de Maria (Legion of Mary) gave the mission a network that reached into distant settlements, encouraging church attendance and daily prayer.[11] Satellite congregations took to making a weekly pilgrimage to Nang'ololo to attend Sunday mass. So evident were the advantages of church membership that almost everyone in the vicinity of the mission sought to be baptized. Reflecting on the soaring interest in baptism at that time, Father João Bruininks told us: "[The mission] had to slow down the process to ensure that people truly understood the catechism."

By 1940, interest in the church was sufficient in the zone north of Nang'ololo to justify the construction of a new mission at Imbuho. Six years later, another mission was built at Nambude in the Shimakonde-speaking lowland region east of the plateau. In 1950, a fourth mission was constructed on the plateau's western edge, in the zone of the *régulo* Mbomela, near the descent to the Lipelwa River. Two more missions were added in Mtamba and in Chitolo, in 1959 and 1960, respectively (see map 3). Each mission deployed a staff of catechists to the surrounding settlements, insuring the reach of the church into virtually every settlement in the plateau region. In 1957, the newly formed diocese of Porto Amélia reported, for that year, 388 baptisms at Mbomela, 444 at Nambude, 1,062 at Imbuho and 1,523 at Nang'ololo (Diocese de Porto Amelia 1957). By the end of 1964, the mission at Nang'ololo alone had baptized 23,533 people and claimed 3,625 Christian families (Cazzaninga 1994: 157).

Despite the astounding evangelical successes of the Catholic missionaries, however, the gospel did not displace *uwavi* discourse. As we shall see in the following chapter, the missionaries themselves ironically came to occupy a prominent place within *uwavi* discourse.

12

Conversation and Conversion

Emiliano Simão Ncimi was among the first in his matrilineage to embrace Christianity. Marcos, Felista, and I sat with him late one afternoon outside his home in the village of Nampanya as he shared with us memories of his earliest conversations with the Montfort Fathers. He told us: "We Makonde used to paint a cross with castor oil on the ground above the place where we had buried a family member. When the *padres* came, they explained that this cross was the one Jesus hung on.[1] The *padres*, it seemed, knew more about what we knew than we did ourselves!"

As we have seen in chapter 11, upon arrival on the Mueda plateau the Montfort Fathers claimed to be the bearers of transcendent truths. In time, many Muedans accepted these claims and embraced Christianity, as testified to by Emiliano Simão Ncimi. Even those Muedans who did not "convert" to Christianity were deeply affected by the broader cultural encounter in which Muedan society was engaged from the mid-1920s onward.

Jean Comaroff and John Comaroff have asserted that as the Southern Tswana "conversed" with the Christian missionaries among them in the nineteenth century—debating the relative powers of rainmakers and prayers to the Christian God, for example—even those who resisted "conversion" to Christianity were "unwittingly and often unwillingly [drawn] into the *forms* of European discourse"; were "seduced into the modes of rational debate, positivist knowledge, and empirical reason at the core of bourgeois culture"; and, therefore, "could not avoid internalizing the terms through which they were being challenged" (Comaroff and Comaroff 1991: 213). To some extent, it would appear, this was true also of the Makonde who "conversed" with Montfortians in the middle decades of the twentieth century.

As also seen in chapter 11, however, the Montfort missionaries who ministered to the Makonde learned to speak like Muedans as much as Muedans learned to speak like them—referring to the Christian God as Nungu, to Christian saints as ancestors, and to Christian souls as *mahoka*. They drummed and danced to Muedan rhythms,[2] dressed themselves as *mapiko*, and acted as masters of initiation rites. In engaging with the world through the Shimakonde language, the missionaries in no small measure internalized Muedan cultural schemas and "unwittingly" affirmed the Muedan logics they sought to challenge.[3]

Consider the "conversation" between Muedans and Montfortians about sorcery. At times—perhaps most often in the early years of the mission's history—the missionaries dismissed *uwavi* as superstition. When I spoke with Simoni Matola, one of the first Nang'ololo Christians, he remembered well the day that he accompanied one of the missionaries on a visit to the house of the elder Shakoma, a healer of great reputation. "The *padre* told Shakoma that the spirit objects in his house were not gods.[4] They were only objects. He told the elder to throw them away, for they were worthless, powerless."[5]

At other moments, however, Montfort missionaries spoke openly, and with certainty, about the existence and the nature of *uwavi*, which they variously "translated" as man's "original sin" or as "the work of Satan" and "his leagues of demons."[6] What is more, they professed to know the appropriate means of controlling *uwavi*'s destructive effects: prayer and regular attendance at mass.[7]

When the Montfort Fathers spoke of sin and the work of the devil as *uwavi*, many Muedans heard them to be proclaiming their abilities to see into sorcery's invisible realm and to fix sorcerers in their gaze. Such claims were not unfamiliar to Muedans,[8] who associated these assertions with ones made by Muedan medicinal specialists and figures of authority. Indeed, most Muedans were convinced that the Montfort Fathers *knew uwavi*.[9] The only question was: What kind of *vavi* were the *padres;* to what ends did they use their power? From the earliest days of the missionaries' presence on the plateau, rumors circulated that they fed themselves on the flesh of young boys (Lebreton and Vloet n.d.: 15)—not surprisingly, considering the *padres'* concerted efforts to attract young boys to the mission to study with them.[10]

Once the missionaries had established for themselves a reputation for benevolence (at least in contrast with government authorities and colonial plantation interests), Muedan looked upon them with greater ambivalence, however. Consider, for example, popular memories of Sister Bendita shared with us by elderly Muedans. Bendita Mattio had come to Nang'ololo from Italy in the 1930s with the first contingent of Consolata Missionary Sisters.[11] She ministered to the mission congregation through the provision of basic health

When I met her in Pemba in 1994, Sister Bendita was eighty-seven years old, but she remained quite active in the Church—prompting me, too, to wonder what kind of *mitela* she had in her bag!

care in plateau settlements. Muedans remembered well the "little black bag" she carried with her as she made her rounds. "Bendita's *mitela*" were the source of anxiety and fascination for children and adults alike.[12] "We used to wonder about what was in that bag," an elder once admitted to me. "We would talk about it with people who had seen her take something from it. It seemed there was no end to her *mitela*. No matter how much she took out, there was still more inside." The many descriptions and accounts of Bendita that other Muedans shared with us betrayed similar mixtures of fear and admiration, reminiscent of Muedan sentiments regarding powerful *vakulaula*.[13]

The *nkulaula* Sinema Kakoli, whose house in Mwambula village looked directly upon the mission, harbored less charitable memories of the missionaries. I once asked him if the missionaries had done away with sorcery. He was astonished by this suggestion. "No way!" he said. "The missionaries practiced *uwavi* themselves. They danced at night to give the church life in the daytime. They had great confidence in themselves, not only in the daytime but also at night!" What the missionaries banned, Sinema told me, was the practice of *kulaula*—healing. This they did to ensure their uncontested power in the realm of *uwavi*, he told me.[14]

Luís Gabriel Mbula told us that the missionaries did not dismiss the existence of sorcery, so far as he could remember. Rather, he told us, they "prohibited it" in much the same way as settlement heads did in their individual settlements.[15] Such "prohibitions"—whether by settlement heads or by missionaries—were broadly considered *to be acts of sorcery*, albeit sorcery of construction. "Around the mission," Mbula told us, "sorcerers were given no place to operate."

Notwithstanding the suspicion and ambivalence with which Muedans looked upon the Nang'ololo mission in the colonial period, many became enthralled with the knowledge they deemed the missionaries to possess. For some Muedans, the missionaries' knowledge—reading and writing, mathematics and engineering, agriculture and commerce—provided keys to the unfamiliar world that had dawned in their midst with Portuguese colonialism. For others, like Emiliano Simão Ncimi, the missionaries offered new insights on a world Muedans previously thought they had known.

One Muedan elder, who was among the first Christians, told us, "The *padres* taught us everything they knew. That was why we loved the church. That was why we joined it." Contrary to the stereotype the Portuguese had applied to the Makonde—"restive toward civilization" (Lebreton and Vloet n.d.: 1)—many plateau residents looked upon the missionaries' knowledge with great curiosity. Luís Gabriel Mbula remembered the earliest days of the mission with nostalgia, wistfully remarking, "The mission was a place where we saw incredible things." Included among these incredible things were simple wonders like the missionaries' orchards of fruit trees (pear, orange, and tangerine) never before seen on the plateau, and the pens in which the *padres* raised pigs. More amazing things included the various mission vehicles and the presses used to extract oil from peanuts. Even the recreational activities witnessed at the mission were strange and exciting to Mbula—whether the singing of the mission choral group (with instrumental accompaniment) or the playing of football. "All of these things which we saw we imitated until we had learned how to do them," Luís told us.

Simultaneous with their interest in and respect for the missionaries' productive techniques and ritual sensibilities, many Muedans were inclined to believe that the missionaries' *mitela* were stronger than the medicinal substances known by Makonde *vamitela*. Many parents, including non-Christians, eventually consented to send their children to the mission to "study with the *padres*" in hopes that their children would learn these powerful new forms of *mitela*.

In time, the mission's educational programs, initially resisted by plateau residents, proved among its greatest attractions. Prior to 1940, the mission at Nang'ololo provided education to Muedan children only informally.[16] Although colonial administrators in Mueda town were pleased that Catholic "converts" and their children spoke a bit of Portuguese, they discouraged the missionaries from "raising expectations" among young Muedans, for whom the only employment prospects were manual labor. With the signing of a concordat between Portugal and the Vatican in 1940 (and the subsequent signings of the 1940 Missionary Accord and the 1941 Missionary Statute), however, the Catholic Church was mandated as the principal provider of education in the Portuguese colonies.[17] In that same year, Father Mentin established the first true elementary school at Nang'ololo, providing education up to grade 3-rudimentary. Separate dormitories were built for boys and for girls. The Montfort Fathers taught the former, while the Sisters of the Consolata taught the latter. In time, graduates of the school would travel to another mission school in Mariri (in southern Cabo Delgado Province) to attend grades 3-elementary[18] and 4. Some would remain at Mariri beyond completion of grade 4 to pursue clerical callings. Beginning in 1957, others would travel to Chiure (also in southern Cabo Delgado) to study to become grade-school teachers. In the meantime, the other missions established in the plateau region between 1940 and 1960 each built their own schools, replete with dormitories. Like Nang'ololo, these missions also sent catechists to teach classes in the surrounding settlements, where adults and children learned the alphabet and cultivated a desire for further education. By 1957, several hundred children were attending mission schools annually, and several thousand were attending classes in their settlements. Where once parents feared that the *padres* would feed on the flesh of their children, many now enforced their children's attendance at school with religious fervor, beating them harshly for truancy, even if they were not, themselves, Christians.

Having one's child initiated at Nang'ololo became as fashionable as clothing imported from Tanganyika. "The *padres'* rites" were certainly more mysterious to most Muedans. They were also widely said to be more effective than those of Makonde *vanalombo* (rites masters). Likewise, many adult Muedans sought baptism because they judged the missionaries' protective *mitela* to be superior to those of their settlement head or their *humu*.[19]

In light of the astounding growth of the Catholic Church on the Mueda plateau in the four decades following the founding of the first mission, and of the great interest shown by plateau residents in learning from the missionaries, one might take Emiliano Simão Ncimi's statement—suggesting that the *padres* knew more about what Muedans knew than Muedans did themselves—as an expression of unqualified Muedan capitulation to what they considered a superior worldview. Of course, many Muedans resisted "conversion," and many Christian "converts" practiced the faith inconstantly. Whereas some Muedans considered Christianity to be a new and improved mode of initiation, some Christians put their children through "traditional" rites of initiation either before or after the mission-sponsored ceremonies, "just to be certain" (Cazzaninga 1994).[20] Some who took Holy Communion and prayed to God to heal their afflictions also consulted *vakulaula.*

Perhaps, to some degree, Muedans' approach to Christianity was similar to that of Afro-Cuban slaves who, according to George Brandon (1993: 97), "used the Catholic saints to mask the worship of their own deities" as part of a broad "strategy of subterfuge."[21] When pressed to convert to Christianity, African slaves in the Americas frequently hid the objects that represented— or housed—their sacred entities (gods, spirits) in shrines beneath the very tables upon which they placed statues of the Christian saints, the Virgin Mary, and Christ.[22] Like these slaves, many Muedans may have embraced Christianity only superficially—perhaps to gain access to the many advantages afforded to "converts" in the colonial context.[23]

In time, however, the missions of the plateau region were filled with Muedans whose embrace of Christianity could not be dismissed as mere charade. The liberal posture of the Dutch Montfortians vis-à-vis "Makonde tradition" allowed many Muedans to regard acceptance of Christianity not as "conversion" from the practice of one religion to another but, instead, as a means of cosmological augmentation.[24] For many, adherence to the church expanded the vocabulary with which they could speak of the meaning of life and social morality, of death and the afterlife, and of relationships between the living, the dead, and unseen forces. These Muedan Christians more closely resembled the *descendants* of Afro-Caribbean and Afro-American slaves—the practitioners of Vodou, Santeria, Candomblé, and so on, who increasingly conceived of Christianity as an alternative language through which to express familiar truths, and who recognized the saints, the Virgin, and Christ as different *aspects* of the entities they also knew by the names of African gods and spirits.[25] To varying extents, then, Muedan Christians acted as "bricoleurs of the spiritual . . . domain" (Jean Comaroff and John Comaroff 1991: 250), exploring and celebrating the compatibility between Christian beliefs and Makonde "traditions."[26] In this, the Montfort missionaries were ultimately complicit in the production of such a mixture (*le mélange,* as Catholic leaders in Haiti referred with alarm to syncretic cosmologies, including Vodou; Métraux [1959] 1972: 338).

Notwithstanding their tolerance of selected Makonde "traditions," however, the Montfort Fathers effectively stood in their sanctuaries and proclaimed to Muedans (including the *vamitela* among them): "We see you! We know you! We know what you're up to!" What is more, Emiliano Simão Ncimi and other Muedans heard the missionaries effectively exclaim: "We know better than you how your world works!" Muedans who flocked to the mission and participated in the *padres'* many rites apparently recognized transcendent force in this confident vision informing the missionaries' practices. Through their actions, Muedans professed their convictions that the *padres* and their god were capable of overturning (*kupilikula*) Muedan visions of the world and remaking the world that Muedans (including the sorcerers and countersorcerers among them) had made.

Still, one might see something other than capitulation in Emiliano Simão Ncimi's words, as well as in Muedans' historical embrace of Christianity. Muedans, after all, began joining the church only after they and the Montfort Fathers had together begun to translate Catholicism into a language and a logic more familiar to Muedans. Muedans, then, did not merely "convert to Catholicism"; they also "converted Catholicism to themselves," to paraphrase Brandon (1993: 98).[27] Muedans thus recognized the prescience of the Montfort Fathers and the power of their Christian vision *even as* they recognized Christian cosmology *through* the discursive genre of *uwavi*.[28] Muedans admitted the missionaries' capacities to see the Muedan world in a novel way, and to bring transformative power to bear upon that world, in the moment that the missionaries' worldview was significantly rewritten in "conversation" with them.[29]

Ultimately, as Muedans constantly scrutinized and perpetually judged the missionaries' actions and the effects produced by their presence among plateau communities, these same Muedans held the missionaries in *their* gaze, claiming to know who *they* were (sorcerers) and what *they* were up to (what kind of sorcery they practiced).[30] Ironically, through surveillance of the mission and the missionaries, these Muedans (although, like any *muntela*, they would have denied it) established for themselves a transcendent vantage point from which they inverted, overturned, or turned around (*kupilikula*) the power that they attributed to the missionaries, along with the Christian cosmology that they increasingly professed to accept.

13

Christians, Pagans, and Sorcery

"There were two kinds of people living in the settlements in those days," Vicente Nkamalila Shuli told us.

"Christians and 'pagans'?" I asked.

Vicente had only just finished telling Tissa and me about his upbringing in the settlement of Kushilindi, a ten-minute walk from the site of the Nang'ololo mission station. He was born in 1926 or 1927, he told us. His parents, Nkamalila Shuli and Lúcia Bonifácio, had been persuaded by the missionaries to send him to catechism classes and, eventually, to the mission school. By age twelve, he had completed first grade, at which time his family migrated to Tanganyika. Vicente pulled weeds in the fields where his father cut sisal until he was himself old enough to cut. Five years on, the family returned to Kushilindi, and Vicente returned to school. He was baptized a year later, and married soon after. As head of a new household, he had to give up study at the mission to work for wages at the Mocímboa Sisal Syndicate. After completing five labor contracts, however, he got hold of a sewing machine and learned to operate it.

"The *padres* at the mission in Nambude hired me to sew clothes, which they sold in the mission shop," he told us proudly. "In time, I moved home and worked for myself making and selling clothes."

"You had a good setup!" Tissa suggested.

"Yes, it was good," Vicente agreed. "But there were dangers in it, too."

"What kind of dangers?" I asked.

"There were envious people back home who tried to demoralize me by ruining my things." Bitterness saturated the elder's words as he continued. "They said, 'You're just trying to provoke us. But in the end, you won't have anything!'"

"*Uwavi!*" Tissa exclaimed, decoding the euphemism for me in case I had failed to recognize it myself.

Vicente nodded, almost imperceptibly, before telling us that many in the settlement of Kushilindi spoke badly of, and to, Christians in those days. "Pagans said that it was Christians, not they, who would go to hell when they died."

Vicente's eyes betrayed his lingering anger. We sat in silence for some time before he offered his statement about there being two kinds of people in the settlements of those days. He ignored my response as he clarified his meaning. "First, there were those who worked hard and earned what they had. Second, there were those who got things in ways that could not easily be explained."

"*Vavi!*" Tissa said, again decoding the euphemism.

"The trouble was," Vicente added, somewhat vexed, "people who worked hard for their wealth were the ones who were attacked."

I wondered if, by "attacked," Vicente meant that he and his fellow "hard workers" were the victims of sorcery or were accused as its perpetrators. I waited for Tissa to decode this euphemism—the first that I did not myself fully understand—but whatever Tissa was thinking, he kept to himself.

Paradoxically, the presence of the Montfort Fathers on the Mueda plateau not only generated among Muedans a consolidated sense of "Makonde tradition" but simultaneously challenged the integrity of that tradition in profound ways. In the very moment that Muedans were encouraged to conceive of themselves as a distinct people with a coherent tradition, Muedan identities were rapidly proliferating, in part as a result of differential responses to the Montfort Fathers. While some Muedans embraced Christianity and sought— like Luís Gabriel Mbula—to emulate the missionaries in varied ways, others opposed themselves to the mission and its teachings. Some settlement heads refused to allow Christians to pray or to sing songs openly, while others themselves joined in the catechism and the prayers.

André Nikutume remembered the strife in his settlement when he was a young man: "Our prayers disturbed them, and their drumming and dancing disturbed us. We couldn't stop what we were doing, and they couldn't stop what they did. It caused great tensions between us."

Not only did residents of many settlements argue over whether or not to allow catechists to hold classes in the *shitala*, some settlements actually divided over the issue, with Christian groups splitting off to found new settlements where they might host a visiting teacher from the mission.

Amaro Mwitu's father was among the early church faithful at Nang'ololo, and he himself became one of the first Makonde ordained as a Catholic priest. He told us that the mission attracted adherents through the construction and maintenance of a progressive economic and social environment: "The missionaries had to show that they were different from the Portuguese—that they had people's best interests in mind. So they set up schools and carpentry classes, and they taught people new agricultural techniques on their fields." Through such endeavors, the missionaries demonstrated their differences with Muedans while inviting Muedans, in practical ways, to become more like them. In doing so, the missionaries further differentiated themselves from Portuguese colonials, who generally sought to preserve distinctions with their colonial subjects.

Indeed, from the late 1930s, the mission became a bustling center not only of religious activity but also of other forms of economic and social commerce, according to oral testimony. Father Vloet, in particular, trained an ever-increasing number of Makonde churchmen as carpenters, masons, tile makers, and brick makers and paid them to work on mission projects. Others were employed by the mission as messengers, assistants, cooks, or tailors. From the time of their arrival at the mission in 1933, the Sisters of the Consolata expanded the mission's activities by treating the ill in the surrounding settlements, assisting in childbirths, and seeking to provide educational instruction in health and hygiene. They also began training women as seamstresses and, eventually, paid these women to sew garments for the mission's Sunday services.

In 1940, the Nang'ololo mission opened a shop on its grounds. According to Lucas Ng'avanga, who worked as the mission shopkeeper, Christians and non-Christians alike traveled to Nang'ololo to purchase cloth, soap, sugar, salt, cooking oil, hoes, *catanas* (machetes), petroleum, matches, and so forth, from the mission store, where prices were considerably lower than in the Indian shops elsewhere on the plateau. The mission used the profits generated by the shop to fund projects such as the construction of the mission school building and dormitories—projects that provided further employment.

By the 1950s, many of the youngsters who had traveled to Mariri to pursue their studies began to return to Nang'ololo, where they found work in the thriving environs of the church. Whereas the earliest catechists had earned 30 escudos a month, the church now paid these young men 150 escudos monthly. Those who worked as teachers in the mission schools on the plateau made between 500 and 600 escudos per month. The mission shopkeeper at Nang'ololo made between 300 and 400 escudos monthly, and skilled tradesmen earned similar wages.[1] This was good money in the economic environment of colonial Mueda. Hut tax, at the time, was between 80 and 100 escudos per year on the Mueda plateau, and church employees could easily pay the tax out of pocket without producing cash crops for sale. The same was not true for those working contracts on colonial plantations or road construction. At the time, the Mocímboa Sisal Syndicate, for example, paid only 60 escudos for six months' work. Even the relatively more generous Nangororo sisal plantation—newly opened in the Metugi area near Porto Amélia—paid only 60 escudos a month for six months of contract labor.[2] "If you worked at the mission, you were wealthy," the former mission teacher Rafael Mwakala remembered. According to oral testimony, many people who derived an income from their association with the mission began conducting small trade: buying goods in Tanganyika and reselling them in Mozambique to multiply their wealth, just as migrant laborers were doing in the same period.

In the short span of forty years, Catholicism had become a defining category *within* Muedan society. As a consequence of opportunities presented by the mission, Muedan Catholics, like labor migrants, began to set themselves apart from others on the plateau.[3] As some Muedans became "more like" the missionaries, the differences that had once been understood to divide Muedans from Montfortians took root *within* Muedan society, penetrating deep into Muedan settlements and their constitutive matrilineages and households.

The employment opportunities provided by the mission to so many members of its congregation contributed to the weakening of ties that bound young men economically to their *vanjomba* (uncles), ties already made brittle by labor migration and the colonial cash economy. In fact, men who found gainful employ at the mission were even less dependent upon their elders than were returning labor migrants, who, upon coming home from abroad, still needed land. What is more, the missionaries encroached upon and undermined the authority of Muedan elders in a variety of other ways. Through their own ritual practices, the *padres* rendered superfluous the roles Muedan elders formerly played in celebrating marriages, arbitrating divorces, and resolving family disputes.

Where young men had once "provided for" (*kukamalanga*) the needs of the entire matrilineage by offering the fruits of their labor to the settlement head for redistribution, they now paid respect and offered tribute to the missionaries, giving a portion of their wealth to the church in the form of tithes and offerings. As diviners, healers, and masters of initiation rites were all denied opportunities to practice their vocations and to secure their economic and cosmological livelihoods, they were pushed toward the margins of Muedan society. Even the status of Muedan ancestors was placed in jeopardy, not only by prohibitions on ceremonies of ancestral supplication but also by missionary inducements to Christians to abandon the names they inherited from their forebears and, instead, to call themselves by the names of deceased Christian saints such as "Pedro" and "Paulo."

The church challenged the economic prerogatives, authority, and counsel of the very elders who decided to send their children to the mission school, even while offering forms of wealth, power, and wisdom that most Muedans—including especially these elders—desired for themselves and for their children. To be sure, church doctrine, in its own way, taught respect for one's elders and condemned what Muedans called *shojo* (ambition). In the end, however, the church's teachings undermined familiar forms of authority in favor of foreign figures, including a distant and incontestable authority to whom the missionaries so often referred: the pope. Some elders themselves entered into the church in attempts to capture its power. To their frustration, however, younger Muedans generally proved more adept at learning to speak the language of Christianity and to see the world in accordance with the novel schemas delineated in the Bible. In the end, even elders who were core members of the church sometimes protested when their children responded to the church's calling, fearing, with good cause, that they would lose control of their progeny to the church.[4] The devout Christian Lucas Ng'avanga admitted to me his fury when his daughter, Ângela, heeded the call of the mission sisters to join their ranks, depriving him of the opportunity to receive bridewealth for her.

Where the fracturing of *likola* solidarities went hand in hand with economic differentiation, the fragmentation of Muedan identities was also accompanied by the proliferation of sorcery. Sorcery, it was said, circulated wildly around the objects that distinguished Muedan Christians from non-Christians, as well as around forms of wealth garnered through association with, or labor at, the mission, as Vicente Nkamalila Shuli told us. Notwithstanding their "faith" in the power of the church, Muedan Christians harbored deep anxieties about the predatory forms of *uwavi* undertaken by envious "pagan" Muedans—anxieties sometimes provoked and exacerbated by the missionaries' talk, in the same breath, of Satan, sin, and sorcery. As a result of persistent fears, some drifted away from the church or gave up wage-paying jobs there.

On the other hand, non-Christian Muedans accused Christians of practicing sorcery as well.[5] Such accusations echoed in the words of Vicente Nkamalila Shuli and other Muedans with whom we spoke. Sinema Kakoli, who never joined the church, told us, "Christians *danced* just as pagans did," referring euphemistically to sorcery. To this he added: "They *ate well* at the mission." Sinema pointed us to the Catholic liturgy—wherein church faithful consumed the flesh and blood of Christ—as evidence in support of his assertion.[6] "What other bodies did Christians feed on with the aid of the *padres' mitela*!?" he asked us.

While Muedan Christians proclaimed to see the world from the revealing vantage point of church doctrine and to know the secret of the transformative power of Christ, then, non-Christian Muedans submitted these "converts" to intensive scrutiny, seeing in them recognizable motives and modes of behavior and thus converting (*kupilikula*) to their own understanding the act of Christian "conversion."

14

Night People

"A *mapiko* dancer was respected when he danced in another settlement," Jacinto Omar told Marcos and me. The elder comported himself with such easy dignity that, despite his sixty-plus years, it was not at all difficult to imagine him cloaked in the *mapiko* dancer's costume, drawing the rapt attention of onlookers. "It was easy to make friends," he continued. "Everyone wanted to get to know me."

Earlier in the conversation, we had learned how much the younger Jacinto had enjoyed what he called "the life of the settlement." "There was a teacher named Nolanda, sent by the missionaries, who taught reading and writing in my settlement when I was a boy," he had told us. "I studied with him for two years, but I never went to the mission school. I enjoyed the life of the settlement too much." The elder smiled. "My friends and I were more interested in hunting bush rats." The shame he attempted to display was superficial. "My sister tried to keep teaching us what she was learning, but we weren't interested."

The conversation flowed easily as the elder told us "the story of his life," interrupted now and then by a question from Marcos or me.

"I never went to Tanganyika," he told us. "I stayed at home after I married."

"Were you married in the church?" I asked.

"Yes," he answered, "but I paid bridewealth too—one *espera-pouco*."

"Where did you work?" Marcos asked.

"Right here. I opened up fields and cultivated them. I paid taxes—until the massacre, at least. After that, people refused to pay."

Jacinto's reference to the Mueda Massacre—a precipitating event in the Mozambican struggle for independence—led us to the topic of his involvement with the nationalist movement. This, too, Jacinto experienced within

During the conduct of my research in 1999, I carried with me a copy of my completed dissertation to show those with whom I had worked. "Nang'olo" (elder), I said to Jacinto Omar, "the stories that you and your friends have told me are in this book." "Read them to me then," he responded. For hours, I excerpted passages from the text, spontaneously translating for my audience of two, Marcos (shown here with Omar) and the protagonist himself. From time to time, the elder would correct me or say, "*ni kweli*" (it is true). When we had finished, he asked me if the work would be housed in the Arquivo Histórico de Moçambique. When I assured him that it would, he clasped my hand and said, "*wambone*" (good).

the context of life in the settlement. As a *mapiko* dancer, he told us, he was often invited to dance in neighboring settlements. The secret of the *mapiko*'s human identity was not the only one Jacinto kept. He took advantage of his travels to do the work of FRELIMO, the clandestine nationalist network that he had recently joined: "I used these occasions to get to know people and to decide who was trustworthy. Some people already knew that I was FRELIMO, but others did not. I spoke a special language on these occasions. I would say to someone I knew about another person I had observed, 'I would like this one to be our friend. What is he like?' and my friend might tell me, 'He's okay; he's fine.' So I would begin to chat with this person. After three or four conversations, I would say, 'I have something to tell you,' and I would talk about FRELIMO. Most people told me that they had been waiting a long time for someone to approach them."[1]

Jacinto's words as a spokesperson for the nationalist movement would have been understood because many Muedans of his age had, unlike him, lived and worked in Tanganyika. Many of these young Muedans had wit-nessed at firsthand the emergence, growth, and eventual triumph of the move-ment that gave birth to an independent Tanzania. In the late colonial period, many migrant Mozambican Makonde workers not only became affiliates of the Tanganyika Federation of Labor but also held Tanganyika African National Union (TANU) membership cards (Adam and Gentili 1983: 66–67). In time, young Mozambicans living and working north of the Rovuma began to envi-sion a similar movement in their Mozambican homeland. In the late 1950s, according to oral testimony, Muedan migrants with protonationalist sympa-thies worked to facilitate linkages between the many dance clubs, football teams, and funeral associations composed of Makonde migrants on Tangan-yikan sisal estates and elsewhere.[2] Their efforts eventually led to the forma-tion of the Makonde African National Union (the English-language name of the organization, and its acronym, MANU, reflected the influence upon it of TANU), which later changed its title to the Mozambique African National Union (still, MANU).[3]

The Portuguese colonial administration responded to the emergent proto-nationalist movement in northern Mozambique by arresting delegates sent across the border, into "the interior," to issue demands pertaining to, among other things, the deflated prices paid to Muedan agricultural producers.[4] On 16 June 1960, a crowd that had gathered in front of the office of the district administrator in Mueda in support of protonationalist leaders detained inside was fired upon.[5] In the aftermath of the event (which would eventually be re-ferred to by nationalists as the "Mueda Massacre"), MANU "mobilizers" be-gan to work clandestinely in Mueda to broaden the protonationalist move-ment's support base, issuing membership cards fashioned after the TANU cards that so many migrant Muedans already held. MANU mobilizers tapped into existing social networks on the plateau, seeking support first and fore-most among adherents to the Catholic missions.[6] Rafael Mwakala, who as a young man was recruited by MANU, told me: "They chose people at the mis-sion because we were educated. We were told that . . . we would be the fu-ture administrators of an independent Mozambique."

On 25 June 1962, at the behest of Julius Nyerere (president of the newly independent Tanzania) and other prominent African nationalist leaders, MANU consented to merge with two other protonationalist parties—the Mo-zambican National Democratic Union (União Democrática Nacional de Moçambique, or UDENAMO) and the Independent Mozambican African Na-tional Union (União Nacional Africana de Moçambique Independente, or UNAMI)—to form the Mozambican Liberation Front (Frente de Libertação

On my first day in the town of Mueda, on an exploratory visit, I awoke to find a delegation awaiting me. In the company of several officials from the District Directorate of Culture was a man of local legendry, namely, Faustino Vanomba, one of the protonationalist leaders whose detention sparked the protests that ended in the Mueda Massacre. Although I was tempted to avail myself of the opportunity to converse with Vanomba about his role in these historic events, I instead explained that I would be returning in a few weeks to begin work on the plateau for a year and a half, during which time I would speak at length with many people. I turned to Vanomba and asked him a few polite questions about himself. He looked at me, annoyed, and said: "This is not serious. If you want to know about me, you must have the proper equipment. When you come back, you bring a tape recorder and a camera. I will not speak about these things just for you to forget them. This story is important, and it must be documented." Once he was certain I had understood his mandate, he said with a grin, "Bring a video camera too. I want to be on video . . . and don't forget cigarettes!" I eventually sat with Vanomba at length as he told me the story of his life. He was greatly pleased when I asked him to pose for a photo in front of the administration building where he had been detained.

de Moçambique, or FRELIMO) under the leadership of Eduardo Mondlane, an American-trained Ph.D. in sociology with experience working for the United Nations Department of Trusteeship.

Within a short time, fissures emerged in the Front.[7] Rival leaders scrambled for a place at the table where, they imagined, the spoils of an independent Mozambique would be carved up. The former officers of the three parties that had merged to form FRELIMO were soon marginalized within the FRELIMO hierarchy by new leaders, many of whom had until recently been students in Europe. Some squabbles were literally over food, as the marginalized complained bitterly that FRELIMO's new officers lived in the finest hotels and ate in the finest restaurants in Dar es Salaam while they, who had worked for years to lay the groundwork for the movement, struggled to make ends meet (Chilcote 1972: 472). Rival organizations led by disgruntled ex-FRELIMO members emerged to challenge the elitist behavior of FRELIMO's leaders— averring that the Front intended to use northern Mozambicans as fodder in its war against the Portuguese. The heads of these upstart organizations, however, were unable to attract the support of African nationalist leaders elsewhere on the continent. At the same time, they failed to cultivate a substantial following among Mozambicans "in the interior," who had transferred their allegiance to FRELIMO.

On the Mueda plateau, FRELIMO picked up where MANU had left off, adopting MANU's clandestine network of mobilizers and recruiting new members through the issuance of membership cards. Muedans referred to those who came calling under cover of night—still mostly young men of plateau origins—as *vashilo* (night people).

FRELIMO mobilizers, including the *mapiko* dancer Jacinto Omar, spoke to Muedans in a language reflecting the Front's revolutionary socialist ideology.[8] Colonialism, they suggested, was unjust because it permitted the exploitation of man by man—be it African by European or African by African. In an independent Mozambique, they asserted, Mozambicans would labor together according to their abilities and reap and consume the fruits of their labor according to their needs.[9] As we shall see, however, Muedans wondered what these young men *knew*—what extraordinary powers they possessed to make them so bold as to challenge the rights of the powerful to eat their fill.

Lucas Ng'avanga, who served FRELIMO as a mobilizer, explained to us the methods adopted by *vashilo:* "We used *likola* [matrilineage] networks. We would find someone we trusted in a *likola,* and we would ask him to approach his family. He would find out who wanted to buy cards, and then we would make the cards. Once there was a large group in the *likola* who had them, these people would go to the elders—the settlement heads, the *humu,* and others—and they would say [to each one]: 'Nang'olo [elder], there is something that we need to tell you, something that you must know about. This "FRELIMO" that we are hearing about—they are very serious. We have bought cards. You don't have a card, and that is dangerous.'"

Of course, having a FRELIMO card was dangerous as well. Albino Mwidumbi Mpelo, who sold FRELIMO membership cards to people living within Nkapoka's *regulado,* remembered this period well: "We were afraid to contact the *régulo.* We only spoke with youths—people of our own generation. My own father had no knowledge of my activities. We approached people outside our own families—sometimes strangers—but we had observed them, so we knew what sort of heart they had. We talked with them about the evils of colonialism, and how things would be better if we had independence. I had been to Tanganyika and seen that things were good there. We told people that FRELIMO could liberate us. But people were afraid of the colonizer. The colonizer was tolerated *because* he was oppressive, *because* he was dangerous."

What made "the colonizer" so dangerous, in large measure, was the network of *autoridades gentílicas* with whom "he" worked. *Régulos*, and to a lesser extent *capitães-mor*, had grown accustomed to "eating well"—accustomed to the power and wealth afforded them in their roles as tax collectors and labor recruiters. With the tacit approval of the colonial administration, many *régulos* even used *chibalo* labor on their own individual *machambas* (agricultural fields). In an independent Mozambique, they imagined, such privilege would be in jeopardy. To protect their interests, many *régulos* and their subordinates collaborated closely with the Portuguese secret police (Polícia Internacional e de Defesa do Estado, or PIDE) to protect their place of privilege at the colonial feast, reporting suspected FRELIMO members in their regions. Others patrolled plateau settlements with the Portuguese, seeking evidence of FRELIMO affiliation in the form of membership cards and registries. On more than one occasion, captured registries led to the imprisonment of large numbers of nationalists or to their flight from Mozambique. On a more continual basis, individual members were apprehended and tortured until they betrayed the names of fellow members (West 2003a).

FRELIMO operatives recognized, as stated above by Mpelo, that fear was the cement that held the Portuguese regime together at the local level. The key to success, they eventually decided, was to transform the dynamic of fear—as foreshadowed in Lucas Ng'avanga's words hinting at the dangers of *not* holding a FRELIMO card. FRELIMO issued death threats to those who refused to join the Front. One mobilizer told us, matter-of-factly: "My job was to deliver FRELIMO pamphlets and letters to those who were not yet with us. The letters would say, 'If you continue to collaborate with the colonizer, we will kill you.'" The houses of particularly influential or vocal FRELIMO detractors were burned. According to the same mobilizer: "It worked with some people. Others had to be killed."

In late 1964 and early 1965, FRELIMO asserted itself even with *autoridades gentílicas*. According to oral testimony, FRELIMO dealt differently with each *régulo, capitão-mor*, or *wajiri* depending upon each one's disposition and behavior. In many instances, FRELIMO sought to recruit *autoridades gentílicas* to the organization, sometimes approaching them directly and sometimes dispatching family members sympathetic to the nationalist cause to speak with them. With others, such strategies were deemed unlikely to work or even dangerous. The *régulos* Naengo, Kavanga, and Lidimo were notorious in the plateau region for their hostility toward FRELIMO. Naengo, the *régulo* in Jacinto Omar's region, patrolled the settlements of his area with government troops, beating and insulting people and participating in the burning of houses of those suspected of nationalist activities (FRELIMO 1964: 6; West 1997b: 151). He eventually paid for his behavior with his life when his own family aided FRELIMO operatives in assassinating him. Kavanga carried a pistol given him by the district administrator and actually killed two FRELIMO operatives when, by chance, they ambushed a bus on which he was riding soon after the outbreak of open hostilities. In November 1964, he was assassinated by a FRELIMO detachment commander, António Saide, who visited him in his own house disguised as a fellow *régulo*. Lidimo's betrayal to the Portuguese of his own brother-in-law brought on a FRELIMO assassination attempt that failed, but he was nevertheless forced to take up residence for the duration of the war under the protection of the colonial army in the town of Mueda.[10] These bold attacks on powerful figures of local authority convinced many people, including other *autoridades gentílicas*, that collaboration with the Portuguese could be as dangerous, if not more so, than collaboration with FRELIMO.[11]

Once the war had begun in September 1964, wherever possible FRELIMO gathered plateau populations close to its bases in the forested lowlands just off the plateau or in the plateau interior. There, FRELIMO suggested, not only would Muedans be safer from Portuguese patrols exacting retribution for FRELIMO attacks, but they would also be capable of contributing to the nationalist campaign by helping to feed FRELIMO guerrillas.

In the first months of 1965, entire settlements and even entire *regulados* moved en masse. In some cases, they were accompanied by the *autoridades gentílicas* who had governed them. In the FRELIMO "liberated zones" that they would call home for the next decade, these populations often reproduced the spatial configurations of the *regulados* in which they had previously lived; that is, the people formerly subject to a particular *capitão-mor* lived clustered together and, within this area, people from a particular settlement lived in immediate proximity to one another. Even in cases where *autoridades gentílicas* accompanied their people, however, they did not exercise authority over them in the liberated zones. Rather, those whom Muedans called *vashilo*—the young men, such as Jacinto Omar, who had joined FRELIMO long before their elders, and who had worked at great risk to mobilize support for the fledgling organization—generally assumed positions of authority within the civilian political structures mounted by the guerrilla force.

FRELIMO now called these liaisons "chairmen" (adopting the English-language term from the political nomenclature of the Tanganyikan move-

ments among which many FRELIMO militants had gained political experience). Clustered settlements formerly under a particular *capitão-mor* or several *wajiri* were now called "town branches" and were placed under the control of a "town branch chairman." The town branch chairman worked in
coordination with two "committees," one charged with responsibility for collecting food for both refugee populations and the guerrillas in nearby bases,
and the other for resolving any disputes arising within the population. Both
committees were generally composed of respected elders from the constituent
settlements, including settlement heads (some of whom had been *régulos,
capitães-mor,* or *wajiri*). The town branch chairman was said to be "elected"
by these committees, but in practice, he was nominated by FRELIMO and he,
rather than the committees, exercised ultimate power as FRELIMO's trusted
intermediary with the people living in his area.

Chairmen and committees were also to be found at the "local branch"
level, which, in most cases, encompassed populations that had once lived in
a single *regulado.*[12] Here, too, the chairman was invariably a young man who
had been a long-standing FRELIMO mobilizer (Jacinto Omar, for example,
served as a local branch chairman), and the ex-*régulo,* if he exercised any
function at all, was merely a member of one or both of the committees. Atop
the local branches, FRELIMO created area branches (corresponding to a colonial administrative post), and these, in turn, were subordinated to a regional
branch (corresponding to an entire colonial district, e.g., Cabo Delgado, Niassa, Tete).[13] These levels were governed by a commissioner and two committees. FRELIMO selected Lázaro Nkavandame—the entrepreneurial Muedan
who had founded successful agricultural cooperatives in the late 1950s—as
Cabo Delgado regional commissioner and gave him responsibility over the
nomination and supervision of area branch chairmen in Cabo Delgado.

FRELIMO structures of authority reproduced the geographical hierarchies
established on the plateau by colonial rule—hierarchies that made only limited historical sense to plateau residents. What is more, chairmen exercised
powers strikingly similar to those of *autoridades gentílicas.* The guerrillas
mandated chairmen to levy tax in foodstuffs or to provide people who would
serve the guerrilla as soldiers, militiamen/women, porters, messengers, and
spies. In this sense, chairmen became the administrators of an independent
Mozambique—or, at least, of FRELIMO's "liberated zones"—as FRELIMO
recruits had been promised in the early days of nationalist mobilization.

FRELIMO did, however, subvert existing political hierarchies in other
senses. In looking to tap all available energies in support of the guerrilla effort, the Front loosened traditional constraints placed upon youths by their
elders and upon women by men (Isaacman and Isaacman 1984; West 2000).

So radical was the guerrilla agenda in these terms that many elders in the liberated zones, as well as several FRELIMO chairmen and even the Cabo Delgado commissioner, Lázaro Nkavandame, openly opposed it (Munslow 1983; Machel 1985: 53).

Tensions between the Tanzania-based FRELIMO leadership and Lázaro Nkavandame and his network of chairmen were exacerbated by other practical and ideological concerns.[14] The success of the FRELIMO campaign depended not only upon uninterrupted agricultural production (with which to feed guerrillas) in the liberated zones but also upon the transport of agricultural surpluses across the border, where they could be exchanged for basic consumer goods needed to sustain a degree of normalcy among civilian populations so as to prevent their mass exodus. Chairmen were responsible for ensuring that people continued to produce marketable surpluses of peanuts, cashew nuts, oil seeds, rubber, and wax, to be carried out of the liberated zones on the heads of civilians protected by guerrilla escorts. Nkavandame was responsible for ensuring that civilian farmers could trade their surpluses at FRELIMO-run shops on the Tanzanian side of the border for the basic goods they required for survival, such as clothing, soap, tools, cooking pots, knives, matches, and kerosene. He was also charged with overseeing the storage of surpluses of maize, manioc, and sorghum produced in the Cabo Delgado interior, with transshipment of these surpluses as needed to other areas in the interior, and with the sale of excess stocks (along with nonconsumable cash crops) on the Tanzanian market to generate revenue to support the war effort.

Nkavandame, however, ran FRELIMO commercial networks as he had run his own business ventures in colonial times, setting up labor pyramids and taking profits for himself wherever they could be found (Machel 1985: 58–59; Negrão 1984: 19). Nkavandame, many said, "grew fat" on the war. When the terms of trade offered in "Lázaro's shops" began to generate discontent among Mozambicans in the interior, and when guerrillas sometimes found themselves without food supplies as a consequence of flagging production and trade (Negrão 1984: 10, 19), FRELIMO military commanders (many of whom were former clients in Nkavandame's cooperative movement) became increasingly concerned and agitated (FRELIMO 1977: 136; Munslow 1983).

When Eduardo Mondlane, the president of FRELIMO, was assassinated by letter bomb on 3 February 1969 in Dar es Salaam, Nkavandame was named as a suspect. He promptly abandoned FRELIMO and fled Tanzania, turning himself in to the Portuguese at a Rovuma River border post.

In the wake of these events, FRELIMO political and military structures were integrated at the highest levels under a single command hierarchy (Munslow 1983). Structures at the local level were also subtly transformed.

Most chairmen at the regional and area branch levels had fled with Nkavan-dame, but chairmen at the local and town branch levels had remained in the interior. Jacinto Omar was among the latter. He and his cohort were required to undergo six months' intensive politico-military training at FRELIMO's principal rear base in Nachingwea, Tanzania, where they were schooled in FRELIMO's socialist ideology and guerrilla methodology and made conscious of their subordination to FRELIMO's military command chain (FRELIMO 1977: 46–47). When they returned to the interior, they were referred to as "secretaries." They now worked in coordination with "councils" formed of local delegates of various FRELIMO departments—for example, Education and Culture, Health, Production and Commerce. The nomenclature of the ar-eas they administered also changed from "town branch" and "local branch" to "*círculo*" (circle) and "*localidade*" (locality), respectively.[15] FRELIMO as-serted that councils and committees at these levels constituted "democratic institutions," but in practice, the FRELIMO central leadership appointed council members at all levels, and it was these councils that now nominated members to the committees.[16]

More importantly, as we shall see in the chapters to follow, the modified command structure facilitated the attempts of FRELIMO leaders to maintain surveillance over guerrillas and civilians alike and, consequently, to gain a decisive perspective on the workings of power in their forest domain.

15

Deadly Games of Hide-and-Seek

On an August morning in 1994, Marcos took me to the place where, at the end of the war for Mozambican independence, FRELIMO's mobile Central Base had been located. A small grove of high trees stood out distinctly on a landscape otherwise cleared of vegetation by the farming families who "guarded" the site more than two decades after the end of the war. After checking our "credentials," a small contingent of men escorted me, Marcos, and another FRELIMO veteran who journeyed with us, Rafael Mwakala, along the paths that cut in and out of the dense bush. Inside, little physical evidence of the base remained. A single thatched-roof *cabana*—which, according to our guides, had to be rebuilt each year—marked the spot of Samora Machel's quarters. Beside it sat a napalm shell with a rusted typewriter on top. The former, I was told, had fallen close to the base without exploding; the latter had been "captured" during a FRELIMO raid on a colonial post.

Light somehow percolated through the forest canopy from the indiscernible sky above us. I imagined planes overhead and wondered what it would have been like to live in constant fear of aerial bombardment. Rafael, it seemed, heard my thoughts.

He said: "When the war began, we all faded into the bush. Entire settlements disappeared overnight [into] the *shilumu*. In Shimakonde, that means a dense, dense bush that has never been cut—so dense that it is dark there in the daytime."

Rafael used a *catana* that one of our hosts had loaned him to cut his way through the growth that constantly threatened to obliterate the pathways traversing the site of the base.

He continued: "[Down in the lowlands and] here in the center of the plateau, far away from . . . water sources and from the roads opened up by

Upon arrival in Pemba, my first research contact informed me that I should meet with Rafael Mwakala. "Rafael has experience with people like you," I was told. Indeed, Mwakala had worked as an interpreter for the team of anthropologists, headed by Jorge Dias, who worked on the Mueda plateau in the late 1950s. As he traveled with the Dias team, Mwakala slipped away after dark to recruit young men to the FRELIMO cause—unbeknownst to Dias and his colleagues (West 2004a: no. 311). Here, he poses with a copy of the Dias team's ethnography, open to a page with a photo depicting his wife.

the Portuguese administration . . . , there was plenty of *shilumu* in which to hide. Here they couldn't see us. We could mount our attacks, ambush troops on [patrol], and melt back into the forest." As he spoke, Rafael mimed the acts he described, riddling his imaginary enemy with automatic weapon's fire.

"We were invisible; they could do nothing. So they had to fly overhead, cut through the forest, and burn the tree cover off to get at us. That was what the war was all about."

We followed Rafael's eyes skyward.

"We had to keep one step ahead, always just out of sight, listening for the planes, ready to take cover or to move at a moment's notice."

⬛

The war for Mozambican independence, as described to us by those who fought in it, was a decade-long, high-stakes game of hide-and-seek. To be visible to one's enemy was to be vulnerable. To be invisible was to be secure. To be able to see one's enemy was to be lethal. The dynamics of the war shifted over its duration, along with the optical relations sustained between combatants.

In the first years of the war, FRELIMO guerrillas operated in squads of six to twelve—combining at detachment strength for larger attacks—and harassed Portuguese military installations and supply routes (Opello 1974: 29). Armed by China, the Soviet Union, and Eastern Europe, many FRELIMO guerrillas carried weapons more sophisticated than those of the Portuguese troops against whom they fought (Henriksen 1978: 32). In any case, land mines accounted for two-thirds of Portuguese casualties, producing mine psychosis and a static defense posture in colonial troops (Henriksen 1983: 44; Monks 1990: 73). Portuguese patrols generally lingered close to their bases— situated along the Rovuma River, in the town of Mueda, and at the Nang'o-lolo mission—returning just before nightfall. When they did venture further afield, the Portuguese were subjected to what FRELIMO called *flagelação*— whiplike hit-and-run ambushes that produced low but constant numbers of casualties (Monks 1990: 71). After attacking, FRELIMO units promptly disappeared into the surrounding bush. Harsh but sporadic Portuguese countermeasures, directed against civilian concentrations suspected of harboring or supporting FRELIMO fighters, succeeded only in generating large numbers of refugees, who fled to Tanzania and, often, recruitment by FRELIMO.

On 17 May 1970, General Kaúlza de Arriaga—a guerrilla warfare expert who had studied with American counterinsurgency specialists to learn the tactics utilized in the Viet Nam War—arrived in Mozambique, vowing that his "Operation Gordian Knot" would finish off FRELIMO by year's end. Kaúlza de Arriaga made use of Caterpillar land movers and defoliant sprays to carve a grid of surveillance corridors in the dense plateau bush. He dropped napalm bombs on guerrilla and civilian targets and utilized heavy air support to protect more than 35,000 Portuguese troops employed in "search and destroy" sweeps. Within months, however, operational costs, army fatigue, and FRELIMO's ability to evade these assaults prompted the Portuguese to undertake less expensive (and less effective) sweeps on foot, supported by bulldozers and mine clearers that could advance only three to six miles per day (Monks 1990: 97).

Kaúlza de Arriaga took another page from the manual of US operations in Viet Nam, implementing a program to win the "hearts and minds" of populations in FRELIMO-held or FRELIMO-threatened areas. "Psychosocial" operatives were dispatched to zones still under Portuguese control (such as Mueda town and the area immediately surrounding the Nang'ololo mission), where they provided vaccinations. Development schemes were presented to local populations as the alternative to the "terror" and "destruction" brought by the guerrillas.[1] Planes flew over FRELIMO-held areas dropping leaflets with images depicting ragged and forlorn guerrillas surrendering to Portuguese authorities, who accepted them warmly and gave them money for their weapons (Henriksen 1983: 103). Other pamphlets conveyed messages from Lázaro Nkavandame—the defected FRELIMO regional commissioner—declaring that FRELIMO had betrayed the Makonde people and that the guerrillas were no longer welcome on Makonde soil. Some planes actually broadcast taped messages in Shimakonde—a tactic pioneered by the French in Algeria and Viet Nam and referred to as "sky-shouting" (Henriksen 1983: 103).[2] The voice most frequently used was that of Nkavandame, who instructed people to leave the bush and end the war in which they, the Makonde, were suffering great losses.[3] In the same period, several Makonde who had been imprisoned by the PIDE after the Mueda Massacre and before the war were given the option of release if they would cooperate with a plan—"organized by Lázaro [Nkavandame]," they were told—to reenter FRELIMO-held areas and to persuade guerrillas and their supporters to give up the war.[4]

The rainy season beginning in November of 1970 forced Kaúlza de Arriaga to suspend Operation Gordian Knot. The campaign had taken a toll not only on FRELIMO[5] but also on the population in FRELIMO's "liberated zones."[6] Kaúlza de Arriaga's claims of victory, however, were premature.[7] Despite "capturing" 61 bases and 165 camps (Beckett 1985: 155), Kaúlza de Arriaga had found most of these installations deserted. The same was generally true of "civilian" encampments. FRELIMO guerrillas and the people among whom they lived effectively disappeared into the forest whenever the Portuguese approached.

By contrast, FRELIMO seemed always to know where the Portuguese were and to be able to attack them with impunity. Portuguese losses during 1970 were considerably heavier than in previous years, as FRELIMO detachments broke up into highly mobile groups of three, mining roads behind the Portuguese troops who opened them, and trapping these troops where they could easily be ambushed.

For FRELIMO and its supporters, however, the worst was yet to come. With the inconclusive "successes" of Gordian Knot, the Portuguese were forced to further modify military strategy to cut costs and limit casualties. Following the American model of "Vietnamization," the Portuguese military in Mozambique was "Africanized."[8] Two elite units of African soldiers were deployed against FRELIMO in 1972: yellow-bereted Special Groups (Grupos Especiais, or GEs) and red-bereted Special Parachutist Groups (Grupos Especiais Pára-quedistas, or GEPs). These units were "90% African" according to most accounts (Wheeler 1976: 243) and gave the Portuguese military increased mobility, allowing for more lethal attacks.[9] GEs could spend considerable time away from base silently pinpointing locations of insurgent concentration and activity, while GEPs could strike suddenly from the air.

Rafael Mwakala described to us the effects produced by the new Portuguese army capabilities: "They would burn a hole in the forest with napalm bombs. Next, helicopters would come and drop soldiers on the zone. They would hit the ground shooting and burn settlements and crops. While this was happening, the helicopters would fly around, shooting people. They would kill, kill, kill, kill. They never took prisoners. All of this left the population in a panic."

These attacks were complemented with expanded use of defoliants to spray not only forest cover but also areas of agricultural production (FRELIMO 1972: 6). FRELIMO eventually responded with the integration of surface-to-air missiles (SAMs) into its weapons repertoire to challenge Portuguese superiority in the air (Beckett 1985: 146), but this did not eliminate the Portuguese reign of terror.[10]

In the memories of most ex-guerrillas and civilians, infiltration and espionage were the distinguishing characteristics of Kaúlza de Arriaga's successor, General Tomás Basto Machado, who took command of the Portuguese campaign in Mozambique in 1973. FRELIMO's English-language publication, *Mozambique Revolution*, reported on Machado's tactics in that year:

> The infiltration of agents into our zones has been intensified over the past few months. Their specific tasks are to foment subversion in our ranks, to assassinate FRELIMO leaders, and to discredit our organization in the eyes of the people. For example, they send groups of Africans dressed and armed like our fighters, who pretend to be FRELIMO soldiers, and massacre the people, violate the women and steal crops.[11] All this in the name of FRELIMO.

As the Portuguese intensified their counterinsurgency campaign, FRELIMO commander Samora Machel and his staff preached tirelessly of the need for "vigilance" among FRELIMO cadres and the populations under their charge (see, e.g., FRELIMO 1973: 4). During this period, FRELIMO's military command post, Base Moçambique, was divided into four sub-bases. Military operations were run out of Moçambique A, also called Base Central. Artillery was run out of Moçambique B, which also provided air defense for Moçambique A. Moçambique C oversaw the production of crops and the raising of livestock. Moçambique D was dedicated entirely to matters of internal security. Provincial Chief of Security Salésio Teodoro Nalyambipano and his adjunct Ladis "Lagos" Lidimo—both Mueda natives—worked out of Moçam-

bique D, in coordination with security operatives and a network of informants scattered throughout FRELIMO's liberated zones; their task was to maintain "vigilance" against potential "enemies within."

Those suspected or accused of sabotage or of collaboration with the
Portuguese were taken by FRELIMO security to Moçambique D. "D" (as the
sub-base was widely referred to) was reportedly divided into two areas. One
of these areas, in the words of a guerrilla who worked as a supervisor on a
FRELIMO collective farm near D, was reserved for prisoners "who had committed little sins." Many of these were women who had "spoken ill of
FRELIMO"; they were reportedly put to work on collective farms growing
food for the base. The other area was reserved for "those whose sins were
greater." Suspected infiltrators, collaborators, and saboteurs were included in
this group. According to the same man: "[These prisoners] were brought in at
night and could not be visited. They did not work in the fields. Anyone who
talked to them would be made to join them. They were mostly men."

Despite the seclusion in which they were held, these prisoners were seen
from time to time by people who lived near D, and word spread about the
conditions to which they were subjected. One witness told us: "They were
kept in trenches in the ground. They were devoured by lice and fleas and other
insects until some of them went mad. Sometimes a trench would collapse,
burying them alive." Other witnesses told horrific tales of vicious torture tactics and summary executions reminiscent of the techniques used by the Portuguese secret police on captured FRELIMO operatives.[12]

Mozambique Revolution offered a rather cheerful account of the successes
of FRELIMO internal security during this period: "[T]he sharp vigilance of
our people and their knowledge of FRELIMO's correct political line thwarts
[Portuguese counterinsurgency] objectives. Many enemy agents have been
arrested by the people themselves and taken to the FRELIMO bases." An ex-
detachment commander remembered the period rather differently. He told
us: "In Machado's time, bombs were nothing. Psychological warfare was
much worse than open warfare. Machado finished off a lot of people. He sent
infiltrators to work in our midst. We all distrusted one another. You couldn't
talk to anyone. So we responded with increased vigilance. We killed a lot of
people. Only later would we sometimes see that they had not been working
with the enemy."[13]

People in the wrong place at the wrong time were falsely accused of espionage. Others were labeled saboteurs for taking too long to deliver a message,
for breaking a piece of "military" equipment as simple as a bicycle, or for
serving a commander tea that was "too hot." One guerrilla said of the air of
suspicion that permeated the liberated zones in this time: "Your own mother

wouldn't receive you and cook your dinner if you did not have marching orders signed by a FRELIMO commander." Another told us: "I would fall asleep at night replaying the day's conversations in my head to make certain that I had not 'compromised myself,' and I would wake up in the morning taking mental roll call of my possible enemies."

As we shall see, the suspicions that permeated the "liberated zones" during the Mozambican independence war found expression not only in the language of insurgency and counterinsurgency (and espionage and counterespionage) but also in the language of sorcery and countersorcery, wherein it was suggested that the deadly games of hide-and-seek that defined the conflict were played not only by soldiers but also by sorcerers.

16

Revolution, Science, and Sorcery

"FRELIMO had better schools in the liberated zones than we have now," Cristiano Lipangati Lipyaluke told me proudly. We sat together in the lounge of the dilapidated Hotel Cabo Delgado in Pemba talking casually about the Mozambican independence war. Lipangati, a Muedan who now lived and worked in Pemba, had told me earlier that he was a student at one of the missions when the war broke out. He fled with his family to a FRELIMO-controlled area. When he expressed his desire to continue studying, FRELIMO leaders asked him to "be a match to light others." After undergoing guerrilla training in Bagamoyo, Tanzania, he was assigned to the interior by the FRELIMO command. His mission: to teach in a bush school in the liberated zones.

"I carried a weapon at all times to defend myself and my students," he told me.

We continued conversing about the resources FRELIMO dedicated to education during the war. Others had told me that FRELIMO looked upon youths in the areas it controlled as the "future of the nation." Lipangati agreed with this but also reminded me that FRELIMO educated adults in the liberated zones as well.

"Guerrilla war is a modern science," he said. "People had to be educated to fight a guerrilla war."

His glance at the notebook I carried with me suggested that I should write down what he told me. He waited as I pulled a pen from my field bag and then continued: "They had to be able to read and write to send messages from one base to another. They had to be able to add and subtract to manage accounts of the materials traded in and out of the liberated zones. They had to be able to do basic equations to fire a mortar. They had to understand the fundamentals of biology to vaccinate people so as to prevent the spread of epidemics in the liberated zones."

He looked at me with intense eyes. "Revolution and ignorance are incompatible," he asserted.

dililii

Even as the threat of violence saturated everyday life in FRELIMO's liberated zones, FRELIMO waged war against poverty, ignorance, and disease among the populations who supported its independence struggle. When, in 1962, FRELIMO declared its intention to oust the Portuguese from Mozambique and to restore the nation to its rightful occupants, it did not promise, nor did it seek, to restore Mozambique to its precolonial state of affairs. On the contrary, FRELIMO set for itself the bold revolutionary agenda of creating a "new man" (and, given its commitment to addressing gender issues within the context of the revolution, a "new woman") to inhabit a new Mozambique (Machel 1985: 2, 33).[1]

Donald Donham writes: "There is perhaps no concept more central to modernism than revolution" (1999: 1). One might also assert that there is no concept more central to revolutionary socialism than modernism. FRELIMO leaders dedicated themselves more deeply than their colonial predecessors ever had to the idea of modernization, envisioning a nation where social needs were determined and met not by market forces but, instead, through "scientific governance." Indeed, for FRELIMO, the objective of modernization could not be deferred until independence. FRELIMO leaders asserted that in order to prosecute modern guerrilla warfare against a modern enemy, Mozambicans immediately had to modernize themselves.

To this end, in the earliest days of the war, FRELIMO began to piece together what would become a vast network of bush-based elementary schools. In these schools, children and adults learned to read and write—mostly in Portuguese (a language that transcended divides between the ethnic groups who contributed to the war effort and who would eventually constitute the Mozambican nation). Students also studied mathematics and natural sciences—subjects that served many of them well as they administered the agricultural cooperatives established by FRELIMO in the liberated zones or as they staffed the health posts maintained by FRELIMO in the interior. Selected "graduates" of these bush schools continued their education in schools funded by international solidarity networks and located in Tanzania or in other foreign nations sympathetic to the FRELIMO cause.[2]

The FRELIMO campaign was animated on all fronts by a deep commit-ment to the idea of "scientific socialism."[3] FRELIMO leaders asserted that, if Mozambicans were to make for themselves a better world, they would have to realize their subjectivity as a modern revolutionary class. Modern educa-tion, among other things, was to help Mozambicans set aside occult expla-nations for their misfortunes — negligent ancestors, evil spirits, sorcery — and to allow them to recognize capitalist-imperialist exploitation as the root cause of their condition.[4]

FRELIMO's commitment to modern science as opposed to "traditional be-liefs and practices" (often glossed as "obscurantism") was motivated, in part, by immediate practical concerns. Marcos, an ex-guerrilla himself, told me that in the first days of the war, *vamitela* distributed to local populations me-dicinal substances that they promised would render them invulnerable to gunfire. FRELIMO leaders and guerrilla commanders preached against the use of such substances out of strategic interest. Marcos, a guerrilla supervi-sor of FRELIMO schools, explained the urgency of the matter to me: "If our guerrillas had trusted in antibullet *mitela* to protect them, they would have been shot down just as Malapende's men were by the Portuguese. We needed them to trust in the techniques of guerrilla warfare, not in *mitela*."[5]

For similar reasons, FRELIMO leaders and guerrilla commanders con-demned *yangele* (divination) and the practice of *kulaula* (healing) (Machel 1985: 21). Not only did the guerrilla command fear the possibility of opera-tives failing to execute orders due to diviners' warnings that the moment was not propitious for an assigned task, but it also feared that sorcery accusations and counteraccusations would give rise to dangerous moments of disunity within and around wartime bush bases.[6]

The FRELIMO prohibition on divination was well known by Muedans and was remembered decades later when we worked among them. On one occasion, a group recited for me a wartime song, sung in Shimakonde, pro-claiming:

> We are the shadow of the people,
> We don't trust in *mitela*,
> We don't trust in *dinumba*,[7]
> *Yangele*[8] causes conflict among us and sets back our war effort.

Concurrent with these prohibitions, FRELIMO also sought to eliminate a wide variety of social practices deemed contrary to the modernist norms of revolutionary socialism, including initiation rites (and the scarification of ini-tiates), *mapiko* dancing, bridewealth, and ceremonies of ancestral supplication. One man, who served FRELIMO as a chairman/secretary during the war, told us: "When leaders started taking this line, the population showed no interest." Such practices persisted in some places during the war, while disappearing in others.[9]

FRELIMO leaders remained particularly concerned about sorcery-related beliefs and practices in wartime Mueda for fear that these might jeopardize the war effort. Leaders campaigned openly against such beliefs and practices, proclaiming them to be dangerous forms of counterrevolutionary false consciousness.[10] At rallies in the liberated zones, FRELIMO leaders led Muedans in call-and-response chants proclaiming: "Down with Obscurantism! Long live FRELIMO!" As we have seen, the threat of violence stood behind such FRELIMO pronouncements and policies. Indeed, the FRELIMO campaign against divination, healing, and medicinal substances was, at times, waged by more assertive means than the chanting of slogans. Several ex-guerrillas told me that, on occasion, FRELIMO commanders dispatched guerrillas to burn down the *cabanas* of practicing *vamitela*. From time to time, according to various oral sources, *vamitela* were threatened, or even killed, by FRELIMO.[11]

It would be grossly inaccurate to suggest that Muedans did not learn the language of revolutionary/scientific socialism. In fact, they gained lethal competence in the tactics and techniques of class struggle and guerrilla warfare. However, despite learning to conceive of and engage with their world through the language of socialism, and despite FRELIMO prohibitions on divination, healing, and medicinal substances, many Muedans continued to interpret events in the discursive genre of *uwavi*—a language that allowed them to sustain a distinctive sense of the operation of power in their turbulent world.

As argued in chapter 15, the Mozambican independence war played out as a deadly contest of hide-and-seek wherein the contestants sought to render themselves invisible to their enemies and/or to expose their enemies to view. As ordinary Muedans were drawn into the conflict, they perceived the defining dynamics of the war in varied ways simultaneously. Even before the war began, Muedans experienced and engaged with the emerging nationalist movement through the cultural schema of *uwavi*, with its attendant ocular logics. For example, those who purchased membership cards from FRELIMO were instructed by mobilizers to hide their cards immediately. Cards were not used for identification within the organization, nor were they used to gain entry to meetings. Since the sale of cards did not generate substantial revenues for FRELIMO, their only tangible purpose was to place members in a situation of shared risk, creating complicity among them. Individuals who refused to purchase cards took no risk and therefore demonstrated no commitment to FRELIMO. Those who bought cards, however, crossed over into the world of a collective conspiracy, effectively hiding themselves from the Portuguese even as they hid the cards that they had purchased. Having done so, they were "recognized" by FRELIMO, whom they trusted to be capable of protecting their collective invisibility—a trust that proved ill founded for those FRELIMO members whose names appeared on membership registries captured by the PIDE.[12]

Vision and power were inextricably bound throughout the war itself. FRELIMO effectiveness depended upon constructing and sustaining a hidden realm, replete with military bases, militia camps, and civilian settlements, deep in the forests of northern Mozambique. Guerrillas cloaked themselves in this forest realm, attacking from it and melting back into it. In the latter years of the conflict, the Portuguese modified their tactics and themselves sought ways to see into, and enter, the invisible forest realm, carving surveillance corridors through the bush, burning off tree cover, and making use of night vision glasses. Ultimately, the Portuguese army deployed African troops deep inside FRELIMO-controlled areas—deep inside a realm previously inaccessible and invisible to them.

For most Muedans, the ongoing battle between the deadly forces of the Portuguese military and the FRELIMO guerrilla insurgency—a battle waged from and within the hidden forest realm—resonated with the struggles Muedans knew to transpire in and over the invisible realm of *uwavi*. Indeed, insurgency and counterinsurgency, for many Muedans, was inseparable from sorcery and countersorcery.

Some Muedans considered the Portuguese actually to be powerful sorcerers. Leonardo Kuvela Nandondo Aligwama told us, for example, that the PIDE used sorcery to decipher where people were hidden in the FRELIMO liberated zones and to communicate this information to the Portuguese military. Most survivors of the war with whom we spoke, however, tied the power of the Portuguese in the invisible realm to the power of fellow Muedans, just as Malapende's contemporaries (and those who shared accounts with us of the Portuguese conquest of the plateau) had done.

Maurício Mpwapwele Moto told us: "Among the Portuguese, there were *vavi*. There were also *vavi* among the Africans serving in the Portuguese military.[13] These *vavi* worked in cooperation with Makonde *vavi* [in the liberated zones]. The black Mozambican *vavi* in the Portuguese army served as liaisons between Makonde *vavi* and Portuguese *vavi*. But they all used the same techniques."

According to some accounts, Portuguese sorcerers initiated contacts with Makonde sorcerers and used them to do their bidding inside FRELIMO-held areas. Marcos himself once told me: "The Portuguese didn't actually send spies into the liberated zones so much as they used people already there. But how were these relationships established? The only way to make these contacts was by means of *uwavi.*"

According to other accounts, it was Makonde sorcerers who initiated these collaborative relationships and who used them to serve their ends. When I asked Inácio Mpupa if there was sorcery in the liberated zones, he exclaimed: "Ehhh! There was lots of *uwavi* during the war. . . . Some people who lived among us used *uwavi* to summon the Portuguese military to come in their planes and their helicopters and to kill people living among us."

Many agreed with Mpupa that Muedan sorcerers were to blame for the attacks of the Portuguese military. Some posited that these sorcerers, who lived among them in the daytime, flew at night to Portuguese bases to report bombing coordinates so as to bring about the demise of neighbors and kin they wished to destroy.[14]

The planes and helicopters used by the Portuguese military in attacks on guerrilla and civilian targets in the liberated zones were the focus of intensive interest on the part of Muedans seeking to discern the role of sorcerers in the war. To some, these spectacular vehicles were the instruments of Portuguese sorcery. Nonetheless, they were often said to have been "summoned" by Muedan sorcerers and piloted or, at least, copiloted from the ground by *uwavi* remote control. To others, these lethal instruments of war were actually the latest inventions of Muedan sorcerers. Limitedi Untonji once asserted in conversation with us: "In the past, sorcerers fabricated animals to kill for them. During the war, they fabricated planes and helicopters."[15]

For some, even Portuguese troops were the product of Muedan sorcery, just as Malapende declared them to have been. Mpwapwele suggested to us that the Portuguese may indeed have made the planes and helicopters, as well as the napalm bombs that these craft dropped from the air, but that Muedan sorcerers still used these instruments of violence to their own ends. Sorcerers, he reminded us, were capable of using the materials and opportunities available to them. By way of illustration, he informed us: "Sorcerers used mines during the war. They didn't make these mines, but they could use *uwavi* to make a person walk to the place where a mine had been laid by the Portuguese and then make that person step on the mine. They could orchestrate people's movements in this way . . . making their deaths look like war casualties when really they were due to *uwavi.*"[16]

Muedans attributed the powers of sorcery not only to those who menaced them but also to those with whom they collaborated in the war effort. Again, such was the case even before the war began. According to popular accounts,

before Faustino Vanomba and Kibiliti Diwani (whose arrests precipitated the
Mueda Massacre on 16 June 1960) were loaded into a vehicle to be taken away
to prison in Mocímboa da Praia, the governor of Cabo Delgado tried and failed
to bind their hands and, finally, to shoot them. According to Leonardo Kuvela
Nandodo Aligwama, a MANU associate of the two men: "The cords kept
breaking when the governor tried to bind their hands. When he tried to shoot
them, water came out of the gun." Muedans celebrated Vanomba and Diwani
as powerful sorcerers even after their imprisonment, much as their forebears
had celebrated the great warlords Malapende and Namashakole even after
their "pacification" by the Portuguese.

The power of *uwavi* was also widely attributed to Lázaro Nkavandame.
According to popular accounts, when the Portuguese came to arrest Nkavandame in 1963 on suspicion of involvement with the nascent FRELIMO organization, he persuaded them to allow him to drive himself to the administrative
post on his own motorcycle. En route, he turned abruptly into the bush and
jumped off his motorcycle. The Portuguese failed to track him down because,
many said, he transformed himself into a cat. Years later, when FRELIMO attempted to arrest Nkavandame on suspicion of involvement in the assassination of FRELIMO president Eduardo Mondlane, he escaped once more, it was
said, by turning into a cat.

Muedans tellingly referred to the very first FRELIMO cadres to appear
among them as *vashilo*, "night people." These men, of course, paid their recruiting visits after sunset when they could more easily escape detection by
the PIDE and by potential informers. The term *vashilo* also called attention
to the fact that these men traveled freely at a time of day when only "the fearless"—a euphemism for sorcerers—were about.[17]

Once the war began, Muedans attributed extraordinary powers to the
FRELIMO guerrillas who moved "fearlessly" among them, just as guerrilla recruits sometimes attributed extraordinary "fearlessness" to their commanders. For example, Wehia Ripua, a guerrilla commander who later achieved
national notoriety by founding his own party and running for the Mozambican presidency in 1994, was legendary for his ability to "play with" enemies
and allies alike. On the battlefield, he was considered invincible. To his men,
he was a constant source of wonder. One guerrilla told me that, after a mission, he often dispatched his men to camp while heading in the opposite direction; when his men arrived, they found him awaiting them with a meal
that he alone had cooked for them. "Ripua!?" one ex-guerrilla said to us. "That
guy was a *mwavi* for certain!"[18]

Ironically, the very FRELIMO cadres who assertively criticized Muedan belief in sorcery, and who banned sorcery-related practices, were generally assumed by Muedans to possess the powers of *uwavi*. These same cadres themselves contributed grist to the mill of Muedan interpretations. Although many of FRELIMO's top leaders were educated in Western Europe and professed disdain for such "rural traditions," most guerrillas (including most guerrilla commanders) were born and raised in the Mozambican countryside. To a great many FRELIMO cadres from Mueda, *yangele* (divination) and *kulaula* (healing) constituted sensible ways of engaging with the world, notwithstanding FRELIMO policy.[19] When these cadres were called upon to implement the FRELIMO ban on sorcery-related practices in FRELIMO-controlled territories, they were placed in the awkward position of policing themselves. As Marcos and I once sat discussing the war with several ex-guerrillas, Marcos admitted that, on one occasion during the war, he and his fellow guerrillas assembled to burn all of the medicinal substances that they had been given by various *vamitela* to protect them: "We said, 'This is the Revolution. We don't need *mitela* anymore!' But a few days later we realized that each of us had already gone to a *muntela* to get more!" As a result of such ambivalence on the part of FRELIMO cadres, the practice of countersorcery *kulaula* continued throughout the war.[20]

In some places, *vamitela* carried on discreetly. Asala Kipande, who served as a FRELIMO guerrilla, told us: "During the war, I didn't practice *kulaula* openly, but I healed a few people at FRELIMO bases when necessary, and I used *mitela* to defend myself and my comrades." By contrast, Limitedi Untonji told us: "During the war, we *vakulaula* didn't have to hide ourselves." Kabaka Nanume Kapembe's experience was the same: "I had a good relationship with [FRELIMO guerrilla commanders] Chipande, Pachinuapa, and Minga during the war. They knew all about my work as an *nkulaula*." Even Asala Kipande suggested that no "serious" guerrilla commander actually prohibited his men from visiting *vakulaula* during the war.[21]

In fact, many FRELIMO commanders themselves consulted with diviners and healers during the war.[22] Marcos told me that he knew of several occasions on which diviners warned detachment commanders of an imminent attack and, as a result, commanders abandoned their camps and moved their men elsewhere. When I asked Limitedi Untonji if FRELIMO leaders ever came to him for treatment during the war, he told me: "We *vakulaula* treated lots of FRELIMO leaders, but we can't say who. There were many, and it was a long time ago." Several of the *vakulaula* we interviewed in fact told us that they had treated FRELIMO commanders, while others told us the names of *vakulaula* colleagues who had treated commanders, as well as the treatments

On the occasion of my first interview with Asala Kipande, the elder was embarrassed that he had no food to share with us because he was preparing to undertake a journey immediately after our conversation. I assured him that it was no problem, but he protested, "A host must warm the bellies of his guests; otherwise, they will think that they are not welcome." Kipande pulled 20,000 meticais (a substantial amount for someone of his means) from a cardboard box that he kept inside his healing storehouse. "Please," he said, holding out the money, "this is for a chicken for your dinner tonight." While some with whom we worked asked *us* for gifts, Kipande, like many, valued our respect for him as a man of independent means more than any charity we might offer him.

that they provided them. Most FRELIMO commanders—including Raimundo Pachinuapa, Alberto Chipande, Virgílio Minga, and even Samora Machel— were widely said to have "visited *vakulaula*."

According to popular accounts, some commanders carried antibullet *mitela* with them when they went into battle. An *nkulaula* named Alabi Makanga, now deceased, was said to have provided Samora Machel with a substance called *nangunagwela* (to ensure that he would be well received by those around him) and to have performed a rite to defend his "house" and the foods he ate against sorcery. Another *nkulaula*, named Dodo Nindo, also now deceased, was said to have provided Samora with *lukalongo lwa ntumi* (lion's throat, to ensure that he would be heard and feared), *lyungu lya ntumi* (lion's spittle, to ensure his strength and long life), and *lulimi lwa ntumi* (lion's tongue, to ensure that his orders would be heard and followed)—all substances formerly associated exclusively with powerful Makonde elders, such as *vahumu*, who were recognized as capable sorcerers in their own rights.[23]

Muedans who interpreted the actions of FRELIMO leaders in accordance with the schema of *uwavi* saw no contradiction in these leaders' behavior. Indeed, what they saw and heard generally reinforced their convictions that the war was being waged, at once, in visible and invisible realms. By simultaneously condemning sorcery and trafficking in medicinal substances, FRELIMO authorities acted much as Muedan authority figures always had. Where settlement heads once stood at night by the *shitala* in the center of the settlement calling out to sorcerers and commanding them to cease their practice of sorcery or face the elders' wrath, FRELIMO officials now stood before assemblies (often held at night) crying out that sorcery was "a problem"—that it (or, at least, talk of it) pitted Mozambicans against one another when they should instead be focusing upon a common enemy.

Of course, FRELIMO leaders said more than that *uwavi* was "a problem." They dismissed it as superstition, and condemned those who spoke of it as purveyors of "obscurantism." Even these proclamations had precedent, however. Had not Malapende dismissed his enemies' *uwavi*, along with the Portuguese troops who laid siege to his settlement, as mere "imaginings"? Like Malapende and those who followed him into battle against Mbavala's lethal imaginings, many of the Muedans who found themselves engaged in warfare with the Portuguese decades later conceived of *uwavi* as the tangible effects of exceptional vision and imagination—a power that could be challenged and overcome only by greater vision and imagination. And many in the liberated zones decided that this was precisely what FRELIMO authorities claimed when they stood before them and chanted, "Down with obscurantism!" Like elders of the past, FRELIMO cadres proclaimed to be the bearers of a vision that transcended the world known to ordinary people—a vision capable of transforming the world.

Time and again, those who remembered the war for independence told us that FRELIMO sloganeering against obscurantism condemned only malicious forms of sorcery: sorcery of danger, sorcery of ruin, sorcery of death. Marcos himself told me that FRELIMO banned only the use of *mitela* for "bad" purposes; FRELIMO permitted *mitela* for "good" purposes, he assured me. Many *vakulaula* who had been practicing prior to the beginning of the independence war continued practicing during the war because they believed that FRELIMO condemned only the use of *mitela* for destructive ends and because they assumed that they themselves had a role to play in policing such acts through their use of *mitela* for socially constructive purposes. Beyond this, many interpreted FRELIMO slogans against *uwavi* as the *enactment by FRELIMO authorities* of *uwavi wa kudenga*—sorcery of construction.[24]

Many confirmed in conversation with us that FRELIMO leaders who lived in their midst and fought by their sides were among the most powerful sorcerers of construction ever known in the plateau region. Paramount among these powerful figures, according to popular perceptions, were FRELIMO security operatives. One man told me in richly euphemistic terms: "FRELIMO had its ways of *knowing things.* It had people who worked at D who *recognized vavi* and *eliminated* them." When I asked him who these men were, he responded as one would when asked to assert the identity of a *mwavi,* looking meekly at the ground and remaining silent—for one never knew what a *mwavi,* or a security agent, might overhear. Others agreed with this man's assertion that FRELIMO security agents were able to see the acts of sorcery that rendered hidden settlements visible to the enemy and that summoned bombers and helicopters to attack these settlements, and agreed that FRELIMO security operatives could identify and overcome the sorcerers responsible for these acts.

Of "Lagos" Lidimo, the most feared security operative on the plateau, one man told us: "He would pass a FRELIMO column in the bush and look each man in the eyes. He would select one from among them and say, 'Come with me!' He would take the traitor to D. He had *seen* something! He saw *everything*! How else could he be a chief?" Most with whom we spoke concurred that Lidimo was able to detect spies, collaborators, saboteurs, and traitors because he was able to see into the dark realm of *uwavi* where these destructive acts were perpetrated. In a word, he, like other FRELIMO security agents, was assumed (despite FRELIMO's antisorcery rhetoric) to be a sorcerer. One *nkulaula* with whom we spoke told us: "Lagos didn't just use *mitela* that *vakulaula* gave him. In fact, he didn't visit *vakulaula.* He didn't have to. He had his own *mitela* because he and his father were both *vavi.* During the war, he slept naked out in the open. He never worried. *He feared nothing and no one.* His men never died when he led them into combat. That's not just *mitela*! That's *uwavi*!"

Just as Muedans considered FRELIMO security operatives to be the quintessential sorcerers of construction, they looked upon the spies, collaborators, saboteurs, and traitors that these operatives caught as the quintessential sorcerers of danger, ruin, and death. When people spoke with us about the war, talk of sorcerers and talk of "enemies within" blended together. One man, for example, told us: "Usually, when a *mwavi* was calling in planes, helicopters, and troops, other *vavi* would report him, because this was considered too much! . . . If the elders couldn't resolve the situation, the case would be taken to FRELIMO authorities. The FRELIMO chairman would confront the person who was doing these things. If things didn't change, a general meeting was called and the case was reviewed. The most complicated cases would reach the point of 'vigilance.' These *vavi* were taken to Base Beira if they were discovered in the first sector or to D if they were discovered in the second sector."[25] Another man assured us that during the independence war, there was little sorcery precisely *because* "it was severely punished by FRELIMO."

Several ex-guerrillas with whom Marcos and I spoke at the site of one of the former FRELIMO bases told us stories of FRELIMO commanders taking counsel from powerful *vamitela* in the region and then, in some cases, turning on them and killing them "because they discovered that they were *working with the enemy.*" One man told us, simply: "When FRELIMO caught the *vavi* who summoned the Portuguese, they were executed." Another put it this way: "Those who were condemned to death were those who traveled to Portuguese bases and collaborated with the PIDE. These trips were made at night, as *vavi.* They were condemned, however, not as *vavi* but as collaborators. . . . They were usually tried in public and executed by popular judgment." Marcos also asserted the same distinction: FRELIMO executed enemies not as sorcerers but as proven spies, collaborators, saboteurs, and traitors. Most witnesses to these executions saw them as both, however. Indeed, on occasion, the idiom of sorcery was predominant in FRELIMO-orchestrated hearings.

In *Witchcraft, Oracles and Magic among the Azande,* Evans-Pritchard suggested that Azande generally believed the oracles' verdicts on the guilt of accused witches to be true until becoming themselves the objects of accusations. The same might be said of Muedans with regard to FRELIMO verdicts passed against "enemies within" during the independence war. Generally, Muedans were inclined to assume FRELIMO judgments to be founded upon extraordinary and certain knowledge and to consider FRELIMO authorities as sorcerers of construction who waged war against a shared and terrible enemy while guarding the well-being of the community against internal maleficence. When they—or close family members—were themselves condemned, however, they generally saw things quite differently.

In any case, Muedans looked upon these powerful new figures of authority with ambivalence, just as they had long looked upon powerful elders. The respect Muedans generally afforded FRELIMO guerrillas and their commanders was inseparable from the fear these men (and, in some cases, women) inspired.[26] Occasionally, those with whom we spoke revealed the dark under-side to attributions of the power of *uwavi* to FRELIMO authorities. One man told us that FRELIMO leaders, especially the heads of FRELIMO security, Nalyambipano and Lidimo, "used *uwavi* to protect themselves more than to protect others. Those who tried to attack [these leaders] with *uwavi* were caught, tried, and killed. The war ended when these people [the attackers] were eliminated, and only then. The war ended when people became afraid to attack these FRELIMO leaders openly, or with *uwavi*—when they became afraid to ally themselves with the Portuguese against FRELIMO."

A respected healer told us that he knew of several cases in which FRELIMO leaders and guerrilla commanders "injured themselves" during the war—a clear reference to using *mitela,* unsuccessfully, to socially destructive ends. Another healer told us that the most frequent victims of poisoning (a form of illness produced by countersorcery *mitela*) during the war were FRELIMO guerrillas who unjustly antagonized the populations upon whom they depended for support.[27]

Indeed, the nickname applied to FRELIMO guerrillas—"lions of the for-est"[28]—was pronounced and heard by Muedans with double entendre, echo-ing the ambivalent associations made in the past between lions and *vahumu.*

FRELIMO authorities sometimes knowingly contributed to Muedan sus-picions that they were powerful sorcerers, notwithstanding their socialist rhetoric. Security operatives found it convenient that people conflated col-laborators with sorcerers; such assumptions only augmented popular per-ceptions of their power to "see" and punish acts of disloyalty. As we have seen, Samora Machel himself played with popular perceptions by visiting *vakulaula* regularly during the war.[29] Machel may have been motivated to make these visits by faith in the power of Muedan healers. On the other hand, he may have visited healers to appease them and their constituents or, cyni-cally, to manipulate local convictions and to consolidate popular respect for (or fear of) himself. We cannot be certain that Machel was even treated in-side the *cabanas* of the healers he is known to have visited. We do know, however, that he *entered* these *cabanas* and that he even once spent the night in Alabi Makanga's house soon after the end of the war. We may be certain, also, that Machel understood that by visiting these healers and, especially, by "going inside" with them—a Muedan euphemism for seeking treatment—he greatly facilitated popular assumptions that he was "well protected."

In any case, just as the Montfort Fathers presented themselves to Muedans as the bearers of a transcendent vision of the world, so too did FRELIMO lead-ers when they preached against sorcery in the liberated zones. Like the Mont-fort Fathers before them, who condemned Muedans for their ignorance and superstition, FRELIMO leaders stood in Muedans' midst and, in essence, proclaimed: "We see you! We know who you are (peasants without revolutionary class consciousness)! We know what you think you see in the world (sorcery)! But *we see* your world more clearly than you (through the lens of scientific socialism)!"

As with the Montfort Fathers, many Muedans lent credence to FRELIMO leaders' claims to possess transcendent vision while, at the same time, understanding these proclamations within the discursive genre of *uwavi*. In concluding that FRELIMO leaders were powerful sorcerers, Muedans themselves ironically reasserted their own transcendent vantage point, overturning (*kupilikula*) the discourse of scientific socialism with their (counter)interpretations, even as they denied (like all sorcerers) the world-making force of their own visions.

17

Rewriting the Landscape

"Now, I am *nang'olo mwene kaja* [settlement head]," Agostinho Simão Shishulu told us.

We sat conversing in Agostinho's yard on the southern side of the village of Matambalale.

"But the *kaja* no longer exists," I said. The construction of the village in which we sat marked the end of the formerly autonomous settlements once inhabited by village residents—or so I had assumed.

"The *kaja* is still there," Agostinho replied, "only we don't live in it anymore."

Agostinho, Tissa, and I had been conversing about the history of the settlement in which Agostinho lived before he and his family fled to the lowlands at the beginning of the independence war. When I expressed surprise that Agostinho had resided as an adult in the settlement of his father's Vashiala matrilineage, and not that of his mother's Vailiu matrilineage, Agostinho told us, "Most young men of my generation stayed in the settlements of their fathers; we turned to our mothers' *likolas* only when we had needs that we could not meet ourselves or that our fathers couldn't meet."

Such were the effects of labor migration and wage employment on Makonde social structure. Not only did Agostinho remain in his father's settlement upon coming of age, but he was ultimately chosen to head the group: "Mpapalola was the founder. He was followed by his younger brother, Dedi. Dedi was replaced by his sister's son, Namiva, who passed his authority on to his mother's sister's son, Henriques Shishulu."

Tissa observed that each of Agostinho's predecessors was Vashiala, but that he was Vailiu. Agostinho responded: "The *nang'olo mwene kaja* has always chosen his successor. What is important is that the one he picks have a good temperament; he must have ambitions that serve the *likola*, not ambitions that destroy it. In the past, the successor could not be a son. Now, it sometimes happens [that way] if the person the *likola* has greatest confidence in is a son rather than a nephew. I consulted with Henriques's nephew until he died. Then, I carried on, alone."

We continued conversing about the changes Agostinho had witnessed. He concluded: "These days, many sons stay with their fathers, so the *likola* is losing its importance." To this, he added, however: "When I die, the position will have to return to the Vashiala."

It was when I expressed surprise that Agostinho would have to select a successor in an era when the *kaja* no longer existed that he informed us not only of the *kaja*'s continued existence despite villagization but also of the continuing existence of *vanang'olo vene kaja.*

"Our lands are there," he told me. "We live here in the village, but we walk each day to tend crops on the same lands we have always cultivated. The *nang'olo* [elder] still watches over the land of the *likola*. Some matrilineages even continue to bury their dead in the *kaja.*"

"How far away are your lands?" Tissa asked, knowing from his own experience growing up in the village of Nimu the importance of the answer to this question.

"We walk for an hour and a half," Agostinho said, pointing south.

"Can't you get land closer to the village?" I asked, astounded that Matambalale's Vashiala were forced to spend three hours of their labor-filled days commuting to and from their fields.

"All the land between here and there belongs to other matrilineages," Agostinho informed us.

"Why was the village built here, so far from your lands?" I asked.

Tissa jumped in: "It's not uncommon. Many have to walk farther. It's the consequence of concentrating so many people into a village."

Agostinho's smile betrayed him as a man only partially resigned to the unfortunate historical circumstances that defined his existence: "Three FRELIMO chairmen came from settlements close to the place where this village was built. Their matrilineages embraced FRELIMO in the early days, before the war had even begun. They were rewarded for their service by those who chose this site."

Agostinho looked at the ground, as if struggling to remain silent, but in the end he allowed these words to escape his mouth: "We asked if another village could be built closer to our lands, but when FRELIMO started to call us 'enemies of the people,' we gave up."

ᜎ

When the war for Mozambican independence ended in 1974, Muedans looked forward to reinhabiting their settlements beneath the groves of trees that provided sweet fruit and cooling shade in close proximity to the tombs of their ancestors. After the withdrawal from Mozambique of Portuguese troops and the granting of Mozambican independence in 1975, however, Muedans were told by FRELIMO that they would instead be constructing and inhabiting settlements of unprecedented size: "communal villages" that would serve as models for the rest of the country in FRELIMO's campaign to bring "socialist modernization" to rural Mozambique (Egerö 1987; Hanlon 1990: 121–131; Casal 1991; Borges Coelho 1993b; West 1997b: 197–199).[1]

FRELIMO presented villagization to the populations of Mueda in the form of a social contract. Rural populations would concentrate into villages of 250 to 1,000 families. They would build their own homes, as well as the buildings that would serve them as schools, health clinics, shops, storehouses, and government and party offices. The government would then provide teachers and health workers, medicine and schoolbooks, basic consumer goods and agricultural tools, machinery and extension workers, and—of utmost importance on the Mueda plateau—a clean water supply. The government would also coordinate transportation and trade between villages and urban centers. In cooperation with villagers, the party would even organize cultural and political events and activities in the village center. According to FRELIMO's vision, communal villages would constitute "cities born in the forests" (FRELIMO 1976).

There were, of course, other dimensions to the villagization initiative. From the outset of the FRELIMO anticolonial campaign, FRELIMO sought not only to free Mozambique from Portuguese rule but also dramatically to *transform* Mozambican society and the operation of power within it (Munslow 1983: 133–148; Pitcher 2002: 85). The decolonization of Mozambique, FRELIMO leaders insisted, required both the end of colonialism and the liberation of Mozambicans from indigenous institutions that had, in the colonial period, colluded with the Portuguese in the exploitation of ordinary Mozambicans (Machel 1985: 41). During the war, FRELIMO guerrillas sometimes found it pragmatic to cooperate with ex–*autoridades gentílicas* and/or other kin-based authority figures, but as early as 1969, FRELIMO's first president, Eduardo Mondlane, asserted publicly that the authority of "chiefs" in contemporary Mozambique derived not from "the original tribal structure" but, rather, from "appointment by the Portuguese," whose instructions they carried out (Mondlane 1969: 40). Over time, FRELIMO leaders increasingly cast these

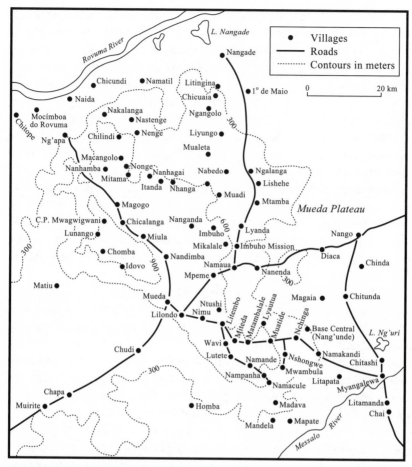

Map 4. Post-independence Communal Villages

figures as corrupted opportunists who had profited personally in the colonial era from their roles as tax collectors, labor recruiters, and local policing agents (Machel 1985: 5). Upon independence, FRELIMO endeavored to exclude these figures from positions of authority. In the first session of the Council of Ministers in 1975, the chieftaincy was summarily abolished (People's Republic of Mozambique [1975] 1990: 4; Monteiro 1989: 14; Sachs and Honwana Welch 1990: 58–60; Meneses et al. 2003: 352).[2]

FRELIMO leaders appreciated that transforming the logic and operation of power at the local level required transforming the conditions of its practice. Villagization was therefore conceived as a means to allow the FRELIMO party/state to rewrite the landscape of power in rural Mozambique through the construction of new village-based political and economic institutions that would supplant the kin-based authority structures that FRELIMO considered "feudal" hierarchies (Munslow 1983: 140; Machel 1985: 41, 55, 57; Meneses et al. 2003: 351). Communal villages were to constitute the substrate upon which Mozambique's "new men" would govern themselves through the exercise of *poder popular* (people's power) in a new classless society (Munslow 1983; Machel 1985: 2, 43; Egerö 1987; Hanlon 1990: 135–146; Casal 1991). Villagers would elect peers to popular assemblies, and these peers would represent the villagers' interests within the postindependence nation. They would also elect judges to popular tribunals, who would resolve conflicts arising among them. Economic affairs, including agricultural production and trade for urban-produced consumer goods, would be mediated by cooperatives whose leaders, too, would be elected from within. All of this would ensure that *poder popular* functioned openly and rationally in the interests of all members of the community—ensure that all "ate well," as Muedans expressed it.

Villagers were not left to practice people's power alone, however. The command culture of guerrilla war persisted within FRELIMO after war's end and was reinforced by the 1977 transformation of FRELIMO into a vanguard party.[3] FRELIMO leaders embraced the mandate to educate the masses and to steer village affairs according to a revolutionary agenda. Village presidents were nominated by the party/state. Most were young men who had the party's confidence but not, necessarily, the confidence of the villagers they governed. Indeed, because FRELIMO considered it potentially problematic to elevate a member of the village community to a position of authority over his peers, many presidents were outsiders to the populations they governed. To ensure that villagers not go astray in their exercise of democracy where the vote *was* extended to them, candidates for popular assemblies (governing bodies that exercised authority over several villages) were chosen by party representatives who orchestrated public discussion of the candidates' merits prior to calling for a show of hands. Former *autoridades gentílicas* were systematically excluded (Hanlon 1990: 170–174; Meneses et al. 2003: 351), meaning that, in most cases, *vanang'olo vene kaja* (settlement heads) were effectively barred from these positions.[4] Because the agenda for elected assemblies was dictated by the FRELIMO political hierarchy, these bodies ultimately served more as organs for the dissemination of state directives than as vehicles for democratic governance (Egerö 1987). Party officials also oversaw the selection of members of popular tribunals and took an interventionist stance in establishing the norms whereby judgments would be rendered (Sachs and Honwana Welch 1990).

Continuity with the former liberated zones was observed not only in the culture of power but also in its structures. The residents of a communal village turned out to be none other than those who had lived together during the war in a single local branch/locality. The residents of one or two wartime town branches/circles were usually placed in a distinct *bairro* (neighborhood), of which most villages had four. The wartime office of town branch chairman/circle secretary was transformed into that of *bairro* president, while that of local branch chairman/locality secretary was transformed into that of village president. Councils at these levels functioned much as they had during the latter half of the war, with appointments made by departmental superiors in the FRELIMO hierarchy.

Where the culture and structures of authority in postindependence villages were continuous with those of the independence war, land use patterns manifested continuity with the prewar past. The postindependence land law stated that all land belonged to the people through the state, but where the state did not exercise claims directly over land demarcated for use by state farms or village collectives, individual families were generally left to clear and cultivate individual plots of land. Although residing in concentrated villages, Muedans walked each day to and from the land they continued to recognize as their own in the environs of their former settlements (sometimes two hours from the village).[5]

The linkages that Muedans maintained with their preindependence settlements ran even deeper than this. When Muedans occupied their new villages, *likola* members normally built their homes on contiguous plots. What is more, if the *likola*'s settlement had been to the north of the village, for example, *likola* members generally built their homes in the northern part of the village so that the walk from the village to their lands would be as short as possible. Those whose former settlements were at a distance from the village normally occupied the village perimeter, while those whose former settlements were close by built near the center (unless the village actually occupied their land, in which case they remained clustered around the trees that had once shaded their independent settlement). In this way, villagers reproduced within the boundaries of the new village (even if in miniature and modified form) the former social geography of the region, and matrilineages silently sustained themselves as distinct units both within the village and upon the lands they cultivated outside the village.

Because people continued to cultivate land that they obtained through matrilineal networks, village officials—especially those foreign to the region in which they worked—were ill prepared to resolve land conflicts when they arose. If they became involved at all, village presidents had to rely upon

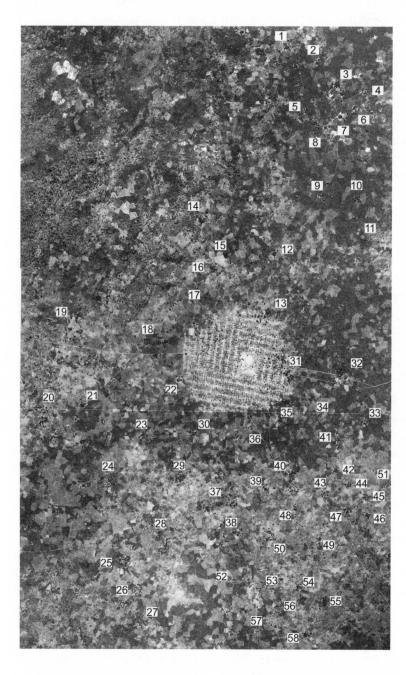

expert witnesses to confirm or deny the validity of claims. In most cases, expert witnesses were none other than the *vanang'olo vene kaja* of the disputants' matrilineages. These elders continued to play a role in other affairs as well. On the Mueda plateau, popular tribunals functioned only sporadically. Because they were established only in villages that also served as locality posts, most villagers had to walk to a neighboring village—and lose a day of work—in order to submit a case. Many villagers felt that the tribunals' rulings were unpredictable. For these reasons, villagers often sought out the *nang'olo mwene kaja* of their former settlement not only when they needed land but also for counsel in family matters or for resolution of conflicts. Depending upon the disposition of the village president, villagers did so either openly or surreptitiously.

Thus, despite the geographic erasure of the settlement (*kaja*) from the plateau, people not only reproduced cognitive maps of preindependence communities on the postindependence landscape but also continued to recognize the political structures that animated the preindependence landscape as well as the authority figures that sat atop these structures—*vanang'olo vene kaja*. For example, the residents of Matambalale village, who once lived in fifty-eight settlements, recognized in their midst fifty-eight *vanang'olo vene kaja* when I worked among them.[6] This was true even when the elder who had held this position before the beginning of the independence war had died, for in all such cases successors had been nominated.[7]

On the other hand, FRELIMO governance produced substantial effects at the level of kin-based political institutions in the postindependence period. Where FRELIMO leaders in the postindependence period disparaged figures of traditional authority as superstitious, self-serving drunkards, young Muedans increasingly looked upon these elders with contempt. The *humu* Windu

Map 5. Matambalale Village and Surrounding Former Settlements (ca. 1994)

The fifty-eight settlements whose residents now live in Matambalale are discernible on the Muedan landscape by the clusters of trees that once shaded their homes.

1. Ntumbati	12. Ntamba	24. Woyo	36. Mpelo	48. Nanda
2. Shimbola	13. Namakate	25. Nandang'a	37. Likabaleni	49. Kolo
3. Malipudya	14. Mashaninga	26. Nauli	38. Tendinyama	50. Shiponda
4. Ndumusha	15. Shilende	27. Pinda	39. Audukile	51. Naengo
5. Mbumila	16. Mang'anyuka	28. Santila	40. Mweva	52. Nandondo
6. Mpalakele	17. Liguguma	29. Ng'oma	41. Minga	53. Nyushi
7. Atibu	18. Mpupa	30. Kakoli	42. Mwalabu	54. Shoongo
8. Niwanje	19. Makuti	31. Namosha	43. Tekuno	55. Kwalata
9. Mapiko	20. Mundumu	32. Nungama	44. Sheka	56. Mbuba
10. Mpapalola	21. Lijega	33. Shileumbutuka	45. Nandembu	57. Namosha
11. Akalimui	22. Kundapanango	34. Mamba	46. Ndaigwashana	58. Ng'oma
	23. Naunama	35. Lilandoma	47. Nding'uni	

told us in 1994 that the institution of *humu* withered in the postindependence period in large measure because of the negative stereotypes with which it was associated by FRELIMO. Where once *vahumu* were revered and respected, following independence they were made to tend their own fields like ordinary Muedans, undermining the prestige of the institution. "Youths today don't want to be *humu*," Windu told us sorrowfully. Indeed, when we conducted research on the plateau in 1994, we discovered that successors were not being appointed when *vahumu* died and that, of the thirty-six matrilineages that once had *vahumu*, only three still had them.

With the passage of time, villagization also made it difficult for *likola* members to reside next to one another. Upon marriage, young couples no longer moved to take up residence with the husband's *njomba* (matrilineal uncle), as they once did.[8] Even when new couples remained after marriage in the village in which they grew up, they often found that they could not build their homes beside a sponsoring elder, for the density of village residences prohibited it. Instead, young people were forced to the village periphery to build next to those with whom they had no kinship ties. Jumbled together with members of many other matrilineages, villagers sometimes lamented their situation with a song asking, "Who is FRELIMO to make me live next to this man who is not my uncle?"

Now and again throughout the 1980s, small groups took the decision to abandon their communal villages and to return to the sites of their former settlements.[9] FRELIMO officials responded to such initiatives forcefully, arresting the leaders of these groups and burning the homes that they had built outside the village. With these measures, FRELIMO demonstrated that it conceived of villagization not merely as a tool to achieve "socialist modernization" in the countryside but, simultaneously, as a component of national security.[10]

Beginning in 1977, Mozambique was, once more, at war. The Rhodesian military had responded to the Mozambican provision of sanctuary to Zimbabwe African National Liberation Army (ZANLA) guerrillas by sending counterinsurgency operatives across the border to attack ZANLA bases. Mozambicans who were disgruntled with FRELIMO, including many who had fought in the Portuguese army against FRELIMO, were recruited by the Rhodesian military to join their counterinsurgency forces. When Iain Smith's white-settler regime yielded power to Zimbabwean nationalists in 1980, the South African Defense Forces adopted these counterinsurgents and, after providing them with additional training, redeployed them inside Mozambique to destabilize a FRELIMO regime that had garnered enmity with South Africa by hosting the headquarters of the African National Congress (ANC) in Maputo.

These counterinsurgents-turned-insurgents, who came to be called the Mozambican National Resistance (Resistência Nacional Moçambicana, or RENAMO), now targeted Mozambican state infrastructure and terrorized rural Mozambicans (Hall 1990; Morgan 1990; T. Young 1990; Vines 1991; Africa Watch 1992; Roesch 1992; Minter 1994).

RENAMO expanded operations throughout Mozambique, recruiting and conscripting new soldiers in areas to which it spread. By the early 1980s, RENAMO had reached Cabo Delgado Province. FRELIMO officials there sought to use communal villages as a bulwark against RENAMO contact with local populations, much as the Portuguese had done with the strategic hamlets they had constructed in Cabo Delgado during the war for independence. Hence, when Muedans abandoned their villages to return to their former settlements, FRELIMO officials responded with vigor.

Although RENAMO never established a lasting presence in the plateau region, in the 1980s Muedans once more felt themselves at war.[11] Officials constantly warned Muedans to remain "vigilant" (Darnton 1979). On the same site where Moçambique D had been located at the end of the independence war, the state security apparatus now maintained a "reeducation camp" called Ruarua (one of several such camps in the former liberated zones) where "enemies of the people" were detained (Amnesty International 1979: 27). Word circulated among plateau residents of the brutal treatment doled out to state prisoners, many of whom died in detention (Carvalho 1981; US Department of State 1984: 253; Africa Watch 1992: 19, 68; West 1997b: 222– 225; 2003a).

Notwithstanding FRELIMO's ability generally to protect the plateau region from RENAMO attack, the specter of violence hung over Mueda's postindependence communal villages. As we shall see, Muedans concerned themselves not only with potentially menacing forces lurking on the margins of FRELIMO's revolutionary heartland plateau but also with dangerous forces concealed inside model postindependence socialist villages—new "enemies within" of disturbingly familiar kinds.

18

The Villagization of Sorcery

"Long ago," Limitedi Untonji told us, "*uwavi wa kulishungila* [sorcery of self-defense] predominated."

Limitedi's son and grandson sat beside him. The grandson was too young to understand the elder's words, but the son listened intently. Earlier, he had told us that he and his wife had begun study with the elder to learn his *mitela*.

"If people wanted to dance *uwavi* in the settlement, the settlement head came out and said, 'Not here!' Now, in the village, it is different."

The elder gave emphasis to his words only with the inflection of his voice, for his eyes were a vacant glossy white.

"The People United from the Rovuma to the Maputo!" he said. The slogan, which made reference to the two rivers constituting the nation's northern and southern borders, was one often uttered by FRELIMO president Samora Machel in the early days of Mozambican independence. "In the villages, *vavi* are also united," the elder continued. "At night, they sound the bell and gather together. They belong to no one *likola*.[1] *This* is *uwavi wa shilikali* [government sorcery]!"

Marcos leaned forward in his seat, respectfully touching the blind elder on his knee to gain his attention before addressing him. "Do *vavi* use the regular village bell?"

The elder responded without hesitation, "Only if the village president is also president of the night!"

"Ummm," said Marcos, indicating his understanding of the euphemism. He then asked, directly, "What's the difference between a village where the president is a sorcerer and a village where he is not?"

"In a village where the president is not a *mwavi*, nothing functions," the

As we conversed with Limitedi Untonji, shown here with his protégé-son and grandson, I was reminded of my own grandfather, whose failing eyesight gave rise to greater sensitivity and acuity of the other senses. A disproportionately high number of the Muedan *vakulaula* we encountered suffered blindness, but they "saw" what ordinary Muedans could not—the invisible realm.

elder answered. "Where the village president is a *mwavi*, everything works well."[2]

"So the president in a village where everything works well practices sorcery of construction?" Marcos asked.

"Yes," Limitedi replied, "if all runs well, he practices sorcery of self-defense on behalf of everyone."

Such cases were, however, quite rare, Limitedi told us.

⸽

James Scott has written:

> Legibility is a condition of manipulation. Any substantial state intervention in society—to vaccinate a population, produce goods, mobilize labor, tax people and their property, conduct literacy campaigns, conscript soldiers, enforce sanitation standards, catch criminals, start universal schooling—requires the invention of units that are visible. The units in question might be citizens, vil-

lages, trees, fields, houses, or people grouped according to age, depending on the type of intervention. Whatever the units being manipulated, they must be organized in a manner that permits them to be identified, observed, recorded, counted, aggregated, and monitored. (1998: 183)

Through the project of communal villagization described in chapter 17, the FRELIMO state dramatically rewrote the Mozambican landscape.[3] In so doing, the FRELIMO leadership hoped to render rural Mozambican society more legible and, thus, more amenable to state intervention.[4] In fundamental ways, the communal village worked like Jeremy Bentham's panopticon (as discussed by Michel Foucault [1977] in his analysis of the modern prison), even if the village did not resemble the hub and spokes of a wheel. Muedans were required to construct their houses in tidy rows on a carefully surveyed grid. Houses stood naked on a landscape almost devoid of vegetation. Villages were divided into four quadrants called *bairros*. Within each *bairro*, houses were assigned to units of twenty-five families. From the level of the village president down to the twenty-five-family unit, the party appointed officials. FRELIMO party offices were constructed in the village center. The spatial concentration of the village rendered subjects directly susceptible to a monitoring eye—embodied in the FRELIMO-appointed village president—that could pass unobstructed through surveillance corridors in a matter of hours where previously it would have taken days to visit all of the settlements represented in the village. When the village president wished to address his charges, he summoned them by striking a "bell"—generally an old tractor wheel hung from a tree beside party offices. Those who failed to appear promptly might later be interrogated and/or chastised.

As FRELIMO took to using communal villages in the Mueda region to deny RENAMO access to plateau populations, FRELIMO vigilance turned inward—as it had during the independence war—with the state monitoring these villages for the appearance of "enemies within." As we have seen, FRELIMO guarded against the reassertion of power within village structures on the part of former *autoridades gentílicas*. The party/state also maintained its wartime prohibitions on all forms of public discourse and practice associated with sorcery, including the use of medicinal substances, the consultation of diviners, and the supplication of ancestral spirits, all of which fell under the category of "obscurantism" explicitly denounced in the constitution (People's Republic of Mozambique [1975] 1990: 7; see also E. Green, Jurg, and Dgedge 1993: 264; 1994: 7; AMETRAMO 1998; Honwana 2002: 169–173; Gulube 2003: 100).[5] In the postcolonial world of "scientific socialism" and "people's power"—where power was said to operate openly, rationally, and to the benefit of all—FRELIMO regarded as political blasphemy the suggestion, implicit in sorcery accusations and counteraccusations, that power operated in hidden and capricious ways.[6]

Ironically, the idiom of FRELIMO governance in communal villages emphasized vision and visibility. Through the construction of communal villages, FRELIMO actualized its bold vision for a transformed Mozambican countryside. Simultaneously, the party asserted its ability to fix rural Muedans in its gaze—to see them and to know, constantly, what they were up to. Such claims were familiar to Muedans, who brought with them to the village not only the spatial logics of preindependence social geography but also the schema of sorcery that conveyed within it distinctive ways of understanding power. Through this schema, Muedans read state power rather differently than FRELIMO leaders intended.

According to Kalamatatu, *vanang'olo vene kaja* could not convincingly claim to exercise control over the members of other *makola* who lived beside them in the villages they now inhabited. In fact, no figure of authority could monitor a domain that neither he nor his predecessors had built. FRELIMO had built the villages and had appointed officials to fill the offices constructed in their centers. In these villages, no *nang'olo mwene kaja* was allowed to build a *shitala* in which to meet with and exercise authority over the members of his *likola*. Therefore, Kalamatatu explained to us, it was incumbent upon village authorities to monitor the invisible realm in these new domains to ensure secure and prosperous environments for those under their charge. In other words, villagers expected village presidents to patrol both the visible realm and the invisible—to practice sorcery of construction. The elder Vicente Anawena, in Matambalale, told us: "Even today's 'chiefs' [referring to state officials] must be *vavi*. How else could they rule?"

Muedans generally interpreted official pronouncements against obscurantism as they had during the war. In other words, they interpreted the FRELIMO ban on sorcery-related practices as a ban on destructive forms of sorcery only. Many healers, certain that their own work did not fall into this category—certain, in fact, that their work constituted a component in the fight against destructive forms of sorcery—continued their practices, even if feeling obliged to keep their countersorcery activities discreet.[7]

Over time, government officials demonstrated increasing laxity in enforcing the ban on countersorcery activities for the same varied and complex reasons as FRELIMO leaders and guerrilla commanders had relaxed prohibitions during the independence war.[8] The *nkulaula* Shindambwanda read the shift this way: "In the beginning, the government made it hard for us to work. But in a short time, they realized that it was best to allow us to treat sorcery so that it would not finish us all off, so we started working more openly."[9]

Some practitioners interpreted FRELIMO's disinterest in enforcing the ban on countersorcery practices as an even stronger mandate to practice. Limitedi Untonji told us that he treated everyone who came to him, including, even, wounded sorcerers. When we asked him why, he told us that he feared *the government would punish him* if he failed to provide treatment to *everyone,* equally.

Many, however, interpreted the loosening of government restrictions on healers as a sign of FRELIMO's weakness in a chaotic invisible realm.[10] Muedans generally concluded that sorcery in the village was of a more complicated nature than was sorcery in the settlements of old. Many referred to the regime of sorcery that existed in parallel with postindependence villages by the same term as had Limitedi Untonji: *uwavi wa shilikali,* "government sorcery." Most understood government sorcery to be sorcery permitted by the government to happen in its villages—sorcery occurring in a realm defined by government power or, perhaps more accurately, lack thereof.[11]

The trouble, Kalamatatu explained to us, was that sorcerers of different matrilineages danced together at night in the village center, exchanged techniques, and even bought sorcery (*uwavi wa kushuma*) from one another.[12] Makudo Shalaga Ntumi Ngole told us: "Villages are veritable schools of *uwavi.*"

The occurrence of death in the village provided constant opportunity for talk of sorcery. When I asked Lucas Mwikumba if there was sorcery in his village, Matambalale, he answered: "Ahhh, yes! In the past, when we lived in settlements, years passed between deaths. Nowadays, deaths follow in each other's tracks." Death visited preindependence settlements only two or three times a year, at most; in the village, death was omnipresent—mortality in some villages reaching as high as two or three per week. Most with whom we spoke saw this not as a function of a much higher population but rather as evidence of the unchecked practice in the village of *uwavi wa kujoa,* "sorcery of danger."[13]

Agostinho Simão Shishulu told us: "In the past, the settlement head controlled sorcery in his own settlement. Now, the village president must call together *vanang'olo* representing all the village matrilineages to do so. It's not as effective." The *humu* Mandia agreed: "*Uwavi* is a greater problem in the villages because no one is truly interested in controlling it. Each one is interested only in himself and his own house. The old authorities have no power. The government asks them who is destroying the village and condemns these acts, but it only has temporary effect." Libata Nandenga concluded: "The village president must act as the *nang'olo mwene kaja* of many *makola*. But he can't prohibit people from killing fellow *likola* members when he is not of the same *likola* as they are.[14] And with *uwavi wa shilikali* [government sorcery], people from one *likola* kill those of another. The village president can't stop this either. That's why village presidents don't last long. All the *vavi* in the village gang up on them, even if they are *vavi* themselves!"

Whereas FRELIMO had suggested, in the language of socialist modernization, that Mozambicans constituted a single family and that the party/ state served that family as a benevolent father (or, in the Muedan case, uncle), assuring that each member ate from the common plate "according to his (or her) needs," the Mozambican family came under intensive strain in the communal villages of civil war Mozambique. Muedans interpreted life in these villages differently, in the familiar language of *uwavi*. Accordingly, they suggested that communal villages not only expanded the family but also intensified the forces that threatened its cohesion. Whereas *uwavi* always festered in the intimate spaces among kin, they now suggested that no father (uncle) figure was up to the task of mediating tensions among such enormous and diverse families as had been borne of communal villages.

Kalamatatu asked us, rhetorically, "Does the village president stand in the village center at night and advise sorcerers against their acts? . . . No, because he can't." The village, according to Kalamatatu, was too complex a social environment, and the sorcery in it too powerful, for any one man to control. On this subject Kalamatatu spoke with a certainty grounded in bitter experience. His own son, Damião, had served as president of the village of Matambalale for a stint that ended with his suicide.

19

Self-Defense and Self-Enrichment

Tissa and I sat together on an *igoli* at the end of an afternoon of work—he whittling, and I reorganizing the items in my field bag.

"Why would a sorcerer make a lion and send it to attack someone's pig corral?" I asked Tissa, referring to a scenario that we had recently heard someone speak about. "What does the sorcerer stand to gain?"

"Sometimes they sell the meat of the stolen pig in the marketplace," Tissa answered, only half interested in my question.

I considered his statement for a moment before asking how it was possible to sell the mauled remains of a pig in the market as meat.

"The carcass people see is fake." Tissa was suddenly more engaged in the conversation. He started tapping on the stick of wood with the knife, accentuating his remarks. "I've seen this. In Nimu [where Tissa grew up], we had a case like this."

I watched Tissa as he composed himself to tell the story. He seemed to be thinking of the case as never before, even as he remembered it.

"A lion was stealing pigs from people's corrals." He paused, running his finger over the grooves he had cut in the stick with his tapping knife. "Eventually, the lion was shot."

"Who killed it?" I asked.

"I don't remember," Tissa answered. "But a few days later, a boy died in the village."

"What did he have to do with the lion?" I asked, somewhat perplexed.

Tissa smiled broadly, as he usually did when delivering the crucial bit of information making a story of interest. He pointed the stick at me. "The boy was the sorcerer behind the lion." He laughed. "He had been selling pork in the marketplace!"

We sat for a time as I mulled over Tissa's tale. Finally, I broke the silence. "How could the carcass be fake?" I asked.

Tissa returned to his whittling, along with his more matter-of-fact tone. "The remains of sorcerers' victims are always fake," he said. "It's the same as when sorcerers kill people. The corpse that is buried is not real. Sorcerers can take a banana tree, make it look like a person they have killed, and substitute it for the body. That's what gets buried."

As I was still ruminating on this point, Tissa further complicated the matter: "Unless, of course, the person hasn't even been killed."

"What do you mean?" I asked.

"These days, more and more, sorcerers don't eat their victims. Their victims are more valuable to them as *mandandosha* [zombie slaves]."

"How so?" I asked.

"Well, in the past, all a sorcerer could do with a *lindandosha* [s.] was put it to work in the fields.[1] Now, sorcerers who have businesses can put *mandandosha* there—to work for them or to guard their riches."

I sat quietly.

Tissa's look betrayed exasperation with my ignorance: "How else could the 'big chiefs' accumulate so much these days?"

⛩

While the violence of the Mozambican civil war was generally experienced as rumor in Mueda, effects of the war were increasingly felt on the plateau in the 1980s. The conflict drained precious national resources and constricted the flow of goods and people necessary to the life of FRELIMO's "cities born in the forest." FRELIMO soon proved incapable of meeting expectations raised by its village-based program of socialist modernization.

The FRELIMO health care system—which had been adopted as a model by the World Health Organization—collapsed nationwide (Cliff and Noormahomed 1988; Mackintosh and Wuyts 1988; Noormahomed et al. 1990; Noormahomed 1991). As real wages for salaried health workers fell (Noormahomed 1991: 46), health posts on the Mueda plateau, as elsewhere, went unstaffed. Intermittent glut and shortage of essential medicines gave rise to a black market in drugs and to popular suspicions of widespread corruption among health workers and government officials more generally (Kappel 1994: 488; Lubkemann 2001: 95).[2]

Similar trends were witnessed in education (Johnston 1990a, 1990b; Marshall 1993). As the education budget declined, teachers were instructed to collect ever-higher school fees as well as the monies students were now required to pay for schoolbooks. Scandals quickly arose in Mueda's school system, as elsewhere, over the alleged misappropriation of funds by underpaid teachers and school officials. Schools that had achieved remarkable success in raising literacy rates among children and adults in the midst of the independence war (Johnston 1984, 1989) now fell into a shambles.

The sophisticated water supply system built on the plateau after independence (UNICEF 1981, 1993; Técnica Engenheiros Consultores Lda. 1994), which had served as a symbolic gesture of national gratitude for the role Muedans had played in the fight for independence, also failed in the late 1980s (Cooperação Suiça 1992; West 1997b: 206–208). Rumor spread on the plateau that system engineers and government officials were selling on the black market the spare parts and diesel fuel needed to keep the system running. Much of the time, however, these essential inputs were simply unavailable.

Also among the social services to fail in the civil war period were *lojas do povo* (people's shops) and producer and consumer cooperatives (Oficina de História 1984; Egerö 1987; Littlejohn 1988). Acute shortages meant that most Muedans went without essential agricultural inputs, such as hoes and seed, and basic consumer goods, such as sugar, salt, cooking oil, and clothes. Cooperatives were overtaken by nepotism and corruption, as ranking members used them to control access to scarce goods that they often sold on the black market (Egerö 1987; Littlejohn 1988).

As the economic crisis deepened, drought touched off famine. In some years, Muedans literally went hungry. All the while, however, ranking party members and state officials "ate well." Indeed, through black-market activities, some "fed themselves" on the misery of ordinary Muedans.

During these same years, Muedans also witnessed opportunism on the part of national-level FRELIMO leaders hailing from the Mueda region. As RENAMO expanded its operations northward into the former strongholds of the FRELIMO anticolonial insurgency, the state feared that growing discontent among veterans of the FRELIMO independence war might provide RENAMO with experienced recruits. As early as 1984, the FRELIMO leadership turned its attention to improving relations with veterans of the independence war. In that year, a state secretariat was established for *antigos combatentes* (former combatants) with the intended purpose of administering retirement benefits to all registered veterans. Priority in the registration process, however, followed military rank. What is more, higher-ranking veterans were not only more likely to have their claims recognized but were also paid substantially higher stipends. The disbursement of checks began in 1986, sparking disputes over benefit levels as well as over the pecking order determining who would be registered first and who would have to wait.

While the vast majority of veterans awaited benefits promised to them, several prominent ex-guerrilla commanders—who now held key positions in the Mozambican government or military—were observed using military transport planes to shuttle materials to the plateau to build European-style tile-roofed stone houses in the town of Mueda or in their villages of origin amid their neighbors' mud and bamboo dwellings. Muedans took to referring to the Soviet-built Antonovs flying overhead as "Linhas Aérias de Imbuho" (Imbuho Airlines) in sarcastic reference to this clique, most of whom had been affiliated in their youth with the Catholic mission at Imbuho.

With FRELIMO socialism unraveling, the government—headed, after the death of President Samora Machel in an airplane crash in 1986, by Joaquim Chissano—adopted austerity measures referred to officially as the Economic Rehabilitation Program (Programa de Reabilitação Económica, or PRE) and, in 1987, conceded to IMF-sponsored structural adjustment and donor-led liberalization of its political and economic institutions (Hanlon 1991). While factions within the ruling party debated whether or not to privatize state assets, Western donors and nongovernmental organizations (NGOs) hosted "workshops" in a variety of institutional contexts to discuss objectives and methods for state divestiture of assets ranging from farms to factories and from fleets to warehouses. Long before the central government made decisions, officials at the provincial, district, and enterprise levels took action, forming "committees" and holding "auctions" through which many of these assets were spontaneously divested, often to the committee members and auctioneers themselves or to their political cronies (Myers and West 1993; Myers 1994; West and Myers 1996).[3]

On the plateau, this "privatization" benefited the most powerful, as it did elsewhere.[4] National-level military leaders from the plateau region took possession of military warehouses, garages, and machine shops. Agricultural officials staked claims to large plots of land in the Nguri State Farm irrigated scheme in the lowlands off the southeastern edge of the plateau. Several of these same officials involved themselves in transactions throughout the northern region and, in a few cases, elsewhere in the country. No longer assured of security and sustenance by state institutions in which they had invested themselves personally, and no longer fettered by the constraining ideological environment of state socialism, state officials looked to enrich themselves in any way possible (West and Myers 1996: 47–51).[5] "The 'big chiefs' found money in the PRE," people often told us.[6]

Further attempts were made beginning in 1988 to shore up the goodwill and loyalty to the party of FRELIMO veterans. On the 7 September anniversary of the beginning of the independence war, the Association of Veterans of the War of National Liberation (Associação dos Combatentes da Luta de Libertação Nacional, or ACLLN) was formed. The association's aim was to valorize the contribution made by war veterans to Mozambican independence and to facilitate their further contribution to the agenda of "national reconstruction" (Elias and Jorge 1988; Henrique 1988). The ACLLN's program mandated it to facilitate economic development among veterans by providing educational, technical, material, and organizational assistance (see Associação dos Combatentes da Luta de Libertação Nacional 1988). The president of the republic, Joaquim Chissano, was named president of the ACLLN national committee, and the association was administratively inserted within the FRELIMO party (Elias and Jorge 1988).

At the provincial and district levels, the ACLLN set up cooperative schemes to generate small funds for its activities. Some schemes were even meant to yield dividends for their individual participants. Simultaneously, the national government began using the ACLLN as a means of disseminating information to veterans about opportunities afforded them by NGO-sponsored development projects and donor-funded credit schemes. In fact, the government took to presenting such projects and schemes to provincial and district branches of the ACLLN as opportunities that it had "arranged" specifically for veterans.[7]

In Cabo Delgado Province, the first major opportunity presented was a credit scheme referred to as the Agricultural Credit Fund for Rural Development (Caixa de Crédito Agrícola para Desenvolvimento Rural, or CCADR), a donor-backed scheme that had actually come on line a year before the creation of the ACLLN. Veterans were informed that, with bank loans handled by the Popular Development Bank (Banco de Desenvolvimento Popular, or BDP) in Pemba, they could purchase a truck, tractor, or grain mill to use for small-business endeavors. Applications were to be submitted to the provincial office of the Veterans' State Secretariat and then vetted by the provincial office of the ACLLN, which would forward them to the bank. Vehicles and mills were imported, beginning in 1988, by local private dealers with the aid of a program sponsored by the US Agency for International Development (USAID) and designed to support the "emerging private sector" through hard-currency conversion at an "official rate" approximately five times the true value of the metical. This allowed the goods to be sold at prices far below those that the "open market" would have permitted.[8] Ultimately, a limited number of loans were made. Influential individuals in the party/state apparatus pressured the BDP to ensure acceptance first of their own applications and those of their close affiliates.[9] These same people also proved to be among the few who could raise the 500,000 meticais required as a down payment for a truck.[10] Thus, when vehicles and mills started to appear on the plateau in 1989–1990,[11] they were largely in the ownership of the already rich and/or powerful, who used them to enhance their wealth and influence. Trucks—and even a few tractors—were put to use carrying passengers to and from the plateau or between plateau villages, for a charge. Others were integrated into agricultural operations. The most influential party/state bosses opened riverbed plots in the lowlands surrounding the plateau. Individuals who commanded sufficient respect and fear from both local government officials and local residents "arranged" land for themselves in the lowlands despite the resistance with which local landholders normally parted with their claims.[12] Two national-level military officials and President Chissano's mother-in-law each eventually put several dozen head of cattle on their new holdings—a practice unheard of at a time when ownership of a single pig was considered a sign of affluence. In the end, FRELIMO programs to assist veterans had the opposite of their intended effect, generating more disaffection among veterans than loyalty.

Indeed, over the course of the two decades following Mozambican independence, the people of northern Cabo Delgado's communal villages were gradually overcome by frustration and resentment (Oficina de História 1986).[13] Where once Muedans had hoped to enjoy the fruits of their victory against the Portuguese, they now complained bitterly of FRELIMO's broken promises to them. Some recriminations were grounded in fantastic expectations, including hopes that all Muedans would have cars soon after winning independence, that a university would be built on the Mueda plateau, or that a new national capital would be constructed in Negomano (the wilderness area just west of the plateau). Nonetheless, as most Muedans reflected on how power operated in their midst, they noted that FRELIMO leaders—men who, as youths, defied their elders by filling, and eating from, their own plates—now controlled the nation's plate. Notwithstanding their revolutionary rhetoric—their articulated dream of a "classless society"—these men had failed to ensure that "each one ate according to his or her needs." On the contrary, Muedans' sarcastic laments conveyed a deep historical irony: "The big chiefs eat everything!"[14]

Economic trends in the 1980s gave Muedans ample opportunity to revisit familiar questions and to interpret and engage with observed phenomena through the language of *uwavi*. Just as in the colonial era, sorcery was said to circulate wildly around the new objects of wealth appearing in the plateau region.

The elder Kabaka Nanume Kapembe, in the village of Nshonwge, once told us: "These days, there is more envy because there is development.[15] *Uwavi* is practiced by those who are envious of others—others who have something for themselves. Generally, *uwavi* is bad; it kills. But these days, *uwavi* has undergone 'modernizations.' People use *uwavi* to find ways to live."

Limitedi Untonji reminded us, however, that one man's survival strategy was often another man's obstacle to survival: "*Uwavi wa kulishungila* [sorcery of self-defense] is complicated," he told us. "It is sometimes self-centered. It is sometimes used to defend only the individual or the matrilineage. That causes problems for others." Indeed, as FRELIMO socialism came undone, Muedans observed the fine line between what they called sorcery of self-defense and what they called *uwavi wa kushunga*, "sorcery of self-advancement" or "sorcery of self-enrichment."

The forms of *uwavi wa kushunga* witnessed by Muedans in the post-socialist era were, at once, fantastic and familiar, as Tissa told me. Indeed, the multiplying effect of *mandandosha* (zombie slaves) labor was seen by most Muedans as the key to unprecedented levels of economic differentiation in the postsocialist era. To achieve success in business, wealthy Muedans were generally assumed to have made *mandandosha* of family members, neighbors, and/or business associates who might have appeared to die but who actually worked as slaves for their sorcerer-masters.[16]

Similarly, Muedans found contemporary forms of sorcery of self-defense at once fantastic and familiar. Tissa explained to me how some recipients of CCADR loans for trucks and tractors were more successful than others in practicing this sorcery of self-defense. He spoke first of those who failed to defend their vehicles:

> If you got a loan for a tractor or a truck, your family thought you had wealth to share. Every time you saw a cousin, he expected you to buy him a beer. Your aunt wanted you to give her, or her children, rides from one of the villages into Mueda town to sell produce in the market. Your wife's father had a grandchild who needed to be taken to the hospital. Your brother wanted to visit a girlfriend. So instead of saving the money you were lent for maintaining the vehicle, you spent it on beer or on petrol. You didn't use the vehicle to do what you had planned. You didn't make any money, and then your vehicle needed a part, or your first payment at the bank was due, and you had no money. So you borrowed from a friend or a relative or maybe even the bank. But you went deeper and deeper. Your vehicle then had a real breakdown. I mean serious. So you had to wonder, "Who has done this to me? Who is using *uwavi* on me?" You went to an *nkulaula,* and he told you that an envious family

member had stuffed an arm or a skull in your vehicle. (Sorcerers will do that. The bones they leave behind are evidence of their cravings for human flesh. They are envious because you have a plan to improve yourself.) A healer removed the skull, but then one of your children became ill. More sorcery. The healer tried, but he told you that you had to take the child to the doctor. So you took a part off your tractor and sold it to someone who needed it so that you would have enough money to pay for the medicine at the hospital. Now you were in trouble. You had no money, the bank was after you, your friend needed his money, and your vehicle was dead. What could you do? So you either waited for the bank to come and take the tractor away, or you sold it.

Tissa then spoke of others who were more capable practitioners of sorcery of self-defense—the "big chiefs," as Muedans called these government and military officials, party bosses, and successful entrepreneurs:

This is how the "big chiefs" wind up with everything. This is how they eat everything. They have the money to buy your tractor. They hire someone from [the southern province of] Gaza to run their business here, so not even their families can eat them. They know how to protect themselves from sorcery. They have a way of "mining" their vehicle or their house. When the sorcerer comes, when the sorcerer gets close, the tractor will disappear, the house will disappear. The sorcerer steps back, and it reappears, but he cannot get close enough to use his sorcery on it!

Others with whom I spoke confirmed Tissa's descriptions of novel forms of sorcery of self-defense. João Chombo once explained to me in detail how objects such as cars, grain mills, sewing machines, and bicycles could be "mined" against sorcery:

With such things, you can't bury a *lipande* [antisorcery mine] inside like you do with a house. So, with a car, for example, you have to take out a couple of parts and put them in a sack along with *mitela* and bury them in the ground somewhere far away. When someone comes with the intention of ruining that car, the *mitela* will draw that sorcerer's attention to the place where the part is buried. They will become confused and they will not be able to see the car.

Verónica Romão, however, told us that there were other, more sinister ways to protect vehicles against sorcery. Just as sorcerers seeking to destroy these things might stuff bones in them to clog them up or to cause breakdowns, their owners might do the same to protect them. The owners might lodge *mandandosha*—usually infants—inside, Romão told us. These zombie slaves guarded against sorcery that might otherwise have ruined the vehicle. It was in such acts that the fine line between *uwavi wa kulishungila* and *uwavi wa kushunga*—between self-defense and self-advancement—disappeared.

Most Muedans who succeeded in capturing and defending the new forms of wealth and power that appeared in the plateau region in the moment of structural adjustment were those who, as young men in the colonial period, had captured novel forms of wealth and power. Where once they had challenged and provoked their more powerful, wealthier elders and, ultimately, colonial rulers on behalf of the nation, they now appropriated and augmented wealth and power on their own behalf, consolidating and accentuating social and economic differentiation in the plateau region.

As we have seen in part 2, Muedans had long looked upon power and wealth, through the schema of *uwavi,* with marked ambivalence. Where most were persuaded that the FRELIMO leaders who moved among them in wartime liberated zones generally practiced a beneficent form of sorcery, in the years after independence many grew skeptical of the argument that these powerful figures policed the invisible realm in defense of the common good.[17] In conversation with us, many let slip from time to time their suspicions that the "big chiefs" now acted in the invisible realm only in defense of their own interests.[18]

Muedans debated the prowess of these "big chiefs" as businessmen, as sorcerers of self-defense and as sorcerers of self-enrichment.[19] When I spent time on the plateau in 1999, many pointed to the scattered "carcasses" (meaning, in Mozambican parlance, abandoned, part-stripped vehicles) of these elites' CCADR trucks and tractors as evidence that they, too, could be victims of envious sorcerers. Others argued that these men were capable sorcerers but miserable businessmen. "They know how to protect themselves," we were often told. "They're *blindado* [armored]," others told us, suggesting that these elites were "loaded up" with antisorcery *mitela* that shielded them from any conceivable attack.[20]

When I asked Muedans if these men had *mandandosha,* many simply responded by rolling their eyes in affirmation.[21] In any case, as the neoliberal era dawned in Mozambique, rarely did Muedans suggest that these figures of authority monitored and quashed the aggressive and accumulative acts of sorcerers of danger.

As ever more powerful elites, in concert with new forces of foreign provenance, remade the world in which Muedans lived, Muedans themselves drew upon the familiar language of *uwavi* to interpret and engage with the transformative processes they witnessed and experienced. Through their judgments and pronouncements uttered in the discursive genre of *uwavi*, they struggled, often in vain, to bring to fruition another world of their own imagining, as we shall see in part 3. If nothing else, as we shall also see in part 3, their suspicions and recriminations constituted a perceptive critique—a discursive "undoing" (*kupilikula*)—of neoliberal reform in the postsocialist era.

III

Part 3 of this volume examines how Muedans have interpreted and engaged with Mozambique's post–civil war transition to a market economy and a multiparty democratic regime through the language of *uwavi*. Whereas over the past century Muedans have sustained a prolonged historical conversation with various Others claiming to be the bearers of transcendent truths that nullified Muedan "traditions," in the postsocialist era Muedans have encountered discursive propositions of a somewhat different kind. In the name of democracy and cultural pluralism, proponents and agents of neoliberal reform have espoused the "validation" and "recognition" of varied Mozambican "traditions." Many of the Western donors, international nongovernmental organizations, and reformist Mozambican officials who have gained ascendancy in Mozambican affairs in the post–civil war period have suggested, for example, that "traditional authorities" constitute key figures in an emergent Mozambican "civil society." Along similar lines, "traditional healers" have been cast as stewards of forms of "indigenous knowledge" worthy of preservation in the new, democratic Mozambique.

Even while inhabiting the "spaces" afforded them in the postsocialist era, however, traditional authorities and healers on the Mueda plateau, as elsewhere in the nation, have proven themselves "complicated" historical agents. Ever in quest of new forms of knowledge that might allow them to overcome those with whom they battle, healers have resisted state regulation and scientific standardization of their practices. In so doing, they have blurred the boundaries with which medical researchers and health officials have attempted to divide one tradition from another, and all of "tradition" from "biomedical science," thereby making of themselves, in the eyes of many, charlatans and menaces to the public health. Concurrently, Muedan *vanang'olo*—like their counterpart "traditional authorities" elsewhere in the country—have on occasion exercised authority in newly opened spaces by meting out economic sanctions, corporal punishments, and community expulsions against those accused of disrupting harmony and social order in their villages. In the wake of such events, some FRELIMO party leaders and state officials have expressed convictions that traditional institutions remain unsuited to participate in the project of modern governance and, more specifically, in the neoliberal agenda of securing individual rights of property and person. Where traditional authorities and healers have "failed" to conform to the expectations of neoliberal reformers, official "recognition" of Mozambican "tradition" has remained uneven and incomplete, producing and enhancing political ambiguities and social insecurities.

Further complicating the picture, the political and economic spaces opened up by neoliberal reform in Mueda have not been occupied by elders and healers alone. Private interests (including foreign and domestic investors and Mozambican officials qua entrepreneurs) have moved into the vacuum created by a receding state. Where the socialist state nominally committed itself to the provision of resources and social services to its citizenry, private interests have extracted local resources while shirking local accountability. As the value of Mozambican citizenship has declined, the recently ended civil war has been followed in Muedan villages by microconflicts sparked by intensive economic differentiation. Muedans have, consequently, experienced neoliberal "development" with deep ambivalence, longing for the "modern" objects that have appeared in their midst while sensing that these objects remain inaccessible to them.

Muedans have expressed their envy and frustration in the postsocialist period in the discursive genre of *uwavi*. In some measure, their discursive engagements with a rapidly changing world have worked to keep economic differentiation in check through fostering fears of supernatural leveling forces. But sorcery's antidevelopmental dynamics have cast an ominous shadow over not only the prosperous but also the poor. In this context, Muedans have sometimes demanded of authorities ("traditional" *and* "modern") that they not only *eat well* but also *feed* those they govern. They have sometimes called upon these authorities to not only *rule the day* but also the *night*. The popular mandate to practice sorcery of construction has been embraced in some locales by village councils of elders (with local state complicity) and in others by local state officials themselves, while in still others it has been declined altogether—all with variable and complex consequences.

Interpreting and engaging with these events and processes in the language of *uwavi*, Muedans have not always succeeded in transforming their world to their benefit. But when reformers have suggested to Muedans in a rather different language that, by embracing the project of neoliberal reform, they might give foundation to their own greater liberty and prosperity, Muedans' have remained skeptical of such claims. Through sorcery discourse, they have sustained their understanding that power, by nature, works capriciously, even invisibly—sometimes constructively and sometimes destructively. They have nurtured their ambivalence toward a modern world on whose margins they perceive themselves to live, preserving their sense that this world is more the product of others' visions than their own. In the language of *uwavi*, they have asked themselves why they are unable to "make something" of their ideas—why decisive knowledge seems always to be held by others. By comparing *uwavi* with the "sciences" of socialist modernization and neoliberal development—by asking if these forms of knowledge are fundamentally the same or different, as well as if one is more powerful than the other—Muedans have pondered whether it is they or those who would transform their world who are truly responsible for their continuing poverty. Monitoring the visible realm for signs of the workings of power in the invisible, they have kept the various powers that shape their world under constant surveillance, occasionally inverting the effects of these powers through their own—albeit tentative—transcendent gaze.

20

The "Resurgence of Tradition"

As Marcos and I entered the village of Nandimba on a cool August morning in 1999, his words were fresh in my memory: "Yes, *mano* [Portuguese for "brother"], that's a good topic for our research. These things must be studied scientifically!"

I was surprised not by Marcos's consent—for he knew me well enough to trust that I would not push any research agenda further than conditions permitted—but rather by his enthusiasm. In previous years, I had felt the need to steer clear of the topic of sorcery when working with Marcos, an active FRELIMO cadre. I had instead cautiously pursued my interests in sorcery alone or in the company of Tissa, a younger man who was somewhat less beholden to the FRELIMO agenda. By 1999, people in Maputo had been talking for several years about the "resurgence of tradition"[1] in Mozambique, and I was determined to make the study of sorcery more central to my research. Notwithstanding five years of multiparty democracy, however, I knew that the Mueda plateau remained "the cradle of the revolution."

Marcos's excited response betokened a shift in the Muedan environment as well. In the coming weeks, I would come to appreciate the subtle complexities of that shift. Some Muedans with whom we worked professed that "times were changing." In the midst of changing times, however, much remained familiar.

Prior to arriving in Nandimba to work, Marcos and I had observed protocol by informing the village president of our intention to conduct research in his village. We had told him that, in particular, we would be interested in speaking with healers. Reciprocating protocol, the village president had agreed to facilitate our introduction to several potential interviewees when we returned to start work, but I had wondered how thoroughly he had accommodated himself to traditions' resurgence in *his* village and, consequently, how obliging he would be.

When we returned later in the week, we found the village president at his home, awaiting us in the company of two other men. The first man he introduced to us as the village vice president. The second was Maurício Mpwapwele Moto. Mpwapwele's title, he informed us, was village chief of security. I interpreted the chief of security's presence as a clear signal that Muedan village officials were not inclined to abandon FRELIMO's historical stance against "obscurantism," regardless of what might be happening elsewhere in the country. My consternation deepened when the three village officials accompanied Marcos and me to the home of our first interviewee, the healer Carmelita Milonge. Although the president and vice president quickly excused themselves, the chief of security remained with us.

Marcos worked astutely to distract the chief of security from the interview that I conducted with Carmelita. When I had finished a short conversation with her, I took Marcos aside, hoping to find a way to handle the problem raised by the official's monitoring of our activities. Marcos first asked me about my conversation. I told him that, to my surprise, the healer did not seem perturbed by the official's proximity. I then asked him, sarcastically, whether he had interviewed the chief of security or the other way around.

"This guy's story is very interesting," Marcos responded, flatly. "His experience in security goes back a long way. He's a FRELIMO veteran of the independence war."

"Perhaps sometime we should do an interview with him about the war," I said. "But for the moment, I'm worried that his presence will make the healers with whom we work nervous."

"That won't be a problem," Marcos quickly answered.

I was taken aback by Marcos's failure to appreciate how the presence of a FRELIMO official—a guerrilla veteran, a security operative—might make it difficult for the healers with whom we planned to converse to speak openly about their work, which FRELIMO had once banned.

"Why won't it be a problem?" I asked, perplexed and somewhat annoyed.

Marcos smiled wryly: "Because the next *muntela* on our list is the village chief of security."

Indeed, it turned out that the third highest-ranking FRELIMO official in the village of Nandimba was among the most respected of "traditional healers" actively practicing.

Mpwapwele informed us that he had begun his career as a *muntela* in 1970—"the year that [the Portuguese general] Kaúlza [de Arriaga] arrived in Cabo Delgado to begin Operation Gordian Knot." When I asked him what healing techniques he knew, he listed them for me, in this order: "antisorcery 'arms,' headache remedies, leg ache remedies, means of treating injured sorcerers, menstrual hemorrhaging remedies, hernia remedies, snake bite remedies, *nshamoko* [a substance ensuring that its user is well liked], urinary tract pain remedies, and poison remedies."

Mpwapwele told us that, after undergoing guerrilla training in 1972, he did not work as a healer until the war ended. He took up his vocation once again in 1975 and had practiced ever since. When he told us that he worked in partnership with Carmelita Milonge, I understood even better why she was unperturbed by his presence during my interview.

"I want sorcery to cease in this village," this village chief of security now told us with conviction. "That is why I often counsel people against its practice."

The word he used—*kulailila*, "counsel"—was the same one Muedans sometimes used to refer to the antisorcery proclamations of preindependence authority figures. I glanced at Marcos to confirm my recognition of this euphemism before asking Mpwapwele, "So you act as settlement heads did in the past?"

"I do," he responded assertively.

Awkwardly, I blurted out the question on my mind: "Do you practice sorcery of construction?" So direct was my question, so strong my language linking this FRELIMO political appointee to sorcery, that I fully expected him to laugh at the suggestion, if not grow angry with me.

The sternness in Mpwapwele's expression as he answered my question, however, seemed directed not at me but instead at prospective sorcerers: "In the settlements of old, our elders used to go out at night to counsel people against the practice of sorcery. They are dead, but we carry on—the same way."

Later, Mpwapwele showed us how he put his wartime training in land mines to good use as village chief of security. He dragged a sack of crushed stones from inside his house and opened it for us to see. These stones, which he told us he had harvested from a secret place in the lowlands, served as the charge in the "antisorcery personnel mines" (*lipande*) that he constructed and laid to protect the settlement against its greatest contemporary security threat: *uwavi*. As I examined Mpwapwele's bomb-making materials, my mind drifted through space and time to guerrilla rear-bases in Tanzania where FRELIMO trainers taught recruits the science of revolutionary socialism. I could scarcely imagine Samora Machel's response to the scene before me.

The encounter left my FRELIMO colleague, Marcos, nonplussed, however. In the following days, he regaled me with stories that betrayed the depths

"Sorcery is a serious problem in our communal villages," we were told by Maurício Mpwapwele Moto, depicted here showing us the materials with which he made antisorcery personnel mines. "Youths today have no respect. You sometimes hear them threatening their elders, saying, 'You better not play around with me! If you do, I'll fix you!'" As we spoke, a group of three teenage boys stood a few feet away, listening to our conversation. Their smiles turned to shameful expressions. "Where there is a lack of respect, there is certainly sorcery," Mpwapwele concluded. "Where there is no fear, you can be certain that people feel secure in what they know."

of the recent "resurgence of tradition" even in the northern FRELIMO stronghold of Cabo Delgado Province. For many, the harbinger of a new era was an *ing'anga* (traveling exorcist) named Ningore, who appeared in the province in the early 1990s. I had heard of Ningore while conducting research for my dissertation between 1993 and 1995, but as he did not operate on the Mueda plateau, I had paid little attention to stories of him. Only now did I come to realize how monumental a presence Ningore constituted in the provincial public consciousness, even in places he never visited.

Ningore traveled widely in Cabo Delgado and quickly gained legendary status for the séances that he held to identify *feitiçeiros* (Portuguese for "sorcerers" or "witches"). Those he accused were forced to ingest medicinal substances that he said would cause them to die if ever they practiced *feitiço* ("sorcery" or "witchcraft") again.[2]

After touring the province, Ningore eventually established semipermanent residence across the bay from Pemba, the provincial capital. People from all over the province, and beyond, traveled by ferryboat to receive his treatments, which generally included cutting a cross over clients' spinal columns or making incisions under their fingernails with a razor blade, a knife, or a *catana* (machete) and inserting medicinal substances into these incisions. Ningore promised that this technique would ensure his clients long life and immunity against *feitiço*.[3]

For his services, Ningore reportedly received payment in money, livestock, and electronic equipment (Membe 1995). As he accumulated riches, provincial officials turned a critical eye upon his practice, but so long as the *ing'anga* enjoyed widespread popularity, he was permitted to continue his work. Support for Ningore waned after a boat filled with his clients capsized in Pemba Bay, drowning dozens of people. Ningore's clients, and the broader public, generally concluded that the healer had used his power to destructive ends, causing the accident himself. Only then did the provincial governor, António Simbine, arrest Ningore, who died in prison soon thereafter.

The "Ningore phenomenon"—as the Mozambican journalist Remígio Membe (1995) dubbed it—was given new life in 1995, however, when a man claiming to be from the village of Namapa, in Nampula Province, appeared in Cabo Delgado "to finish Ningore's work" of eliminating *feitiço*. His followers called him "Pergunta Bem" (Ask Well), but he referred to himself as "Perseguido Sem Motivo" (Hunted/Persecuted without Cause). Asserting that he had learned his methods with the famed Naparama guerrillas, who operated in Zambezia Province and held both government and RENAMO forces at bay late in the Mozambican civil war (K. Wilson 1992), Pergunta Bem promised to purge villages and urban neighborhoods of *feitiço*, house by house. With his many followers beating drums, Pergunta Bem descended upon communities and danced to identify *feiticeiros* within them. His followers beat anyone who resisted him or challenged his judgments. Many of those he accused of *feitiço* were forced by their neighbors to flee their homes and to take up residence elsewhere.

According to Membe, who tracked the traveling exorcist, Pergunta Bem, like Ningore before him, accepted payment in money, animals, and electronic equipment. FRELIMO officials in Pemba remained wary of offending his many supporters and permitted him to carry on without impediment. He left Pemba, according to Membe, only when he chose to, proceeding to the southern part of Cabo Delgado, where he met with hostility in the villages that he visited and, eventually, disappeared.[4]

Although Ningore and Pergunta Bem practiced for only short periods, they heralded changing times in the province—times in which the "resurgence of tradition" would become a celebrated topic of public discussion.

21

Neoliberal Reform and Mozambican Tradition

"Nós queremos que a autoridade tradicional exista."

President Chissano's words reached me via Internet Listserv all the way in Virginia, where I was writing my dissertation. As he addressed the media after meeting with a group of former *régulos* in the province of Niassa in June of 1995, the leader of the party that had two decades previously abolished the chieftaincy now declared: "We want traditional authority to exist" (Mohomed 1995b; see also Mohomed 1995a).

Chissano's statement reflected, and contributed to, a dramatic transformation in Mozambican public discourse on topics that many now glossed as "traditional authority" and "traditional healing." Complex historical forces animated the Mozambican president's words. Since Chissano's accession to power, the Berlin Wall had fallen, the Soviet Union had collapsed, and the Cold War had come to an end. No longer receiving assistance from Eastern bloc allies, FRELIMO had abandoned its socialist identity, adopted austerity measures, and, ultimately, accepted IMF conditions to ensure the flow of Western aid. As apartheid drew its last breaths and the flow of South African military assistance to RENAMO abated, FRELIMO had also consented to the liberalization of Mozambican politics, making possible the cessation of armed hostilities and the transformation of RENAMO into a political party that would contest FRELIMO at the polls rather than in the bush.

In the run-up to the nation's first multiparty elections, RENAMO made issues of "traditional authority" and "traditional healing." Indeed, as RENAMO had spread throughout the country in the previous decade and a half, the insurgency had not only destroyed all vestiges of FRELIMO's program for socialist modernization but also reversed FRELIMO bans on the chieftaincy and the practices of divination, healing, and ancestral supplication. RENAMO policy paid dividends in many regions. Having been embarrassed, abused, and marginalized by the FRELIMO state, healers, spirit mediums, and ex–*autoridades gentílicas* were in many cases disposed to support the anti-state insurgency (Geffray and Pedersen 1988; Geffray 1990; Englund 2002: 69–74). In areas RENAMO came to control during the war, *mambos* were identified and used as intermediaries in the insurgency's administrative hierarchy.[1] Where RENAMO destroyed FRELIMO-constructed health clinics and killed or chased off clinic staff, "traditional healers" were permitted to work unimpeded.

To be sure, the RENAMO-orchestrated "revival of Mozambican tradition" was a complex phenomenon that played out in vastly different ways in various places.[2] As often as not, rather than vesting authority in popularly sanctioned chiefs or ex–*autoridades gentílicas*, RENAMO "recognized" figures who would serve as pliant intermediaries (Alexander 1995: 26–31). RENAMO's wartime relations with traditional authorities and traditional healers nonetheless laid the foundation, in many places, for postwar mobilization of voters over whom these figures exercised influence.[3]

Cognizant of the advantages that good relations with traditional authorities and traditional healers might afford RENAMO in postwar electoral politics, some FRELIMO leaders soon recognized the potential value in cultivating rapport with such figures. President Chissano himself met with groups of ex–*régulos* in several Mozambican provinces in the months leading up to the 1994 elections as part of a FRELIMO party initiative to "charm the *régulos*" (*Notícias* 1995c).[4] Party officials at lower levels made similar overtures in many places; in some cases, they had been doing so for years. Concurrently, FRELIMO officials demonstrated growing awareness of the alienating effects of party policy on traditional healing (E. Green, Jurg, and Djedje 1994: 7; E. Green 1994: 120; Honwana 2002: 175). At the FRELIMO Fifth Party Congress in 1989, the ban on traditional healing was lifted. Thereafter, officials in the Ministry of Health began to speak more openly and sympathetically about, and with, traditional healers (Honwana 2002: 174).[5]

Western donors also played a substantial role in the production of public discourse on traditional authority and traditional healing. Donor interest in these entities was bound up with the neoliberal project of "democratic decentralization." At war's end, the FRELIMO health care system lay in ruins. With austerity measures making the system's full reconstruction inconceivable, donors demonstrated interest in the idea of working in collaboration with traditional healers to hold down costs while reestablishing a health care network that reached into the nation's rural areas.[6] Advocates argued that, even during the heyday of FRELIMO socialism, Mozambicans had continued to consult traditional healers (E. Green, Jurg, and Dgedge 1993: 264; 1994: 7). During the war, they suggested, traditional healers had effectively filled in where the state system had collapsed (Nordstrom 1998), often providing more culturally appropriate treatment for war-related trauma than "modern" health care workers might have (E. Green 1996: 75).

Donors similarly argued that the institutions of traditional authority might be drawn upon to render local government more efficient and more effective in the postsocialist era of structural adjustment. The institutions of traditional authority constituted vehicles through which rural residents could manage their own affairs and resolve their own problems at little or no expense to the state, it was argued. What is more, where the postcolonial state had ceased to collect taxes, these socially embedded institutions might afford the postwar regime a legitimate means to levy a national reconstruction tax (Buur and Kyed 2003).

In 1991, the Ministry of State Administration agreed to host within its walls a Ford Foundation–funded research project (administered by the Africa-America Institute) designed to produce recommendations for legislative and policy reform in relation to the issue of traditional authority. The project was extended in 1995 with funding from the US Agency for International Development (USAID) under the rubric of its Democracy in Mozambique project.[7] Between September 1995 and October 1996, project researchers in the ministry's Administrative Development Center (Núcleo de Desenvolvimento Administrativo, or NDA) toured the country, organizing workshops in eight of the ten provinces (Africa-America Institute 1997; Ministério da Administração Estatal/Núcleo de Desenvolvimento Administrativo 1997). The workshops were designed to facilitate discussion on how traditional authorities might be accurately identified both within their communities and by government officials; on what functions they might serve; and on how their mandate might be made more certain. Researchers prepared a series of five brochures to educate local state officials about the role of traditional authority in Mozambican society.[8]

In parallel with these activities, the European Union provided funding in 1990 for a consultant to advise the Ministry of Health on policy formation and legislative reform in relation to traditional healers (E. Green 1994: 121). The consultant—American medical anthropologist Edward Green—proposed that the government adopt the World Health Organization definition of "traditional medical practitioners"; that it allow these practitioners to form associations; and that it recognize the members of legally constituted associations (E. Green 1994: 124–125). In 1991, with Green's assistance, the ministry's Department for the Study of Traditional Medicine (Gabinete de Estudos de

Medicina Tradicional, or GEMT) "proposed a three-year program to begin public health collaboration between the National Health Service and the indigenous health practitioners of Mozambique" (E. Green, Jurg, and Djedje 1994: 8). USAID subsequently funded field studies undertaken by Green and a team of researchers working in the GEMT to examine existent and potential contributions of traditional healing to the prevention and treatment of sexually transmitted diseases and infant diarrhea (E. Green, Jurg, and Dgedge 1993; Gaspar and Djedje 1994; E. Green, Marrato, and Wilsonne 1995).

Advocates cast these reforms both as practical necessities and as desirable objectives in their own right. In repressing Mozambican tradition, many argued, FRELIMO socialism had stifled democratic participation and thereby quashed the creative and productive capacities of the nation. Postwar freedom and prosperity, they argued, were contingent upon the flourishing of Mozambican "civil society." But what would Mozambican civil society look like in the new democratic era? As a result of historical subjection first to an authoritarian colonial regime, then to a highly centralized socialist state, and, finally, in many places, to RENAMO's military hierarchy, Mozambicans had long experienced strong disincentives to forming spontaneous social institutions (trade unions, religious associations, rural cooperatives, groups organized around expressive and communicative media, and so forth). The forms of Mozambican civil society would thus necessarily differ from those of Europe, Latin America, and other parts of the world.

Some reformers asserted that kinship constituted a historically enduring form of social organization—a local variant of civil society that might carry the load of popular political expression within an emerging modern democracy (cf. de Sousa Santos 2003: 79).[9] Hence, some saw in the kin-based institutions of traditional authority a crucial component to a reinvigorated Mozambican civil society and a thriving Mozambican democracy (Lubkemann 2001: 90–91).

Among them were NDA project researchers, led by Brazilian-born Swedish anthropologist Iraê Baptista Lundin. In their published works, these researchers celebrated the institutions of traditional authority as "a sociocultural affirmation of Africanness" (Lundin 1995: 10). Project publications presented these institutions as enduring traditions—"customs and beliefs practiced from long ago" (Africa-America Institute 1997: 14)—and heralded them as essentially democratic in nature. Lundin wrote that the institutions of traditional authority were subject to the popular restraints of councils of elders, who acted as "electoral college[s]," monitoring the actions of chiefs—sometimes verifying their authority, sometimes holding it in check, and sometimes challenging their legitimacy (Lundin 1995: 27; see also Lundin 1996; Nhan-cale 1996). So clearly legitimate and so clearly democratic were traditional authorities according to Lundin that they did not need to have their author-ity confirmed through state-sponsored multiparty electoral contests, as some proposed, for they adhered to their own internal democratic principles.[10] In-stead, she suggested that the government merely identify these figures and "recognize" them through the issuance of uniforms, as had been done with *régulos* in the colonial period.

Reformers also cast traditional healers as essential to a revitalized Mo-zambican civil society. They were, many emphasized, bearers of distinctive forms of "local knowledge" (or "indigenous knowledge") that might comple-ment other resources within the context of neoliberal development. When I visited the Ministry of Health in Maputo in 1999, a staff member in the GEMT told me: "Traditional healers are the stewards of a Mozambican medical cor-nucopia." In Pemba, in that same year, an officer of the Provincial Directorate of Health told me: "Traditional healers are Mozambique's doctors and Mo-zambique's medical textbooks." In Mueda, the district director of health said: "Traditional healers know cures for diseases that Western medicine cannot heal. They even know cures for diseases that Western medicine has not yet diagnosed."[11]

Even in the early 1980s, the Mozambican Ministry of Health had shown some interest in traditional healing. Paradoxically, while the state expressly prohibited the practice of traditional healing, GEMT researchers gathered data on the medicinal plants used by healers throughout the country.[12] In the mid-1980s, the ministry published a four-volume catalogue of Mozambican medicinal plants and their various uses in the practice of traditional healing (Jansen and Mendes 1983–1984).[13] Green, however, suggested that the GEMT's focus on materia medica obscured more valuable findings, namely, the knowledge healers bore not only of remedies but also of illnesses (E. Green 1994: 44–45).[14] Building upon the traditional-medicine paradigm elaborated by the World Health Organization from the mid-1970s onward (World Health Organization 1978, 1995; Bannerman, Burton, and Wen-Chieh 1983; E. Green 1994: 21), Green argued that the "indigenous knowledge" possessed by Mo-zambican "traditional healers" made their participation in collaborative re-search and health care an invaluable national resource. "A society's creativ-ity and genius is embodied in its IKS [indigenous knowledge systems]," Green wrote. "An understanding of health-related indigenous knowledge is . . . essential for health planners and implementers, if plans and programs are to be culturally appropriate and therefore effective" (E. Green 1994: 21).

Notwithstanding the apparently stark contrast between neoliberal perspectives on Mozambican "tradition" and those of colonial administrators, Catholic missionaries, and revolutionary socialists, reformers nevertheless envisioned the world rather differently than the "traditional" subjects of their advocacy did, as we shall see.

22

Limited Recognition

"How long does one of those blades last?" I asked.

As we conversed, Vantila Shingini was at work "vaccinating" an adult woman.[1] Naked from the waist up, the patient sat quiescently on a reed mat, legs extended, her back to the *muntela*. The razor blade that Vantila held in his hand had an ocher hue—whether from rust or dried blood I could not tell. He carved into her skin with focused attention.

"I buy a new one several times a year," he answered confidently, as if certain that he had assuaged my concerns.

Earlier, he had told me that he "vaccinated" several patients per week. I quickly performed calculations in my head. Assuming that "several" meant half a dozen in both instances, I figured that he used the same blade on as many as fifty people.

Vantila continued his work. He made approximately a dozen pairs of parallel cuts—perhaps a centimeter and a half in length—in a patterned array on the woman's arms, chest, and back. He then turned around to retrieve a small jar containing a black pasty substance. Using the blade like a putty knife, he smeared the substance into the incisions he had made.[2]

"What is it?" I asked, in reference to the substance.

"*Mitela*," he said.

"Yes, I know," I responded. "But what kinds of *mitela*?"

When he had finished with the pair of incisions on which he was working, he paused to give an only slightly more revealing answer. "It is made of various leaves that have been burned and pulverized." He reached for a mortar and pestle that sat on the edge of the mat and used them to mime the method by which he had processed these unspecified substances. "Oh, and this," he added, picking up a disassembled AA battery. Perhaps anticipating

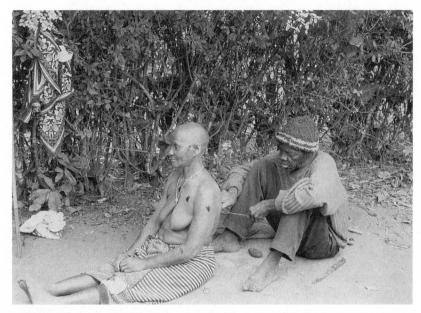

Vantila Shingini, shown vaccinating a patient, treated both what he described as "ordinary illnesses" (headaches, stomachaches, backaches, and leg pains) and sorcery-related illnesses. He treated victims of sorcery as well as those who had wounded themselves in the act. Many of his patients were children, he told us. "Sorcerers sometimes feed small pieces of human flesh to children to make them sorcerers, too. These children are brought to me with stomachaches, but I can tell what the problem is from the way they look at me with wide-open, questioning eyes. Children can be cured by inducing vomiting or diarrhea, but once they are adults, it is too late. Then, you can only try to contain it."

that I would once more ask "What kind?" he volunteered, "It's the kind you use in a radio."[3]

As Vantila Shingini completed the procedure on this woman, two others visited him, making appointments to return later in the day. Some came for treatment of backaches, he told us; others for defense against sorcery. The composition of the *mitela* he used to vaccinate his patients depended upon the nature of their afflictions.

Like his patient, I too sat quiescently, pondering whether or not the AIDS virus or hepatitis could survive exposure to battery acid.

᛫᛫᛫

At first glance, it would appear that the neoliberal era has constituted a moment of complete reversal in the ongoing conversation between rural Mozambicans and their many Others on the issue of "tradition." Where once Muedan Others had asserted themselves as the bearers of transcendent truths—had claimed to fix rural Mozambicans in their gaze and to see their world more clearly than they—Muedan Others now proclaimed a desire to understand rural Mozambican "traditions" of authority and healing and expressed an inclination to find value, even wisdom, in "traditional" institutions, practices, and beliefs.

Not only have government officials begun to speak of "tradition" more openly and more sympathetically, but they have also deliberated legal and institutional reforms that would give formal recognition to traditional institutions. What is more, representatives of domestic and international NGOs working to reconstruct the war-torn Mozambican countryside increasingly have made it their practice to identify and collaborate with "traditional authorities" and "traditional healers" in the implementation of relief and development projects. Along with the Western donors who have funded many of these interventions, NGOs have often considered traditional authorities and traditional healers to be better counterparts than state institutions. Through them, many have suggested, one might more directly get to "the people in need," circumventing still overly centralized state bureaucracies and/or escaping the clutches of increasingly corrupt officials.

Upon closer examination, however, the conversation about tradition conducted between rural Mozambicans and their Others since the early 1990s has proven rather complex. As we shall see, despite their more sympathetic rhetoric, these new Others, like their predecessors, have read Mozambican tradition through the filter of their own logics, "recognizing" traditions that are as much of their own making as of rural Mozambicans'. Notwithstanding reformers' designs, traditional institutions have proven unwieldy vehicles for the rationalization of Mozambican society in accordance with the enlightened and enlightening visions articulated by neoliberal institutions. Ultimately, even many reform-minded state officials, representatives of international donors, and NGO project managers have found *unrecognizable* the Mozambican traditions they sought officially to *recognize.*

In the area of traditional healing, for example, researchers in the GEMT had long taken an interest in the medicinal properties of plants used by Mozambican healers, but due to government policy that declared traditional medical practices to be inseparable from obscurantism (Meneses 2000: 5), they had pursued this line of inquiry to the exclusion of interest in the nonmaterial dimensions of Mozambican healing (Meneses n.d.: 15–16). Like health officials and researchers working elsewhere, GEMT researchers had conceived of traditional healing as the administration of substances whose active ingredients might be isolated, tested, and validated in the scientific laboratory.[4] As we have seen in chapter 21, Edward Green counseled the GEMT to broaden its conceptions of "traditional healing" so as to recognize "traditional healers" as the bearers of distinctive forms of local knowledge. Green himself, however, conceived of indigenous knowledge through a restrictive scientific lens and argued that researchers typically overemphasized the "magical" components to African notions of health and healing (E. Green 1999). Much of African indigenous knowledge of healing, he asserted, had nothing to do with witchcraft and/or sorcery (1994: 139): "indigenous and biomedical etiological models are, in fact, not very different in fundamental and important ways" (1999: 12). Seemingly exotic cultural expressions worked as symbols (or as metaphors); once decoded, these expressions were altogether compatible with biomedical categories and concepts of disease and its treatment (1999: 16, 18, 90). For example, African concepts of "pollution" constituted an "indigenous contagion theory," Green suggested; and the "invisible snake" (which many southern African peoples suggest resides in the body of a healthy person)[5] constituted an "indigenous theory of resistance" to disease (E. Green 1997, 1999).[6] The "indigenous theories" Green *recognized* were, as he happily admitted, strikingly similar to those of the biomedical paradigm that he and other consultants carried with them to places like Mozambique. At the same time, more dissimilar notions, such as witchcraft and/or sorcery, were denied the status of indigenous theories and given diminished, if any, consideration in Green's celebratory portrayals of Mozambican "traditional healing."[7]

Mozambican health officials and researchers in the GEMT took the same line when I conversed with them in the 1990s. When I asked them about divination, sorcery, or spirit possession—practices that rural Mozambicans themselves considered essential to healers' activities—I was often gently reminded that healing was "rooted in" physical substances with medicinal properties.[8] Indeed, topics such as these were rarely raised unless by me. These advocates of traditional healing spoke of healers as "medical textbooks" but insisted upon editing—even censoring—essential passages in these "texts" before recommending them to a wider audience.[9] In so doing, they acted more than they cared to admit like FRELIMO leaders at the Third Party Congress (in 1977) who called for the study of "Traditional Medicine" with the objective of "valorizing its positive aspects" and "eliminating [from it] obscurantist practices" (Jansen and Mendes 1983–1984: 1.6; see also Meneses n.d.).[10]

Nevertheless, after the ban on healing was lifted in 1989, healers practiced more openly throughout the country. On instructions from the provincial level, officials on the Mueda plateau began in 1991 to register healers practicing in the district. Registration procedures were improvised at the local level.

Tellingly, the process was overseen by the Mueda District Directorate of Culture rather than the Directorate of Health.[11] The identity cards issued to healers were the same ones the directorate had long used to register Mueda's famous ebony wood sculptors. In other words, healers were literally credentialed as "artists" who worked in various "media" (as noted on their cards): divining, healing, exorcizing spirits, initiating youths, and so on. The Directorate of Culture continued registering healers through the mid-1990s. When it exhausted its supply of blank artists cards, it began to issue Letters of Credential. The letter that Luís Avalimuka showed us was dated 1996. It declared that he had been a *curandeiro* since 1986 and that, for this reason, he was "officially recognized as a *curandeiro traditional.*" District Director of Culture Sanyula's summary of the registration initiative was revealing of the political dynamics of the undertaking: "The healers with whom we had contact never gave us any trouble."

In the same period, however, government officials in Maputo, the capital, debated the advantages and disadvantages of registering healers. While registration potentially enhanced the government's ability to monitor and assess the practices of registered traditional healers and/or to collaborate with them in the provision of medical services or train them as biomedical paraprofessionals, the Ministry of Health's limited capacity and resources in an era of structural adjustment militated against the realization of such initiatives on a national scale. Edward Green made substantial contributions to the debate, arguing not only that registration was impractical but also that it presented risks. Registering healers entailed the involvement of government in the evaluation of individual healers' legitimacy or, short of this, the implicit legitimation of *all* registered healers and the sanctioning of their varied practices (E. Green 1996: 20).[12] Notwithstanding their celebration of the indigenous knowledge of Mozambican traditional healers, this was a step that even sympathetic reformers were unprepared to take. Even in a democratic Mozambique, many argued, practices that jeopardized the health of clients could not be permitted (Lubkemann 2001: 99). Green himself raised the issue of the dangers presented by nonsterile invasive procedures such as "vaccination" (E. Green, Jurg, and Dgedge 1993: 272–273, 274; E. Green 1994: 144).[13] As a consequence of these reservations, Green advised the government, as mentioned in chapter 21, to facilitate the formation of healers associations, whose members would enjoy the "recognition" so provided, and to leave to these associations the tasks of assessing member credentials and monitoring member activities.

In 1992, with the consent of the government in Maputo, the Mozambican Traditional Medicine Association (Associação da Medicina Traditional de

Moçambique, or AMETRAMO) was formed. With the aid of legal counsel, AMETRAMO drafted bylaws that stated its objectives and the rights and responsibilities of its membership (E. Green 1996: 32). Among AMETRAMO's professed aims were the following:

- Mobilizing, registering, and fostering cooperation among traditional healers throughout Mozambique
- Raising awareness of the preventative and healing potential of the country's medicinal plants
- Taking inventory of the practices and plants used in traditional medicine in Mozambique
- Contributing to individual and community health
- Promoting professional training for its members and others interested in traditional medicine
- Promoting research on the value of traditional medicine in Mozambique
- Protecting patients and the community against false practitioners of traditional medicine and the use of its techniques in ways detrimental to the public
- Collaboration with the national health system in public health initiatives
- Collaboration in community health education
- Aiding doctors in mental health
- Promoting exchanges with international organizations
- Aiding and collaborating with foreign health institutions (AMETRAMO 1998)

Founders of the organization saw it not only as a vehicle for the collective expression of healers' perspectives in the postsocialist environment but also as a vehicle for the enhancement of healers' status in a democratic society (Luedke n.d.). Entrepreneurial figures asserted themselves under the aegis of the organization and spawned a bureaucracy around them to consolidate their legitimacy as self-regulating professionals and to certify "true" healers while excluding "charlatans" (Meneses 2000: 9).

New members were required to fill out a questionnaire. The form evoked the authority of the very state that had permitted the association's formation in order to avoid direct involvement in the oversight of healers. At the top of the form, above the name of the organization, Associação da Medicina Tradicional de Moçambique, appeared the Mozambican state seal and the words "República de Moçambique." Below the space allotted for applicants to affix a passport-style photo of themselves, the form asked applicants to identify themselves by name, national identity number, residence, place and date of birth, parents' names, and marital status. It also asked whether or not they were literate, what level of education (if any) they had, and what religion they "currently practiced." It further asked them what year they "completed training" as a "traditional doctor," whether they had any "other profession beyond medicine," and whether they were training their own students. Finally, it asked them to check off the illnesses that they were able to treat or cure and the practices of which they were capable, from a list that included, in this order, "tuberculosis; skin illnesses; diarrhea; kidneys; *érola* [a term no Mozambican doctor was able to translate for me but which may have been a misspelling of "Ebola"]; heart pains; asthma; vomiting; hemorrhaging; discharges; sexual impotence; evil spirits; *oessessos* [probably a misspelling of "abscesses"]; female sterility; sexually transmitted diseases; *britharziose* [a misspelling of "bilharziasis" (schistosomiasis)]; cholera; mental illness; marital conflicts; bad luck; driving away sorcerers [*feitiçeiros*]; divining; coughs; bronchitis; pneumonia; anemia; and Can you cure AIDS?" The list was immediately followed by a blank line after the words "Other illnesses" and by the questions, "Have you ever traveled outside the country to cure illnesses?" and "Where?"

In time, AMETRAMO generated a fees list for use by members to determine the cost of various treatments.[14] Researchers reported that members used the inflated rates on the list to gouge patients (Pfeiffer 2002).

Healers themselves often fell prey to the burgeoning organization, which in many respects operated as a pyramid scheme as it spread from Maputo to provincial capitals to district seats to rural villages. Ambitious individuals donned the mantle of AMETRAMO authority and collected "dues" from healers who believed them when they asserted that membership in the association was now compulsory by law (Luedke n.d.).

AMETRAMO's expansion into the province of Cabo Delgado was beset with scandal. When I met with the Cabo Delgado president of AMETRAMO, Paulo Niuaia, he told me that his predecessor, a man named Mutocha, had been an "imposter": "He came to Pemba from Nampula and set himself up as a healer. Then, he went to Maputo and convinced the president of AMETRAMO to delegate him as AMETRAMO president in Cabo Delgado. He was given materials to register members, but he kept the dues—55,000 meticais per person—for himself. When he had sold all of the AMETRAMO membership cards that he had been given, he started selling copies of his own business card for as much money as he could get. He was a complete imposter. He didn't even know the basic kinds of cures that all healers know. He just collected money and used it for his own affairs in Nampula."[15] Accounts such as these—betraying corruption and bureaucratic incompetence within the healers' association—caused health care staff working for, and associated with, the National Health System throughout the country to look upon AMETRAMO and its members with deep suspicion, despite increasingly liberal proclivities toward traditional healing (Honwana 2002: 176–178).

AMETRAMO's subsequent arrival on the Mueda plateau was closely monitored by the district government. Mueda AMETRAMO assistant president Terezinha "Mbegweka" António informed us that, in 1998, an AMETRAMO representative from Pemba—a woman she identified only as "Joana"—came to Mueda to organize healers. Joana first met with the district director of culture and other representatives of the district government. She then began to register healers and to issue membership cards. Long after Joana departed Mueda, the district government remained engaged with the association. When Marcos and I first approached Mbegweka to inform her and Mueda AMETRAMO president João Chombo that we wished to conduct interviews with AMETRAMO members on the Mueda plateau, Mbegweka informed us that if we wanted to work with Muedan healers, we should first visit "AMETRAMO's office" in Mueda town. We followed her directions, only to discover ourselves seated at the desk of Mr. Sanyula, district director of culture. When we asked him about AMETRAMO, he showed us the association's registry book, which *he* kept in his drawer. He had little to say about AMETRAMO, except that he was relieved when *they* had taken over responsibility for registering healers in the district. Marcos and I looked at one another in confusion but pushed the issue no further. "There is good cooperation between AMETRAMO and [the Directorate of] Culture," Mbegweka later "explained" to us. Indeed, as we came to appreciate, she and other AMETRAMO members in Mueda looked upon Sanyula as their (un)official patron and derived legitimacy from his disinterested oversight. Mueda AMETRAMO president João Chombo's claim to be the most powerful healer on the Mueda plateau simultaneously derived from his reputed powers in the realm of the invisible *and* from his AMETRAMO title, duly "recognized" by the state.

Mbegweka had greater difficulty portraying good relations between AMETRAMO and the District Directorate of Health. At first, she told us that AMETRAMO members referred cases they could not treat to the district hospital, while the hospital referred cases that it could not resolve to AMETRAMO healers. Once we came to know her well, however, Mbegweka admitted to us that this was not so; hospital staff almost never referred hospital patients to *vakulaula*.[16] She speculated: "They don't really know who among us can cure which ailments, so they can't really recommend any one of us specifically."

More likely, Muedan hospital staff—including Muedans, Mozambicans from other parts of the country, and *cooperantes* of international origin—

knew too well the practices of Muedan traditional healers and had greater difficulty than Edward Green in reconciling them with the biomedical paradigm
in which they had been trained. Living as they did in close proximity to
Muedans and their traditional healers, they knew that *vakulaula* like Vantila
Shingini "vaccinated" people with battery acid as treatment for backaches
and as prophylaxis against sorcery. They also knew the risks this practice
posed for the transmission of infectious disease. Like health care workers and
policymakers elsewhere in the country, they raised eyebrows at AMETRAMO
classification of diseases (on its membership questionnaire) in broad categories such as "skin illnesses" or "coughs," at the equation of biomedical categories such as tuberculosis with "bad luck" and "driving away sorcerers,"
and at inquiries about healers' capacities to cure AIDS.

Whether or not they personally vested confidence in *vakulaula* when
they themselves faced certain kinds of afflictions, as some hospital workers
did, many understood *kulaula* (healing) and biomedicine to be (contra
Green) "different in fundamental and important ways." Where *kulaula* depended upon transcendence of rival visions of the world, it resisted biomedical attempts to suborn it through translation and scientific validation.[17] Its
logics remained *unrecognizable* to those who did not practice it—those who
did not enter into its invisible realm. Where hospital workers did recognize
the fundamentally similar ways in which biomedical and traditional healers
asserted transcendent visions of the world, many also recognized the perils
to their profession of granting such claims equal status. "If traditional healers are so effective," one hospital nurse asked us rhetorically, "why did I have
to be trained in Maputo?"[18]

Proponents of "traditional authority" similarly crafted a purified object of
advocacy. When neoliberal reformers cast traditional authority as an essential component of Mozambican democracy, they glossed variable and complex histories of authority. As we have seen in part 2, the institutions of traditional authority in Mueda were shaped and reshaped time and again in the
cauldron of violent historical events and processes. Precolonial *vanang'olo*
ensured the continuance of their matrilineages by mounting raids on neighbors and selling youths as slaves. Colonial-era *autoridades gentílicas* acted
as intermediaries for a harsh, extractive regime. What is more, these figures
of authority simultaneously exercised power in visible and invisible realms,
"feeding" their subordinates by "eating" their rivals. Subjects' respect for
these elders was inextricably bound up with the fear they inspired.

FRELIMO abolished the authority of chiefs within its liberated zones during the independence war, and elsewhere thereafter. As the NDA researchers
traveled throughout Mozambique in 1995 and 1996, however, the NDA's na-

tional director, Francisco Machava, told ex-*régulos* and other workshop participants: "The Mozambican government committed a grave error when it abolished traditional authority right after independence and, today, recognizing this error, is disposed to the return of traditional power" (*Notícias* 1995b). For all intents and purposes, the gatherings constituted rallies on behalf of former *régulos*. Those traditional authorities invited to attend were encouraged to call for official "recognition" as well as for a mandate similar to that granted *autoridades gentílicas* in the colonial era. After the workshop held in Manica Province, for example, the ex-*régulo* Dandja Viracadjua told reporters: "We want to control taxes as we did in colonial times" (Gauth 1996). Everywhere workshops were held, participants met with approval when they expressed desires to mobilize "lazy populations" to labor as they once had in the colonial era or to discipline those in their communities who committed crimes or demonstrated "disrespect" for authority (Fry 1997: 15).

Demands for restoration of various colonial-era privileges enjoyed by *autoridades gentílicas* were also validated. In the Manica workshop, Machava stated that the NDA was studying the possibility of offering "*régulos*" gratuities for work they performed (*Notícias* 1996h); in subsequent workshops, invitees asserted that they should, in fact, be paid (Gauth 1996). Ex-*régulos* also voiced the need for bicycles—necessary for them (or their appointed messengers) to make rounds in the territories under their jurisdiction.[19] State-issued uniforms and flags, as well as state-sanctioned monopoly rights to symbolic objects, also figured among the demands of NDA workshop participants concerned with demonstrating to their subjects that they represented greater powers, as they had in the colonial era (*Notícias* 1997f).

Most of the "*régulos*" invited to the workshops left with hopes raised that they would soon receive what they had (with official encouragement) asked for (*Notícias* 1995b, 1995d). Many awaited a "green light" in the form of new legislation. Workshop participants in Manica, for example, were quoted by journalists as saying: "We ask the government to renew our authority so that we may better organize society" (*Notícias* 1996c).[20] Others, however, simply took the workshops as a mandate. "*Régulos*" throughout Inhambane Province were reported in October 1996 to have begun exacting tribute from their populations (Chicuque 1996). "*Régulos*" in Niassa, according to a newspaper report, had effectively replaced local state structures in activities ranging from arresting criminals to judging civil and criminal cases. Inhambane provincial governor Francisco João Pateguana told reporters: "I have met with some *régulos* who have asked me to deport to São Tomé [where the Portuguese sent serious offenders in the colonial era] people accused of not paying taxes" (*Notícias* 1996a).

In cases throughout the country, self-sanctioned *régulos*, acting without the consent or knowledge of local officials, bound and beat people accused of criminal or "political" infractions or merely of "indiscipline" (*Notícias* 1995d, 1996a, 1996b, 1997b, 1997c, 1997e). Taking the NDA's final workshop in Inhambane as a license to resume his colonial-era role, the ex-*régulo* Machavela, in Homoine District, began to administer corporal punishment to "reestablish order" among his people; one man nearly died after reportedly being "tortured" at Machavela's instructions (*Notícias* 1997e). When I asked him about this incident during an interview in July 1997, Machavela brandished the NDA workshop handbook and told me that it catalogued his responsibilities—past and future.[21]

Muedans witnessed no such behavior on the part of ex-*régulos*. Ndyankali was the only *régulo* in the southern half of the plateau who survived from the colonial period. Unlike elsewhere in the country, where the dimensions of *regulados* corresponded to precolonial jurisdictions, Muedans did not recognize successors to these offices and considered *régulos* (contra the NDA project) not as the embodiment of "customs and beliefs practiced from long ago" (Africa-America Institute 1997: 14) but instead as the creation of the colonial administration. Muedans viewed as preposterous the idea that power should once more be vested in such figures. As no successors to these authorities had been named, *régulos*, as such, no longer existed in Mueda.[22]

Muedans looked upon *vahumu* and *vanang'olo vene kaja* with deeper ambivalence. In the postcolonial period, *vahumu* had also died without naming successors, even though Muedans considered the institution to be an "authentic Makonde tradition." So essential to the life of the matrilineage was the *nang'olo mwene kaja*, however, that, as we have seen in chapter 17, successors to these figures *had* been named throughout the independence war and the period of FRELIMO socialism. Nonetheless, because the Mueda plateau remained under FRELIMO control throughout the civil war, these figures were not "reinstated" as were their counterparts under RENAMO administration in areas that the insurgency came to control. In the post–civil war period, Muedan *vanang'olo* consequently asserted their authority more tentatively than traditional authorities elsewhere in the country, acting only within the spaces granted them by local government officials.

In any case, in the wake of the reassertion of traditional authority elsewhere in the country, local-level state officials raised valid concerns about empowering individuals whose model of authority derived from the colonial era, when African subjects were recognized to have only limited rights. What is more, many of these same state officials questioned the competence of ex-*autoridades gentílicas* to oversee projects such as the construction and staffing of village-level schools and health posts or to facilitate local cooperation with international NGOs working in their regions—activities with which colonial-era governance provided them no experience. Filipe Sitoe, administrator of Homoine District, in Inhambane Province, shared his concerns with me when I spoke with him in July of 1997: "How will traditional authorities facilitate development in their regions when they cannot read and write? How will they restore order in a world so different from colonial times? How will they combat car thieves armed with AK-47s, hashish smugglers, or even today's surly youths if they are not armed and are not permitted to beat people as they did in colonial times? How will they be respected if they are not feared—if the government behind them is not feared like the Portuguese were? But we do not seek to govern through fear anymore."[23] As Mueda District Administrator Ambrósio Vicente Bulasi might have put it, ex–*autoridades gentílicas* were not prepared to "govern scientifically."

Some FRELIMO leaders in Maputo echoed these concerns. The violent behavior of reemergent traditional authorities—often motivated and/or validated by diviners, witch finders, and/or healers—undermined reformers' claims that these institutions could be rationalized and incorporated into the framework of state governance.[24] Consequently, many doubted whether the reconstitution of traditional authority was compatible with "good governance" and the protection of basic human rights[25] in the new democratic era, just as health officials looked warily upon the idea of collaboration with traditional healers. Despite an increasing official rhetoric of tolerance for rural "tradition" then, the state continued to hold "traditional" authorities at arm's length.

To be sure, party politics also played a role in this. Because claimants to traditional authority in most locales had suffered under FRELIMO rule, and because many had been "reinstated" by RENAMO, RENAMO now enjoyed a competitive advantage over FRELIMO in cultivating such figures as political constituents. Even as FRELIMO leaders became intrigued with the idea of subverting this trend, in more places than not the endeavor presented great risk. Where FRELIMO party cadres had supplanted *autoridades gentílicas*, many advocates of traditional authority (often including former *autoridades gentílicas*) now envisioned the state withdrawing its representatives from the levels of government at which traditional authority was to be restored.[26] Collaborating with traditional authorities thus entailed making concessions that might weaken or completely marginalize FRELIMO's most loyal and most influential cadres at these levels.[27]

In any case, expectations raised by the NDA workshops among claimants to traditional authority went unfulfilled throughout the 1990s. Whereas Alfredo Gamito, minister of state administration, had promised repeatedly in the mid-1990s that President Chissano would soon make a public proclamation defining the new role of traditional authority in postwar Mozambique (*Diário de Moçambique* 1995, 1996; Gauth 1996; Mohomed 1996; *Notícias* 1996d, 1996h), and although Chissano himself stated in 1995 that he "*want[ed]* traditional authority to exist" (Mohomed 1995b), the president was unable to state anytime thereafter that traditional authority *did* exist and that it was empowered to act in a specified way. On the contrary, in December 1996, Prime Minister Pascoal Mocumbi publicly stated that "all those who demand a law on traditional authority are demagogues who only wish to create problems for us" (*Domingo* 1996). Amid rising criticism, the NDA project—originally scheduled to present its findings and recommendations to a national audience in Maputo in April 1997—staged its final conference in obscurity in the relatively inaccessible provincial capital of Inhambane.

Advocates of official recognition of traditional authority suffered another setback when, in 1995, Law 3/94 (passed weeks prior to the 1994 elections) was declared unconstitutional. Law 3/94 had provided for the devolution of responsibility over a variety of governmental functions to "municipalities" to be formed of urban and/or rural districts. The law stated explicitly that municipal governments would "listen to the opinions and suggestions of *traditional authorities* recognized as such by the communities" (my emphasis) even if it left unspecified how such figures would be identified and how their counsel would be given force.[28] A subsequent piece of legislation passed in 1997, Law 2/97, established a framework for the creation of democratically elected local governments, called "autarchies," only in cities and large towns and mandated devolution of key governmental functions to these bodies. Under the new law, democratic process failed to reach into rural areas, where traditional authority was a salient political force (António n.d.; Trindade 2003: 121).

In June 2000, the Council of Ministers issued Decree 15/2000, which mandated government consultation and cooperation with "community authorities" everywhere in relation to a variety of governance issues and activities, including tax collection, voter registration, policing, judicial proceedings, land distribution, oversight of public education and public health, environmental protection, road construction, and other development initiatives (Hanlon 2000; Buur and Kyed 2003). While the decree granted such "community authorities" the right to wear uniforms and to use "symbols of the Republic," it neither stipulated that government was required to heed their counsel[29] nor strictly delineated who they were. Included among "community authorities" were not only "traditional leaders" but also "village or neighborhood secretaries" (FRELIMO government appointees), and "other legitimate leaders" (Hanlon 2000; Buur and Kyed 2003; de Sousa Santos 2003: 83; Meneses et al. 2003: 358). Such leaders, the decree stated, needed to be duly "recognized as such by their respective communities" (Hanlon 2000); the decree did not specify what constituted a "community" nor the mechanism for "recognition" (Buur and Kyed 2003).

The autarchies law (Law 2/97), as well as the community authorities decree (Decree 15/2000), ultimately left it to the discretion of local state officials to craft relationships with the traditional authorities in their jurisdictions in accordance with their governing strategies and agendas. In some areas of the country, especially where RENAMO relations with traditional authorities undermined FRELIMO hegemony, local government officials organized ceremonies of formal recognition for traditional authorities (Buur and Kyed 2003; Institutions for Natural Resource Management n.d.), seemingly in attempts to rob RENAMO of a point of political contention while rendering these figures more beholden to the ruling party.[30] Some even used such duly recognized "community authorities" as tax collectors, granting them a subsidy for their services in accordance with the provisions of the decree (Buur and Kyed 2003).

District-level officials in the Mueda region adopted a different strategy. To preempt claims to traditional authority, administrators organized ceremonies in each village to *recognize* village presidents *as* "community leaders." These village-presidents-turned-community-leaders sustained relations with *vanang'olo vene kaja* and/or councils of elders as they saw fit—as many had been doing for years—but the only "tradition" underlying their authority was that of the postindependence FRELIMO state.[31]

As socialist-era institutions of popular governance (including popular tribunals, popular assemblies, and village-level dynamizing groups) withered with the contracting postsocialist state, district and village officials indeed allowed these *vanang'olo* to (re)assert themselves in spaces the state no longer occupied. From time to time, authority exercised by village elders yielded problematic effects, namely, sorcery accusations and trials, followed by the meting out of violent punishment, such as that suffered by Sefu Assani Kuva in the village of Kilimani (see the prologue). Despite the fact that district officials sometimes "decoded" such incidents as the playing out of "family tensions" or "village politics" in a symbolic register, they often insisted that profound differences existed between the logics of traditional authority and, as Ambrósio Vicente Bulasi called it, "scientific governance." They—not traditional authorities—were the protectors of democracy and human rights (contra Lundin).

While local officials on the Mueda plateau could ill-afford to manifest disdain for the tradition of "traditional authority" in the new democratic Mozambique, neither could they fully and unqualifiedly *recognize* the authority of "traditional authorities" within their jurisdictions. To do so, they generally realized, not only would be to jeopardize completely the "rule of law"—and with it the rule of FRELIMO—in the world of everyday politics but also would be to throw into question among their constituents their own abilities to "move beyond" all others, to hold their subjects in their gaze, and to (re)make the world they governed in accordance with their visions.

23

Transcending Traditions

"Recently, I have been possessed by spirits that come to me from Tanzania," Mbegweka told us. "They live in caves there, in a region filled with wild animals. It is a very dangerous place."[1]

Marcos and I were passing the night with Mbegweka in her compound as she presided over a healing ceremony for a woman having difficulties nursing her newborn child. The woman's breasts were greatly engorged—each one nearly as big as her head. When her child suckled, she had reported to Mbegweka, her breasts did not let down milk. She had lost her previous child because she was unable to nurse it; she feared that she would lose this one as well.

Mbegweka continued to speak of the distant caves whence her healing spirits came. "Lots of Tanzanian healers go there to consult these spirits, but I have been fortunate; they come to me, here." She paused, as if allowing her mind to travel over the landscape. "I am waiting to be authorized to go there myself some day soon. I am waiting for the healers there to tell me that the spirits have authorized my visit."

On the preceding day, Mbegweka had asked Marcos and me to take her nephew with us as we traveled outside the town of Mueda to conduct interviews. According to her instructions, we had dropped the youngster along the way, in the village of Mpeme, and fetched him on the return trip. By that time, he had organized a small troupe. They carried with them several drums, which they would play for Mbegweka's healing rite. When we arrived in her compound late the following afternoon, we encountered the place transformed. From a pole driven into the ground in the center of the yard flew a flag adorned with a red crescent and a star above Arabic script. Two fires burned at the edge of the yard, around which young men heated drum skins.

Once darkness settled, the drumming began. The ritual more closely re-sembled the healing practices of Ngoma (Janzen 1992; van Dijk, Reis, and Spierenburg 2000) or Zār (Boddy 1989: 125–165) healers than the methods of other Makonde healers with whom we had worked. Mbegweka led the pa-tient out of the small closed pavilion in which she kept her *mitela* and seated her at the base of the flagpole. She then came to greet us, explaining that they would dance tonight to help the woman receive the spirit that afflicted her. Once the woman had learned how to host her *jini*, Mbegweka told us, she would be able to nurse her child. When Mbegweka stepped away, Marcos leaned close to me and said, simply, "*majini*" (pl.). Like me, he was struck by Mbegweka's use of the term—prevalent among the Swahili populations of the Tanzanian coast but foreign to Mozambican Makonde.[2]

Mbegweka next led a dozen women out of her house. As they seated them-selves in a circle around the pole, Mbegweka stepped close to us to continue her quiet narration of the proceedings over which she officiated. These women, she explained, were also patients under her care, each one learning to work with the *jini* spirit that possessed her.

Mbegweka took her place in the circle as the women began to sway with the rhythm of the drums. The tempo steadily increased until the women's up-per bodies thrashed forcefully, to and fro. In time, the women rose and be-gan circling the pole. The drums beat out a frantic tempo as the women raced around the flag. When they slowed—as they did from time to time—two or three of the women would begin grunting and snorting, eventually falling on the ground in a hysteria between laughter and sobbing. They were summon-ing their "Arab spirits," Mbegweka now told us, asking if we did not recog-nize them by the cutlasses the women brandished.[3] Indeed, the women men-aced one another—as well as onlookers—with *catanas*.

Deeper into the night, the rhythm of the drums noticeably changed. Mbegweka passed by to tell us that the women were now summoning their "Makonde spirits." As she spoke with us, one of the women lunged from the circle toward a fire burning at the side of the yard, sending the drummers who huddled around it reeling and scattering bright orange coals. She was pulled away but left lying prostrate on the cold ground, weeping, for more than a quarter of an hour, after which she arose and slowly approached the fire once more. The assembly—with onlookers numbering more than fifty people—closed around her as she stepped on the hot coals, extinguishing them one by one with her bare feet.

As I observed the scene before me, I worried that my amazement might somehow, invisibly, disrupt this enactment of "tradition" which those around me considered ordinary, even routine. I consciously averted my gaze from fellow onlookers for as long as I was able before quickly glancing out of the corners of my eyes at those around me. To my surprise, they appeared more astonished than me. Conversing with them later, I discovered that many were most amazed by the "Arab spirits" that possessed Mbegweka's group of women.[4] As I observed the women possessed by Arab *majini*, my mind's eye wandered over the plateau landscape, crossed the Rovuma, and settled somewhere in an ill-defined, dangerous, cave-filled region of Tanzania to which I had never been but from which Mbegweka told us her *majini* came. In the midst of Mbegweka's compound, I soon learned, Muedans too experienced a foreign land, both enchanted and frightening, filled with powerful spirits from places that most had never seen and that many had never heard of.[5]

Mbegweka later told us that she was first possessed by the spirits of her own ancestors but that, eventually, she came to be possessed by spirits that her patients—and even she—considered exotic.[6] As it turns out, soon after she began to treat her own patients, Mbegweka embraced Islam—a religion strange to most Muedans, who know of it only from their travels to the Cabo Delgado coast (whose Mwani and Makua populations are predominantly Muslim) or to Tanzania (whose Makonde people are mostly Muslim). Mbegweka took the Muslim name Atija and began study in an Islamic school to learn to read.[7]

Whereas advocates of traditional healing began to sing the praises of "indigenous knowledge" in the dawning neoliberal era, Mbegweka and other Muedan healers challenged the notions of tradition, locality, and indigeneity in myriad ways. The healing practices of many *vakulaula* with whom we worked were dependent upon the remaking of Makonde "tradition" and the transgression of geographical and cosmological borders by which "tradition" might be defined.[8]

Asala Kipande boasted an "international practice."[9] He proudly told us when we met with him that he had traveled to Tanzania the previous year and, while there, joined a Tanzanian association of healers.[10] What is more, Kipande was learning to read and write so that he might be able to "interpret" the Koran to his patients. Among the predominantly Christian Makonde of Mozambique, Islam is both exotic and modish. "Most *vakulaula* are not Muslim," Kipande told us, "but there is a growing tendency these days for *vakulaula* to become Muslim."

Of course, even celebrants of "indigenous knowledge" proclaim that "traditional healing" manifests a historical dynamism (E. Green 1999: 29). Such aphorisms as "tradition is dynamic," however, fail altogether to convey the innumerable ways in which these practitioners perpetually and profoundly remake the institutions and practices of healing even as they reproduce them.

Mbegweka expected us to spend at least part of the day with her when we were in the town of Mueda and to report to her when we had safely returned to Mueda after a journey. Her great self-assurance allowed her gracefully to compete with rival healers for our attentions. At the end of our research stint in 1999, to show her our gratitude for the warm reception she always afforded us, we purchased a goat to be slaughtered for a feast in her compound. She invited fellow AMETRAMO members, as well as her patients. By hosting the event, Mbegweka consolidated her already-considerable prestige in the world of Muedan healing.

Whereas sorcerers are "always studying to improve their techniques, to advance their *science,*" as the *humu* Mandia told us, *vakulaula* with whom we worked sought to assure their clients that they were improving and advancing even *further beyond.* Generally, the *vakulaula* Muedans recognized as most powerful were precisely those known for their innovation.[11]

Consider Júlia Nkataje, of Namande. When Marcos and I first entered her compound, Júlia invited us to share with her the shade beneath an open-air zinc-roofed pavilion. As we spoke with her, she sat with her back against one of the wooden poles holding up the roof. She rested a primary school exercise notebook on her lap. With great deliberation, she used a blue ballpoint pen to draw what looked to me like curlicues on each line of a strip of paper torn from one of the notebook's pages. As we conversed, she focused her

eyes on her drawing, never looking at us. I wondered if she doodled to alle-
viate anxiety produced by our visit, but I quickly learned otherwise.

In response to our questions, Júlia told us that her healing career began
with her own illness soon after independence. She suffered from headaches
for more than three years. During that time, she told us, her body was always
hot. Eventually, a healer named Lapiki Madigida, in the village of Miteda, dis-
cerned that Júlia's illness was due to sorcery. He did not reveal to her the
identity of her attacker but cured her nonetheless. Once she was healed, she
told us, she heard voices telling her to get a pen and paper.

"The voices told me to draw these figures," she said, holding up a strip
of paper. "They told me to put these writings in a pot of water and to boil
them. Then, they told me to give the water to my mother to drink. She suffered from leg pains at the time, and the water cured her."

Thus began Júlia's career as an *nkulaula*. As she demonstrated for us
later in the day, she replicated the process she first used years ago to heal her
mother. Patients came to her suffering from sore throats and headaches, from
gonorrhea and HIV, from impotence and infertility. They sometimes suffered
"God's illnesses," and they were sometimes the victims of sorcery. No matter, Júlia told us, she healed them all the same. Whatever the affliction, she
prescribed three glasses per day.[12]

Later in the day, as she took out a recycled five-liter British Petroleum motor oil jug and poured water—prepared earlier—into cups for her patients to
drink, I asked Júlia what she wrote on the strips of paper. "*Sibila*," she told
me. I wondered if she took the term from the Portuguese "*sílaba*," meaning
"syllable." In any case, I associated her technique with accounts I had read
of healers who used the pages of sacred texts like the Bible or the Koran in
healing rites.[13] I later learned that Lapiki—the man who healed Júlia—was
Muslim, and that he sometimes tore pages from the Koran, rolled them up,
and placed them in a bottle that he gave to patients afflicted with mental illness. Lapiki, Júlia told us, could not read the Koran. Júlia was herself illiter-
ate; what is more, she was not a Muslim. Still, Júlia's marks—written on the
page from left to right, from top to bottom—looked vaguely like Arabic script.
I asked her about this.

"It's not the Koran that I write," she told me.

"What is it then?" I asked. "Does it have meaning?"

"Yes," she answered, confidently. Then she smiled, adding, "But *I* don't
know what it means."

As she summoned the patients assembled in the compound to approach,
she told us that she was, in fact, a Christian. "The Virgin Mary has appeared
to me four times," she said, in confirmation of this.

Júlia Nkataje informed us that she was told in her dreams each night where to go to collect the water in which she boiled her healing scripts.

The patients now lined up at the edge of the pavilion. As there were four glasses, the patients were treated in groups of four. They kneeled in front of the glasses and picked them up. As they drank, together, they made the sign of the cross over their hearts.

It seemed to me absurd to categorize Júlia as a "traditional healer" in the Muedan context, for she used no *mitela*. I wondered, even, by what criteria Muedans determined that she was a legitimate *nkulaula* and not a charlatan, for her healing practices differed greatly from those of all other *vakulaula* whom we encountered.[14] I asked Júlia if her work had ever been criticized by anyone, including the government. She informed me that long before the local government started registering healers, she asked for documents to legitimate her practice. "The district administrator responded by send[ing] word to the village authorities to protect me," she assured us.

Ironically, Júlia's was, perhaps, the most frequented healing practice on the plateau. Her compound was a far busier place than the market in the center of her village. Within the boundaries of the bamboo fence that delimited her property, more than a dozen people rested in scattered patches of shade, while almost twice as many attended to tasks around a large house under construction. All of these people were patients, we were told. Some were "in-patients" who resided for days, weeks, or even months at a time in the eighteen-bed dormitory adjacent to her house. Others came to see her by day and returned home at night. Those who were able labored for her in exchange for the care she provided. They would soon finish the second dormitory, she told us, pointing to the house under construction.[15] Once Marcos had surveyed Júlia's establishment, he gleefully pronounced it "a healing factory."

Just as Muedan healers like Asala Kipande, Mbegweka, and Júlia Nkataje drew power from the geographical and cosmological borderlands that separated them from and connected them to their Others (rendering specious the idea that their practices could accurately be described as "indigenous" or "local"), they also challenged the idea that their practices were "traditional," not only in the sense of "handed down from generation to generation . . . from time immemorial" (World Health Organization 1978: 8) but also in the sense of "antimodern." Many *vakulaula* with whom we spent time drew power from working on the edges of the "official" world of medical "science" as they understood it, and they sought legitimation to secure the safety of their practices vis-à-vis authorities. Many cultivated relations with the state and with official health care institutions in accordance with their convictions that such relations enhanced their credibility with their clientele (E. Green 1996: 24) and/or augmented their skills as healers. Healers often displayed their government-issued documents for clients to see, just as medical doctors hang framed diplomas on the walls of their treatment rooms.

Some *vakulaula* studied and replicated practices they witnessed in official health care settings.[16] When I asked Luís Avalimuka to tell us about recent cases that he had successfully treated, he ducked inside his house and reemerged with a school student's notebook. He put it on the table in front of us, the back cover facing up with the print upside down. He opened the notebook, revealing a list of names. It was his "patients' register," he told us.[17] The first entry was dated 18 August 1991. He had begun keeping the register, he informed us, when he was instructed to do so in a dream. He turned the pages. The entries were numbered up to 230, although several dozen unnumbered entries appeared at the end. He pointed out columns that indicated follow-up treatments and reports from patients on treatment success or lack thereof. I counted 54 successful treatments among the first 230 entries— a decent rate of success, I thought, when adjusted for "patient noncompliance" with treatment and for survey nonresponse.

Asala Kipande also fashioned himself as a "traditional healer" who practiced "modern medicine." Kipande specialized in treating illnesses related to sexuality. He told us that many of his patients were men suffering from impotence. The most common problem he saw was that of men who had had sex with prostitutes. He explained: "When menstrual blood gets inside a man's penis, it causes impotence. Normally, this doesn't happen. Most women have shame; they do not have sexual relations with their husbands when they are menstruating. The trouble is that prostitutes have no shame. They are concerned only with money, so they will have relations with a man while they are menstruating. And that can make the man impotent. We say of such a man that he cannot climb the *njala* tree!"

Kipande also treated female patients suffering from what he called "blockage of the vaginal canal." He was proudest, however, of his ability to treat the diseases that he had heard his "colleagues at the hospital" refer to as "sexually transmitted diseases": syphilis, gonorrhea, and AIDS.[18]

When the topic of sexually transmitted diseases arose in a conversation we had with him one day in his compound, Kipande stepped inside the small covered pavilion that he used for healing and reemerged with a shoebox. He opened it and pulled out a strand of JeitO condoms, the brand then being distributed throughout rural Mozambique by an NGO concerned with HIV education and prevention (Agha, Karlyn, and Meekers 2001; Karlyn 2001). Kipande said, matter-of-factly, "I give my patients one of these to use."

More importantly—as if in fulfillment of the prophesies sometimes made by advocates of indigenous knowledge—Kipande told us that he knew how to cure AIDS. He explained that he knew of a small tuber essential to the cure. Between the thumb and first finger of his left hand he squeezed the pinky finger of his right hand at its first joint to show us the size of the tuber. "When you boil it, a red juice comes out," he told us. "You put that juice in a bottle and shake it well every day. People with AIDS should drink some of that juice each day. They will begin to urinate a lot—red foamy urine. AIDS passes out of them with that urine."

In my best attempt to emulate an ethnobotanist, I asked Kipande if he could supply me with a specimen of the root. He told us that he could not reveal his secret, but he assured us that his cure was effective.[19] He had already healed three people afflicted with AIDS, he assured us. "One woman from Ndonde had tested positive for AIDS before coming to see me," he said. "After my treatment, she was tested again, and this time the test was negative."[20]

Among the other procedures Kipande performed were "vaccinations." His technique was almost identical to that of Vantila Shingini, as described in chapter 22. Just before I left Mueda at the end of my research stint in 1999, Kipande asked me for two items: razor blades and latex gloves. When I asked him why he needed these things, he told me that he feared contaminating his

patients by using the same blades again and again, and that he feared contracting diseases in the course of his work by getting his patients' blood on
his hands. Kipande had been "reached" by public health educators.[21]

I knew, however, that inexpensive razor blades were available in the marketplace. If he could not afford to buy enough of them to use a new one on
each patient, he might have easily required each patient who came to him for
"vaccination" to bring his or her own razor blade; Marcos, I knew, did this
when he was "vaccinated."[22] In time, it became apparent to me that Kipande
wanted better-quality razor blades than he could buy in the local market.
Such quality "instruments" would set him apart from his *vakulaula* competitors. Similarly, latex gloves were a component of a more official "uniform" that would enhance Kipande's credibility with potential clients.[23] Already one of the most respected and feared *vakulaula* in Mueda, Kipande
wished to consolidate his practice by upgrading his professional identity to
"traditional *doctor.*" Doctors, both he and his patients knew, wore gloves.[24]

Like Mbegweka, Asala Kipande was an officer in the Mueda chapter of
AMETRAMO. Like Luís Avalimuka and Júlia Nkataje, Asala Kipande and
Mbegweka were among the plateau's most widely respected and commer-
cially successful traditional healers. None of these *vakulaula* sat idly by
awaiting researchers from the Ministry of Health or elsewhere to validate
their knowledge and to harvest their medicinal substances and techniques
into the stores of medical science. Rather, they scoured their world at its margins in their attempts to expand their own knowledge, demonstrating dis-
regard for the boundaries that others placed around "traditional healing" and
"modern medicine" alike. Indeed, their power as healers depended upon
their transgressions of these boundaries. Through their transgressions, these
vakulaula redrew the boundaries that divided local from global, traditional
from modern, indigenous from exotic, and sorcery from science, situating
themselves as gatekeepers between a world known to their clients—and
their competitors (including biomedical practitioners and health officials)—
and an unknown world that lay beyond. As they drew power from mediating
these interstices of their own invention, they asserted their abilities to transcend (*kupilikula*) even those reformers who, through liberalizing patronage
and patronizing liberalism, sought to remake them as "traditional healers."[25]

24

Uncertain Knowledge

The night fire danced over our faces like a gurgling stream. From time to time, Felista, on my right, registered short complaints about how long Tissa was taking inside the healer's pavilion. When I made comments about the interviews that the three of us had conducted earlier in the day or about the agenda for the next day's work, in lieu of words Felista merely drew audible little gasps of air, as she often did when bored or annoyed. She had no right to be annoyed with Tissa, I thought, for even if this visit to the *nkulaula* was for the purpose of attending to Tissa's health rather than our research, she, like me, had agreed to come along for lack of anything else to do in Matambalale between eating the evening meal and going to sleep.

On my left sat Eusébio. Later, once we had left the healer's compound, a reanimated Felista would ask Tissa and me with astonishment and revulsion: "Did you see his face?!" Placing her hand halfway between her nose and her right ear, she exclaimed: "His mouth was all the way over here!" Such facial distortion, I had often been told, was the effect of illness caused by sorcery.[1] Rather than admitting to Felista that I had not noticed Eusébio's symptom, I answered her question with an audible little gasp of my own. Eusébio had given me other things to think about.

As we had huddled around the fire, Felista's silence had a chilling effect upon Eusébio. He sat slumped and silent. When Felista rose and stepped away from the fire for a moment, Eusébio sat up. A sense of urgency hung about him. He emerged from the darkness as he leaned closer to me. He hesitated. He seemed profoundly confused. His breath reeked of *lipa* (cashew liquor). Finally, he looked me in the eye. For a moment, he seemed to gain clarity of mind.

"Andiliki," he said, and then, in Portuguese, "I have a question to ask you."

Eusébio Matias Mandumbwe was Marcos's "brother" (Eusébio's father, Matias, and Marcos's father, Agostinho, were each sons of Mandumbwe). Wherever we traveled on the Mueda plateau in the conduct of our research, Eusébio was there. We found him awaiting us in the town of Mueda, where many of the more successful members of his family lived. We found him also in Matambalale, where some of his father's family resided, and in Namande, where his maternal grandmother lived. Eusébio, however, could show up anywhere. As we sought out *vakulaula* in villages all over the plateau, we might come upon Eusébio in any of their compounds. I sometimes wondered if it was the healers whom Eusébio had come to see, or me. He seemed to know where we would be even before I did, and to get there ahead of us despite the fact that we had a vehicle at our disposal and he did not—a disparity to which Eusébio often drew my attention.

Marcos did his best to deny Eusébio access to me. Like most of Eusébio's "friends" and family members, Marcos described Eusébio as "a man without a program." If Eusébio had any "program," when he was around Marcos and me it generally involved asking Marcos to ask me for something—whether an article from my field research gear, a ride from one place to another, or a few meticais with which to buy *lipa.* Considering him an embarrassment, Marcos sometimes shooed Eusébio away with the word generally used to chase a dog or a duck from the cooking area: "*Suca!*"

Even Marcos recognized, however, that Eusébio was a deeply troubled young man. Eusébio once described his physical maladies to me using a medical vocabulary that included "seizures" and "insomnia." I wondered if he had sought treatment in a hospital at some point, perhaps in Pemba or in Nampula. He had, we knew, sought treatment from a multitude of Muedan healers, many of whom interpreted his illness as the work of troubling spirits. In any case, Eusébio was an incorrigible patient. *Vakulaula* everywhere told him that he must abstain from drinking alcohol and smoking *suruma* (cannabis) while under their care, but Eusébio invariably wandered from his healers' compounds only to return drunk or stoned.

Such was Eusébio's state when he posed his question to me in the moment of opportunity afforded him by Felista's absence from the warming fire in the healer's compound. He placed his hand on my shoulder and let loose his first word.

"Russian," he said.

His head bobbed slightly as he paused to allow me to appreciate the weight of what he was to ask me. He then continued, slowly measuring his words.

"Is it a science?" he asked, his voice hanging suspended for a moment. "Or is it a drug?"

ılı

The medical anthropologist Byron Good (1994: 15–17) has argued—following Needham (1972) and Smith (1977)—that Western science displays unfounded arrogance in its assumption that "we" (scientific thinkers) *know*, while "they" (unscientific thinkers) only *believe*. From the scientific perspective, he tells us, "[k]nowledge requires both certitude and correctness; belief implies uncertainty, error or both."[2] Good warns that the concept of belief, so easily attributed to others, is a distinctively Western one that has come to connote conviction to a given idea or principle within the modern context of, and despite, uncertainty.

Good argues that people who understand their world in terms of sorcerers and spirits do not "believe in" these entities but instead "know" them to be real and true. In certain ethnographic contexts, "[a]ny sensible person believes in their existence; that isn't even a meaningful question" (Good 1994: 15). Jean-Pierre Olivier de Sardan has come to the same conclusion with reference to the "banal" categories of sorcery, spirits, trance states, and magic charms in contemporary Africa: "[they] are all familiar concepts in regard to which 'disbelief is suspended,' and *which need no justification*. There is no question of believing or not believing: it is not a case of belief, but of fact, not of the fantastic but of the routine" (1992: 11).

In accordance with this line of argument, increasing numbers of anthropologists have chosen, over the past decade, to describe such discursive formations not as "belief" but rather as "knowledge" (e.g., Lambek 1993; Humphrey and Onon 1996; Stephen 1996; Kapferer 1997). Beyond this, many have argued that Western science has much to gain by recognizing the value of other forms of knowledge such as these. Ethnobotanist Mark Plotkin comments: "Western medicine does *not* have all the answers—where is the cure for the common cold or for AIDS?" (1993: 237). In his view, shamans and witch doctors scattered around the globe constitute libraries of "accumulated human wisdom" (236) about "a world that, for the Western scientist, is not supposed to exist" (266).[3]

Most Muedan *vakulaula* with whom we worked, as well as those they treated, would have agreed that they—like their biomedical "colleagues" (to use Asala Kipande's phrase)—were the bearers of *knowledge* rather than mere *believers*. Indeed, most Muedans generally considered *kulaula* to be a matter of *knowledge.* When Muedans spoke euphemistically of sorcerers, they said, "*andimanya shinu shoeshoe*" ("he/she *knows* a little something"). To engage with the hidden powers shaping their world, Muedan diviners, healers, mediums, exorcists, and masters of preventative and protective rites also had to "*know* a little something."[4]

Muedans' knowledge of the world of sorcery and countersorcery healing was, however, saturated with ambivalence, ambiguity, and doubt. Where reformers and development practitioners have sought to cast what Muedans and their *vamitela* know as a corpus of indigenous knowledge to be gathered, tested, and incorporated into the universal body of scientific knowledge, Muedans have sustained among them a body of knowledge about *uwavi* and its treatment that resists scientific rationalization and bureaucratic instrumentalization—a body of knowledge that proves unwieldy even in the hands of Muedan *vamitela* themselves.

In conversations that I attended, Muedans often pondered the relationship between sorcery and science (putting their own twists on what Walter Mignolo has termed "border thinking" [2000]), at times concluding that these categories were diametrically opposed and at times concluding that they were one and the same.[5] On a variety of occasions, the hapless Eusébio Matias Mandumbwe shared profound reflections with me on this topic.

We sat together one day beneath the eaves of a relative's house. Marcos and I had seen Eusébio the previous night in Mbegweka's compound. He had wandered into the circle of Arab-spirit-possessed, *catana*-wielding dancers in a mild stupor. He had mimicked these mediums, moving with them and dancing their steps, if somewhat incompetently. From time to time, like the dancers receiving spirits, Eusébio collapsed on the ground. He took care, however, always to collapse on the reed mat near the flagpole—upon which the evening's principal patient also sat—so as to avoid soiling his clothes. Whereas his dancing among the women raised eyebrows, his contrived collapses produced howls of laughter from onlookers. "That *jini* is afraid of the dirt," one bystander had said to me through peals of laughter. When we had left that evening, Eusébio had quickly lifted himself up off the ground and out of his "possessed" state and asked, politely, if I could give him a cigarette.

Marcos had laughed raucously at Eusébio that evening, but in the morning, he berated his brother for his embarrassing behavior. "How will you ever overcome this illness if you don't do what Mbegweka tells you!" he scolded. "You know that you aren't allowed to drink while you're being treated. It messes everything up!"

Eusébio sat motionless, speechless.

"If you're going to break the healer's rules and drink *lipa,* at least stay away from her compound while you're still drunk!"

As soon as Marcos stepped away, Eusébio turned to me.

"Can you give me a lift to Pemba when you go?" he asked.

I was astonished at how quickly Eusébio recovered from Marcos's tongue-lashing. "Pemba?" I asked. "What do you want to do in Pemba?"

"João Chombo and I have plans there."

"What kind of plans?" I asked, doubtful that João Chombo, the president of Mueda AMETRAMO, would involve himself in any enterprise with Eusébio.

Eusébio looked to make sure that no one was listening: "We're going to buy a vehicle."

I knew that Eusébio depended upon the goodwill of others to keep himself clothed and fed. I knew that he had no money at all, let alone enough with which to buy a vehicle. "What do you plan to do with a vehicle?" I asked him.

He grew confident. "There are all kinds of things that you can do to make money if you have transportation. There's fish at Lake Ng'uri that you can sell on the plateau. There are cashew nuts from the plateau that you can sell at the coast. There's lumber. There's tourism."

What Eusébio envisioned was not at all uncommon among young men in northern Cabo Delgado. All around them, they saw economic activity: things moving to and fro, money being made. Those who succeeded in commerce were rich. And they all had "transport." That was the key, Eusébio had decided.

"Mozambique is filled with riches," Eusébio assured me. "If you have transport, there is money to be made."

I thought of the many conversations that I had had with Joseph Amissy, a Burundian consultant working for a French NGO in Pemba that tried to assist aspiring entrepreneurs in planning small-business ventures. "The downfall of nearly every failed business in this province is the obsession with vehicles," Amissy once told me. "Most good business ideas go bad the moment people try to put a vehicle into the budget. The trouble is, for many people, having a vehicle is the reason for doing business!"

I now told Eusébio what Joseph had told me: "Vehicles don't make money. Not here. Not on these roads. It costs a fortune just to keep a vehicle running. The cost of fuel is too high. The cost of maintenance is too high. Vehicles don't make money, Eusébio. Vehicles eat money."

He looked at me as if I were testing him. He decided to test me in return: "Why, then, do all the big bosses have them?"

"They were rich and powerful before they got vehicles. Lots of these guys use their political ties and influence to get vehicles. Lots of them never pay the true cost of a vehicle, or of its maintenance. One thing's for certain, vehicles didn't make them rich."

"But they make money with them," Eusébio insisted.

"I don't think they do," I responded. "They move a lot of things around. And a lot of money passes through their hands. But even the big bosses seem to have trouble keeping their vehicles on the road. Look around you. These guys leave carcasses everywhere."

We sat quietly for several minutes.

Finally, Eusébio said, "I have ideas in my head." His gaze remained fixed on the ground. After a few moments, he added, "But how do you turn ideas into inventions?"

He spoke with the same mixture of hope and frustration as he had several years earlier when he asked me if Russian was a science or a drug. I suddenly understood the question he had posed that night. During his formative years, Eusébio had lived in a world where Soviet and Eastern European technicians served as stewards of the Mozambican project of socialist modernization. In Mozambican public discourse, "African tradition" was unfavorably compared with Soviet-style "scientific socialism." Then, only a few years before my arrival, the Russians (and Cubans and Romanians and North Koreans, etc.) who advised Mozambicans in hospitals, in factories, and on state farms had been replaced by aid workers from countries such as Norway, Italy, Japan, and the United States. These newcomers espoused a new "science" called "development" (to use these terms as Eusébio and other Muedans did), condemning their predecessors for their mismanagement, their inefficiency, and their ignorance—undoing (*kupilikula*) socialism with their transcendent neoliberal vision of the world. In many regards, "development" and "socialist modernization" looked much the same to Muedans like Eusébio: big projects, big machines, big budgets, and big bosses.[6] So, was this new "science" any different? Had the Russians truly been the bearers of "science," or when seen from the perspective of a "superior" American "science," were they, too, a "backward" people? Did Russian knowledge and power more closely approximate the sorcerer's and/or the countersorcerer's knowledge—based, as this knowledge was, in "drugs" (*mitela*)? Or were all of these forms of knowledge and power essentially the same? Eusébio remained uncertain.

In his classic essay "African Traditional Thought and Western Science," Robin Horton ([1967] 1970) suggests that witchcraft beliefs serve Africans in some of the same ways as science serves Westerners. Witchcraft, he asserts, constitutes an explanatory paradigm through which the unknown is "modeled," events are placed in broad causal contexts, and complex and disorderly phenomena are simplified and ordered.[7] Building upon Horton's ideas, one *might* conclude not only that Muedans modeled the unknowns of their world through *uwavi* discourse but also that the power they attributed to sorcerers and countersorcerers was nothing other than the ability to fashion reality from their models—to use Eusébio's words, to transform their ideas into inventions.

Muedans themselves remained undecided, however, as to whether or not sorcery and science operated in the same way, whether or not these visions of the world were equally powerful, and whether or not their power was productive in the same ways. Muedans turning to *vakulaula* to aid them against illness and misfortune asked themselves, endlessly, what manner of knowledge these *vakulaula* possessed, and how such knowledge stacked up to other forms of knowledge circulating in their world.[8]

In the village of Matambalale, Mariano Makwava once told me: "You Americans have your science. You have your *uwavi*. You know how to make airplanes and other incredible things. We Makonde know how to make airplanes, too—ones that don't even need water and gasoline [Makwava refers here to planes made by sorcerers and used to carry out sorcery attacks].[9] But we have to figure out how to use these things to develop ourselves rather than to destroy one another. We haven't figured that out."[10] Makwava's phrasing—"you have your science . . . you have your *uwavi*"—betrayed his indecision as to whether American science *was,* indeed, American *uwavi* and whether Makonde *uwavi* was essentially the same as one, the other, or both.[11]

Whereas Muedans often professed to us to not understand the foreign "sciences" to which they were exposed, they generally assumed them to "make sense" to those who did understand them. Muedans often bemoaned the fact that, by contrast, *uwavi* "made no sense." Through *uwavi's* practice, lives were destroyed; but to what ends?[12] *Uwavi,* they said, inevitably escaped the intentions, and undermined the interests, even of those who enacted it. *Uwavi,* as a form of knowledge, was too unwieldy and dangerous to be used instrumentally.[13] Because *uwavi* was a battlefield upon which rivals competed and challenged one another, sorcerers suffered as many losses in the hidden realm as they achieved victories. The prizes sorcerers sought, including human flesh, were nearly all protected with countersorcery devices that wounded would-be attackers. Sorcery, as most Muedans understood it, was a high-risk venture that ultimately undid those who did it.[14]

What is more, *uwavi* was a form of knowledge that the vast majority of Muedans only suspected others of possessing and that those assumed to possess invariably denied having. Where sorcerers were euphemistically identified by the phrase *"andimanya"* (he/she knows), rarely was the phrase *"nindimanya"* (I know) uttered in the context of *uwavi* discourse, even by self-assured countersorcery specialists. Most Muedans knew that *shikupi* provided the "key" with which sorcerers and countersorcerers entered the invisible realm, but most admitted that they did not know what *shikupi* was or how it worked.[15] In the end, what ordinary Muedans *knew* was that *other people knew uwavi.*[16]

I am reminded of the words once spoken to me by a college friend who concluded, after a particularly unsuccessful semester: "What I have learned in college is that everything in life comes down to physics or economics, and that I don't know shit about either one." Eusébio often uttered similar laments. He would have agreed with Bacon's adage: knowledge is power; he often expressed frustration that he had neither. Whether power belonged to Russians or Americans, to scientists, sorcerers, or countersorcerers, he knew that it did not belong to him. From his perspective, socialist modernizers and democratic developers, like *vavi* and *vamitela,* "knew a little something." His only certainty was that whatever they knew, he did not. If power lay in the ability to "see" the hidden dynamics of the world—to interpret the way the world worked and, thus, to act decisively upon it—this Eusébio was sure he could not do.[17]

More often than articulating a vision of the world, Eusébio called attention to that which he could not see. His—like many, ordinary Muedans'—was an anti-vision derived from a life mostly led on the uncertain edges of human experience.[18] His perspective implicitly challenged reformers' assertions that, through the realization of a neoliberal vision in and over Mueda, power could be rationalized, rendered "transparent,"[19] and metabolized on behalf of the commonweal and that a better world could thereby be brought to fruition. Ironically, by coloring power in postsocialist Mueda opaque, the hapless Eusébio's anti-vision subtly subverted (*kupilikula*) reformers' claims, whether he knew it or not.[20]

Postwar Uncivil Society

"Ahhh, we don't want development here!" Tissa exclaimed. It was a phrase that I had heard him utter with exasperation on several occasions. On this day, Marcos, Tissa, and I—en route from Matambalale to the town of Mueda—were visiting Tissa's brother, Germano, at his home in Nimu. It was the first time we had taken a meal at Germano's house. His wife tended to a chicken roasting in the fire close by while contributing to our conversation. The children—excited but shy—soaked up the attention of their *tios* (Portuguese for "uncles") Tissa, Marcos, and Andiliki.

Germano, Tissa reminded me, was a carpenter.

"This guy knows his trade," Marcos said enthusiastically, returning as he spoke from the back of the yard. "He makes the most incredible things."

"What do you know about carpentry?!" I said, jokingly, to Marcos.

Stifling the urge to laugh at himself, he mustered a glare before ordering me to follow him to the back of the yard where there sat an exquisite little "house" with tightly fitted glass windows and a tidy new thatch roof.

"What is this?" I said with awe.

"*This* is what I'm trying to tell you!" Marcos responded, triumphantly. "Go inside."

I lifted the wooden latch on the precisely engineered wooden door and peeked inside. Where I had nearly expected to find a shrine of some sort, I discovered a bathhouse, divided into two rooms—one housing a toilet, the other a shower stall. Never had I seen anything like it on the Mueda plateau. Muedan villagers ordinarily bathed on a small space of bare earth lined with slender tree trunks and fenced off from the rest of the yard by panels made of reed or bamboo. To one side of the same space, a latrine was normally located—a ten-foot-deep pit covered over by a latticework of small tree trunks, straw, and pounded earth that left a small hole in the center. Germano, how-ever, had installed a level floor of finely planed lumber over his latrine and mounted upon it a wooden box-commode with a seat and a hinged cover. He had left sufficient space between the flooring slats of the shower stall for the drainage of water. Covering the platform floor was a "house" of finely plas-tered walls beneath a tidy thatch roof. The glass windows let in light and, when opened, air; when closed, they kept out flies and other insects. Germano had mounted hooks on the walls from which towels hung; small wooden shelves held a bar of soap and candles (to light the bathhouse after dark); and a roll of toilet paper was spooled on a wooden hanger.

"It's a five-star hotel!" Marcos said gleefully. "It's nicer than the Hotel Cabo Delgado!"

I had to agree that it was.

When Marcos and I returned from the back of the yard, I told Germano how impressed I was with his craftsmanship. "Where did you learn to do this?" I asked. Germano seemed pleased by our flattery, but also ill at ease. He looked away, and remained silent.

Tissa spoke for his younger brother: "I arranged for him to apprentice with a carpenter in Pemba. He learned some things there, and he teaches himself other things by reproducing what he sees in pictures in magazines that he sometimes gets hold of. Sometimes, he gets his own ideas and invents things himself. He's quite clever."

"I've never seen anything like this in a village before," I said.

I turned to Germano: "I imagine that your skills are in great demand here. It's not everyone who can make such things!"

"Ahhh, it's not so difficult," Germano said, still looking away, shyly. "Lots of people could do this if they wanted to. But they choose not to."

"What do you mean they *choose not to*?" I asked. I couldn't imagine why anyone would choose not to have an improved bathhouse—or a chest of drawers or a comfortable chair or any of the other things that I saw under con-struction in Germano's workshop. I could only imagine that most Muedans could not make them and could not afford to buy them from someone, like Germano, who could.

Tissa drew a deep breath and then let out an audible sigh. A smile passed over his face, turning, in time, into a pained expression. "This is a very com-plicated thing," Tissa said to me. "But if you really want to understand Mueda, Andiliki, you have to understand this."

I looked at Tissa with amusement: "I need to understand your brother's toilet to understand Mueda?"

"Yes," Tissa responded with sincerity. He paused, as if gathering strength

Germano was not only a skilled carpenter but also the proud owner of a bicycle that he used to visit friends and family in neighboring plateau villages. At the end of a day of fieldwork, we would often be visited by Germano in the various villages in which we stayed.

to make his case to someone he knew would have trouble grasping such obvious truths. "Life in the village is difficult. People here have nothing. You've seen it. They have one or two shirts to wear, and a pair of trousers. Their children go without shoes. They eat *ugwali* [porridge] with *shidudu* [ground cassava leaves] every day. Some of these kids don't know the taste of meat. But it doesn't have to be this way. People here could live better if they chose to. They have that possibility. They have everything they need here to make a better life. My brother is telling you the truth. Anyone could make a toilet like that."

"So why don't they?" I asked, perplexed.

Without hesitation, Tissa pointed to a goat tethered a few meters away. "Do you see that?" he asked me.

I had noticed the goat even before Tissa pointed to it. There was something peculiar about the animal. It constantly bobbed its head to one side as if trying to escape invisible pestering insects. From time to time, it lost its balance, nearly toppling to the ground. The image reminded me of a cow afflicted with mad cow disease.

"What about it?" I asked.

"*That,*" Tissa said, still pointing to the goat, "is the result of *that*"; he now pointed to the bathhouse.

"I don't understand," I admitted.

"Villagers may suffer out here—they may have nothing—but their suffering only gets worse when they dare build something for themselves, when they try to pull themselves up a little bit."

Tissa put his head in his hands for a moment before continuing. "People in this village treat Germano very badly. They insult him all the time. All because he has made something for himself."

Marcos now hummed with comprehension. I struggled to catch up. I continued to look at Tissa inquisitively. He now looked at his brother. "He's a Christian. He doesn't waste his money at the drinking stalls in the marketplace. He saves it to buy materials to work with. And he works hard, building things for himself, and for my father. When other people ask him to do something for them, he saves the money he makes. He doesn't drink it away. He invests it in livestock and other things."

"But what does that have to do with the goat and the bathhouse?" I asked, impatiently.

"Every eye in the village is on that bathhouse. People say that Germano thinks he's too good to shit in a hole like everyone else—that he's proud and ambitious, that he's showing off."

Tissa shook his head before concluding, simply: "*Uwivu*" (Kiswahili for "envy").

"So they're envious of your brother and his bathhouse," I said, slowly catching on.

Tissa's response confirmed my statement, if only implicitly: "But they don't say so. Instead, they steal his livestock. Or they beat his animals when they stray from his sight. That one [pointing to the Mad Goat] was fine until, one day, Germano found it in the center of the village, blood running down the side of its head. Someone had beaten it until it lost its senses. Look at it! It's no good to anyone now. Now, it just suffers—like everyone here."

I shook my head in sympathy with the goat, with its beleaguered owner, and with the village that they somehow indexed.

"The village is a violent place, Andiliki. Life out here is a war—all the time."

As Tissa spoke, I thought of how the international community of nations conceived of Mozambique as an African model for conflict resolution. Whereas *other* nations, such as Angola, Liberia, Sudan, and Congo, were cursed with riches (oil, diamonds, coltan,[1] etc.) that fueled protracted military conflict, by contrast, in the absence of wealth, Mozambique had found durable peace—or so it was said. The portrait Tissa painted, however, was one of a nation still at war, where Mozambicans, pushed to the margins by structural adjustment, waged among themselves myriad minuscule wars.

Tissa looked toward the center of the village as he continued: "Sometimes, you can see people going at one another in plain daylight. Sometimes it takes place at night. But it never ends, this war."

With his euphemistic allusion to nighttime skirmishes, Tissa introduced sorcery into his picture of a village at war. His younger brother, who generally looked upon him with admiration when he spoke, now sat quietly, somewhat disengaged from the conversation. I wondered if, as a Christian, he professed disbelief in sorcery. I wondered if, despite his silence on the matter, he feared sorcery's effects. I wondered if his "fearless" air provoked fellow villagers to *suspect him* of sorcery. I stole a quick glance at Germano, who I somehow expected, in light of my passing thoughts, to appear slightly sinister. He did not.

Tissa continued: "To live without hope of improvement is misery." His voice hung suspended. We waited for him to complete his thought. He turned to me: "But remember what that *nkulaula* in Matambalale told us, Andiliki, . . . that young woman, Verónica Romão."

"What was that?" I asked.

"She told us that the guy who sits alone picking *matakenya* [fleas] from his feet is the one who is safe. No one takes note of him. While those who do something to improve their situation are in danger. They are insulted from every direction. They live in fear. They know that anything they do will eventually get ruined and that they may be ruined in the process."

Prompted by these words, I now placed Tissa's brother in a category with Sefu Assani Kuva: daring "self-improvers" subject to attack by *vavi va lwanongo,* sorcerers of ruin. I again glanced at Germano to see if he looked the part. On the contrary, by comparison with these men—"ambitious," high-stakes players around whom sorcery inevitably swirled—Germano now appeared as young, unassuming, and innocent as ever.

As we shared the meal of roasted chicken in Germano's yard, I pondered the words Tissa attributed to Verónica Romão. I had assumed them to mean that there existed two distinct categories of Muedans: the ambitious and the complacent. I had assumed them to mean that the ambitious were the objects of potentially lethal envy—an envy manifested by the complacent, an envy to whose effects the complacent were themselves immune. This envy might take the form of sorcery perpetrated by the complacent against the ambitious or of the accusation of sorcery made against the ambitious by the complacent. At any rate, it was the ambitious who were held back—even damaged—by it.[2]

I now considered another reading of these words—a reading that rendered problematic the strict dichotomy between two categories of people and instead conceived of these categorical profiles as aspects of experience shared by all Muedans. Most Muedans with whom we worked, it seemed to me, coveted a better life *as well as* feared the consequences of its achievement. Most, seemingly, struggled to find a comfortable place between "making something" for themselves and "laying low." Most betrayed envious desire, from time to time, for something beyond their grasp, while on other occasions jealously guarding something already in their possession which they feared might provoke the envy of others. Most hid what wealth they had, revealing just enough to hide their poverty.[3]

"We don't want development here!" Tissa said; but he, and the Muedans for whom he spoke, *did* want that nebulous, elusive thing they called "development." Tissa's was an ironic, exasperated lament, whose "we" might have been "they," and whose "development" might have been qualified as "our"—even "my"—("*they* don't want *our/my* development"),[4] were it not impossible to separate the ambitious from the complacent, sorcerers from their victims, and "them" from "us." Through their contributions to the discourse of *uwavi*, Muedans both held their neighbors and kin in check *and* contributed to the (re)production of a vision of the world by which they were themselves held back.

Democracy only complicated the matter. Where the socialist state had claimed the wealth of the nation—and had exercised the right to dole it out—on behalf of "the people," the receding neoliberal state now left villagers to their own devices simultaneously to "develop" themselves and to police one another against dangerous displays of "ambition." In an environment of scarce resources, this contradictory mandate rendered individual "improvement" of even the most modest proportions a precarious endeavor, for Muedans easily recognized their own "ambitions" in the acts of their neighbors and kin. In this environment of acute mutual suspicion, anything that might be accomplished by anyone was undone (*kupilikula*) even in the moment of its doing, making impossible not only advancement on the part of the "ambitious" but also maintenance of the dwindling commonweal upon which Muedans of all ambitions depended—a truth underscored by Tissa as we departed Germano's house.

Pointing to the standpipe at the center of the village in front of Germano's yard, Tissa exclaimed: "How many millions of meticais have been spent on that?! And now it sits there, dry. Do you know why?!"

I awaited his answer.

"Sorcerers have clogged the tubes with arms and legs and children's skulls so that it doesn't run. Can you imagine that?! Just to keep others from living a better life!"[5]

Tissa lowered his head and forced a deflated laugh before concluding his commentary: "Ah, no, Andiliki. We don't want development here!"

26

Democratization and/of the Use of Force

"What have you learned this year, Andiliki?" asked Rafael Mpachoka, the FRELIMO first party secretary in Muidumbe who had, for several years, graciously facilitated my work in his district. His tight grin betrayed amusement at the anthropological enterprise.

"Well . . ." I said, wondering how forthright to be. I then confessed, curious to see what his response would be: "We have spent most of our time this year studying *uwavi.*"

"*Feitiço*?!" Mpachoka replied, translating the term into Portuguese, the language in which we spoke. He smiled broadly and then laughed. I returned his smile but not his laugh.

"I have heard some of the most astonishing things," I told him, reproducing language used by many of my informants. "People turning into lions, people making helicopters . . ."

Mpachoka looked at me now as if pondering how forthright *he* would be. He shot a quick glance at the door. The walls of his office rose only halfway to the roof. Beyond the closed door, we clearly heard the voices of his staff as they talked to one another. If we could hear them, I assumed, they could hear us.

Mpachoka proceeded nonetheless: "These things happen, you know. The Portuguese had trouble believing it, but these things do happen. In the old days, Makonde *curandeiros* could graft the heads of slaves onto the deceased and bring them back to life. When I was young, I saw this. I remember seeing a woman who had a dark-skinned body and a light-skinned head! I saw it with my own eyes!"

Mpachoka was the highest-ranking FRELIMO official to speak with me about sorcery without asserting disbelief. Just as I had wondered how genuine was Mueda District Administrator Ambrósio Vicente Bulasi's dismissal of sorcery (see the prologue), I now wondered how genuine was Mpachoka's embrace. I wondered: were Mpachoka's words those of a "true believer" or of a savvy politician in the emergent neoliberal environment defined by "tolerance" for Mozambican "tradition"?

The conversation turned to a case that had occurred in Mwambula in the past year, a case of which I had first heard only a few days earlier from others with whom we spoke. Mpachoka now gave me his account.

"The guy was an *antigo combatente,*" said Mpachoka, himself a veteran of the independence war: "He lived here in Mwambula, but he was traveling on foot down to Chitashi, where he was going to catch a ride to Pemba to collect his veteran's benefits. Apparently, as he traveled the pathway through the lowlands, he was attacked by a lion. People discovered his mauled body and followed a trail of blood until they found the lion. The man was big and strong. He had wounded the lion with his knife before the beast killed him."

Mpachoka looked at me as if deciding whether or not to end his account there. I looked back, inquisitively, conveying that I knew there was more to the story than he had told. He carried on.

"When the lion was killed, it turned out that it was an elder in the man's family."

I had been told in previous conversations about the case that the lion carcass had taken on the appearance of one of the victim's elder kinsmen, and that the relatives summoned to collect the victim's body saw, and recognized, this family member.

"Why had the elder attacked the man?" I asked.

"Envy," Mpachoka said. "The guy was getting veteran's pension checks. He had put a zinc roof over his house.[1] He had his life all arranged."

We sat quietly for a moment, reflecting on the tragedy before Mpachoka broke the silence. "This kind of thing is common. Just a few days ago, here in Mwambula, a man came running out of his house in broad daylight yelling that another guy had shot down his helicopter."

It took me only a moment to realize the self-incriminating nature of the man's grievance. "His helicopter!?" I exclaimed. "So he was admitting that *he* was a *mwavi.*"

"Yes!" Mpachoka responded, shaking his head in exasperation.

The first party secretary continued: "Then the guy went out to the [Muidumbe] district administrator's office [located at the edge of Mwambula village] and submitted a claim for restitution!"

We laughed together. Mpachoka sighed. I drew closer to his desk. He looked at me.

Zinc roofs serve as veritable lightning rods for *uwavi*.

"So, how do you handle such situations . . . as a FRELIMO leader, I mean?"

Mpachoka immediately grew tense, as if he realized, suddenly, that he had admitted too much to me. The familiar tone that he ordinarily took with me gave way to that of a spokesperson taking the party line—albeit a "reformed" line.

"Most of these matters are resolved at the family level. We rarely even hear about them. When we do, it's best that we not get involved."

Indeed, in the case of the FRELIMO war veteran who had been mauled by a lion, Mpachoka and the government *had* limited their involvement. Just as Ambrósio Vicente Bulasi had handled the cases of lions in Namaua and in Kilimani, Mpachoka and his colleagues in the Muidumbe District administration (who ordinarily took their cues from Mpachoka, a higher-ranking party official) left it to the villagers of Mwambula to "work it out among themselves" in this, the new era of "democracy."[2] In this case, the consequences were even graver than they had been for Sefu Assani Kuva (who, remember, was beaten, fined, stripped of his land, and evicted from the village of Kilimani). Mpachoka reluctantly admitted to me that a group of villagers assembled to confront the suspected sorcerer. The old man was pulled from his house in the middle of the night, accused of the crime of killing his kinsman,

and unceremoniously beaten to death.[3] Only after the killing did local officials intervene—detaining those who had instigated the killing, reprimanding them, and releasing them a short time later.

The grimace I now saw on Mpachoka's face betrayed the dilemma that
such incidents posed for him and other FRELIMO officials, a dilemma rooted
in the complex, and ever-changing, relationship between daytime governance
on the Mueda plateau and governance of the night. Whereas the Portuguese
had been relatively "tolerant" of occult discourse in the colonial period (as
seen in chapter 10), FRELIMO had, for nearly two decades, attempted (at least
officially) to suppress witchcraft/sorcery accusations, ordeals, and trials (as
seen in chapter 18), differentiating themselves from their Portuguese predecessors (whom they accused of using Mozambican superstition against
Mozambicans) but acting, ironically, rather like colonial authorities had elsewhere on the continent.[4] While colonial "witchcraft ordinances" elsewhere
were often interpreted by colonial subjects as the exercise of power on behalf
of, or in collaboration with, witches and/or sorcerers (who, as a result of these
new regimes, were left unchecked by counter-witchcraft/sorcery measures),[5]
Muedans (who were mostly sympathetic to the nationalist cause) generally
understood FRELIMO's wartime ban on *uwavi* discourse *not* as the expression
of alliance with sorcerers but instead as *the exercise of* sorcery of construction (as we have seen in chapter 16). Only with the collapse of FRELIMO socialism did most Muedans begin to wonder whether FRELIMO authorities
worked in league with malevolent sorcerers. Elsewhere in Mozambique—
where FRELIMO was not so easily accepted as in Mueda—rural populations
had long looked upon FRELIMO as accomplices to occult forces whose local
control they disallowed in the name of antiobscurantism. RENAMO had
seized upon these sentiments, translating them into popular support in some
regions of the country and into a political critique of FRELIMO—as intoler-
ant of Mozambican "tradition"—that resonated with neoliberal Western donors. FRELIMO's lift of the ban on "traditional healing" and its adoption of a
more "tolerant" stance vis-à-vis occult discourse could be understood only in
light of these historical dynamics, exacerbated by shrinking state budgets
and postwar administrative fatigue.

In the spaces afforded by neoliberal reform, Muedans now tentatively asserted themselves. The "traditions" that came to the fore, however, were as
much the product of novel circumstances as of historical precedent, for the
FRELIMO state neither disciplined sorcerers (as *vanang'olo* had in times
past) nor specifically mandated "traditional authorities" to do so.[6] Muedans
were left to their own devices to police the invisible realm and to constitute
social practices and institutions through which justice might be applied.

They did just this, sometimes administering fines and beatings and occasionally evicting or lynching the accused—acts by which they threw into question the state's monopoly claim on the legitimate use of lethal force.[7]

In late 2002 and early 2003, this state of affairs reached intense crisis with a spate of lion maulings in and around the villages on the southeastern edge of the plateau. Shabani Shamambo, an elder in the village of Namakandi, expressed suspicions shared by many villagers in the region when he spoke with Radio Moçambique reporter Óscar Limbombo (Limbombo 2003): "This phenomenon is inexplicable. Normally, lions don't make people their main quarry. What kind of lion is it that attacks people again and again? When a lion is hungry, it may, by chance, attack a person to feed itself, but then it leaves the area in which people live, contrary to what happened here."

Word circulated that some victims' wounds appeared to be made by knives. Hunters tracking the lions reported paw-prints turning into human footprints or sandal-prints. Rumors circulated of letters found proclaiming: "You won't kill us. We are too many."

Pedro Agostinho, also of Namakandi, told Limbombo: "We met many times. I said to the eldest of the elders: 'What's this?! If someone knows that this is a magical lion, it would be best to tell us. You must inform us when so-and-so is saying he will do this so that the government can take measures before he does.' But no one said anything. The elders themselves were shocked."

Even more shocking to most residents—more "inexplicable" (although prompting various explanations nonetheless)—was the "failure" of government to act on its own initiative. As fear intensified, villagers abandoned their fields, provoking famine in the region. Women could fetch water only en masse, accompanied by men armed with bows and arrows. Schools shortened classes so that children could be home by midafternoon. Residents shut themselves inside their homes before sunset, urinating and defecating in gourds or old cooking pots in lieu of visiting the latrine after dark (Limbombo 2003). And still, the killings continued.

According to Pedro Seguro, the Muidumbe District administrator, the district office had no arms with which to hunt lions, and his requisitions went unmet. Villagers were more vexed by Seguro's public silence in the midst of such sinister events. "One of the district administrator's great failings," Limbombo told me, "was that he never came out and *condemned* what was happening." As Seguro failed to resolve the crisis—or even to address it publicly—villagers took it upon themselves to deal with the threat that menaced them, lynching neighbors and kin they suspected of making or transforming themselves into lions (Limbombo 2003). The young Tadeu Jonas, of Mwambula, told Limbombo that his uncle was summoned to the village center, where he was set upon by a mob, dowsed with gasoline, and burned; when Tadeu tried to intervene, he was accused of being an accomplice to the accused sorcerer and his own life was threatened. On at least one occasion, district police arrested mob leaders, but the district administrator expressed frustration that arrests could only be made after crimes were committed and frenzied mobs dispersed (Limbombo 2003). Such events, he suggested, had to be allowed to play themselves out.

Over the course of a year, local hunters succeeded in killing six lions. The maulings stopped soon after another—reputedly the most ferocious—was killed by hunters dispatched from Pemba. Fifty-two people had fallen victim to lions (forty-six dead, six seriously injured). Another eighteen had been lynched by fellow villagers (Limbombo 2003) largely left to "work things out among themselves."

Whereas neoliberal reformers envisioned the reinvigoration of Mozambican "tradition" contributing to a postsocialist fluorescence of *civil society*, Muedan society became increasingly *uncivil* in the post–civil war period. What is more, the extralegal justice pursued by villagers in the new democratic era (in which, as Mueda District Administrator Ambrósio Vicente Bulasi suggested, "each one has the right to believe what he believes") threatened to undermine the rights to safety of person and security of property enshrined in the new Mozambican constitution.[8]

Through their invocation of the schema of *uwavi*, vigilante villagers focused attention on the logics whereby a privileged few among them benefited by the largess of the ruling FRELIMO party as it sought to consolidate the support of core constituents such as FRELIMO guerrilla war veterans. Ironically, violence was often directed at those (such as the mauled veteran's elder family member) who embodied the envy social differentiation engendered—an envy with which vigilante villagers themselves might have empathized every bit as much as with emergent elites' "ambitions" for "self-improvement." According to Limbombo's report, people of relatively greater economic means often *were* accused of sorcery when family members were killed by lions. When his brother died by lion mauling, Emiliano Lucas, owner of a market stall in Mwambula, came under suspicion of killing him to make of him a *lindandosha* (zombie slave). "Anyone who owns something is suspected," Lucas told Limbombo. Lucas, however, escaped lynching, as did many suspects of relatively greater means. In any case, in an environment were *uwavi* operated unrestrained, the strong and the weak, the rich and the poor, suffered alike. Anyone might be attacked, whether by sorcerers or by vigilante villagers accusing them of sorcery. Anyone might be ruined, anyone undone (*kupilikula*). *Uwavi*, as Muedans said, "made no sense." This, at least, was the *sense* that Muedans assertively *made* of *uwavi* as they (re)produced the world in accordance with their *uwavi*-filled vision of it.

To FRELIMO authorities such as Ambrósio Vicente Bulasi, Rafael Mpachoka, and Pedro Seguro, however, the greatest irony was this: in spite of FRELIMO's new "respect" for "tradition," Muedans turned a critical eye upon *them*. The aloof liberality that officials such as Seguro demonstrated in relation to sorcery accusations and suspicions was read as abdication of responsibility for policing *uwavi*. Indeed, because of their *tolerance* of *uwavi* discourse, many suspected them of *complicity* with maleficent sorcerers. If men such as them, who undoubtedly *knew a little something* ("How else could they have risen to positions of such power?"), did not act as sorcerers of construction, many assumed, they must be sorcerers of danger.[9] Before the killings subsided in Muidumbe, District Administrator Pedro Seguro had in fact become the principal suspect in the eyes of most; Muidumbe residents not only petitioned the provincial police commander and the provincial governor to have this "dangerous man" removed as district administrator but ultimately threatened to drive him from Muidumbe themselves (Limbombo 2003).[10]

27

Governing in the Twilight

On a cool August morning in 1999, Tissa and I sat conversing with Mariano Makwava, president of the village of Matambalale. As we talked, one of Makwava's grandsons—perhaps seven or eight years old—ferried around the yard on a rudimentary scooter made of scrap material. Clad in a filthy sweatshirt that was more holes than material, the boy bobbed up and down as he scooted forward on unevenly worn wooden wheels.

Makwava, who had been president of Matambalale for as long as I had been working in the Mueda region, confessed to us that in recent years he had found his job increasingly difficult. At the same time that the state passed on to him fewer and fewer resources to satisfy the expectations of his constituents, it relied upon him more and more to consolidate order in the village. When villagers appealed to the state to assist them in the resolution of their problems, and when—in the name of democratic decentralization—district-level officials pushed problems back down to the village-level, demanding that they be resolved there, the paradox of a state that was simultaneously absent and present was embodied in village presidents like Makwava.

In more ways than this, Makwava, like other village presidents, occupied an interstitial space in village affairs. Whereas district administrators, like Ambrósio Vicente Bulasi and Pedro Seguro, and first party secretaries, like Rafael Mpachoka, earned salaries that allowed them to maintain residences in the provincial capital, where they might invest in economic activities, village secretaries received no pay for their services and derived their livelihoods within the village economy. Makwava and his family tended agricultural fields, like ordinary villagers. A couple of times a month, however, this president traveled to Pemba to purchase bulk quantities of essential consumer goods—*capulanas*, cooking pots, utensils, salt, soap, and matches—

with which he stocked a shop in the village marketplace. Makwava was *of* the village, but *not completely in* it.

Makwava's liminal status in village affairs became clearer to me as he explained to us the disarray that we witnessed in his yard. He had recently demolished his house. During this, the (cold) dry season, he and his family slept in a temporary *cabana* while a new house was being built, in part from materials recuperated from the old house and in part from materials recently purchased in Pemba. Construction had not gone smoothly, however.

"Not long ago, my confidants informed me that someone had arranged a lion to kill me," Makwava told us.

The corrugated zinc sheets that lay propped up against a half-demolished wall of the old house were essential elements to the story. Makwava had purchased them with the proceeds of his trade and intended to use them to cover his new, improved house. The zinc sheets, however, had attracted the envy of village sorcerers, including, apparently, members of Makwava's own family.

His own life in jeopardy, Makwava responded swiftly and assertively: "I called a council of elders and informed them of the situation. The council summoned family members of mine who had been identified as suspects and scolded them: 'Why are you trying to kill our president?' they asked. 'If you proceed with this, we will know that it was you and we will bring you to justice,' they said. And so, these people who were trying to kill me desisted."

In stark contrast with higher-ranking FRELIMO officials like Bulasi, Seguro, and Mpachoka, who transposed such events into moments of "democratic decentralization," Makwava confronted the problem in the language of *uwavi*. When we questioned him, Makwava explained to us in greater detail how he learned of activities in the realm of *uwavi* and how he responded to them: "Among the sorcerers in this village, there exist a few who take pity on the victims. When they find out about other sorcerers' plans, they come report to me. I call together the accused and tell them that I know about their plans. I tell them that if they don't desist, I will expose them to the village and that they will be ridiculed, beaten, or imprisoned. In this way, these problems are resolved." The president hastened to add, proudly: "No one has yet been killed by a lion in this village."

I then said to Makwava: "I have often been told that, in the days of old—when people still lived in settlements—the settlement head would respond to the occurrence of sorcery by going out at night and crying out that he knew who the sorcerers were and that if they did not refrain from attacking people he would deal with them himself."

"Eeh," Makwava said, confirming my account.

"I have been told that, in order to do this, the settlement head had to be a sorcerer."

"It is true," Makwava said.

"I have been told that what the settlement head did was called sorcery of construction."

"Eeh."

"So," I asked, "isn't your way of handling sorcery the same? Don't you perform sorcery of construction?"

I fully expected Makwava to deny my charge, for the embodiment of the FRELIMO party in the village of Matambalale could scarcely admit to being a sorcerer.

Makwava tilted his head back and gently laughed: "What I do and what the settlement head did are indeed the same, Andiliki . . . only I do it in the daytime in my office, or in the village center, while the settlement head did it beside the *shitala* at night."[1]

Tissa and I were both astonished.

I remembered a village meeting I had witnessed in Matambalale in September 1994 over which Makwava had presided. He had stood on a low platform at the center of a crowd of several thousand villagers. Well into the meeting (which lasted for hours and during which such pressing issues as the upcoming elections were addressed), Makwava had called out: "It has come to my attention that there is a problem in the marketplace."

The crowd, which had grown bored and restless, went silent. Makwava's voice grew louder. "I am told that people are treating the notes that they spend so that these notes return to them at night. These treated notes mix with others in the cashboxes and take these other notes along with them when they return to their owners."[2]

A muted murmur arose from the crowd, eventually giving way, in my ears, to distinct voices.

One of them said: "Yes, I have seen this happen!"

Another said: "Treated notes?! Ha! Those notes never leave the marketplace! Look for them in the cashboxes of the *lipa* vendors! That's where they all go at night! That's where the merchants lose them!"

Another insisted: "No, no, it's true. It has happened to those who don't even drink *lipa*! Something must be done about this!"

The president ran his fingers through his beard as the crowd quieted once more. Then he spoke, firmly but simply. "This behavior must stop," he said. Soon thereafter, the meeting was adjourned.[3]

Only now, speaking with Makwava five years later, did I realize that, on

Mariano Makwava (left, conversing with Eusébio Tissa Kairo) did not fight for FRELIMO during the war for Mozambican independence but instead passed the war years in Tanzania. Because of this, he would never have been appointed village president in the period of FRELIMO socialism. More than a decade afterward, however, he was chosen for the post by FRELIMO due to his steady demeanor and skillful diplomacy.

that day, in an official village meeting, the village president had practiced sorcery of construction.

In the political space that Makwava occupied, somewhere between the state and the people of Matambalale village, neoliberal reformers had imagined something rather different. This space was to be inhabited by "civil society"—social institutions and configurations at once independent of the state and acting in harmony with it in the project of "rationalization" of Mozambican political life. Makwava's presence in this space simultaneously evinced the messy convergence of state and occult power in the plateau region *and* the divergence of state and rural conceptions of power and its mandate.

I asked Makwava: "Isn't there a danger in this?"

He gazed intently at me as I explained my question. "If, for example, I didn't like my neighbor, I could simply accuse him of sorcery and bring trouble to him—get him fined, beaten, or evicted?"[4]

Makwava hummed in acknowledgment of the vexing problem I had raised. He then explained: "In dubious cases, I summon an *nkulaula,* who was once a *mwavi*, to advise me. He has ways of knowing if the accused is actually a *mwavi* or not."[5]

"He uses *yangele* [divination]?" I asked.

"Yes," Makwava answered.

"Doesn't *yangele* sometimes lie?" I asked, echoing words I had heard many Muedans speak.

We sat quietly for a few moments before Makwava spoke again: "Most accusations are true. Most of them are made by *vavi*. They know these things. And they tell the truth because that way they gain favor with me. They know that I will protect them from those upon whom they report and, in turn, they promise to protect me."

Makwava's words only exacerbated my concerns. Sitting, as we were, amid scattered construction materials in Makwava's yard, I found it impossible to dissociate his caretaking authority from his personal interests. Through his commercial activities, Makwava had become one of the wealthier men in the village. Villagers—including Makwava's family members—had good cause for envy, and Makwava had good reason to feel threatened, whether in the daytime or at night. Indeed, the more successful Makwava was in "defending himself," the wealthier he became, making him an ever-greater target for sorcery and giving him greater justification to "protect himself." In defending his interests and consolidating his power, Makwava drew upon diverse resources, including his trading partners, his sorcerer-advisors, and the FRELIMO party. In the body of this village-official-cum-sorcerer-of-construction, party/state authority, economic status, and occult power mixed, reinforcing and accentuating existing hierarchies in ways that neoliberal reformers could scarcely have imagined, let alone desired.

I was not alone in my concerns. Villagers in Matambalale debated whether it was good or bad that the man who governed them knew the invisible realm as well as Makwava, apparently, did. To some, Makwava's words and deeds gave evidence of his predatory potential; he was a man with ample appetite, as well as the ability, apparently, to satisfy his cravings. Others argued that order in Matambalale depended upon Makwava's ruling the night, just as he ruled the day.

To Makwava's credit, Matambalale was among the more harmonious villages in the plateau region. During the time I spent there over the years—and I spent more time in Matambalale than in any other Muedan village—I did not once hear a story of violent conflict between villagers, nor did I hear any account of village justice involving beatings, evictions, or executions. And Makwava told the truth: no lions had killed a Matambalale villager while he was in office. The most dramatic forms of sorcery known to Muedans, it seemed, were held in check in Matambalale.

I had the impression, however, that the unusual peace in Matambalale was tenuous, as was the legitimacy Makwava enjoyed. Like all plateau villages, Matambalale knew too much sorcery; too many died, too young, to be dismissed as the result of "God's illnesses." Unable, in the moment of structural adjustment, to deliver to his charges goods and services passed on to him by a higher authority—unable to ensure that his people's plates were full—he remained vulnerable to their frustrations and suspicions. In the enduring Muedan interstices between vanguard socialism and democratic decentralization, Makwava's authority rested neither in the assertive mandate of a bold revolutionary party nor in the voice of the people he served. Neither "traditional" nor "scientific," Makwava, it seemed, governed in the gray space between the state and village residents—in the twilight between the visible realm and the invisible—with just as much dexterity as was required.[6]

28

Constitutional Reform and Perpetual Suspicion

"Look at this, *mano*," Marcos said excitedly. "They're making Papa Chissano a *humu*!"

It was the first day on which candidates for the 1994 elections were permitted to campaign, and the president of the republic, Joaquim Alberto Chissano, had descended upon Mueda. Marcos and I stood together on the airfield tarmac with thousands of Muedans. Several women's choral groups, dressed in bright, new, uniformed dresses sewn from *capulanas*, competed with one another in demonstrating their enthusiastic support for the leader of the FRELIMO party, singing songs in praise of "Papa Chissano."

Chissano's decision to inaugurate his campaign in Mueda was at once symbolic and strategic. He wished to remind the nation of FRELIMO's heroic origins in the armed struggle for Mozambican independence, as well as to remind Muedans of their long-standing historical affiliation with his FRELIMO party. On this day, he would speak, not Portuguese, the language of state, but instead Kiswahili, the lingua franca of the *luta armada* (armed struggle) bush paths.

A small group of FRELIMO veterans, gathered on the tarmac, had their own symbolic agenda. They had "mobilized" the local population over the preceding weeks, prepared the town, built the speakers' platform, rehearsed the choral groups, and drilled the ceremonial rifle corps. They had "delivered Mueda to Papa Chissano," and now they would have a word with him. After the president descended the plane and greeted local officials and representatives of the press, he found himself standing, unwittingly, before these veterans. They instructed him to remove his shirt, whereupon they clothed him in the regalia of a *humu* (replete with robe, headband, and spear), placed him upon a litter, and carried him through town to the site of the campaign rally.[1]

"*Humu* Chissano" on the campaign trail in 1994. During the war for Mozambican independence, Chissano served FRELIMO as chief of internal security.

As we followed the procession, I thought of Mandia's account of his own nomination as *humu*—of how his matrilineage sought to domesticate his wild energy and to limit his insatiable appetite by forcing him to swallow power on behalf of his kin. I wondered if Chissano, who had spent time in Mueda during the independence war and who had married a Makonde woman from Mueda, appreciated the complexity of the veterans' gesture. Apparently, the media did not. With perhaps a bit of interpretative assistance from Chissano's high-priced Brazilian campaign advisors, one paper reported that Muedans had crowned Chissano "emperor" (*Savana* 1994: 1). Clearly, the meaning of Mozambique's "transition to democracy" depended greatly upon the language through which one interpreted it.

As I have suggested throughout part 3 of this book, agents and advocates of liberalization of the Mozambican economy and polity spoke of various reforms as means of "opening up space" for the greater participation of Mozambicans in a prospering postwar economy and a flourishing postsocialist civil society (Weinstein 2002). Muedans, however, experienced neoliberal reform rather differently. For many plateau residents, the end of "socialist modernization" and the beginning of "democracy" and "development" constituted a historical moment marked not by the opening up of spaces for their greater participation but instead by the abandonment of these spaces—and of the obligations their occupation entailed—on the part of the state.

Indeed, Mozambique embarked upon the path of neoliberal reform in accordance with the exigencies of the historical moment: the end of the Cold War, the termination of support from once-socialist allies, and the imperatives of (Western) donor-driven structural adjustment. With the contraction of budgets, the state receded from essential spheres of Mozambican life. As we have seen, rural schools went without books and teachers, health clinics without doctors and drugs, and water supply systems without fuel and spare parts. Where the state had once exhorted rural Mozambicans to contribute to the national project of socialist modernization by producing in their fields the wealth of the nation (Machel 1978) and had supported these efforts by means of producer cooperatives, state farms, and agricultural extension (Saul 1985), it now withdrew almost completely from the sphere of peasant agriculture. With agricultural production in decline, the state neither taxed its rural residents[2] nor involved itself in the trade of their harvest. To the state, rural Mozambicans had become increasingly irrelevant.

In the era of structural adjustment, the state turned elsewhere for sources of revenue. Inefficient state enterprises were sold off; concessions were granted on others from which rent could be derived; and partners were sought for participation in joint ventures in the exploitation of key national resources (Pitcher 2002). In Cabo Delgado Province, the state focused attention on graphite and marble mines, generating employment for a few hundred provincial residents while sharing substantial profits with foreign investors.[3] The presence of the state was thus concentrated in sites of intensive economic investment and exploitation and was diluted over the remainder of the national territory, where "low-intensity governance" (Hansen and Stepputat 2001: 16) was practiced.

Where international relief and development agencies established a presence in the countryside, the state conceded to them governmental functions ranging from the monitoring and resolution of social conflict, to the maintenance of infrastructure, to the provision of essential goods and social services. On the Mueda plateau, only schools with NGO sponsorship sustained access to the materials necessary to function. Only health clinics staffed and supplied by Catholic missionaries or NGOs were able to dispense appropriate medications. Only with the support and supervision of a Swiss NGO did the water supply system continue to function. To a significant extent, the state ceded to these organizations sovereignty over areas it deemed of little or no value.[4]

Whereas the state withdrew from vast areas of Mozambique and from large swaths of Mozambican life, state officials and party leaders did not. Indeed, *as private entrepreneurs,* elites occupied some of the same spaces from which they simultaneously withdrew *as agents of the state.* Government officials and party bosses—or their clients—captured valuable resources by working with, or as agents of, foreign NGOs (Lubkemann 2001: 98).[5] They also captured lucrative profits through facilitating and/or partnering with foreign investors.[6] Elites of Muedan origin scrambled to register claims over forestland in the plateau center and to broker concessions to Japanese or South African lumber companies. Others steered foreign investors through the would-be hostile state bureaucracy to establish provincial predominance in economic sectors such as public transportation and tourism. Privatization, in the words of one analyst of Mozambican affairs, *"open[ed] new space* for a reconfiguration of established elites in conformity with new international interests" (Alden 2001: 123, my emphasis)—quite a different opening of space than promised by neoliberal reformers.

In their richly provocative discussion of the neoliberal state, Ferguson and Gupta (2002) argue that Western donors, NGO representatives, and international investors create the context for the emergence of new forms of "neoliberal governmentality" which involve the continuance, in the same space, of the state and its agents, and *not* the "rolling back" of the state that neoliberal reformers promise.[7] In Mozambique, however, neoliberal governmentality emerged unevenly on the landscape and became concentrated in the limited spaces of commercial investment and/or NGO intervention. Elsewhere, the salience of the state diminished or the state disappeared altogether.[8] Even in areas of concentrated investment or intervention, the value of Mozambican citizenship declined with the dilution of Mozambican sovereignty. In the eyes of many NGO representatives, Muedans were "beneficiaries," not citizens. To many investors, as well as local elites with whom they partnered, Mozambicans (with the exception of a limited number of employees) were nothing more than potential (albeit weak) counterclaimants to denationalized resources and the profits to be derived therefrom. Needing nothing from these rural residents, investors and their intermediaries had no reason to offer them anything—no cause to cultivate their deference and loyalty.[9] The spaces opened up by neoliberal reform thus sheltered and consolidated an elite that insulated itself, to an unprecedented degree, from broader social networks (whether expressed in the idiom of the nation or in the idiom of kinship), a process referred to by Mbembe as the "privatization of sovereignty" (2001: 78). As elsewhere in the country, elites of Muedan origin constructed for themselves luxurious residences and hired private security companies to protect their assets, giving rise to enclaves of wealth in a sea of poverty.[10]

Of course, as Joaquim Chissano stood before Muedans on the airfield tarmac, he *did*—for a brief moment—need something from them. He was interested, above all else, in persuading them to vote for him and for his FRELIMO party. Western donors funding the 1994 Mozambican elections were interested in more than this. They sought to persuade Mozambicans that, through the ballot box, they could give definitive shape to the exercise of power in Mozambique. Where corrupt officials had abused power, "disinterested" election sponsors now informed Mozambican voters that they could simply expel them from office. Where other candidates promised good governance, voters could grant them a mandate. Through the rational and transparent exercise of public choice, destructive powers could be brought to heel and made to work on behalf of the commonweal.

Most Muedans with whom we spoke considered elections more a burden than a boon (West 1997a, 2003b). Many were, undeniably, displeased with current political and economic trends. To most, however, FRELIMO was a historical identity that encompassed them. As FRELIMO, Muedans had given birth to a new nation, and Chissano was the party's chosen leader, their father ("papa"), and they were his supporters, his children. One could not "expel" one's father, no matter the circumstances. And what choice was there in any case? Dhlakama, "the bandit" whose troops had attacked plateau villages and killed Makonde sons and daughters?

Concurrently, most Muedans saw peril, not promise, in the idea of democratic decentralization. To be sure, many were displeased with local administrators. Most, however, responded to questions about the idea of *electing* such officials with their own question: "Who would rule us then?"[11] Their response was no mere capitulation to authoritarianism. They appreciated the inherent complexities of governance. They understood the establishment of a mutually beneficial order to be inextricably bound up with the exercise of superior force, and, at the same time, legitimate authority to be dependent upon the cultivation of consent. They considered a ruler's power to be commensurate with his ability to tap resources beyond the reach of others. The power and authority of local officials, in their conception, derived from the state, in whose voice these officials spoke. An official of their own nomination, they feared, would not speak for the state—would not bring the force of the state to bear in the maintenance of local order and in the resolution of local problems. An official of their own choosing would speak only with their voice—a voice they had no reason to believe the state would hear. They feared, in fact, that a state that allowed them to appoint their own officials was a state no longer interested in ruling—a state no longer prepared to bestow its largess in the interest of cultivating consent, a state preparing to abdicate its authority and/or evade its responsibilities.[12]

Many Muedans saw ominous signs in the staging of elections in 2001 and 2002 for the posts of village president prior to Muedan administrators' cynical recognition of such officeholders as "community leaders." To many, a state that no longer cared who occupied such positions was a state no longer interested in the social domains over which these officeholders exercised authority.

The same fears motivated Muedan antipathy for the neoliberal idea of "empowering" "traditional authorities." Whereas most Muedans embraced the notion that state officials should consult with *vanang'olo vene kaja* in the administration of local affairs, none with whom we spoke saw sense in the restoration of the colonial-era hierarchy of *autoridades gentílicas*. "Traditional authorities," Muedans knew, would be even more poorly positioned to bring the force of a superior power to bear on local problems—would speak even less with the voice of the state—than would elected village officials.

The *régulo*, of course, was a particularly contrived invention on the Mueda plateau—a "traditional authority" of rather more dubious "tradition" than elsewhere in Mozambique. In dismissing the idea of reinvestiture of power in traditional authorities—indeed, in dismissing the neoliberal idea of devolution of power more generally—Muedans did not, however, reveal themselves as a "traditionless" people. It was, in fact, through their suspicions of democratic decentralization that, in the context of neoliberal reform, Muedans most cogently expressed a distinctive *tradition of authority*, an enduring (albeit dynamic) logic that animated Muedan understandings of power in an ever-changing world. According to this logic, legitimate rulers not only ate well but also necessarily fed those they ruled. In the moment of Mozambican "transition to democracy," Muedans judged those who ruled them in accordance with this logic and found them wanting. Incumbent officials, they suggested, ate well but brought little, if anything, to the collective plate. Rather than calling for the recognition of traditional authorities, who few believed could feed them, Muedans focused attention on the behavior of state officials, demanding *their* reform.

Standing on the airfield tarmac, Muedans dressed the president of the republic in accordance with their vision of legitimate authority. Fixing him in their gaze, they worked to transform him and, thus, to remake a world riven with violent conflict and obscene chaos. They bestowed upon him, qua *humu*, the voice of a lion, authorizing him to speak to them as a figure of authority. They demanded, however, that he enact authority responsibly. They mandated him to protect them—and Mozambicans generally—from the destructive forces of war, economic crisis, and political standoff that had afflicted them for decades. Whereas the representatives of his state had taken to "eat-

ing everything," they conveyed their expectations that he, and his party, ingest power on behalf of the Mozambican people rather than themselves.
They demanded that he, and his party, behave as stewards of the nation
rather than as predators—as sorcerers of construction rather than as sorcerers of danger.

Whereas the architects of Mozambique's emergent democracy suggested
that the operation of power within the nation could be rationalized (rendered
transparent and accountable) through the electoral process,[13] Muedans,
through invocation of the schema of *uwavi*, sustained and expressed a rather
different view of power. They remained suspicious that power was defined
not by constitutional arrangements but rather by exceptional abilities to fix
the world in one's gaze, to see its operative logics, and thereby to secure and
protect one's interests. Truly decisive power, Muedans told themselves, was
accessible only to an extraordinary few;[14] to all others, it remained unattain-
able—often, even imperceptible.[15] What is more, the schema of *uwavi* nurtured Muedans' ambivalence toward power,[16] an ambivalence deriving from
Muedan appreciation for power's inherent capriciousness. Power, in accordance with the schema of *uwavi*, was at once essential to the creation of prosperity and social well-being *and* potentially destructive of individual lives
and social harmony. Considered through the schema of *uwavi*, politics (contra the neoliberal perspective) was an unending contest with ever-changing
rules—one in which no victory was final, and no defeat complete. Moreover,
it was an unavoidable contest; those who did not enter risked being devoured
unawares, while those who did enter risked inevitable loss in the face of superior force.

"Life is war," as Tissa told me. Seeing life's nature through the schema
of *uwavi*, Muedans armed themselves for battle. From the tenuous vantage
point afforded them by the schema of *uwavi*, Muedans subjected power to
perpetual suspicion, and figures of authority (of any kind) to unremitting
judgment. Using *uwavi* as a diagnostics of power, they fixed those who governed them in their scrutinizing gaze, seeking to discover the decisive forces
that animated their world and to steer these forces as best they could.[17]

Of course, ordinary Muedans denied the power of their gaze, denied the
ability to remake their world in accordance with their vision for it. Like healers who denied being sorcerers—"*Nangu? Mene!*" (Me? No!)—most Muedans
would have expressed shock at the idea that their suspicious perspectives
somehow remade their world—"*Wetu? Mene!*" (Us? No!). Engaging with ongoing political and economic transformations through the language of *uwavi*,
they did not claim to be able to *see* the operation of power so much as *to see
that it operated invisibly.*[18] Indeed, through *uwavi* discourse, Muedans often

expressed resignation to the idea that one cannot always truly see, or know with certainty, the reality in which one is suspended[19]—that one is sometimes left to trade secondhand accounts about how the world works, and why.

In perceiving the world's irreducible complexity through the language of *uwavi*, Muedans carried on making their world complex.[20] Indeed, in engaging with the world through the schema of *uwavi*, Muedans failed more often than they succeeded in (re)producing a better world and, within that world, better lives for themselves, as Tissa lamented in his brother's yard. In perceiving a world at war through the language of *uwavi*, they carried on waging innumerable, interminable wars.[21]

This is not to suggest that Muedans did not aspire to a different world, a better world. Whereas Max Marwick suggested decades ago that sorcery beliefs "conserve indigenous norms threatened by modern ones" (1965: 258), through the language of *uwavi* Muedans have long manifested profound ambivalence vis-à-vis the momentous historical transformations they have experienced.[22] Indeed, in the moment of Mozambique's "transition to democracy," they did not so much "resist" the neoliberal rationalization of power as sustain doubts in the face of assertions that power in their midst could actually be made to operate openly, fairly, and to the benefit of all. Through the language of *uwavi*, Muedans expressed similar ambivalence vis-à-vis modernity,[23] betraying at once their desires for things modern, their anxieties over the troubling consequences of uneven "development,"[24] and their frustrations with modernity's failure to materialize in their midst.[25] Through *uwavi* discourse, Muedans "plumb[ed] the magicalities of modernity," as Jean and John Comaroff have phrased it, attempting "to penetrate the impenetrable, to unscrew the inscrutable, to recapture the forces suspected of redirecting the flow of power in the world" (1993: xxx).

In the language of *uwavi*, however, Muedans expressed their sense that the world in which they lived is largely the product of others' creative visions—others' fantastic "sciences." They reflected upon the complex truth that the world generally eludes their attempts to (re)make it, and often violently and unpredictably (re)makes them. In short, they reconciled themselves with the indomitable dialectics of life as they experienced it. In their diffidence, however, lay their wisdom, for power behaved in the world they knew just as they suggested, inverting constitutional arrangements and evading the rationalizing gaze of neoliberal reformers. Insofar as this was true, through the elaboration of their anti-visions of the world Muedans transcended—even inverted, overturned, and/or negated (*kupilikula*)—the visions of neoliberal reformers.

Epilogue

Lines of Succession

"That's where you'll find the new *humu* Mandia," Marcos said, pointing to a house nestled between the roads to Mueda from Muidumbe and from Mocímboa da Praia at their junction in Lilondo.

"Mandia has moved from Nimu?" I asked.

"No, no," Marcos replied, playing with my confusion. "This is the *new humu* Mandia!"

"I don't understand," I admitted.

Marcos laughed at me.

It had been five years since, in 1994, I last visited with the elder in Nimu, where he lived. During the many times that we conversed together in that year, Mandia had told me about how the institution of *humu* had been brought to the plateau region by Makua captives, how it had been reshaped to suit the needs of Makonde matrilineages, and how, at one time, there had been thirty-six *vahumu* in the plateau region. He had described for me the lengthy process whereby *vahumu* were installed by their peers, the medicinal substances that gave them the power to protect their people and to resolve disputes, and the role that they played in preserving *likola* unity. He had lamented that there were at present only three *vahumu* still living in the plateau region. As the others were even more aged than he, Mandia feared that he would be the last to die and that no *humu* would remain to treat his body for burial, which would place the members of his matrilineage in grave danger of being attacked by the lethal predators that his untreated body might spawn when the medicinal substances he had ingested upon becoming a *humu* escaped him.

"Why are there only three *vahumu* now when once there were so many?" I had asked him.

"When *vahumu* die, they are not replaced," he told me, simply.

When I pressed him on the matter, he told me: "Young people today don't want to become *vahumu.*"

He eventually confided in me that this was because in the postindependence period FRELIMO had openly condemned the institution and publicly ridiculed living *vahumu.* In fact, no *humu* had been succeeded since the beginning of the independence war—since the time when most Muedans had found themselves living under the authority of FRELIMO in the liberated zones.

I was in the United States when I received a letter from Marcos informing me that the *humu* Windu, with whom I had also conversed during fieldwork in 1994, had passed away. Mandia had told me that when a *humu* dies, the sun is encircled with glowing rings. I tried to find the sun in the overcast Virginia sky above me and wondered what it had looked like, in Mueda, just after the death of which I was only months later being informed.

Now, back in Mueda in 1999, I could not believe that Marcos, who so consistently informed me when Muedans I knew passed away, had not told me of the death of a friend so dear to me as Mandia. Even so, I asked him, with trepidation: "The elder Mandia has died?"

"No!" Marcos answered at once to relieve my anxiety. "But he has appointed a successor!"

"Really!?" I was surprised to hear this.

"Good news, isn't it?" Marcos responded.

Mine was the response of an anthropologist: "We'll have to interview him soon!"

Within a few days, we returned to the junction at Lilondo and turned off the road into the yard of the new *humu*'s house. As we climbed out of the pickup and approached the house, the figure in the doorway took shape. At first, I noticed the *humu*'s regalia: the kiltlike wrap, the sport-coat, the scarf around his neck, and the headband. So accustomed was I to seeing these vestments worn only by aged *vahumu,* I was taken aback when I came close enough to appreciate the new *humu*'s upright posture and the glow of his youthful face. He was, I guessed, younger than Marcos.

The new *humu* invited us to sit with him in chairs that a young attendant dragged out of the house and into the sun on this cool, windy morning. We told him who we were and the nature of our research. He told us that he already knew our agenda. The elder Mandia had kept him abreast of the work we had done with him years earlier.

"You were already working with the elder then?" Marcos asked.

"The council of Vashitunguli elders nominated me to succeed Mandia in

1988," he informed us. "For the next eight years, the elder worked to prepare me."

I was astonished. I addressed myself to Marcos: "Mandia told us nothing about this when we worked with him!"

The new *humu* laughed gently. "It was still early then. We didn't yet know what would happen." His conspiratorial manner now conveyed to us the message that the secretive preparation of the new Vashitunguli *humu* was motivated by uncertainty about the government's potential response.

"Things are different now?" Marcos asked, delicately.

The young Mandia—the embodiment of his *likola*'s bold assertion—smiled coyly: "Times are changing."

The figure of the new *humu* played on my senses as Marcos and I sat conversing with him. His upright frame somehow captured the essence of dignity that defined a *humu*. His mannerisms were strangely ornate for a man of his generation, and yet, they highlighted his youthful face and lithe hands. His Portuguese was strikingly fluent, but the tenor of his voice, the cadence of his words, and the imagery of his spoken thoughts all led me to forget that we were not speaking in Shimakonde. The new *humu* was at once a throwback to the bygone days of his elders' youth and a vision of a future inhabited by new *vahumu*.

"Mandia told us a few years ago that there were no young people interested in becoming *vahumu*," I said to him, as if not yet convinced of his existence. "He told us that the last *vahumu* were all dying without successors."

I was, perhaps, a bit wounded by the fact that the elder had not revealed to me that he was preparing a successor.

The young Mandia sat patiently, abiding my words. He responded by saying: "Many of the young people in the villages today have no direct experience with *vahumu*. They were not yet born when there were last *vahumu* in their matrilineages."

"So how do they receive you?" Marcos asked.

"They are starting to get an idea of what our tradition has been."

It seemed to me that the young Mandia was trying to reassure himself of this as much as us.

"And the elders?" Marcos asked.

"There are Vashitunguli in nearly all of the villages of the plateau. I am treated with respect not only by them but by everyone. I am a *humu* for everyone. Everyone is proud of me."

The young Mandia might have been a beneficiary of the contemporary crisis of authority on the Mueda plateau. Tired of corrupt and abusive officials,

Muedans might have hoped for better from new *vahumu*. Where Muedans condemned "official" authorities for the abuse of power or for the use of resources for personal gain, however, it occurred to me that they might as easily dismiss new *vahumu* for lacking the resources with which to exercise any influence at all.

The new *humu* Mandia, however, apparently had some resources at his disposal. As he provided a brief autobiography in response to Marcos's questions, I studied the environment in which we found ourselves. The atmosphere contrasted sharply with the isolated and forlorn homestead of the elder Mandia that I had come to know so well in years past. Several young men sat on the verandah of the new *humu*'s house, sculpting in the tradition of Makonde ebony-wood carvers.[1] People came and went. Occasionally, Mandia exchanged money with these visitors. He was, I realized, running a bustling little sculptors' cooperative out of his home.

The young Mandia informed Marcos and I that he was born in Mueda in 1959. His father, Feliz Focas, and his mother, Ernestina Magwogwe, named him Jorge. He would have attended a Catholic mission school, he told us, were it not for the fact that the independence war broke out when he was still a small child. Along with his family, he fled to the FRELIMO-controlled bush in the center of the plateau. There, he began his studies in a FRELIMO bush school in 1969. By 1976, he had reached fourth grade, but that year, at the age of seventeen, he was conscripted into the army. He trained in Boane in southern Mozambique and served until 1984. After leaving the army, he returned to the Mueda plateau, where he learned to sculpt. For a brief stint, in 1987 and 1988, he lived in Beira, where he sculpted and sold his works, but he soon returned to the plateau.

"In the past, *vahumu* were prohibited from work," I said. "They weren't even permitted to cultivate their own fields. But I see that you are doing business here."

"This is the evolution of society," Mandia responded. "In the past, people gathered around the *humu*. His home was a focal point in the settlement. People brought him food. There was so much food in his warehouse that he could share it out with the community when times were hard. Today, this is no longer true."

I remembered what the elder Mandia had told me years earlier—that young people didn't want to become *vahumu* because, in contemporary Muedan society, there was no dignity in the role. Young men wanted to travel, to do business, to be men of experience. Money had become for them a new kind of *mitela*, the knowledge of which measured the worth of men. It occurred to me, however, that the first *vahumu* on the Mueda plateau—the founders of "tradition"—were actually men of bold innovation. Many were the descendants of slave mothers or grandmothers taken from the Makua-speaking lowlands surrounding the plateau. In becoming *vahumu*, they re-established their ties to these distant places and made of their humble origins a source of prestige. They were inducted as *vahumu* not on the plateau but in the lowlands, by—to Muedans—foreign, exotic Makua *mahumu*. The currency of their knowledge was rooted in their travels and in their commerce with those they encountered elsewhere. The new *humu*, it seemed to me, scoured Muedan horizons, just as his predecessors once had, finding hidden sources of wealth and power and repatriating them to the plateau, even as he sought to reinvigorate the "traditional" institution of *humu*.

As if to punctuate my thoughts, a bright-red pickup truck pulled off the road at the edge of the *humu*'s yard. Its driver blew the horn. The *humu* rose and walked casually toward the car as the horn blew again, more insistently. A red-faced man leaned his head out the driver's-side window. "*Pressa! Pressa!*" (Hurry up!), he said, in broken Portuguese, with a distinct Boer accent. I later learned that he was, indeed, South African—a manager at the lumber camp that had recently opened at the eastern edge of the plateau.

Mandia continued to amble, preserving his dignity as best he could. After a brief conversation with the Boer, he called out to one of the younger members of his sculpting cooperative, who loaded two roughly identical five-foot-high statues on his shoulders and ran, frantically, toward the road. One of the statues was purchased, the other rejected. When I later looked at the refused one more closely, I discovered that it was a sculpted rendition of the impish cartoon character that appeared on the wrappers of the condoms then being distributed in rural Mozambique by a public health NGO called PSI (Agha, Karlyn, and Meekers 2001; Karlyn 2001). The little imp and the condoms were called "JeitO," meaning "knack" in Portuguese. As sculptors, too, Mandia and his apprentices had breathed new life into Makonde "tradition"—the kind of life that tourists and airport shoppers often found endearing but that Western art critics frowned upon as "inauthentic" and undignified (West and Sharpes 2002).

When Mandia returned from the roadside, he sat deliberately, trying to compose himself—to reestablish the atmosphere in which he was being interviewed as *humu* by a foreign social scientist. His prestige, I now realized, was wrested precariously from a world filled with rival forms of authority that threatened constantly to challenge the dignity of his office. In more ways than one, the new *humu* embodied the identity and the experience of his people.

When I met with the young *humu* Mandia, he informed me that the elder Mandia, who was spending his days working his lowland fields and his nights sleeping in a *cabana,* had recently lost his balance, fallen into the cooking fire, and badly burned himself. As Marcos and I were scheduled to depart the Mueda plateau soon, and as the only means of visiting the elder was by journey on foot, we were unable to see him. Mandia asked if I knew of any good treatments for burns. I retrieved my medical kit and gave him materials with which to dress the elder's wounds—sharing, for a change, a bit of my healing knowledge.

As if sensing my thoughts, the new *humu* returned to the stream of our conversation, remarking, simply: "These days, we must support ourselves. I do what I know how to do."

Near the end of our conversation, Mandia told me: "There was a time when we feared that all *vahumu* would die without successors. No one wanted to become a *humu*, because the *humu* no longer had a role. We are still wary of transgressing the government's rules and laws. Up to now, our duties are still limited. We are waiting for the government to clarify what our new role will be. We will not displace the structures of government. There will not be a return to the traditional authority of the past. This much we know. But we can play a crucial role in society if the government chooses to work with us."

In the following year, while I was on a short visit to Pemba, Marcos told me, with a heavy heart, "*Mano,* Mandia has died."

"The elder?" I asked, saddened by the notion that I would not again see this longtime friend.

"No," Marcos answered. "The young Mandia."

I looked at him, mouth agape. Although I was not as close to the young Mandia as I was to the elder, I sensed greater tragedy in the death of the only new *humu.*

Marcos had been informed by a relative that the *humu* had taken ill and died while in Beira, where he was attending to the children of a nephew who had also recently fallen ill and passed away. The disease(s) that had taken these young men were not specified. I did the arithmetic in my head: Mandia had died at the age of forty.

Marcos and I sipped our beers as the still night air enveloped us in silence. I wondered if, wherever I was on that day, the sun above me was encircled with somber rings and, if so, how I had failed to notice. I wondered, too, if Mandia the elder had time to prepare another successor.

Glossary

autoridades gentílicas (Port.). Native authorities.

cabana (Port.). Temporary hut that is built close to agricultural fields and in which people sleep during seasons requiring intensive agricultural labor.

capitães-mor (pl.). See *capitão-mor.*

capitão-mor (Port.). Intermediate-level native authority in Mueda region.

capulana (Moz.). Printed cloth worn by women as a wrap (see Lopes, Sitoe, and Nhamuende 2002: 42).

catana (Moz.). Machete.

chibalo (Moz.). Colonial-era term for forced labor (see Lopes, Sitoe, and Nhamuende 2002: 148).

cooperantes (Moz. Port.). Foreigners rendering technical assistance in Mozambique.

curandeiros (Port.). Healers.

dimika (pl.). See *imika.*

escudo (Port.). Unit of Portuguese currency.

espera-pouco (Moz. Port.). "Wait a little"; used as slang for muzzle-loaded firearms.

feitiçeira/feitiçeiro (Port.). Sorcerer or witch.

feitiço (Port.). Sorcery or witchcraft.

FRELIMO. Frente de Libertação de Moçambique (Port.); Mozambican Liberation Front.

humu (Shimakonde). Arbitrator of disputes and ritual counselor of a Makonde matri-lineage.

igoli (Shimakonde). Knee-high platform made of braided reed cord lattice stretched over a rectangular wooden frame and elevated from the ground by four wooden legs.

Moz. = African term with currency throughout Mozambique; Moz. Port. = Mozambican Portuguese; Port. = Portuguese.

imika (Shimakonde). Piece of any of certain species of wood used to make lion, etc.

ing'anga (Shimakonde). Healer who identifies sorcerers and eliminates sorcery from the community; generally from outside the community. Regional cognates are used in reference both to healers and/or to witches/sorcerers; see, e.g., Janzen 1989: 240; 1992: 63, 67–68; M. Green 1994: 24; Ciekawy 1998: 128; Niehaus 1998: 104; Pels 1999: 237; Ashforth 2001b; Ciekawy 2001: 164; Fisiy and Geschiere 2001; Sanders 2001.

kaja (Shimakonde). Settlement. For a regional cognate, see Beidelman 1993: 53.

kulaula (Shimakonde). To heal. Beattie (1967: 212) reports the term *kuragura,* meaning "to divine," among Bunyoro in Uganda; while Muedan *vakulaula* do sometimes divine, the verb does not mean "to divine" in Shimakonde; the terms may nonetheless be inexact cognates.

kulipudya (Shimakonde). Ceremony of ancestral supplication.

kupilikula (Shimakonde). To turn around, to overturn, to invert, to undo. Most commonly used to refer to the act of turning sorcery back on its sender.

kushulula (Shimakonde). Literally, to drip. Used to indicate a craving for meat.

likola (Shimakonde). Matrilineage. For regional cognates, see Beidelman 1993: 42; Pels 1999: 246. Mombeshora (1994: 75) reports use of the same term among Bena in Tanzania to refer to the patrilineage.

lindandosha (Shimakonde). A sorcerer's living-dead slave (zombie). For a regional cognate, see van Dijk 2001: 110.

lipa (Shimakonde). Liquor made from cashew fruit or sugarcane.

lipande (Shimakonde). Antisorcery mine or bomb.

luta armada (Port.). Armed struggle. Used by FRELIMO in reference to its military campaign for independence.

machamba (Moz.). Agricultural fields (see Lopes, Sitoe, and Nhamuende 2002: 84).

makola (pl.). See *likola.*

Makonde. "People in search of fertile land"; ethnic name used by majority of Muedans.

mandandosha (pl.). See *lindandosha.*

mano (Port.). Brother. Commonly used by Mozambicans as a form of familiar address with boys or men not biologically related (see Lopes, Sitoe, and Nhamuende 2002: 96).

mapande (pl.). See *lipande.*

mapiko (Shimakonde). Masked dance performed at initiation rites.

matanga (Shimakonde). Funerary rites.

meticais (pl.). See *metical.*

metical (Moz.). Unit of postindependence Mozambican currency.

mitela (pl.). See *ntela.*

muntela (Shimakonde). Medicinal specialist.

mwavi (Shimakonde). Sorcerer. Among Lungu in Zambia, the strychnine-bearing *Erythrophloeum guineense* tree is called *mwavi* (Willis and Chisanga 1999: 176 n. 26); the use of a substance by this name (or one of a number of cognates) as poison oracles is reported by Marwick 1950: 111; Mair 1969: 145; Mombeshora 1994: 74; Probst 1999: 119; Fry 2000: 126. As sorcerers have commonly been identified in Africa through the use of strychnine-based poison oracles (e.g., Evans-Pritchard [1937] 1976), one might speculate that the use of the term in reference to a sorcerer derives from the use of such substances in detecting witches and/or sorcerers.

mwene (Shimakonde). Chief, lord, steward.

nang'olo (Shimakonde). Elder.

nang'olo mwene kaja (Shimakonde). Settlement head (literally, elder-steward-of-the-settlement).

nang'olo mwene shilambo (Shimakonde). Elder-steward-of-lands.

njomba (Shimakonde). Uncle (specifically, mother's brother). For a regional cognate, see Pels 1999: 161.

nkulaula (Shimakonde). Healer.

ntela (Shimakonde). Medicinal substance.

ntumi (Shimakonde). Lion.

obscurantismo (Port.). Derogatory term for traditional practices, implying ignorance, superstition.

regulado (Port.). Area over which a *régulo* exercised jurisdiction.

régulo (Port.). Upper-level native authority figure (see Lopes, Sitoe, and Nhamuende 2002: 130).

RENAMO. Resistência Nacional Moçambicana (Port.); Mozambican National Resistence.

shidudu (Shimakonde). Ground cassava leaves, eaten as a relish.

shikupi (Shimakonde). Medicinal substance used to render a person or act invisible.

shitala (Shimakonde). Men's meeting pavilion in the center of the settlement.

takatuka (Shimakonde). A practice whereby a deceased person is revived by grafting a new head on the body. *Takatuka wanalyuva* refers to a healing practice whereby a wound is transferred from a person's body to an object such as a tree.

ugwali (Shimakonde). Porridge, once made exclusively with sorghum flour, now made with manioc flour or cornmeal.

ushaka (Shimakonde). Demonstration of bravery; provocation.

uwavi (Shimakonde). Sorcery. For regional cognates, see Gray 1969: 175; Beidelman 1993: 139; Abrahams 1994: 9; Mombeshora 1994: 71; Ciekawy 1998: 122; Ciekawy 2001: 165.

uwavi ndenga kaja (Shimakonde). Settlement-building sorcery.

uwavi wa kubyaa (Shimakonde). Sorcery of killing/murder.

uwavi wa kudenga (Shimakonde). Sorcery of construction.

uwavi wa kujoa (Shimakonde). Sorcery of danger, or dangerous sorcery.

uwavi wa kulishungila (Shimakonde). Sorcery of self-defense.

uwavi wa kulogwa (Shimakonde). Sorcery of killing/murder.

uwavi wa kunyata (Shimakonde). Dirty/ugly/bad sorcery.

uwavi wa kushunga (Shimakonde). Sorcery of self-advancement, or sorcery of enrichment.

uwavi wa lwanongo (Shimakonde). Sorcery of ruin.

uwavi wa shilikali (Shimakonde). Government sorcery.

vahumu (pl.). See *humu.*

vakulaula (pl.). See *nkulaula.*

vamitela (pl.). See *muntela.*

vanang'olo (pl.). See *nang'olo.*

vanang'olo vene kaja (pl.). See *nang'olo mwene kaja.*

vanang'olo vene shilambo (pl.). See *nang'olo mwene shilambo.*

vanjomba (pl.). See *njomba.*

vantumi (pl.). See *ntumi.*

vavi (pl.). See *mwavi.*

waing'anga (pl.). See *ing'anga.*

wajiri (Moz.). Lower-level native intermediary in Mueda region.

yangele (Shimakonde). Divination.

Notes

Prologue

1. A *capulana* is a printed cloth worn by women as a wrap.

2. I generally refer to those with whom I worked as Muedans—i.e., residents of the Mueda plateau region—rather than as Makonde. The Makonde ethnic identity, as we will see in part 1, was forged among people of disparate origins fleeing the regional trade in slaves from the seventeenth century onward. To this day, included among the residents of this region are small numbers of people who identify with other regional ethnic groups such as Makua, Yao, or Angoni. In the postindependence period, a smaller number of people identifying with ethnic groups from the center and south of Mozambique have also taken up residence on the plateau, as have a limited number of non-Mozambicans. While non-Makonde residents of the Mueda plateau region some-times conceived of the events, processes, and phenomena described in these pages dif-ferently than did Makonde residents, many in fact spoke and acted as their Makonde neighbors did. At the same time, not all Makonde in the region conceived of these events, processes, and phenomena in the same way. In any case, my research focused not on "the Makonde" per se but instead on those who lived in, and contributed to the collective life of, a particular place, namely, the Mueda plateau. I therefore use the ethnonym Makonde only when and where the topic at hand and/or my informants/ sources lead me to emphasize ethnic identity as a defining social category.

3. Ambrósio himself did not use the term "cosmopolitan," but he nonetheless em-braced the cosmopolitan style defined by Ferguson (1999).

4. A *cabana* is a temporary hut providing shelter close to one's fields during peak agricultural seasons.

5. A *chamboco* is a wooden paddle introduced by colonial authorities to administer beatings (Lopes, Sitoe, and Nhamuende 2002: 45).

Introduction

1. See also Ellis and ter Haar 1998: 201; Palmié 2002: 20. Compare this stance with the call made by Cameroonian writer Daniel Etounga-Manguele for an African "cultural adjustment programme" to solve the continent's present ills (in Chabal and Daloz 1999: 128).

2. I quote Bakhtin's work from Todorov due to the quality of translation.

3. Scholars have debated whether Bakhtin's longtime associate Voloshinov in fact authored the many works published under his name or whether the name was used by Bakhtin as a pseudonym.

4. See also Leach 1954 and Wagner 1975 on culture as an "as if" system.

5. Medvedev, like Voloshinov, was a member of Bakhtin's circle; scholars also debate whether he or Bakhtin authored the works published under his name.

6. I include within the notion of sorcery discourse (qua language of power) not only verbal exchanges but also—in rather more Foucaldian fashion—related nonverbal practices. John Bowen (1993: 179) and Diane Ciekawy (2001: 182–183) also take "sorcery discourse" ("*utsai* discourse" in the latter case) as their objects of study.

7. Translation of *uwavi* as "sorcery" is not unproblematic. When Muedans with whom I worked translated *uwavi* into Portuguese, they used the word *feitiço,* which derives from an antiquated form of the verb "to make" and which means, literally, "a made thing" (see Rosenthal 1998: 1). The Portuguese term *feitiço,* however, may be translated into English either as "witchcraft," as "sorcery," *or* as "magic."

In his groundbreaking work among Azande, Evans-Pritchard differentiated between *mangu,* which he translated as "witchcraft," and *ngwa,* which he translated as "magic." *Mangu,* as he understood it, was founded in "hereditary psycho-physical powers" (sometimes unleashed subconsciously). By contrast, *ngwa* was founded in the conscious use of medicinal substances and spells that had to be learned (Evans-Pritchard [1937] 1976: 176). According to Evans-Pritchard's Azande definitions, witchcraft was malicious. Magic, however, comprised two categories. Magic used to avenge the killing of a family member by a witch—"vengeance magic"—constituted a form of "good magic" (which Evans-Pritchard also labeled "white magic"). By contrast, magic used to harm or to kill others, unprovoked, constituted a form of "bad magic" (which he also labeled "black magic"). This latter category Evans-Pritchard also translated as "sorcery" (Evans-Pritchard [1937] 1976: 176, 189; [1931] 1970: 25, 26; [1929] 1970).

While Muedans did, sometimes, suggest to me that *uwavi* may be passed down from parent to child (like Azande "witchcraft" as defined by Evans-Pritchard), they generally placed greater emphasis on the idea that *uwavi* must be learned (like Azande "magic" as defined by Evans-Pritchard). What is more, Muedans with whom I worked understood certain physical substances (called *mitela*) to be essential to the practice of *uwavi,* even if these substances were not alone sufficient for *uwavi*'s practice. Considering all of this, it would seem that "magic" is the best English-language term by which to translate the Muedan concept *uwavi.* However, in translating *uwavi* by the Portuguese term *feitiço,* Muedans explicitly avoided the Portuguese term *magia*—a word whose form and meaning are more unambiguously linked to the English "magic."

In any case, the English term "sorcery" more effectively conveys the "somber" (Geschiere 1997: 58), even sinister, sense adhering to the concept of *uwavi* (see also Ciekawy 2001: 158–159). Although, as we shall see, the practice of *uwavi* is not always considered to be evil, *uwavi* is always recognized as *potentially* menacing.

8. Along with Todd Sanders, I have taken up this theme in the introduction to an edited volume that presents contemporary ethnographies of occult discourses ranging from sorcery and shamanism to urban legend and conspiracy theory (West and Sanders 2003).

9. Wyatt MacGaffey (1980) has argued that concepts such as *uwavi* are ultimately untranslatable. See also Turner 1964; Fadiman 1993: 14–15; Abrahams 1994: 10; Saler 1967: 72. Geschiere, by contrast, argues that Africans have themselves translated such concepts into the European languages that they speak, and that scholars can, and must, follow suit (1997: 14).

10. In espousing dialogical engagement with other languages, I take inspiration from Rosaldo (1980: 20) and Limón (1994). See also Pels 1998: 201.

11. Helen Verran, who studied learning and logic among mathematics students in Nigeria, suggests that, even *within* a sphere such as mathematics, "many logics [are] possible as the result of different methods of symbolizing in representing," and that the worlds that emerge from these distinctive logics are not "hermetically sealed off from one another" (2001: 218–219). Verran asserts that distinctive logics "constitute worlds of knowing that can be slipped into and out of by individual knowers," depending upon their expertise, and that, consequently, "individual knowers can learn to work in multiple symbolic domains and formulate determinate methods of translation between the codes."

12. Evans-Pritchard apprenticed his field assistant to the witch doctors whom he studied ([1937] 1976).

13. Pace Stoller, who provides a rather nuanced account of an investigative journey replete with interruptions and detours, from which he retired before completion, telling his readers: "to have walked further down that unknown path would have prevented me from telling my story" (Stoller and Olkes 1987: 229). (Cf. Van Binsbergen, who tells his readers that after he "became a Sangoma," anthropological discourse became irrelevant to him [1991: 333].)

14. This never happened, as Mpalume left ARPAC before Felista's work with me was completed.

15. Mandumbwe, it turned out, had written a Shimakonde grammar in collaboration with Mpalume (Mpalume and Mandumbwe 1991).

16. While Andiliki is a transliteration of the Portuguese name Henrique (which I told Muedans most closely resembled my English name, Harry), it is a name many Muedans themselves bear; others, by contrast, go by the Portuguese version, Henrique.

17. I did go over substantial portions of the manuscript with them when in Cabo Delgado in 2004, undertaking what Steven Feld (1987) has referred to as "dialogical editing."

Chapter One

1. Muedans with whom we worked generally bore several names. Children were named at birth—often, although not always, for a deceased family member. At various moments—including, for example, passage through rites of initiation, conversion to Christianity or Islam, or induction into warfare—they may have received nicknames that sometimes, but again not always, supplanted previous names. Upon rising to positions of authority, men often took not only their predecessors' titles but also their names. Men and women alike generally appended to their own names the names of their fathers, followed by the names of their fathers' fathers, and so on, as far as they wished to recite; these patrilineal forebears' names served in some ways as surnames (complementing matrilineal, or *likola,* identities), although over the course of generations, the name of each forebear came later in the chain of names by which the living called themselves until being dropped completely. (On the changing names of Makonde individuals, see also Dias and Dias 1970: 287; Gengenbach [2000] provides a fascinating account of the complexity of naming in southern Mozambique.) In this volume, I refer to Muedans by the names I most often heard used to refer to them in my presence.

2. I have written at length about the relationship between O'Neill's rhetorical and geopolitical strategies in West 2004b.

3. The interviewee takes his name from this elder.

4. Beidelman (1993: 12) similarly portrays the East African people eventually known as Kaguru as both victims and perpetrators of the slave trade.

5. Here, Marcos actually refers to a female ancestor, perhaps his mother's mother or his mother's maternal grandmother.

6. The "Angoni" descended from splintering Nguni bands moving northward through the region after the politico-military upheaval referred to as the Mfecane in the mid–nineteenth century (Omer-Cooper 1966; Cobbing 1988; Ngcongco 1989; Hamilton 1997).

Chapter Two

1. Beidelman (1993: 78) describes similar dynamics between founder-hosts and latecomer-guests among Kaguru in Tanzania.

2. Alpers (1969) describes how caravan trade similarly led to the concentration of populations among Yao in the precolonial period.

3. Concerning schismatic dynamics elsewhere in precolonial and colonial Africa, see also Turner [1957] 1996; Forde 1958; Marwick 1967: 114; Beidelman 1993: 17; Fields 1997.

4. Oral testimony indicates that the institution of *humu* was imported with captives and refugee migrants from the Makua-speaking regions south of the plateau around the turn of the century and was modified to fit the needs of Makonde matrilineages. Among Makua, the *nihumu* was a sort of settlement head who represented the geographically broader authority of a *mwene* (Martinez 1989: 69). Makonde matrilineages inverted the hierarchy between [*nang'olo*] *mwene* [*kaja*] and [*ni*]*humu.* Many of

the elders that we interviewed indicated that the first *vahumu* they knew were the first ones named by their respective matrilineages. The three surviving *vahumu* with whom we worked in 1994 asserted that there were once thirty-six *vahumu* among plateau Makonde.

5. The first *vahumu* among plateau Makonde were initiated by Makua counterparts. Subsequently, Makonde *vahumu* initiates were "trained" by *vahumu* from other Makonde matrilineages as well as, often, by Makua counterparts.

Chapter Three

1. Kaspin (1993: 52) describes conceptions of gluttony and the desire for meat among Chewa in Malawi in similar terms.

2. In their time, Dias and Dias (1970: 363) observed similar means being undertaken by Makonde healers to kill suspected sorcery lions. Turner (1968: 115) describes rites undertaken among Ndembu to deal with lion "familiars."

3. Fabian (1990) describes in rich detail how the verb "to eat" connoted power among Luba with whom he worked in Zaire (now Congo). Bayart (1993) argues persuasively that "eating" constitutes an essential euphemism for power in contemporary African politics more broadly. Along similar lines, Schatzberg (1993) argues that the central motif in African political discourse is *consumption*. See also MacCormick 1983: 56; Ferguson 1995; Shaw 1996; Chabal and Daloz 1999: 36; Ellis 1999a: 223; Masquelier 2000; Mbembe 2001: 102–141. Bayart asserts that political idioms of consumption have been radically transformed in the postindependence era to legitimate growing social differentiation (26). (See also Ellis 1999a: 223.) Fabian provides evidence in support of this with his observation that, where once Luba expressed the values of sharing in proverbs about "eating," today they say (exclusively in French, the contemporary language of state), "Power is eaten whole" (1990: 28–31).

4. Turner ([1957] 1996: 31) similarly describes the sharing out of meat as a means of reproducing social relations. So vast is the comparative literature on this topic that Whyte sarcastically alludes to it as the "'right foreleg of the cow' school of ethnography" (1997: 96).

5. See also Piot 1999: 113; Sanders 2001: 171.

6. Middleton (1967: 60) describes Lugbara with whom he worked as assuming that those who ate alone were witches/sorcerers. In fact, because he often ate alone while conducting his research, Middleton was himself assumed to be a witch (61). See also Mair 1969: 43; M. Green 1997: 325.

Chapter Four

1. Epidemics are often blamed on sorcery in Africa. For example, Turner (cited in Mair 1969: 134) documented the attribution of an outbreak of malaria in the Ndembu village of Mukanza to a sorcerer's activities.

2. The phrase "to die in so-and-so's house" is a common euphemism in Africa for dying in the act of attacking so-and-so by means of sorcery (see, e.g., Mair 1969: 96).

3. On another occasion, Marcos told me the story of a 100-seat helicopter that was said by many with whom he previously worked to have carried 100 sorcerers from the village of Myangalewa in an attack upon the legendary healer Manda, also of Namande. The vehicle was said to have crashed in the bush near the village of Miteda, where Manda habitually staged boys' initiation rites. Marcos told me that he visited the scene of the crash the day after it was reported and that, while he saw no mechanical parts, he did see a circular patch of bush that had been flattened in a way that ordinary men with ordinary tools would never have been able to accomplish. His story reminded me of witness accounts of "crop circles" in the English countryside.

4. The division of the world into visible and invisible realms is documented in diverse regions of the globe; see, e.g., Eliade 1964: 205; M. Brown 1986: 50; Atkinson 1989: 16, 37–39; Boddy 1989: 269–309; Stoller 1989: 14; Humphrey and Onon 1996: 76; Stephen 1996: 89; Gufler 1999: 182; Mueggler 2001: 196–197.

5. See also Mbembe 2001: 143–146. Cf. Horton 1993: 326, who equates ideas of the "hidden" to "secondary theories" invoked when first-order explanatory theories fail.

6. Whyte (1982: 2060; 1997: 28, 180) also reports the use of battery acid as a medicinal substance in Uganda.

7. Dias and Dias (1970: 367) suggest that medicinal substances deriving from trees mediated between the living and their ancestors, whose graves were marked by trees, which absorbed their corporal substance.

8. Ambivalence toward medicinal substances and the powers they generate is a common theme in the ethnographic literature on Africa; see, e.g., La Fontaine 1963: 191; M. Green 1994: 25; Ashforth 1996: 1194; Whyte 1997: 28; Ciekawy 1998: 128; see also Taussig 1987: 140. Kluckhohn (1944: 51) reports Navaho beliefs that healing chants could also be used to harm. John Bowen gives evidence of the Koran itself being similarly viewed as a neutral source of power that might be used "to kill or to heal, to clarify or to obscure" among Gayo in Sumatra (1993: 187). See also Lambek 1993: 260.

9. Sorcerers are reported in varied ethnographic contexts to be able to render themselves invisible. Evans-Pritchard ([1937] 1976: 14), for example, reports Azande convictions that witches rub a special ointment into their skin to make them invisible. Goody (1970: 210) describes how Gonja *begbe* (mystical agents) similarly rendered themselves invisible to all but fellow *begbe*. See also M. Green 1994: 25.

10. The use of exotic substances to see persons or things that remain invisible to others is also widely reported in the ethnographic literature. Turner describes Ndembu convictions that a substance called *nsomu* allows its users to see hidden things: "*Nsomu* is like a torch at night whereby [the diviner] can see witches openly" (1968: 28–29). *Nsomu* as described by Turner apparently differs from *shikupi* as described to us by Muedans, however, in that the latter is also used by sorcerers to hide themselves in the first place. Simmons reports Badyaranke in Senegal telling him that people of extraordinary power have "a remarkable ability to 'see' . . . spirits and events that are invisible to others" owing to their "eyes of the night" (1980: 452). On vision and (in)visibility in relation to occult powers more generally, see also Lienhardt 1951: 309; Eliade 1964: 348; Atkinson 1989: 91; Lambek 1993: 243; Plotkin 1993: 235; Bongmba 1998: 173; Gufler 1999: 183; Nyamnjoh 2001: 43. Cf. Ferme 2001: 4, who reports Mende convic-

tions that power derives from the ability "to see beyond visible phenomena and to interpret deeper meanings" but who suggests that Mende do not consider the exercise of this acuity to be limited to the realm of the occult.

11. See also Willis and Chisanga 1999: 3, 173. According to Nyamnjoh, the invisible realm has a name among inhabitants of the Cameroonian grass fields; he describes *msa* as "a mysterious world of abundance and infinite possibilities" that exists in parallel with the visible world (2001: 44). Eliade (1964: 259–260) famously suggested that "the pre-eminently shamanic technique is the passage from one cosmic region to another"; this is precisely what is accomplished by Muedan sorcerers—and, as we shall see, countersorcerers.

12. Among Fore in highland New Guinea, according to Lindenbaum (1979: 56), the word for sorcery, *kio'ena*, expressly means "it is hidden." While this was not so on the Mueda plateau, sorcery and invisibility implied one another in Muedan sorcery discourse. See also Beidelman 1963: 65.

13. See also Lattas 1993; Devisch 2001: 111; Ferme 2001: 209–212.

14. The association of witchcraft and/or sorcery with dancing is reportedly common in the southeastern part of Africa; and such dancing is often said to be done naked. Lambek, for example, gives account of sorcerers dancing naked together in Mayotte (1993: 251). Van Dijk's informants suggested that witches made their practices attractive to prospective witches by combining them with two irresistible activities: dancing and nakedness/sexual congress (van Dijk 1992).

15. Middleton (1963: 271; 1967: 65) similarly argues that witches "invert" social norms. Van Binsbergen asserts: "Witchcraft . . . is everything which falls outside the kinship order, is not regulated by that order, [or] challenges, rejects, [or] destroys that order" (2001: 241). Mair (1969: 42) describes witches as forming an "anti-society." Boddy uses the same phrase—"anti-society"—to describe the *zār* world of spirits among Hofriyati in the northern Sudan. She writes that "the behavioral traits of *zayran* both surpass and invert those of humans: in some regards, *zayran* are antitheses of Hofriyati; in others, they are their caricatures." She further suggests that the language used within *zār* operates as an "anti-language" (1989: 156–157, 273–274). See also Beidelman 1963; Forth 1993; Devisch 2001: 113–114.

16. See also Devisch 2001: 111.

17. Cf. Humphrey and Onon 1996: 352.

18. Muedan sorcery, as described to us, in many ways resembled "deep knowledge" as described to Apter by Yoruba (Apter 2002: 234–238) insofar as it constituted a capacity for "revision and reversal." See also Kapferer 1997, who portrays Sinhalese Buddhists as conceiving of sorcery as the power to make the world through the constitutive act of seeing it.

19. Beattie (1963: 29) suggests that one need not view the use of poisons as "magical," for their effects can be explained in chemical or physiological terms. See also Fields 1997. Muedans, in any case, considered the use of *shongo* to be, by definition, an act of sorcery.

20. Lambek (1993: 242) describes similar devices used by sorcerers in Mayotte.

21. Cf. Lienhardt 1951: 305, who suggests that, when Dinka said witches "eat" their victims, they meant that witches consumed the well-being of others, not that they actually consumed their victims' flesh.

22. Dias and Dias (1970: 394) use the term *machatwani* in reference to slave-dead (*mortos-escravos*) among Makonde in the late 1950s. The phenomenon of living-dead slave laborers appears in the ethnographic record throughout Africa. See, e.g., Beidelman 1963: 66; 1993: 155; Ardener 1970: 147; Geschiere 1992: 170–174; 1997: 147–149; 1998: 822–824; Mesaki 1994: 49; Reynolds 1996: 90; Stadler 1996: 92; Jean Comaroff and John Comaroff 1999; Sanders 1999: 123; 2001: 170; Ashforth 2000: 182; Niehaus, Mohlala, and Shokane 2001: 69–71. Willis (1999: 144–146) specifically mentions the use by Lungu sorcerers of banana trees to replace the bodies of their victims. Curiously, Beattie (1963: 46) informs readers that, in precolonial days in Bunyoro, convicted sorcerers were tied up in dried banana leaves and burnt to death; see also Fadiman 1993: 250 for evidence of the execution of witches in this same manner among Meru in colonial Kenya. Whitehead (2002: 82), by contrast, reports Patamuna corpses being wrapped in banana leaves to ward off *kanaimà* (dark sorcerers).

23. The idea of sorcerers making or transforming themselves into animals—often called "familiars" in the literature—is widespread in Africa and beyond. See, e.g., Evans-Pritchard [1929] 1970: 33 n.; [1937] 1976; Kluckhohn 1944: 26; Krige [1947] 1970: 265; Wyatt 1950; Lienhardt 1951: 308; M. Wilson [1951] 1970; Deren 1953: 65; Beidelman 1963: 65; 1993: 141; Gray 1963; Middleton 1963; 1967: 59; Eliade 1964; Ginzburg [1966] 1992: 3; M. Nash 1967: 127; Saler 1967; Castenada 1968; Turner 1968: 177; Mair 1969: 39; Ruel 1969, 1970a, 1970b; R. Brain 1970: 164; Goody 1970: 208; Hammond-Tooke 1970: 366–368; Marwick 1970: 461; Mayer 1970: 56; Pitt-Rivers 1970; Schapera 1970: 111–113; Willis 1970: 219; Wyllie 1970: 135; Reichel-Dolmatoff 1975; de Heusch 1985: 98; M. Brown 1986: 50; Stoller and Olkes 1987; Taussig 1987: 246, 358–363; Jackson 1989; Auslander 1993: 180; Ellen 1993b: 10; 1993a: 91; Forth 1993: 100; Schmoll 1993: 200; Mesaki 1994: 49; Goheen 1996; Humphrey and Onon 1996: 101, 328–329; Kapferer 1997; Shaw 1997; Prechtel 1998; Ellis 1999a; Gufler 1999; Willis and Chisanga 1999: 115; Bastian 2001; Niehaus, Mohlala, and Shokane 2001: 45–62; Whitehead 2002. See also Saul Bellow's novel *Henderson, the Rain King* (1959); Bellow studied anthropology before turning to a career in writing fiction.

24. In the late colonial period, Dias and Dias wrote: "For the Makonde, the power of sorcerers is unlimited. Frequently, they use animals, like lions, leopards, or snakes, creating ones which chase whomever they instruct and which no one can kill without the aid of powerful *ntela*. At times, the sorcerers themselves transform into these animals. . . . In general, it is believed that people considered to have been killed by lions are eaten at nighttime feasts. So deeply rooted are these beliefs that, when a lion killed in 1957 close to Mueda and left mutilated remains spread on the ground, the Makonde said that this was fake, and that the man was being kept alive in the house of the sorcerer, who was fattening him up to eat him later" (1970: 369, my translation).

25. See also Ashforth 2000: 126.

26. La Fontaine (1963: 208) reports envy among co-wives as the most common cause of witchcraft accusations among Gisu. See also LeVine 1963: 242.

27. Jones (1970: 325) describes a similar logic of "flesh debts" among Ibo witches, and Danfulani (1999: 171) among Eggon witches. Karen Brown (1989: 280) describes how Haitian *manbo* and *oungan* sometimes find it "impossible to extricate themselves" from "an ascending spiral of obligations" produced by involvement in sorcery.

28. Van Dijk (1992) reports witches in Malawi demanding in-kind repayment of flesh debts according to body parts—literally, an eye for an eye, a uterus for a uterus, a penis for a penis, etc.

29. Masquelier (1997) describes how Mawri, in Niger, are understood to enter into deals with Doguwa *spirits,* whose insatiable hunger for flesh they must feed by identifying victims among neighbors, friends, and even strangers.

Chapter Five

1. Lambek was told a similar story by one of his informants (1993: 298).

2. Cf. Whyte 1997: 179; Bongmba 2001: 53–54.

3. Salapina most often divined to discern the cause of a difficult delivery. According to her, such births were generally the result of either the woman or her husband having had intercourse with someone else during the woman's pregnancy. Her oracle told her which of the couple had been unfaithful. Once the guilty party had confessed, she told me, the mother usually gave birth without losing the child.

4. Willis and Chisanga (1999: 104) also give an account of the use of bottles, albeit containing medicinal substances, in divination.

5. Cf. Marwick 1967: 104, who presents the term "deaths of God" as one of long standing among Chewa. Maxwell (1999: 85) describes the dichotomy between "diseases of God" and "diseases of man" as a precolonial phenomenon among Hwesa. Janzen (1978: 67–74) reports the categories "disease of God" and "disease of man" being used among Bakongo in Zaire but does not tell us whether the dichotomy predates colonial encounter. Whyte (1982: 2057) reports Nyole suspicions that illnesses that prove untreatable are "of God."

6. By contrast, Rasmussen (2001b: 30) reports that Tuareg conceived of "illnesses of God" as those that could be cured by Koranic healers.

7. By contrast, Azande oracles, according to Evans-Pritchard's descriptions ([1937] 1976), informed those who consulted them of the identity of their assailants.

8. Cf. Ciekawy 2001: 181.

9. Colonial policy and administrative practice (to be discussed in part 2) may have played a role in quashing sorcery accusations and ordeals.

10. A substantial literature on "witch-finding" or "witch-cleansing cults" in the region dates to the colonial period; see, e.g., Richards [1935] 1970; Marwick 1950; Tait 1963; Willis 1968, 1970; M. Green 1994, 1997; Fields 1997; Maxwell 1999; Probst 1999.

11. Maia Green (1994: 25) reports use of the term *hirisi* to refer to similar objects used among Pogoro in Tanzania. Davis-Roberts (1992: 388) also reports the use of such amulets among Tabwa in Zaire (now Congo) to render potential victims invisible to their attackers. See also Whyte 1997: 133.

12. Curiously, Ginzburg ([1966] 1992: 24) writes that *benandanti* of sixteenth- and seventeenth-century southern Europe were said to arm themselves with stalks of fennel to do battle against witches armed with stalks of sorghum. Maia Green (1994: 38) tells us of Pogoro healers who administer millet flour to patients' heads and bodies as a medium for ancestral blessings.

13. Beattie (1963: 38–49) describes the production and use of similar instruments among Nyoro. See also Devisch 2001: 115–116.

14. Krige ([1947] 1970: 271) describes Lobedu in Northeastern Transvaal similarly defending villages through camouflaging.

15. Not all *vamitela* cured (some only divined and/or undertook preventative activities), and a very small number of *vakulaula* used no *mitela* in their healing practices.

16. The term *kupilikula* resonates with conceptions of countersorcery healing elsewhere in Africa and beyond. Devisch reports Yaka healers in Zaire (now Congo) fighting illness by "turning it back against itself autodestructively" (1990: 220–221). Joralemon and Sharon describe Peruvian *curanderos* similarly "send[ing] [sorcery] back to its source" (1993: 253). John Bowen tells of Gayo healers in Sumatra achieving "retribution" by "returning" harmful spirits to their senders (1993: 179). See also Luomala 1989: 291; Rodman 1993; Whyte 1982: 2057; 1988: 219; 1997: 3. Muedans also use the verbs *kupindula* and *kupindikula* to express similar meanings.

17. Lienhardt (1951: 304) similarly uses the term "counter-witch" to describe Dinka who combat witchcraft.

18. Like Yaka healers described by Devisch, Muedan healers worked "beyond the usual cognitive maps of space-time limits" (Devisch 2001: 106).

19. See also Gufler 1999: 181; Devisch 2001: 108.

20. Again, see Devisch 2001: 109.

21. See also Beidelman 1993: 2, 204.

Chapter Six

1. An *igoli* is a knee-high platform made of a braided reed cord lattice stretched over a rectangular wooden frame and elevated from the ground by four wooden legs. It may serve as a bed or as a bench on which to sit.

2. See also Gufler 1999.

3. Danfulani (1999: 176) describes a similar means of divining witches among Eggon in Nigeria.

4. Rodman (1993: 232) tells of an accused sorcerer in Abmae, Vanuatu, who ultimately admitted to him uncertainty as to whether or not he was, indeed, guilty of the charge. Muedans similarly sometimes express doubts about their own innocence.

5. Maia Green (1994: 35) describes Pogoro antiwitchcraft rites in which, by contrast, no distinction is made between accused witches and their accusers.

6. See also Geschiere 1997: 55. The scenario is far from universal, however; e.g., Kluckhohn's (1944: 49) Navaho informants connected the confession of a witch to the recovery of the witch's victim rather than to the recovery of the witch.

7. According to Kluckhohn (1944: 54), Navaho healers attributed any illness that did not quickly pass to a witch's attack rather than diagnosing it as the product of a failed attack on someone else. See also Mesaki 1994: 48.

8. Such encounters are driven by healers' accusations and not by patient confessions; see also Wyllie 1970: 132.

9. See also Mayer 1970: 65–66; Ruel 1970b: 333; Devisch 2001: 120.

Chapter Seven

1. Cf. Turner 1968: 203, where the making of a *nyalumaya* (young girl) "familiar" among Ndembu in Zambia is described.

2. Beattie (1967: 229–230) documents Nyoro convictions that *mahembe* ("fetishes"; i.e., "made things") present similar dangers of escaping their makers.

3. See also Ashforth 2000: 189.

4. See also Willis 1970: 219.

5. Laderman (1991: 59) describes a similar induction among Malay shamans.

6. The same pattern has been frequently observed elsewhere in Africa and beyond. See, e.g., Turner 1968; Redmayne 1970: 103; Fry 1976: 38; D. Brown [1986] 1994: 94; Masquelier 1987; Taussig 1987: 447; Devisch 1990: 220; K. Brown 1991: 352; Janzen 1992: 105–106; Reynolds 1996: 6; Willis and Chisanga 1999: 152; Ashforth 2000: 90; Rasmussen 2001b: 60. Vaughan suggests that the first African medical assistants engaged by missionary doctors were generally ex-patients who "lingered on in the hospitals long after they had recovered from their illnesses" (1991: 61).

7. Chavunduka (1978: 19) details the importance of the guidance of spirits to healing in Rhodesia (now Zimbabwe).

8. By contrast, according to Tracy Luedke (personal communication, January 2004), some healers in the Mozambican province of Tete emphasized the importance of medicinal substances, and others emphasized the importance of possessing spirits; each category accused those falling into the other category of sorcery.

9. When Kalamatatu told us that only the "complicated" ate lion meat, he referred to sorcerers. Whereas ordinary people would be wary of eating the meat of an animal that may have eaten people, sorcerers, of course, would have no aversion to cannibalism. Kalamatatu's sly tone, however, left open the possibility that he himself had tasted lion flesh—that he was himself a "complicated" man.

10. Evans-Pritchard ([[1937] 1976: 31) observed the same among Azande.

11. Karen Brown (1989) describes a similar dynamic of mutual suspicions and accusations among Haitian Vodou priests and priestesses.

12. Such is reportedly the case elsewhere in Africa and beyond; see, e.g., Kluckhohn 1944: 61; M. Brown 1986: 63; Atkinson 1989: 98; Lambek 1993; Pigg 1996: 169; Stephen 1996: 86; Kapferer 1997: 6; Voeks 1997: 105; Ellis 1999a: 233; Willis and Chisanga 1999: 140; Ashforth 2000: 109; Rasmussen 2001b: 32. Cf. Chavunduka 1978: 97. Hofriyati in Sudan described *zayran* spirits to Boddy in similarly ambivalent terms (1989: 342–343). Wafer (1991: 14) reports practitioners of Candomblé as looking upon the healing *exus* with similar ambivalence.

13. See also Lienhardt 1951: 312; Mair 1969: 24; Whyte 1997: 60–61.

14. The notion that healers are sorcerers (or witches) is reportedly common in Africa. See, e.g., Evans-Pritchard [1937] 1976: 79; Gray 1963: 144; La Fontaine 1963: 195; LeVine 1963: 236; Mair 1969: 77; Mombeshora 1994: 83. Geschiere (1997: 51) reports Maka in Cameroon saying that the *nkong* (healer) is "a witch who has beaten all records." See also Shaw 1997: 867–868, 872 n. 17.

15. Whitehead (2002: 224) makes the same point in reference to shamans among Patamuna of South America.

16. The belief that healers are cured or reformed sorcerers is reportedly widespread. Taussig (1987), for example, discusses shamans in the South American highlands in this light. Stephen (1996) suggests that in some Melanesian societies, sorcerers themselves are considered the preeminent ritual experts in the community and, being capable of mediating sacred power, act in many regards as shamans. See also Nadel 1970: 287; Nitibaskara 1993: 126; Ashforth 2001b: 214; Rasmussen 2001a: 150.

Chapter Eight

1. Mitchell (1956: 136–137) speaks of this phenomenon in colonial Nyassaland.

2. Similar practices are described by M. Wilson [1951] 1970: 278; La Fontaine 1963: 198; LeVine 1963: 239; Mair 1969: 58; Goody 1970: 211–212. Evans-Pritchard ([1937] 1976: 39–40) describes how Azande victims' families themselves made public orations expressing their convictions that they had been attacked by witches.

3. Unlike the Beng authority figures described by Gottlieb (1989), who consolidated popular legitimacy by showing their willingness to sacrifice their own kin in the interests of the larger social group, settlement heads were not expected by Muedans to practice such "destructive" forms of sorcery. In this regard, Muedan authority figures resembled the *benandanti*—southern European pagan practitioners tried by the Inquisition. These *benandanti*, Ginzburg tells us, were generally assumed to be capable of destructive forms of witchcraft ([1966] 1992: 78) but, *as benandanti*, were expected to do battle against witches rather than the work of witchcraft. Cf. Turner ([1957] 1996: 112), who characterizes suspected Ndembu sorcerers as unsuitable for positions of authority.

4. Geschiere (1997: 13) gives an account of the use of the term "constructive" to describe certain acts of sorcery in the Cameroon. Elsewhere, Fisiy and Geschiere (1990: 142) speak of "witchcraft of authority" practiced by elders in the context of village palavers.

5. Muedan ambivalence regarding sorcery resembled the ambivalence of Safwa, as described by Harwood, regarding the occult capability called *itonga*. According to Harwood's account, Safwa conceived of *itonga* simply as "the power to understand and perform 'hidden things,'" as "doing things to others without being seen," or as "the power to act, unperceived by others" (1970: 57). Such power could be used to either moral or immoral ends. One informant described people with *itonga* by saying: "They are like keys, which can both open and close doors" (59). Based upon his understanding of Safwa *itonga*, Harwood questioned Evans-Pritchard's assertion that Azande always considered *mangu* (witchcraft) to be bad, citing evidence from within *Witchcraft,*

Oracles and Magic among the Azande that the witch doctors who detected witchcraft were themselves believed to use *mangu*, but to "good" effect (Harwood 1970: 70–71). The notion that witchcraft or sorcery is inherently neutral is widespread; see, e.g., Parsons [1927] 1970: 235; Kluckhohn 1944: 6; Krige [1947] 1970: 267; Gilbert 1989: 60; Joralemon and Sharon 1993: 167, 175; Danfulani 1999: 169.

6. See also Goheen 1996: 145.

7. Stephen (1996: 92) reports that the power of Mekeo (Melanesia) sorcerer-healers was sometimes attributed to their having ingested the flesh of a poisonous snake.

8. De Heusch (1985: 32–33) reports Tetela (Zaire, now Congo) lineage chiefs—who dressed as leopards in ritual dances—abstaining from eating leopard flesh because "the leopard does not eat the leopard." Authority figures throughout Africa have often been closely identified with lions and leopards. For example, Turner ([1957] 1996: 11) documents Ndembu chiefs sitting on leopard or lion skins. De Heusch (1985: 104) reports Swazi kings playing the role of "'sacred' monsters" by becoming lions among their people. Lan (1985: 32–34) records convictions in the Dande region (of Zimbabwe) that royal ancestral spirits take up residence in the bodies of lions. Goheen (1996) speaks of Nso' chiefs, in Cameroon, transforming themselves into lions (and their counselors into leopards) in order to patrol their chiefdoms and to protect their inhabitants from evil sorcerers. Douglas reports Lele ideas that a diviner could "transform himself into a leopard, to meet other sorcerers at night and out-wit them on their own ground" (1963: 130).

9. According to many elders with whom we conversed, the practice of ingesting *lukalongo* eventually spread to include many settlement heads.

10. Cf. Lan's account: "Some people say that a few days after a Zande chief is buried, a tiny lion without a mane crawls up through the hole left for it at the side of the grave and scampers off into the forest. When I asked why this happens to chiefs and not to other men, I was given one of two answers. Either I was told that it is simply because chiefs are chiefs. They own and rule the land when alive and it is the same when they are dead. Or I was told that chiefs eat certain medicines which at their deaths transform them into *mhondoro*. Only chiefs know these medicines. They have the monopoly on power now and for all time" (1985: 32–34). See also Ruel 1970a: 54–55.

11. Cf. Harwood 1970, who writes of Safwa differentiating between good *itonga* and bad *itonga*.

12. Geschiere (1997: 57–58) makes this point eloquently.

13. In Evans-Pritchard's account, Azande kept their own rubbing boards and consulted them alone; termite oracles were also consulted alone; *benge* oracles were consulted in the presence of another person, but this person did not deliver the oracle's verdict.

14. See also Whyte 1997: 178, 197.

15. Dias and Dias (1970: 345) do report cases in which individuals were submitted to ordeals to produce confessions; in each of the cases they present, however, sorcery was deemed to have produced effects that menaced an entire settlement.

16. Kluckhohn (1944: 113) advances a similar argument with reference to witchcraft among the Navaho.

17. Chowning (1987: 170) offers a similar description of the effects of sorcery among Kove in Melanesia. See also Mombeshora 1994: 177 on similar effects produced by cursing among Bena in Tanzania.

Part Two Introduction

1. Horton (1993: 319) himself later argued that "the 'closed'/'open' dichotomy [was] ripe for the scrap heap," although yielding primarily on the grounds that a continuum existed between these two poles. See also Hountondji 1983: 156–169.

2. Shaw (2002) argues that in Sierra Leone the beliefs and practices associated with witchcraft are traceable to the social disruptions produced by the slave trade. Rosenthal (1998) links sorcery, historically, to the slave trade. Hartwig (1971) links the rise of sorcery among Kerebe in East Africa to the inequalities fostered by caravan trade. Along similar lines, Gow (1996) hypothesizes that *ayahuasca* shamanism emerged in western Amazonia only after "contact," taking form in the racialized interstices between indigenous communities, European colonizers, and mestizo populations.

3. Vaughan argues, along similar lines: "For many people in Africa the fluidity of identity and the necessity of constructing new individual and collective identities for political purposes [have been and] are real and immediate experiences" (1991: 204).

4. Cf. Horton 1993: 317; Rasmussen 2001b: 186.

5. See also Geschiere 1997: 59, 166; Ashforth 2000: 123.

6. Mayer (1970: 67–68) argues that, among Gusii in western Kenya, the witch is always marked as one of "them" and not one of "us," although often as a result of betraying former family, friends, and/or allies—that is, the witch is an Other who was once self. See also Bond and Ciekawy 2001: 11.

7. Van Dijk (2001: 112) has argued that witchcraft itself provides a "creative space" where new identities are produced.

Chapter Nine

1. Because the conquering Portuguese came to Mozambique by way of the sea, Muedan elders often refer to them as *dyomba*, "fish."

2. Aged settlement heads appointed war chiefs in their stead, and Namashakole may have been one of these. Others with whom we spoke told us that Namashakole was the war name by which Maunda himself was known, but these informants were not Maunda's Vashitunguli nephews, as was Ng'upula.

3. Here, it was unclear if Maunda Ng'upula was referring to the same, or another, Mbavala. Had Mbavala died, his successor might have inherited the name Mbavala along with his title. But our interviewee did not explicitly state that Mbavala died. Through the practice of *takatuka*, Makonde *vamitela* of the time were said to have been able to place the severed heads of captives on the bodies of the deceased, thereby bringing them back to life. For that reason, it is plausible that our interviewee credited Mbavala—a powerful *muntela* in his own right—with having survived decapitation.

4. During this period the Portuguese feared German incursions from Tanganyika.

5. That is, their fathers were each Vamwanga.

6. Two years earlier, Ensign António Pires claimed to have "divided the rebel Makonde region of Nyassa in the middle" (Pires 1924: 18), but the path of his campaign to link the Rovuma River to Porto Amélia had skirted the plateau's southwestern margin and avoided areas of concentrated population (see map 2). Subsequent accounts (Costa 1932) give evidence that Makonde engaged in skirmishes with Portuguese troops only months after Pires's passage.

7. According to Maunda Ng'upula's account, the Portuguese, with Mbavala's aid, pursued Malapende and Namashakole to the lowlands near the Messalo River. Eventually, Malapende and Namashakole returned to the plateau, but Maunda refused (like Malapende in Lyulagwe's account) to surrender. Instead, he sent Shiebu on his behalf.

8. This is, of course, a common motif in African war stories. The most famous example relates to the Maji Maji uprising in German East Africa in 1905 (Adas 1979). See also Fry 1976: 107; K. Wilson 1992; Rosenthal 1998: 113; Wild 1998; Rasmussen 2001a: 140. Bastian (2001) reports that members of some Nigerian university fraternities claim immunity to gunshots. See also Worsley 1968: 141 on similar phenomena in Melanesia.

9. Muedans described similar strategies for escaping danger—including transforming oneself into clouds—to Dias and Dias (1970: 371).

10. For a similar account of an Mbugwe chief widely acknowledged to have summoned troops (German, no less) by means of witchcraft to punish his enemies, see Gray 1963: 147.

11. Dias and Dias report being told by one of their informants: "Whites know how to make machines and fly through the air, but . . . Mbavala was able to do/make better things [*fazer coisas superiores*] than whites" (1970: 364, my translation).

Chapter Ten

1. A *regulado* was a geographical domain of colonial authority encompassing the domains of many formerly autonomous settlement heads.

2. A *régulo* was "chief" of a *regulado*.

3. Portuguese control of the plateau was tenuous during the war, especially when German incursions prompted Makonde revolts. The Nyassa Company retook the plateau in 1919 and 1920, putting down scattered revolts (Serra 1983: 118; Pélissier 1994: 416).

4. *Capitão-mor* is a Portuguese military term meaning "greater (or "superior") captain" and was originally applied to commanders of forts or expeditionary forces in the Portuguese overseas territories. Ironically, it was applied to native authorities at the moment these figures were subordinated to a superior authority.

5. The term *wajiri* is a transliteration of the Kiswahili term *wajili,* which is in turn derived from the Arabic word *waziri,* meaning "minister" or "envoy."

6. This can be verified by comparing the personnel notices in the *Boletim da Companhia do Nyassa* with those in the colonial *Anuários de Moçambique.*

7. The Portuguese curiously adapted the term *gentílica* to refer, not to non-Jews, but instead to "tribal," "pagan," non-Christian peoples.

8. The term *régulo* means "kinglet" or "native chief" in Portuguese. It was used everywhere in Mozambique to refer to *autoridades gentílicas* at the highest level, while subordinates of the *régulos* were referred to by titles that varied throughout the country.

9. According to Mitchell, the colonial administration in Nyassaland similarly "incorporated . . . indigenous organization in its framework" (1956: 48–49).

10. Mair (1969: 139) reported that Ndembu crossed the border from British-administered Northern Rhodesia into Portuguese-administered Angola when they wanted to consult diviners about witchcraft cases.

11. See Portaria no. 292 de 17 de Julho de 1911; cited in Gulube 2003: 100.

12. See Lei no. 32.171 de 29 de Julho de 1942; cited in Gulube 2003: 100.

13. See Lei no. 23.229 de 15 de Novembro de 1933; cited in Gulube 2003: 101.

14. Meneses (2000: 9, 22–23) suggests that colonial authorities ultimately permitted the practice of "traditional medicine" owing to the short supply of colonial doctors and nurses.

15. See Pereira 1998: 167–177 for the story of a colonial-era district administrator in Mueda to whom a man—accused of killing a family member suspected of sorcery—was brought by *autoridades gentílicas* for judgment. The administrator recounts the details of the case with dreamlike curiosity before telling how the death of the accused by means of countersorcery rendered irrelevant the decision he faced between, on the one hand, applying the penal code and finding the accused guilty of homicide or, on the other hand, pardoning the accused due to "extenuating circumstances" arising from culturally sanctioned "convictions."

16. One of the most common forms of dispute in the plateau region took the following form. Soon after conquest, a settlement head nominated a subordinate to interact with the colonial regime. The settlement head used the opportunity to consolidate unity among his people by nominating one from among the descendants of a slave mother, whose loyalty to the matrilineage (not genuinely their own) was tenuous. When the post in the colonial hierarchy proved lucrative, however, the settlement head (or his heir) sought to dislodge the nominee (or his heir) by questioning his line of descent. See also Dias and Dias 1970: 307.

17. Africanist anthropologists have long observed that the use of "native authorities" by colonial administrations placed these figures in awkward—"intercalary"—positions (Gluckman, Mitchell, and Barnes 1949). Fadiman (1993) provides a fascinating account of this dilemma as experienced by Meru in Kenya.

18. Dias and Dias (1970: 305) attribute declining popular respect for *autoridades gentílicas* to the fact that authority was not exercised at the level of the *regulado* in the precolonial period, but they ignore how the colonial administration also transformed the nature of authority enacted by these figures.

19. Ex-Mpanga workers with whom we spoke remembered that the blanket, sleeveless shirt, and shorts provided to them by the company were more valuable than the wages they received.

20. See also Harries 1993, who suggests that labor migration has long served southern Mozambicans as a rite of passage into status as financially independent heads of household.

21. Some of these goods, such as bicycles and sewing machines, soon became available in shops built on the plateau by coastal-based Indian merchants. Even so, prices were far better in Tanganyika. Oral testimony indicates that, in the mid-1940s, for example, a migrant worker in Tanganyika could buy a bicycle for between 250 and 350 shillings. In Mozambique, a bicycle cost between 1,250 and 1,500 escudos in the same period. Considering the rates of exchange (e.g., 100 escudos to the pound in 1946), the range of prices was almost the same; but the quality of bicycles available in Tanganyika was substantially higher, meaning that the cheapest ones there were comparable to the most expensive in Mozambique. Sewing machines cost 300 shillings north of the Rovuma River and 3,000 escudos to the south, despite their poorer quality.

22. Lindenbaum (1979: 74) suggests that Fore in highland New Guinea experienced a similar proliferation of forms of sorcery after colonial contact.

Chapter Eleven

1. The Montfort missionaries (also commonly referred to as the Company of Mary) are one of three Catholic congregations founded in early-eighteenth-century France by Louis-Marie Grignion de Montfort (canonized in 1947).

2. Emakua is the language spoken by Makua.

3. Peel (2000: 249) has argued persuasively that it is with great uncertainty that we read religious conviction in practical expressions of belief; "conversion," he suggests, can be defined only as the adoption of a social identity. Accordingly, I place the terms "conversion" and "convert(s)" in quotes.

4. See also Meyer 1992: 98.

5. Pels (1999: 115–157) details how Christian missionaries among Luguru, who also sponsored initiation rites, similarly "tried to pull Luguru initiation practices apart" (135). Ellis (1999a: 241) provides an account of how the British colonial government in Liberia organized initiation rites that omitted all practices associated with Leopard Societies (said to be behind ritual murders enacted in the guise of leopards). See also Fadiman 1993: 205–228 for an account of how missionaries among Meru in Kenya selectively embraced local "tradition."

6. Pels (1999: 7) argues that "initiation" serves as a better metaphor for Christian evangelization in Africa than does "conversion"; the Dutch Montfort Fathers took this metaphor literally.

7. Pels (1999: 136) documents how missionaries among Luguru attempted to supplant African rhythms with others they considered better suited to Christian sensibilities. The Montfort Fathers at Nang'ololo similarly taught their congregation European hymns, but they also apparently demonstrated greater tolerance for African rhythms than the missionaries of which Pels writes. In this regard, the Montfortians acted more like missionaries among Hwesa as described by Maxwell (1999: 92).

8. The same term is reportedly used to mean ancestral spirit among Pogoro (M. Green 1994: 32; 1997: 331) and Bena (Mombeshora 1994: 75) in Tanzania.

9. Ranger (1992: 280–281), Beidelman (1993: 113), and Maxwell (1999: 92) report missionaries encouraging similar transpositions elsewhere in Africa.

10. As Landau (1995: 132) has suggested, too little attention has been paid by historians to the critical role played by Africans themselves in Christian evangelization.

11. The Legion of Mary is a lay Catholic association founded in 1921 in Dublin, Ireland, by Frank Duff. It stresses "a Marian spirituality inspired largely by the writings of Louis Grignion de Montfort," founder of the Montfort missionary order (McBrien and Attridge 1995: 763).

Chapter Twelve

1. Voeks cites evidence that the sign of the cross was similarly "already a traditional sacred symbol to [Brazilian] slaves who hailed from Dahomey" (1997: 158).

2. See also Pels 1999: 40.

3. Meyer (1999: 54–82) points out in her work on Christian missions among Ewe in Ghana that missionaries struggled, sometimes unwittingly, with the paradox generated by translating Christianity into local languages: translated Christian terms inevitably carried within them significance deriving from Ewe cosmology.

4. Here, Matola's account is inflected with the language of Christianity, for Shakoma would not have called these objects "gods." Some of the objects might have been vessels used in *kulipudya* ceremonies. Others might have been vessels containing Shakoma's *mitela,* including substances that allowed him to see into the invisible realm of *uwavi.*

5. See also Pels 1999: 257.

6. Meyer (1999: 83–111) has called similar transpositions of Christian notions of the devil onto African cosmologies acts of "diabolisation."

7. Other missionaries to Africa—particularly those of Protestant sects—prescribed more dramatic measures, developing rituals to exorcise sorcery from their congregants. See, e.g., Maxwell 1999: 81–83. Such rites gave foundation to the healing emphases of many contemporary African Independent Churches.

8. Cf. Jean Comaroff and John Comaroff 1991: 208–209, 245.

9. Of course, the missionaries had in other ways cast themselves as powerful operators not only in the mundane world but also in affairs that Muedans associated with the invisible realm by, for example, staging their own rites of initiation at the mission (cf. Jean Comaroff and John Comaroff 1991: 212, 213).

10. Such rumors were common wherever missionaries went in colonial Africa. See, e.g., White 2000: 182–183.

11. The Congregation of the Consolata Missionary Sisters was founded by Giuseppe Allamano in 1910 in Turin, Italy.

12. Dias and Dias (1970: 365) similarly report that those with whom they worked referred to Western medicine by the term *ntela/mitela.* Vaughan (1991: 60) reports that

Swahili also used the same term (*dawa*) to refer both to missionary medical substances and to the substances used by their own healers.

13. Pels (1999: 239, 259) suggests that Luguru similarly conceived of missionaries as *waganga* (healers). Landau (1995: 113) suggests that this conception was common in African encounters with missionaries. See also Rekdal 1999: 472.

14. White (2000: 184) reports that the White Fathers in Northern Rhodesia, among other African missionaries elsewhere, were widely assumed to be powerful sorcerers. Pels (1999: 262) suggests that missionaries among Luguru were considered capable only of beneficent forms of magic.

15. M. Green (1994: 41, 43) similarly suggests that Catholic prohibitions on witchcraft beliefs and practices among Pogoro in Tanzania were interpreted as the expression of church opposition to "actual witches."

16. Until 1929, Portuguese policy limited education for "native" children to vocational training that would enhance their labor skills (Hedges 1985: 7). In 1929, new regulations permitted African children to study with white children, but only if their families had achieved *assimilado* status through an official process whereby they demonstrated "civilized" modes and manners of eating, speaking, and dressing, etc. (Penvenne 1991). "Indigenous" children (non-*assimilados*) were limited to a "rudimentary" education, including grades 1, 2, and 3-rudimentary (a simplified version of grade 3).

17. These agreements required that the school curriculum meet with the satisfaction of the colonial administration and that it foster a sense of Portuguese nationalism among students by providing instruction in the Portuguese language and in Portuguese history and geography (Sheldon 1998). Indigenous children were still limited to a fourth-grade education, after which they were permitted to study only in vocational schools.

18. Grade 3-elementary completed grade 3 for students who had previously taken grade 3-rudimentary.

19. Pels (1999: 258) describes how rosaries and baptism medals were similarly taken by Luguru as replacements for protective amulets once provided by *waganga* (healers). Maxwell (1999: 90) describes the same phenomenon among Hwesa.

20. See also Pels 1999: 137. In later years, mission students who underwent traditional initiation or scarification risked being expelled from the mission school.

21. Métraux ([1959] 1972: 324–326) makes this argument regarding Haitian Vodou, which he then contradicts by portraying Vodou practitioners as "convinced of the efficacy of the Catholic liturgy and therefore wish[ing] their own religion to benefit from it" (328). Murphy (1988: 32) discusses this argument in relation to Cuban Santeria. Voeks (1997: 60) presents a similar argument regarding Brazilian Candomblé but adds that it is unlikely that Catholic officials were duped by such maneuvers, especially given the church's policy of gradually substituting images of the Catholic saints in the place of "pagan deities."

22. See also Deren 1953: 56. Murphy (1988: 122) describes such shrines among practitioners of Santeria; Brandon (1993: 121) illustrates one. See also Fry 1977 regard-

ing how practitioners of Umbanda descend from slaves who "[kept] the traditions of Africa alive by hiding the Gods of Africa . . . behind the Catholic Saints." Danfulani reports that Eggon members of the *ijov* cult in Nigeria "make use of the bible" but "accuse the writers . . . of substituting spirits with the name of Christ" (1999: 191).

23. Such "converts," if nothing else, adopted Christian identities (Peel 2000: 249).

24. Bond (2001: 147) similarly suggests that Yombe "augmented" their "ritual field" through appropriating Christianity. See also Gilbert 1989: 61.

25. Murphy (1988: 40, 114, 122) suggests that Santeros consider Catholic saints to be "personae," or "attitudes," of the *orishas,* and Catholicism to be one "way of the *orishas*" in the New World. See also Bastide 1978: 123 and Apter 2002: 238 regarding Vodou, and Fry 1977 and D. Brown [1986] 1994 regarding Brazilian Umbanda.

26. See also Horton 1993: 317.

27. See also Behrend 1999: 116. Métraux has referred to similar dynamics in Haiti as the "veritable seizure of Catholicism by Voodoo" ([1959] 1972: 331).

28. See also Barker 1990; Meyer 1992: 122.

29. See also Landau 1995: xxi, as well as Masquelier 2001, who similarly describes the complex relations obtaining between Bori and Islam in Niger.

30. Cf. Jean Comaroff and John Comaroff 1991: 229.

Chapter Thirteen

1. Data on salaries are drawn from oral testimony provided by dozens of Muedans who worked at the mission in the colonial period.

2. Wage levels were reported to us by dozens of ex–plantation laborers.

3. Maxwell (1999: 108) describes how a "mission elite" emerged in similar fashion among Hwesa.

4. Maxwell (1999: 109) suggests that many young Hwesa became Christians precisely to escape the constraints of "traditional commensality."

5. Fadiman (1993) offers a similar account of Christian Meru coming under suspicion from non-Christian Meru in colonial Kenya.

6. See also White 2000: 189.

Chapter Fourteen

1. *Mapiko* dances had long provided a forum for subtly veiled criticism of the Portuguese through the use of masks that caricatured administrators, plantation owners, or cotton board officials. Dances thus constituted environments pregnant with subversion (Alpers 1983: 149). In this regard, *mapiko* resembled the *hauka* among Nigerien Songhay, as described by Stoller (1989: 147–163).

2. Mozambican political leaders followed the example of TANU mobilizers, who also recruited support among migrant workers (Iliffe 1969), especially members of dance clubs and other migrant workers' social organizations (Ranger 1969).

3. See West 1997b: 145–151 for a more detailed discussion of the history of MANU, including citations of the relevant literature.

4. At the time of these arrests, the many associations and organizations that would eventually coalesce had not yet merged to form one group calling itself MANU; this would happen only in 1961.

5. This event is also discussed in detail in West 1997b: 147–149; see also Borges Coelho 1993a for documents conveying the colonial version of these events, and Chipande 1970 for an account provided by Alberto Chipande, a survivor of the incident and future FRELIMO leader.

6. According to oral testimony given by former mobilizers and mission clergy alike, even the Dutch Montfort Fathers sometimes offered material support to mobilizers and, later, to FRELIMO guerrillas. Maxwell (1999: 125–127) reports that, in Rhodesia, Zimbabwe African National Liberation Army (ZANLA) and Zimbabwean People's Army (ZIPA) guerrillas enjoyed similar support from some missions during the Zimbabwean nationalist struggle.

7. The absorption of MANU and other protonationalist parties by FRELIMO, and attendant tensions and schisms, are treated in greater detail in Chilcote 1972: 470–475 and Opello 1975; see also West 1997b: 149–151.

8. Over the course of our research, we interviewed dozens of men and women who worked as FRELIMO mobilizers.

9. Lan (1985: 127–128, 208) gives an account of how ZANLA guerrillas in Zimbabwe similarly "educated the peasantry" in the language of revolutionary socialism— albeit with greater ideological flexibility.

10. Kriger (1992: 104) offers similar accounts of ZANLA attacks on chiefs in Rhodesia.

11. Of the eighteen *régulos* in the southern half of the plateau, eight eventually sided with FRELIMO, and one was imprisoned by the Portuguese. FRELIMO killed three. Two took refuge with the Portuguese. Three fled to Tanzania (I was able to gather no account of the remaining one) (West 1997b: 164–168, 312).

12. By war's end, many *regulados* had fractured into more than one administrative domain at this level in the FRELIMO administrative hierarchy.

13. At this time, what are today provinces were classified by the Portuguese as districts.

14. Tensions between Nkavandame and other FRELIMO leaders are treated in detail in Opello 1975; FRELIMO 1977; Munslow 1983; Negrão 1984; Machel 1985; de Brito 1988: 21–23. See West 1997b: 174–177 for an expanded discussion.

15. At the same time, "area branches" became "districts," and "regional branches" became "provinces."

16. See Machel 1985: 19 for a statement of the party's vanguard role in elections. Richard Gibson concludes that "virtual guerrilla autarkies grew up in the areas inside Mozambique under guerrilla control" (1972: 279).

Chapter Fifteen

1. The cornerstone of these schemes were *aldeamentos*—planned villages that were supposed to provide health care, clean water, and education to their inhabitants,

but which in fact served as strategic hamlets. While many *aldeamentos* were constructed in the southern part of Cabo Delgado, the northern part of the colonial district saw only a few built (around the town of Mueda and along the Tanzanian border), despite ambitious plans to line the Rovuma River with them (see Opello 1974: 33; Calvert 1973: 83).

2. Lan (1985: 7) reports the use of this technique by Rhodesian forces during the war for Zimbabwean independence.

3. A great many interviewees insisted that Lázaro Nkavandame's words were carefully crafted so as to communicate a message contrary to that intended by the Portuguese. Whether or not this was true, it indicated not only popular refusal to believe FRELIMO's vilification of Nkavandame but also enduring popular commitment to the idea of the armed struggle for independence.

4. In 1967 the PIDE, renamed the General Security Directorate (Direcção Geral de Segurança, or DGS), began to operate a "reeducation center," called the Centro de Recuperação de Terroristas da Machava, to "rehabilitate" political prisoners (see Melo et al. 1974: 223; Opello 1974: 33). Most of those chosen to "work with Lázaro" were taken from this program or from Mabalane prison (see FRELIMO 1970: 12 for an account by Muarabu Shauri, who was "recruited" to participate). Upon entry into FRELIMO areas, many of those who "accepted to work with the Portuguese" told FRELIMO authorities why they had been sent. They were "debriefed" and "reeducated" by FRELIMO security and, in some cases, eventually permitted to rejoin the FRELIMO cause. Others apparently honored their commitments to the Portuguese—the most famous being Atanásio Chitama, who was accused of "collaboration" and executed by FRELIMO. For a more detailed treatment of these events, see West 2003a.

5. Henriksen (1983: 51) reports the defection of commanders and commissars along with rank-and-file guerrillas in the wake of Operation Gordian Knot.

6. Monks asserts that "thousands of Makonde tribesmen (among others) defected, in response to Nkavandame's call for the Makonde to lay down their arms and Portugal's own propaganda leaflet campaign" (1990: 104).

7. In the same year, FRELIMO increased the intensity of its operations in Tete Province, crossing the Zambezi River for the first time. This forced the Portuguese military to meet the new threat and provided breathing room for FRELIMO in Cabo Delgado.

8. Kriger (1992: 112) gives an account of a similar strategy to Africanize the Southern Rhodesian army in the late 1970s.

9. Henriksen (1983) places the numbers of these forces at approximately 6,000–8,000 GEs and 3,000 GEPs by the end of the war. According to Calvert (1973: 82), GEs and GEPs were mostly captured FRELIMO guerrillas who agreed to join the colonial army.

10. Beckett (1985: 154) reports that by 1973–1974 the Portuguese were using twelve Fiat G-92s, fifteen Harvard T6 converted trainers, fourteen Alouette helicopters, two Puma helicopters, five Nord-Atlas transports, and seven DC-3 transports in Mozambique. He places the number of Portuguese ground missions in 1971 (in all of

Mozambique) at 3,657, the number of air missions at 14,398, and the number of air sorties at 28,060 (1985: 156).

11. Munslow (1983: 130) suggests that these imposters were GEs and GEPs.

12. Elsewhere (West 2003a), I have written at greater length on the topic of the FRELIMO security apparatus and violence against Mozambicans during the independence war.

13. Kriger (1992: 156) presents similar accounts of the execution of suspected traitors by Zimbabwean guerrillas.

Chapter Sixteen

1. See also Pitcher 2002: 55.

2. For accounts of the social services provided to civilians by FRELIMO in its liberated zones, see Melo et al. 1974; Gabriel and Stuart 1978; Negrão 1984; Johnston 1989.

3. In 1981, President Samora Machel declared: "The victory of Socialism is a victory of science, it is prepared and organized scientifically" (quoted in Pitcher 2002: 76).

4. June Nash ([1979] 1993: 159) reports the use of similar language by union organizers in Bolivian tin mines to criticize miners' beliefs in a protective God.

5. FRELIMO's relative success in such initiatives sets its guerrilla insurgency apart from movements such as the Holy Spirit Mobile Forces in Uganda described by Behrend (1999), whose leadership not only ritually armored its fighters but also actually prohibited them from taking cover when attacked (57) and blamed battlefield losses on infractions of such rules and the lack of faith such infractions betrayed.

6. By contrast, Niehaus (1998, 2001) reports cases in which African National Congress (ANC) "comrades" in apartheid South Africa actually acted as witch finders in their efforts to consolidate popular support, notwithstanding prohibitions on such activities by ANC leaders. In the course of processes initiated by these comrades, accused witches were "necklaced" (i.e., executed by being beaten and then having a tire placed over their heads that was doused with petrol and set alight).

7. *Dinumba* are pumpkin gourds used to mix and carry medicinal substances.

8. *Yangele*, "divining."

9. Mueggler (2001: 164) describes similar attempts by communist Chinese officials to abolish the festivals and rituals associated with the *ts'ici* headmanship system.

10. Kohnert reports that Kérékou's Marxist regime in Benin labeled beliefs in the occult as "obscurantist" forms of "false consciousness" (1996: 1351). Leaders in socialist Ghana also dismissed occult perspectives as "false consciousness" (Meyer 1998).

11. In his classic account of the Zimbabwean struggle for independence, Lan (1985) suggests that spirit mediums facilitated popular support for ZANLA guerrillas by treating them as the legitimate successors to chiefly authority where chiefs had become discredited during the colonial era for collaborating with colonial interests. Lan further suggests that these same mediums imposed restrictions on guerrilla behavior on behalf of their communities. Lan's account, which portrays the relationship between guerrillas and mediums as generally cooperative, has been challenged by Kriger (1992), who suggests that relations between guerrillas and spirit mediums were satu-

rated with the threat of violence (see also Maxwell 1999). The relationship between ZANLA and rural Zimbabweans differed greatly from the relationship between FRELIMO and rural Mozambicans owing to the fact that ZANLA was unable to open and sustain "liberated zones" (Kriger 1992: 95). Rural Zimbabwean communities thus found themselves "between two armies," to borrow a phrase from Stoll's account (1993) of the Guatemalan civil war. Notwithstanding this, FRELIMO relations with civilian populations in the liberated zones were saturated with the threat of violence in ways that more closely resemble Kriger's account of the Zimbabwean independence war than Lan's.

12. In 1963, many of the members whose names appeared on two registries that fell into PIDE hands were imprisoned and tortured (West 2003a).

13. Mpwapwele was here referring, I believe, to the elite GEs and GEPs.

14. Fry (1976: 23–24) tells us that, in Rhodesia, Zezuru labeled informers who betrayed their kinfolk to colonial police as *uroyi* (witches), but that they used the term metaphorically. Muedans, however, used the term *vavi* quite literally in reference to those they suspected of collaboration with the Portuguese.

15. The anthropologist J. D. Krige once compared the "night-witches" that "prowl[ed] over" Lobedu villages to the "[World War II] night bombers over our cities" ([1947] 1970: 264). Muedans, by contrast, perceived substantial linkages between sorcerers and bombers.

16. See also Behrend 1999: 27 regarding similar perspectives in the context of the Ugandan civil war.

17. Middleton (1967: 61) reports that Lugbara similarly suspected that those who walked about at night were witches/sorcerers.

18. Lan (1985: 128) reports rural Zimbabweans attributing to ZANLA guerrillas the "ability to vanish into thin air."

19. Cf. Lan 1985: 147.

20. According to Lan (1985: 158, 162), ZANLA guerrillas made use of medicinal substances provided them by healers—including antibullet medicines—more openly than did FRELIMO guerrillas. Maxwell (1999: 140) reports ZANLA guerrillas in Zimbabwe consulting with *n'angas* (diviner-healers). Eric Young (1997: 257) tells of the use of *n'angas* by commanders in the postindependence Zimbabwe National Army.

21. In Henriksen's words, "[C]adres in the field winked at the practice of rituals and the wearing of amulets for safety" (1983: 76).

22. See also Honwana 2002: 179–180 for accounts of FRELIMO military commanders consulting diviners and healers in the civil war against RENAMO in the south of the country.

23. Accounts of African political and military leaders seeking the protection of occult practitioners are legion. See, e.g., Stoller 1995: 186; Kohnert 1996: 1351; Shaw 1996, 2002: 257–261; Ellis and ter Haar 1998; Meyer 1998: 17; Piot 1999. See also Apter 2002: 244 regarding similar phenomena in Haiti.

24. Kohnert (1996: 1351) reports a similar popular reaction to antiobscurantist state rhetoric in Benin. Cf. Humphrey 2003: Buryati Buddhists interpreted Stalin's anti-

Buddhism campaign as the playing out of a Buddhist saga, namely, the reincarnation of the Blue Elephant, whose destruction of Buddhism three times over had been predicted.

25. Maxwell (1999: 140) documents ZANLA guerrillas killing "sellouts" (those who collaborated with the Rhodesians) *as witches.* Cf. Kriger 1992: 132.

26. Kriger (1992: 116–169) implies that the fear rural Zimbabweans had of ZANLA soldiers precluded any possibility of genuine popular support for the guerrilla campaign.

27. Even if Muedans conceived of FRELIMO guerrillas according to "local social categories" (Lan 1985: 19), Muedans looked upon these guerrillas with ambivalence befitting such identities—an ambivalence that Lan's account of the Zimbabwean independence war does not admit.

28. Cf. Lan 1985, which reports ZANLA guerrillas being referred to as "the lions of rain" due to their association with *mhondoro* spirits, who inhabited the bodies of lions and brought rain to their descendants.

29. Shaw (2002: 257) argues that politicians in contemporary Africa must balance the benefits of being thought to possess occult powers against the suspicions that such assumptions arouse concerning their proclivities to act malevolently. See also Ferme 1999: 171.

Chapter Seventeen

1. The same terminology was used in other revolutionary socialist contexts. See, e.g., Mueggler 2001: 270 on China.

2. See also Law 1/77, art. 14 (published in *Boletim da República*).

3. As Pitcher (2002: 78) points out, this command culture manifest itself in the language through which FRELIMO governed; they initiated literacy "campaigns" and "offensives" against poverty and disease, for example.

4. Dinerman (2001) has suggested that in the areas of Nampula Province where she conducted research, former *autoridades gentílicas* often retained control of post-independence local organs of state (often through orchestrating the appointment of family members to these posts). In Mueda, however, where FRELIMO had established itself in the context of guerrilla war, the party more rigorously excluded former *autoridades gentílicas* from such positions of influence.

5. The land law actually protected these historical claims, stating that no cultivator could be dispossessed of land so long as he or she continued to use it. Thus, land claims continued to be founded upon occupation and inheritance.

6. This was, of course, thirty to thirty-five years after they had abandoned their settlements, and twenty to twenty-five years after the chieftaincy had officially been abolished in Mozambique.

7. See West 2001 for a more extensive treatment of Mueda's communal villages and the enduring institutions of kinship therein.

8. Even before independence, this practice was waning. As wage labor took on greater importance and access to land became less essential, fewer incentives existed

for young men to seek out the sponsorship of matrilineal kin in setting up their households.

9. For detailed accounts of such incidents, see Oficina de História 1986; Egerö 1987: 160–161; West 1997b: 213–219; 2001.

10. Cf. Dinerman 2001: in Nampula Province, state officials encouraged residents to abandon their communal villages so that they might participate in state cotton-growing schemes.

11. RENAMO did occupy several villages in the lowlands around the plateau and dispatched spies to seek out sympathizers on the plateau, but only once attacked a few plateau villages.

Chapter Eighteen

1. See also Simmons 1980: 455.

2. See also Geschiere 1997: 64.

3. Fitzpatrick (1994) and Donham (1999: 28, 179) describe similar attempts to "rewrite the landscape" undertaken by socialist regimes in Russia and Ethiopia, respectively.

4. Although Scott criticizes "high modernist" state projects for their arrogance and ignorance of social complexity, he also gives evidence that modernizers have often justified rewriting the landscape as a means to provide beneficial social services, including health care, education, sanitation, and other infrastructural components. This was certainly true of the FRELIMO campaign—undertaken in the moment of postcolonial exuberance—to bring about socialist modernization of the nation's rural areas.

5. Honwana (2002: 171) reports how FRELIMO prohibitions on rain ceremonies, fertility rites, and ancestral supplication were experienced in the southern region of the country where she worked. She reports that in some cases healers were included among those detained and transferred to the north of the country under the rubric of "operation production," a 1983 FRELIMO program nominally dedicated to expelling unemployed migrants from urban areas (172).

6. Feierman reports the position taken by the socialist Tanzanian government that "socialism and superstition [were] incompatible" (1986: 210). Humphrey reports shamans in Siberia, Mongolia, and Manchuria being "imprisoned and killed by Communist governments," which cast shamanism as "a primitive superstition" (Humphrey and Onon 1996: 1). According to Brandon (1993: 101–102), although the socialist state in Cuba showed a greater official tolerance for "folk beliefs and practices," it sometimes authorized antagonistic measures. Karen Brown (1991: 378) refers to recurrent "anti-superstition campaigns" in Haiti.

7. *Waing'anga* (traveling witch doctors) constituted a notable exception; FRELIMO aggressively enforced the official ban on their activities. Makudo Shalaga Ntumi Ngole told us that *waing'anga* came to fear the government because it supported claims for restitution made by people professing to have been "falsely accused," even if he assured us that FRELIMO punished only *waing'anga* who were, indeed, "liars."

8. Honwana reports similar findings in reference to southern Mozambique. In fact,

she gives evidence that high-ranking FRELIMO leaders adhered to FRELIMO prohibitions "during the day time" but visited healers and participated in "traditional" rites "at night" (2002: 172).

9. According to Maia Green (1994: 30), the Tanzanian government attempted to ban antiwitch specialists from working in its *ujamaa* villages in the 1970s but relented to prevent the breakup of these villages as a consequence of witchcraft fears and festering accusations.

10. Cf. Mueggler 2001: 131, who describes how villagers in southwest China blamed postrevolutionary turbulence on the state's abolition of the ancestrally sanctioned headmanship.

11. Maia Green (1994: 29) notes that the Tanzanian government allowed antiwitchcraft activities to be undertaken and that villagers called the agent of such activities an *mganga wa serikali* (government witch doctor), owing to assumptions that he or she worked *for,* or even *as,* the government.

12. Ashforth (2000: 188) states that people in Soweto considered witchcraft more virulent there because of the many different kinds of herbs that migrant witches carried with them. Sanders quotes an Ihanzu woman in Tanzania: "today, anyone can buy medicine," unlike in days past (2001: 175). See also Lattas 1993: 59.

13. Behrend (1999: 28) reports that the rising death rate in Acholi, Uganda, was similarly interpreted as a sign of increasing levels of witchcraft. Mesaki (1994: 55) reports that villagization in Tanzania exacerbated witchcraft in the view of village residents. James Brain (1982: 383) links the rising incidence of witchcraft accusations in Tanzanian *ujamaa* villages to high child mortality rates. See also M. Green 1997: 337–338. On rising rates of witchcraft in South African "betterment schemes," see Stadler 1996: 100.

14. Geschiere (1997) argues that, where sorcery was once constrained by the boundaries of kinship, this is no longer the case in many places in Africa.

Chapter Nineteen

1. Lambek (1993: 249–250) gives an account of this phenomenon in Mayotte.

2. Van der Geest (1988) suggests that black market medicine is so omnipresent in contemporary Africa as to constitute a fundamental component of the category of "traditional medicine."

3. The Mozambican attorney general sarcastically referred to these auctions as "silent privatizations" (in Harrison 1999: 543).

4. Because it gave rise to dramatic social differentiation, Mozambicans cynically referred to the Programa de Reabilitação Económica (PRE) as the Programa de Reabilitação Individual (PRI) (Marshall 1990: 29).

5. In this period, high-ranking Mozambican officials were implicated in drug smuggling, money laundering, bank fraud, and other forms of organized criminal activity (Ellis 1999b). Whereas Chabal and Daloz (1999: 79, 99–101) argue that such activities may provide means whereby elites cultivate patron-client relationships, ordinary Muedans reaped few benefits from the good fortunes of Muedan elites.

6. Hibou (1999) argues persuasively that elites elsewhere on the African continent effectively turned structural adjustment to their own individual gain through privatizing to themselves the powers of the state, including taxation, labor mobilization, the regulation of trade, and the limited provision of security to clients. See also Bayart 1993: 60–86.

7. In many cases, veterans had, in fact, been identified as target groups for such projects and schemes, but rarely were these opportunities designed exclusively for them.

8. Tim Born, USAID, personal communication, 19 September 1994.

9. The fund was meant to be a revolving source of credit but was exhausted by the end of 1988 due to nonpayment by its first group of borrowers. Many of these individuals demonstrated the attitude that the money loaned them was "compensation" for their sacrifices to the nation during the war. Some also came to realize that a high rate of inflation, coupled with the low interest rate on their loans, created conditions in which the hard-currency value of their debt would actually decrease over time even as they failed to make payments against it.

10. Many state officials actually turned to Indian merchants to arrange the money they needed for a down payment. In return, these merchants secured political favors from officials who had, until recently, treated them with great hostility.

11. In Cabo Delgado Province, approximately forty-five trucks and thirty tractors were imported in 1989, and twenty-six more trucks in 1990.

12. Between the passing of the land law regulations in 1987 (permitting the issuance of land titles to occupants) and my dissertation research in 1994, the Provincial Office of Survey and Cadastre received thirty-five requests for titles to land in the plateau region. The vast majority of these were submitted by state officials for areas in excess of 100 hectares in the lowlands. A select few officials also applied for and received large concessions to cut and sell timber in the plateau region.

13. See also Borges Coelho 1998 for a description of similar trends in Tete Province.

14. Shaw (1996: 37–39; 2001: 65; 2002: 258) reports popular recriminations uttered in the same idiom in postindependence Sierra Leone.

15. See also Lattas 1993: 53; Sanders 2001: 173.

16. Pfeiffer (2002) argues that economic differentiation, spawned by Mozambican structural adjustment, similarly gave rise to increased suspicions of witchcraft, sorcery, and avenging spirits in central Mozambique. Whereas those Pfeiffer worked among commonly turned to prophets in African Independent Churches instead of to *curandeiros* (because the former charged no fees), Muedans were only beginning to witness the rise of such churches in their midst when we worked among them.

17. Chabal and Daloz warn that elites "who fail to redistribute, or are perceived to redistribute too little, run the risk of facing hostility and suspicion" (1999: 107). On the Mueda plateau, these suspicions found expression in the discursive genre of *uwavi*.

18. For a similar discussion, see Geschiere 1997: 6.

19. Goheen (1996: 161) describes the occurrence of similar debates among Nso' in Cameroon.

20. Geschiere (1997: 9, 43) reports use of the same term—"armored"—to describe sorcerers in Cameroon.

21. Ardener (1970: 147–148) writes of the suspicion held by Bakweri in western Cameroon in the late colonial period that those who were relatively more prosperous had built their tin-roofed homes with zombie slave labor. Simmons (1980), however, describes common villagers among Badyaranke in Senegal as reluctant to accuse people more powerful than themselves.

Chapter Twenty

1. Similar expressions have appeared in other neoliberal contexts; see, e.g., Morris 2000; Kendall 2003.

2. Feierman (1986: 209) suggests that traveling witch finders emerged in the African colonial context when and where government attempted to ban witchcraft accusations and trials at the local level. In northern Mozambique, however, traveling witch finders were among the first to test new spaces afforded by neoliberal reform.

3. Witch finder/exorcists such as Ningore are reported throughout contemporary Africa; see, e.g., Geschiere and Fisiy 1994; M. Green 1997; Yamba 1997; Danfulani 1999.

4. In Montepuez, Pergunta Bem and his followers reportedly desecrated mosques and forced sheiks to drink urine and to urinate on the Koran (Membe 1995).

Chapter Twenty-one

1. *Mambo* is a term for "chief" in the Shona languages spoken in the central Mozambican regions where RENAMO was strongest during the war and from which many key RENAMO leaders originated. In some regions of Mozambique, RENAMO used other local terms instead of *mambo,* but the term was applied well beyond the boundaries of the area in which it had historical significance.

2. Englund (2002), for example, provides a subtle account of the variable scenarios witnessed in the Mozambique-Malawi border region in Tete Province.

3. Manning in fact concluded that "traditional authorities were likely decisive in RENAMO's strong electoral showing" in 1994 (2001: 159).

4. After the 1994 elections, the FRELIMO governor of Inhambane Province, Francisco João Pateguana, counseled his party to take note of the fact that FRELIMO did poorly in those areas where they did not have good relations with ex-*régulos* (*Notícias* 1995c).

5. Oyebola (1986: 227) suggests that Nigerian politicians courted traditional healers in the 1979 elections and that the winners granted them political appointments, all in recognition of their influence over voters.

6. This echoed World Health Organization justifications for their traditional-medicine paradigm articulated as early as 1983 (Bannerman, Burton, and Wen-Chieh 1983: 326).

7. For detailed reports on the project, see VeneKlasen and West 1996; Fry 1997. For a more substantial critique of the project, see West and Kloeck-Jenson 1999.

8. The mandate for these brochures is articulated in the first one: Cuehela 1996: 7. See also Alfane 1996; Fernando 1996; Mucussete 1996; Nhancale 1996.

9. Based upon work in Uganda, the anthropologist Mikael Karlström has made a similar argument: "If ethnicity-based solidarities and associations are likely to remain a central element of the organizational sector that articulates state and society in Africa, then the analytical task will be to try and understand the conditions under which they can perform this mediating role constructively and the circumstances under which they become divisive and destructive. . . . If it is thus empirically the case that traditional, ethnically based political institutions provide at least the potential for a positive articulation of state and society, then the exclusion of such institutions from the definition of civil society does not seem particularly helpful" (1999: 110–111). See also Durham 1999: 196.

10. Most ex-*régulos*, of course, agreed with Lundin when she met with them, arguing that their legitimacy derived from succession and that it would be undermined should their subordinates be able to oust them with a vote (Mohomed 1996).

11. Janzen (1978: 62) suggests that such views are common among African elites. Such perspectives, however, echo those of medical anthropologists and ethnobotanists working in diverse locales. The medical anthropologist Sjaak van der Geest (1997) argues that such hopes justify biomedical overtures toward traditional medicine. See also Plotkin 1993: 13, 236.

12. Semali (1986: 88) and Feierman (1986: 214) describe similar initiatives undertaken in socialist Tanzania in the mid-1970s by the Traditional Medicine Research Unit at the University of Dar es Salaam.

13. Joralemon and Sharon (1993: 163) suggest that similar research served to legitimate *curanderos* in Peru.

14. Edward Green (1994: 44–45) further argued that only minimal benefits could be derived from bioprospecting of medicinal substances owing to the high cost of laboratory analysis and pharmaceuticals testing. On this issue, see also Chavunduka and Last 1986: 255; Pearce 1986: 255; Greene n.d.

Chapter Twenty-two

1. White (1994: 363; 2000: 99) reports that injections have long been the object of fear and fascination in Africa. Vaughan (1991: 59) suggests that this fascination led Africans to assimilate the medical practices of Western missionaries into their healing repertoires. By contrast, Whyte, van der Geest, and Hardon (2002: 104–116) not only document the widespread existence in contemporary Africa of "injectionists" (unofficial practitioners who use hypodermic needles to inject clients with medicinal substances of a wide variety) but suggest that this practice is linked to long-standing indigenous therapeutic practices: "Making a cut, or several small incisions, with a knife or razor blade, and then rubbing in medicine, is still common in many African settings" (112). See also Whyte 1988: 220. In any case, "vaccination" is a common component of the repertoire of many contemporary Africa healers. See, e.g., Marwick 1950: 104; Beattie 1963: 42; LeVine 1963: 235; Redmayne 1970: 113; Janzen 1989: 241; M. Green 1994: 37; Yamba 1997: 214–215; Willis and Chisanga 1999: 138; Ashforth 2001b:

213; 2000: 48, 116. See also Wafer 1991: 91 regarding similar practices in Brazilian Candomblé.

2. Dias and Dias (1970: 375) report similar techniques being used by Muedan healers in the late 1950s.

3. Virtually every healer and every patient with whom we spoke verified that battery acid was an essential component to vaccination *mitela*. See also Whyte 1997: 28, 180.

4. Agrawal (1995: 430; 2002: 290) points out that "indigenous knowledge" exists as such only in the moment of being "validated" by scientific means and absorbed into the purportedly universal corpus of "scientific knowledge." The validation of indigenous knowledge, Agrawal further suggests, is a process fraught with power—one in which the bearers of indigenous knowledge are perpetually subordinated to the stewards of science, made to act as "eyes and ears" to a scientific brain (Howes and Chambers 1980: 327). Purcell and Onjoro remind us that "the Western bias toward scientific knowledge as the *a priori* standard for all 'true' knowledge is as old as science itself" (2002: 173). On the use of biomedical knowledge as the standard against which traditional medical knowledge is measured, see also Last and Chavunduka 1986: 3; MacCormick 1986: 155; Oyebola 1986: 230; Greene 1998: 640, 642; Langford 2002: 8.

5. See also Stoller and Olkes 1987: 171.

6. Green's approach was by no means unique among medical anthropologists and ethnobotanists. Consider, for example, the work of Wade Davis (1988), the famed Harvard ethnobotanist who, in the early 1980s, investigated reports of the existence of zombies in Haiti. Davis took seriously Haitian legends suggesting that powerful *bokor* (Vodou priests) could raise the dead from their graves and keep them as zombie slaves. In the course of his research, Davis isolated pharmacological substances that he concluded to be capable of producing the zombie effect as described in Haitian folk narratives. In doing so, he suggested not only that Haitian zombie beliefs were grounded in truth but also that the truth of this "indigenous knowledge" could—indeed, had to— be validated by Western science. See also World Health Organization 1978: 29. Plotkin (1993: 237) expresses greater ambivalence regarding the scientific paradigm as a standard of verification, although he uses it as such in any case.

7. Ashforth argues that such portrayals "involve a serious misrepresentation of the politics involved in the business of healing" (2000: 247–248).

8. Honwana (2002: 174) suggests that researchers in the GEMT widened their view of traditional healing in the late 1980s and early 1990s to include "symbolic and ritualistic components," but I saw little evidence of this in the mid-1990s.

9. Langford (2002: 17) suggests that Ayurvedic healing has been (re)invented in the Indian national-cultural imaginary with similar precautions.

10. Reynolds (1996: 23) observes and criticizes this same phenomenon in her work on healers in Zimbabwe.

11. In postcolonial Tanzania, Ngoma healers were also licensed by the Ministry of Culture rather than the Ministry of Health (Janzen 1992: 171).

12. Twumasi and Warren (1986: 127) describe how the Zambian government attempted to distinguish between indigenous healers and "quacks" in the registration process. See also Hopa, Simbayi, and du Toit 1998.

13. Yamba (1997: 215) raises similar concerns about "vaccinations" performed by healers in Malawi. Ashforth (2000: 184) gives an account of biomedical practitioners' criticisms of the practices of traditional healers in South Africa, including the use of mercury in "vaccinations" and the administration of toxic (e.g., chromium) enemas for diarrhea.

14. Sanders (2001: 175–176) presents a photo of a Tanzanian healer's menu of items for sale in the market that is similarly conceived.

15. According to Niuaia, Mutocha was eventually imprisoned for fraud.

16. See also Fry 2000: 140. Pearce (1986: 239) reports health care workers in Nigeria demonstrating a similar reluctance to refer their patients to traditional healers.

17. See also Meneses n.d.: 13.

18. Langford (2002: 229) suggests that when practitioners of magical medicine mime the techniques of professional medicine, they upset the divide between the two, ultimately exposing the magic within professional medicine.

19. Sofala governor Felisberto Tomás actually distributed bicycles to *"régulos"* in Chibabava District, scoring political points nationwide for his FRELIMO party by appearing in news photos with one of the recipients, RENAMO leader Afonso Dhlakama's father, the *"régulo"* Mangunde (*Notícias* 1996e). Manica governor Artur Canana followed suit, offering mopeds to *"régulos"* in Dombe District, where, only months before, *régulo*-claimants had been involved in resisting the postelectoral reestablishment of state structures (*Notícias* 1997d). See also Gauth 1996; *Notícias* 1996g.

20. See also *Notícias* 1996i; Bento 1996; *Notícias* 1996f.

21. For accounts of similar incidents in Nampula Province, see *Notícias* 1996b, 1997c.

22. For more detailed discussion, see West 1998.

23. See also *Notícias* 1997e.

24. Meneses et al. (2003) provide details of witchcraft/sorcery cases in various parts of the country being adjudicated by *"régulos"* in collaboration with healers and/or diviners in the neoliberal era. Ironically, the control exercised by traditional authorities in and over the realm of the invisible served as an index for their popular legitimacy while simultaneously delegitimating them in the eyes of policymakers. On this paradox elsewhere, see Geschiere 1996: 308, 314.

25. When FRELIMO expressed concerns about traditional authorities undermining human rights, neoliberal reformers sometimes countered that FRELIMO had itself abused the rights of traditional authorities and their subjects after independence. As Mamdani has argued, such contradictory assertions arise from a historical substrate of colonial rule where a limited number of "citizens" were treated as members of civil society in possession of civil rights while the claims of a majority of "subjects" could be pressed only in the idiom of culture and custom (1996: 18). The legacy of this bifurcated colonial state is competing modernist and traditionalist discourses of rights (3). In Mamdani's view, radical regimes such as FRELIMO replaced the "decentralized despotism" of colonial indirect rule with "centralized despotism" in their efforts to "detribalize" politics in the postcolonial era (26–27, 291).

26. See, e.g., *Notícias* 1997a.

27. Tensions between local-level FRELIMO cadres and claimants to the title of *régulo* in the neoliberal era are reported in Meneses et al. 2003: 370, 381.

28. See article 8.2 of the law. Alfredo Gamito, minister of state administration, went so far as to state in 1995 that, "in fact, the municipal phenomenon and that of traditional authority have the same law, so the one, just as the other, are expressions of the community will to organize itself and govern itself" (*Diário de Moçambique* 1995). See also *Notícias* 1995a, 1995b.

29. Local government bodies are expected, according to the decree, to "ask [community authorities'] opinions on how best to mobilize and organize the participation of local communities in the realization of plans and programs for economic, social, and cultural development" (Hanlon 2000).

30. Meneses et al. (2003: 370, 380) report several cases in which FRELIMO recognition of traditional authorities led to RENAMO condemning such figures as "sell-outs."

31. In some villages, referenda were held to validate the authority of village presidents before making them community leaders; in some cases, villagers selected other candidates. Such democratic mechanisms actually highlighted the fact that these figures were *not* traditional authorities in the sense celebrated by Lundin and other advocates.

Chapter Twenty-three

1. Maia Green writes of Pogoro healers in Tanzania who often work with the aid of spirits that inhabit "pools of still deep water in a section of unviolated forest" (1994: 37).

2. Janzen (1992) discusses the role of *majini* spirits in healing practices on the East African coast. Boddy (1989: 143) refers to the *zayran* spirits possessing Hofriyati women as a class of *majini*. Willis and Chisanga (1999: 147, n. 4) provide an account of the appropriation of the Kiswahili term *majini* by Lungu people in Zambia to refer only to "evil spirits." Gray (1969: 174) reports that, among Segeju on the northern Tanzania coast, *majini* do not possess people; rather, a category of spirits referred to as *shetani* do. These same *shetani* have inspired a genre of sculpture among Makonde migrants to Tanzania (Kingdon 2002; West and Sharpes 2002).

3. Boddy (1989: 284–288) reports that Hofriyati also classify some of the *zayran* who possess them as "Arab spirits." The appearance of "foreign" spirits in rites of possession is common. See, e.g., Stoller 1995.

4. Janzen (1989: 239–240) suggests that spirits of distant provenance have come to be regarded as increasingly more powerful in central and southern Africa.

5. Boddy (1989: 165) reports that Hofriyati *zayran* spirits also generally "originate in locales exotic to that of the village." Gray (1969: 179) makes note of the fact that *mganga* chant "in an esoteric tongue not understood by ordinary people" in the course of their healing rites. Engelke (2004) describes the use of "deep" (archaic) Shona by healers in Zimbabwe. See also Eliade 1964: 347 on the use of esoteric language in healing.

6. When she spoke of the spirits of her own ancestors, Mbegweka used the Shimakonde term *mangonde;* when she spoke of the other spirits that eventually possessed her, she used the term *majini.*

7. Prior to this, she had attended school for just one year in a FRELIMO bush school in the liberated zones during the independence war.

8. See also Geschiere 1998: 821.

9. Azande witch doctors did this even in Evans-Pritchard's time (Evans-Pritchard [1929] 1967: 18). Last (1992: 398) reports that among Nigerian Hausa, the value of "foreign" remedies is greater owing to their "strangeness."

10. As evidence of his claim, Kipande produced for our inspection a receipt in the amount of 500 shillings for payment of dues to an organization called TAMOFA (the Tanzania-Mozambique Friendship Association). (To my knowledge, TAMOFA has no formal function in relation to traditional healing.)

11. Atkinson suggests that, similarly, among Wana shamans, a "premium is placed on seeking new and powerful forms of knowledge" (1989: 65).

12. Danfulani (1999: 190) reports "holy water" being similarly administered for "all diseases" by Eggon healers in Nigeria. Ashforth (2000: 46) tells of a South African healer prescribing the same herbal concoction for all ills.

13. See Gray 1969: 175; Knipe 1989: 92; Peletz 1993: 162; Whyte 1988: 225; 1997: 165; Harries 2001: 420; Rasmussen 2001a: 142; Shaw 2002: 253; Stoller 1989: 50; Obbo 1996: 190. Cf. Lambek 1993: 244, who reports that while sorcery in Mayotte often entails writing, the healing of sorcery's effects does not.

14. Langford (2002: 188–230) provides a fascinating account of her attempts to discern how those with whom she worked differentiated between "genuine" Ayurvedic healers and "quacks." She observes that, upon application, every standard she tested proved problematic.

15. Redmayne (1970: 108) encountered similar healing compounds, replete with dormitories, in colonial Nyassaland.

16. Bongmba (1998: 176) tells of Wimbum healers in Cameroon bottling and labeling their medicinal substances so as to make them attractive to a "modern" clientele.

17. Dillon-Malone (1988: 1160) also describes the use of patient record books among healers in Zambia; Maia Green (1997: 320–321) describes written records kept by witch cleansers in southern Tanzania.

18. Healers in the region claiming to know cures for AIDs are common. See, e.g., Probst 1999.

19. See also Forster 1998: 538.

20. At the time of our conversation, Mozambique did not yet have facilities for HIV testing even in Maputo. The few Mozambicans who wished to be tested, and who could afford it, generally traveled to South Africa.

21. According to Tracy Luedke (personal communication, 17 April 2002), AMETRAMO members in Tete Province participated in NGO-sponsored AIDS awareness workshops that alerted them to the potential dangers of razor blade "vaccination."

22. Marcos took this precaution after working for a stint as a public educator in an NGO-sponsored HIV awareness campaign.

23. See Langford 2002: 188–230 for an interesting discussion of how an Ayurvedic

healer with whom she worked enhanced his credibility among his clients through what she describes as the fetishistic deployment of objects and procedures associated with medical science. See also Rekdal 1999: 471. Langford is quick to point out that biomedical practitioners sometimes deploy these objects in ways that might be described similarly.

24. I prepared for field research by training as an emergency medical technician. In the emergency medical kit that I carried with me in the field were several pairs of gloves. When Kipande made his request, I promised myself that I would give him a pair before leaving. Over the next few days, I imagined Kipande using and reusing the gloves—as I had sometimes seen health workers do in Mueda's hospital—turning them inside out once they had become "too soiled." I also imagined how these gloves might assist Kipande in assuring his patients that his "vaccinations" were sterile and safe, and I questioned whether I wanted to contribute to this impression. When I next saw him, Kipande had forgotten the requests that he had made of me, and I decided not to remind him.

25. See also Greene 1998: 653, who suggests that where biomedical practitioners have attempted to "scientize" Aguaruna shamans, these shamans have indeed "shamanized" biomedical science.

Chapter Twenty-four

1. Stoller and Olkes (1987: 118) describe similar signs of illness among Songhay in Niger.

2. Good tells us, "[Wilfred] Smith's favorite illustration of the juxtaposition of belief and knowledge is an entry in the Random House dictionary which defined [sic] 'belief' as 'an opinion or conviction,' and at once illustrates this with 'the belief that the earth is flat'! Indeed, it is virtually unacceptable usage to say that members of some society 'believe' the earth is round; if this is part of their world view, then it is knowledge, not belief!" (1994: 17). (See also Lewis 1994: 565–566.)

3. See also Rouch 1989.

4. Willis and Chisanga (1999: 17) tell us that the term commonly used in southern Africa for healer—ng'anga—literally means "knower." See also Lévi-Strauss 1963: 179–180, who reports Wintu labeling shamanic relations with the supernatural as forms of "knowledge."

5. Cf. Humphrey and Onon 1996: 329.

6. Ferguson (1995) suggests that "scientific socialism" has been replaced in many African nations by "scientific capitalism"—a donor-driven project that looks in many ways the same notwithstanding the substitution of technical prescriptions for moral considerations.

7. Horton (1993: 320–327) argues that such paradigms as sorcery are deployed as "secondary theories" to "explain, predict and control" the world where "primary theories" have failed to do so.

8. See also Pigg 1996: 161; Langford 2002: 200.

9. Van Dijk (2001: 106) tells us that Malawian witches are said to make planes

from human skeletons and to use human blood as fuel. By contrast, Gottlieb (1992: 127, 132) tells us that Beng in Côte d'Ivoire consider cameras, typewriters, automobiles, and airplanes to be the inventions of Western witches: "Who but a witch could invent [such things]?"

10. In taking this line, Makwava put a twist on words once penned by Charles Taylor: "Whatever happens / We have got / The Gatling gun / And they have not" (quoted in Pels 1998: 203).

11. Worsley (1968: 240) suggests that similar questions animated participants in Melanesian "cargo" cults, who witnessed Europeans in possession of fantastic goods but never saw them *work* for such riches. Muedans pondered if the *kudenga* (work) undertaken by foreigners in their midst was indeed *uwavi wa kudenga* (sorcery of construction).

12. Ashforth (1998a: 57–58) argues that Africans often consider the powers of an "African science" to be relatively more effective for destructive ends than productive ends—the inverse of what they consider Western science to be. See also Shaw 1997: 860; Sanders 1999: 126; Bond 2001: 142.

13. I was sometimes told that the most powerful of all sorcerers were those who practiced it as pranksters—playing tricks on their victims, such as switching the shirt and pants on their bodies as they slept. Tellingly, these sorcerers demonstrated their disinterest in using sorcery to discernible ends.

14. See also Taussig 1997: 83.

15. Whyte (1997: 24) suggests that, for reasons such as these, Nyole manifest "subjunctivity" in their assertions about illness, misfortune, and occult forces.

16. Werbner (2001: 193) and Ashforth (2001b: 217) make similar points. Humphrey and Onon (1996: 5) emphasize that shamanic knowledge is always "partial"—*shinu shoeshoe*, "a *little* something," in Shimakonde.

17. See also Last 1992; Ashforth 1998a: 57; Bastian 2003; Sanders 2003.

18. Cf. Whyte 1997: 68, 81–82.

19. See also Kendall 2003; West 2003b; pace Kohnert 1996: 1352.

20. See also Sanders and West 2003: 16.

Chapter Twenty-five

1. Columbite-tantalite (commonly referred to as coltan) is a metallic ore used to make capacitors for laptop computers, pagers, and cell phones. Recent conflicts in Central Africa have been financed, in significant part, by illicit coltan mining in Congo.

2. The literature on witchcraft/sorcery is filled with similar ideas. Ashforth's (2000: 128) informants told him that witches "don't want any progress"; consequently, they seek to destroy the material manifestations of any attempts at self-advancement or improvement (see also Ashforth 1996: 1202). Geschiere (in Fisiy and Geschiere 2001: 233) portrays Cameroonian villagers as afraid to join in the riches of that country's cocoa boom for fear of attracting the envy of their poorer relatives; those who did grow cocoa, Geschiere tells us, were assumed by others to have some sort of unusual "occult protection" (see also Danfulani 1999; Bond 2001: 143). Bailey (1994: 4, 206)

suggests that witchcraft serves as an invisible hand, promising ill to those who act in self-interest—pace Adam Smith, who argues that the invisible hand of the marketplace guides those who act in their self-interest toward a mutual good (see also Sanders 2001). Bailey offers the example of a successful entrepreneur in an Indian village who is eventually brought down by accusations of sorcery (5); he describes his story as "the nightmare of all the liberal-inclined free-enterprise-touting planners and developers that the United States sprinkled around the Third World from the 1950s onward" (206). See also La Fontaine 1963: 217; MacCormick 1983: 58; Geschiere 1997: 143, 147.

3. Gable (1997) similarly suggests that, while fear of supernatural retribution gives rise to attempts to "keep behind the Joneses" among Manjaco in Guinea-Bissau, people also hide the shame of having nothing that might truly provoke envy.

4. Geschiere (1988: 49) reports Cameroonian officials saying that "the villagers spoil everything by their sorcery" (see also Fisiy and Geschiere 1990: 143). In Mueda, however, villagers themselves suggested as much, presuming malice on the part of their neighbors and kin (as also noted in Ashforth 2001a: 17).

5. Water (or the lack of this essential resource) provides a fertile site for occult expressions of vulnerability and suspicion. Serra (2003) tells the story of residents of the Mozambican province of Nampula who blamed the depositing of chlorine tablets in local wells by health officials and aid workers for the outbreak of cholera these workers said they were seeking to contain. Serra concludes that such expressions do not constitute resistance to modernity so much as frustration with its empty promises (91). In any event, in the case described by Serra, as well as on the Mueda plateau, it can be argued that such expressions foster an atmosphere that impedes "the work of development."

Chapter Twenty-six

1. Maia Green (1994: 27) describes Pogoro villagers in Tanzania as being reluctant to build improved homes for fear of being attacked by witches. See also Ashforth 2000: 73. By contrast, Geschiere (1992: 172) suggests that Bakweri in Cameroon long hesitated to build zinc-roofed houses for fear of being *accused* of witchcraft.

2. Gomes et al. (2003: 300) offers further evidence of the ambivalence of the state toward intervention in sorcery-related cases in their account of the Maimio neighborhood community court in Mueda town—a quasi–state institution—which refused to hear such cases but did refer them to "an elder" of the court's confidence.

3. Geschiere (in Geschiere and Fisiy 1994: 335) tells a similar story.

4. Witchcraft ordinances were enforced in Africa with variable vigor in different places and times. Niehaus (2001) suggests that the apartheid-era South African state enforced the ban on witchcraft accusations and trials only halfheartedly, allowing such activities to go on as long as no one was killed. Semali (1986: 87) notes that the Tanzanian ordinance differentiated between witchcraft and *uganga* (healing), allowing the latter although not "promoting" it. See also Slaats and Portier 1993 regarding the measured enthusiasm with which the Dutch enforced the ban on sorcery in colonial Indonesia.

5. See Beattie 1963: 49; Simmons 1980: 455; Mombeshora 1994; Fisiy 1998: 149, 151; Fisiy and Geschiere 2001: 237. Redding argues that British officials in Transkei "maintained control . . . by allowing themselves to be translated into African idioms of power" (1996: 556). Fadiman (1993: 302–322) suggests that Meru, in Kenya, interpreted colonial attempts to eradicate witchcraft beliefs as the enactment of witchcraft because colonial authorities demanded that Meru ritual specialists renounce their beliefs in the form of oaths spoken, for all intents and purposes, in the discursive genre of witchcraft. O'Neil (1991) provides evidence that colonial suppression of the poison ordeal in Cameroon undermined popular confidence in the local leaders through whom the colonial government exercised rule. Fields (1982: 576–577) argues that by banning witchcraft accusations and trials, the British simultaneously stripped African rulers of their sovereignty *and* made of them accomplices to murder in the eyes of ordinary Africans who witnessed their failure to police witchcraft. Behrend (1999: 118) argues that antiwitchcraft laws in Acholi, Uganda, rendered spirit mediums suspect by forcing them to "tie" and "untie" witchcraft secretly, at great personal risk, and that the resulting high prices charged for such work provoked popular resentment and engendered assumptions that they worked in their own self-interest and to the detriment of others.

6. Elsewhere, postcolonial African regimes undertook such measures. In South Africa, a postapartheid state commission "accepted witchcraft as real" (Niehaus 2001) and established an occult crimes unit to investigate witchcraft cases. In Cameroon, the postcolonial government declared "any act of witchcraft, magic or divination" punishable by law and, in the eastern part of the country, judges allowed witch finders to testify as "expert witnesses" in witchcraft cases (Geschiere and Fisiy 1994; Fisiy and Geschiere 1996; Geschiere 1997: 169; Fisiy 1998: 143; Geschiere 1998). Courts in Sierra Leone similarly allowed diviners to provide oracular findings as testimony in court (Shaw 1997: 866). Maia Green (1994: 24) reports that the postcolonial Tanzanian state referred witchcraft accusations back to the villages from which they came, but that it eventually established a procedure whereby witch finders were required to secure permission before undertaking witch-cleansing activities (M. Green 1997: 336); where the state allowed witch finders to practice, villagers sometimes assumed that they *worked for* the government (M. Green 1994: 29). In any case, she suggests, the granting of permission was generally politically motivated to create an environment in which accusations might arise rather than following upon such accusations. Slaats and Portier (1993) describe how the postindependence Indonesian state enforced punishment of accused witches by rendering judgments in parallel with popular suspicions but without admitting into evidence occult testimony.

7. Niehaus (2001) describes similar forms of spontaneous justice against accused witches in postapartheid South Africa, including "necklacing" (see also Stadler 1996: 107; Crais 1998). In Tanzania, where the colonial-era witchcraft ordinance officially remained in effect into the postcolonial period, Bukurura (1994) and Mesaki (1994) report vigilante justice in some regions being attributed to popular sentiments that, where the government protects witches, the people must protect themselves.

8. The same erosion of individual rights has been observed as a consequence of postcolonial liberality toward witchcraft accusations in Cameroon (Fisiy 1998: 143;

Geschiere and Nyamnjoh 1998: 87; Fisiy and Geschiere 2001: 226) and in Tanzania (M. Green 1994: 23). Fisiy writes: "The feeling one gets when reading witchcraft [court case] files is that alleged witches are treated as if they do not possess any civic or human rights" (1998: 155). Ashforth (2001a: 15–16) concurs, suggesting that witches are denied human rights because people generally do not consider them to be fully human.

9. Recognizing this same dilemma, Ashforth (1998b: 531) argues that the postapartheid South African state ultimately had to choose between actively restraining witches or being perceived as defending them.

10. Seguro was widely suspected to have "sold" rights to attack the district's residents by means of sorcery to "three whites" for the price of "three sacks of money." Included among the suspect "whites" was a dental technician working at the Nang'ololo mission. Like the health workers in Serra's account (2003), this technician was suspected of harming the clinic's intended beneficiaries, a suspicion perhaps provoked by the fact that dentists remove elements from the bodies of their patients. For his part, Seguro had recently obtained ownership of the former town school building and was transforming it into a *pensão* (a hostel), the only one in the district. When we visited him, the building was filled with sacks of grain harvested from his fields. He also had a thriving restaurant in the town marketplace. Despite his successful businesses—indeed, because of them—many sought to know the true source of his relatively great wealth.

Chapter Twenty-seven

1. For a similar account, see Geschiere 1997: 4 n. 7.

2. Meyer (1995: 238) tells a similar story of bewitched currency serving as a means to steal the wealth of others. Schmoll (1993: 198) tells of "wind money," among Hausa, that disappears from the market sellers' coffers.

3. Geschiere (in Fisiy and Geschiere 2001: 229) tells a similar story of a government official in Cameroon publicly admonishing villagers for their practice of sorcery.

4. One of Ashforth's (1998: 523) South African informants raised this issue as well. Bailey (1994: 3, 73, 204–205) describes such a scenario in an Indian village, suggesting that the accused, Tuta, was treated as a "troublemaker" in part because he had achieved greater financial success than villagers were willing to grant a man of his caste—because he had "broken from the chains of the past."

5. Like settlement heads of the preindependence period, Makwava shielded himself from popular suspicions that *he* was a sorcerer by attributing his knowledge of the invisible realm to sorcerer-advisors.

6. When I returned to Matambalale for a brief visit in 2004, I discovered that Makwava had, in fact, been replaced as village president in elections held prior to transformation of the position into that of "community leader." The winner of these elections, Romão Geraldo Nankuta, was among fourteen candidates who challenged Makwava. Although some characterized this process as democratic, residents of Matambalale expressed concerns that an elected community leader represented only those who voted for him, whereas previously the village president, having been appointed by district authorities, governed them all.

Chapter Twenty-eight

1. I describe this event in greater detail elsewhere (West 1997a).

2. See also Hibou 1999: 86–88.

3. See Alden 2001: 86–89 for a detailed account of foreign direct investment in Mozambique in the period following structural adjustment.

4. Hanlon (1991) and Saul (1993) offer stimulating commentary on the challenge such trends posed to Mozambican sovereignty.

5. Hibou refers to this process generally as the "privatization of development," arguing that it goes hand in hand with the "erosion of official administrative and institutional capacity" and "a reinforcement of the power of elites, particularly at the local level" (1999: 99–100). Chabal and Daloz describe this phenomenon as the "decentralization of corruption" (1999: 105).

6. See M. Bowen 1992: 270; Harrison 1999: 543; Alden 2001: 92; Pitcher 2002: 140–178.

7. See Bayart, Ellis, and Hibou 1999: 3.

8. Pitcher offers a subtle discussion of the ways in which the Mozambican state sustained itself as a powerful force, notwithstanding neoliberal transformation, becoming "leaner and meaner" in the process (2002: 145); while this is true, to many rural Mozambicans, the state effectively disappeared, receding from many spheres of activity that had previously brought it into contact with the rural populace.

9. This is reminiscent of the transformations wrought by the "green revolution" in Malaysia as described by Scott (1985), wherein, with the onset of mechanization, landholders no longer depended upon landless laborers to assist them in the harvest and, therefore, no longer cultivated their loyalty as clients through the offering of "gifts."

10. See also Alden 2001: 96, 118.

11. Cf. Bailey 1994: 202–203.

12. In other words, Muedans were more anxious to secure political patrons than to change the complexion of the political order (cf. Chabal and Daloz 1999: 14, 44).

13. Along these lines, Manning asserts that "elections can . . . serve to demonstrate to all parties that even at the height of its intensity, political competition obeys impartial, mutually agreed upon rules, both in letter and in spirit" (2001: 166)—this notwithstanding her own admission that Mozambique's transition to democracy has suffered from a lack of transparency (156).

14. See also Meyer 1998.

15. Whereas Scott (1998) suggests that subalterns sustain "hidden transcripts" that animate their understandings of and engagements with the world, the message conveyed by *uwavi* discourse—for all to hear—was that *power* was hidden. Peek argues: "Many African peoples maintain that 'real' knowledge is hidden, secret, available only to certain people capable of using it properly" (1991: 14). Nyamnjoh writes: "If the reality of politics were limited to the apparent and the transparent as prescribed by liberal democracy, there would hardly be reason to explain success or failure otherwise. In general, if people had what they merited, and merited what they had in liberal democratic terms, there would be little need for a hidden hand of any kind, real or imag-

ined. But because nothing is what it seems, the invisible must be considered to paint a full picture of reality" (2001: 37).

16. See also Ciekawy and Geschiere 1998.

17. Through *uwavi* discourse, Muedans attempted to discern the "clandestine power structures" or "shadow structures of power" of which Africanist political scientists such as Bayart, Ellis, and Hibou (1999: 22–23) write. See also Ellis and ter Haar 1998: 177.

18. See also Kendall 2003; Sanders 2003.

19. See also Beidelman 1993: 8; Ashforth 2002: 219.

20. See also Kapferer 1997: 15.

21. See also Stewart and Strathern 2003.

22. See also Lattas 1993: 70.

23. Englund and Leach (2000), who challenge the notion that discourses such as *uwavi* stand outside of and critique a singular modernity, remind us that turn-of-the-twentieth-century sociologists posited a definitive link between modernity and ambivalence.

24. Worsley (1968: 44) suggests that Melanesian ambivalence toward the goods of European modernity was similarly expressed through cargo cults. June Nash ([1979] 1993: 164) argues that Bolivian tin miners expressed both frustration and desire for things modern through the cult of Supay.

25. Like Patamuna as described by Whitehead (2002: 176), Muedans have experienced modernity as "highly episodic and fleeting, a series of one-night shows, short runs, and rapidly-folding productions."

Epilogue

1. See Kingdon 2002; West and Sharpes 2002.

References

Abrahams, Ray G. 1994. *Witchcraft in Contemporary Tanzania.* Cambridge: African Studies Centre, University of Cambridge.

Adam, Yussuf, and Anna Maria Gentili. 1983. O Movimento Liguilanilu no Planalto de Mueda 1957–1962. *Estudos Moçambicanos,* no. 4:41–75.

Adas, Michael. 1979. *Prophets of Rebellion: Millenarian Protest Movements against the European Colonial Order.* Cambridge: Cambridge University Press.

Africa-America Institute. 1997. *Relatório sobre Círculos de Trabalho e Discussão.* Maputo, Mozambique: Africa-America Institute.

Africa Watch. 1992. *Conspicuous Destruction: War, Famine, and the Reform Process in Mozambique.* New York: Human Rights Watch.

Agha, Sohail, Andrew S. Karlyn, and Dominique Meekers. 2001. The Promotion of Condom Use in Non-regular Sexual Partnerships in Urban Mozambique. *Health Policy and Planning* 16 (2): 144–151.

Agrawal, Arun. 1995. Dismantling the Divide between Indigenous and Scientific Knowledge. *Development and Change* 26:413–439.

———. 2002. Indigenous Knowledge and the Politics of Classification. *International Social Science Journal,* no. 173:287–297.

Alden, Chris. 2001. *Mozambique and the Construction of the New African State: From Negotiations to Nation Building.* New York: Palgrave.

Alexander, Jocelyn. 1995. Political Change in Manica Province, Mozambique: Implications for the Decentralization of Power. Computer printout, Oxford University.

Alfane, Rufino. 1996. *Autoridade Tradicional em Moçambique.* Brochura 3, *Educação Cívica na Sociedade Tradicional.* Maputo, Mozambique: Ministério da Administração Estatal/Núcleo de Desenvolvimento Administrativo.

Alpers, Edward. 1969. Trade, State and Society among the Yao in the Nineteenth Century. *Journal of African History* 10 (3): 405–420.

——. 1975. *Ivory and Slaves in East Central Africa*. Berkeley and Los Angeles: University of California Press.

——. 1983. The Role of Culture in the Liberation of Mozambique. *Ufahamu* 12 (3): 143–189.

——. 1984. "To Seek a Better Life": The Implications of Migration from Mozambique to Tanganyika for Class Formation and Political Behavior. *Canadian Journal of African Studies* 18 (2): 367–388.

Alves, Armando Melo Nobre Teixeira. 1995. Análise da Política Colonial em Relação à Autoridade Tradicional. In *Autoridade e Poder Tradicional*, edited by I. B. Lundin and F. J. Machava. Maputo, Mozambique: Ministério da Administração Estatal/ Núcleo de Desenvolvimento Administrativo.

AMETRAMO. 1998. Associação da Medicina Tradicional de Moçambique (AMETRAMO): Estatuto. Maputo, Mozambique.

Amnesty International. 1979. *Amnesty International Report 1979*. London: Amnesty International.

António, V. n.d. Local Government Reform in Mozambique. Harare, Zimbabwe: SADC Regional Information Centre on Local Governance.

Apter, Andrew. 2002. On African Origins: Creolization and Connaissance in Haitian Vodou. *American Ethnologist* 29 (2): 233–260.

Ardener, Edwin. 1970. Witchcraft, Economics and the Continuity of Belief. In *Witchcraft Confessions and Accusations*, edited by M. Douglas. London: Tavistock.

Arens, W., and Ivan Karp. 1989. Introduction to *Creativity of Power*, edited by W. Arens and I. Karp. Washington: Smithsonian Institution Press.

Ashforth, Adam. 1996. Of Secrecy and the Commonplace: Witchcraft and Power in Soweto. *Social Research* 63 (4): 1181–1234.

——. 1998a. Reflections on Spiritual Insecurity in a Modern African City (Soweto). *African Studies Review* 41 (3): 39–67.

——. 1998b. Witchcraft, Violence, and Democracy in the New South Africa. *Cahiers d'Études Africaines* 38 (2–4): 505–532.

——. 2000. *Madumo: A Man Bewitched*. Chicago: University of Chicago Press.

——. 2001a. AIDS, Witchcraft, and the Problem of Power in Post-apartheid South Africa. School of Social Science Occasional Paper no. 10, Institute for Advanced Study, Princeton.

——. 2001b. On Living in a World with Witches: Everyday Epistemology and Spiritual Insecurity in a Modern African City (Soweto). In *Magical Interpretations, Material Realities: Modernity, Witchcraft, and the Occult in Postcolonial Africa*, edited by H. L. Moore and T. Sanders. London and New York: Routledge.

Associação dos Combatentes da Luta de Libertação Nacional. 1988. Estatutos e Programa. Maputo, Mozambique.

Atkinson, Jane Monnig. 1989. *The Art and Politics of Wana Shamanship*. Berkeley and Los Angeles: University of California Press.

Auslander, Mark. 1993. "Open the Wombs!" The Symbolic Politics of Modern Ngoni

Witchfinding. In *Modernity and Its Malcontents: Ritual and Power in Postcolonial Africa,* edited by J. Comaroff and J. L. Comaroff. Chicago: University of Chicago Press.

Bailey, F. G. 1994. *The Witch-Hunt; or, The Triumph of Morality.* Ithaca, NY: Cornell University Press.

Bannerman, Robert H., John Burton, and Ch'en Wen-Chieh. 1983. *Traditional Medicine and Health Care Coverage.* Geneva: World Health Organization.

Barker, John. 1990. Encounters with Evil: Christianity and the Response to Sorcery among the Maisin of Papua New Guinea. *Oceania* 61 (2): 139–155.

Bastian, Misty. 2001. Vulture Men, Campus Culturists and Teenage Witches: Modern Magics in Nigerian Popular Media. In *Magical Interpretations, Material Realities: Modernity, Witchcraft, and the Occult in Postcolonial Africa,* edited by H. L. Moore and T. Sanders. London and New York: Routledge.

———. 2003. "Diabolical Realities": Narratives of Conspiracy, Transparency, and "Ritual Murder" in the Nigerian Popular Print and Electronic Media. In *Transparency and Conspiracy: Ethnographies of Suspicion in the New World Order,* edited by H. G. West and T. Sanders. Durham, NC: Duke University Press.

Bastide, Roger. 1978. *African Religions of Brazil: Toward a Sociology of the Interpenetration of Civilizations.* Translated by Helen Sebba. Baltimore, MD: Johns Hopkins University Press.

Bayart, Jean-François. 1993. *The State in Africa: The Politics of the Belly.* London and New York: Longman.

Bayart, Jean-François, Stephen Ellis, and Béatrice Hibou. 1999. From Kleptocracy to the Felonious State? In *The Criminalization of the State in Africa,* edited by J.-F. Bayart, S. Ellis, and B. Hibou. Oxford: International African Institute.

Beattie, John. 1963. Sorcery in Bunyoro. In *Witchcraft and Sorcery in East Africa,* edited by J. Middleton and E. H. Winter. London: Routledge and Kegan Paul.

———. 1967. Divination in Bunyoro, Uganda. In *Magic, Witchcraft, and Curing,* edited by J. Middleton. Austin: University of Texas Press.

Beckett, Ian F. W. 1985. The Portuguese Army: The Campaign in Mozambique, 1964–1974. In *Armed Force and Modern Counter-Insurgency,* edited by I. F. W. Beckett and J. Pimlott. London: Croom Helm.

Behrend, Heike. 1999. *Alice Lakwena and the Holy Spirits: War in Northern Uganda, 1985–97.* Oxford: James Currey.

Beidelman, Thomas O. 1963. Witchcraft in Ukaguru. In *Witchcraft and Sorcery in East Africa,* edited by J. Middleton and E. H. Winter. London: Routledge and Kegan Paul.

———. 1993. *Moral Imagination in Kaguru Modes of Thought.* Washington: Smithsonian Institution Press.

Bellow, Saul. 1959. *Henderson, the Rain King.* New York: Viking Press.

Bento, Eliseu. 1996. Chefes Tradicionais Querem Reconhecimento e Espaço de Acção. *Notícias,* 10 April.

Boddy, Janice Patricia. 1989. *Wombs and Alien Spirits: Women, Men, and the Zār Cult in Northern Sudan.* New Directions in Anthropological Writing. Madison: University of Wisconsin Press.

Bond, George Clement. 2001. Ancestors and Witches: Explanations and the Ideology of Individual Power in Northern Zambia. In *Witchcraft Dialogues: Anthropological and Philosophical Exchanges,* edited by G. C. Bond and D. M. Ciekawy. Athens: Ohio University Center for International Studies.

Bond, George Clement, and Diane M. Ciekawy. 2001. Contested Domains in the Dialogues of "Witchcraft." In *Witchcraft Dialogues: Anthropological and Philosophical Exchanges,* edited by G. C. Bond and D. M. Ciekawy. Athens: Ohio University Center for International Studies.

Bongmba, Elias K. 1998. Toward a Hermeneutic of Wimbum Tfu. *African Studies Review* 41 (3): 165–191.

———. 2001. African Witchcraft: From Ethnography to Critique. In *Witchcraft Dialogues: Anthropological and Philosophical Exchanges,* edited by G. C. Bond and D. M. Ciekawy. Athens: Ohio University Center for International Studies.

Borges Coelho, João Paulo, ed. 1993a. Documento: O Estado Colonial e o Massacre de Mueda: Processo de Quibrite Divane e Faustino Vanombe. *Arquivo,* no. 14:129–154.

———. 1993b. Protected Villages and Communal Villages in the Mozambican Province of Tete (1968–1982): A History of State Resettlement Policies, Development and War. Ph.D. diss., University of Bradford.

———. 1998. State Resettlement Policies in Post-colonial Rural Mozambique: The Impact of the Communal Village Programme on Tete Province, 1977–1982. *Journal of Southern African Studies* 24 (1): 61–91.

Bowen, John R. 1993. Return to Sender: A Muslim Discourse of Sorcery in a Relatively Egalitarian Society. In *Understanding Witchcraft and Sorcery in Southeast Asia,* edited by C. W. Watson and R. Ellen. Honolulu: University of Hawaii Press.

Bowen, Merle L. 1992. Beyond Reform: Adjustment and Political Power in Contemporary Mozambique. *Journal of Modern African Studies* 30 (2): 255–279.

Brain, James L. 1982. Witchcraft and Development. *African Affairs* 81 (324): 371–384.

Brain, Robert. 1970. Child-Witches. In *Witchcraft Confessions and Accusations,* edited by M. Douglas. London: Tavistock.

Brandon, George. 1993. *Santeria from Africa to the New World: The Dead Sell Memories.* Blacks in the Diaspora. Bloomington: Indiana University Press.

Briggs, Charles L. 1986. *Learning How to Ask: A Sociolinguistic Appraisal of the Role of the Interview in Social Science Research.* Cambridge: Cambridge University Press.

Brown, Diana D. [1986] 1994. *Umbanda: Religion and Politics in Urban Brazil.* New York: Columbia University Press.

Brown, Karen McCarthy. 1989. Afro-Caribbean Spirituality: A Haitian Case Study. In *Healing and Restoring: Health and Medicine in the World's Religious Traditions,* edited by L. E. Sullivan. New York: Macmillan Publishing Co.

———. 1991. *Mama Lola: A Vodou Priestess in Brooklyn.* Comparative Studies in Religion and Society 4. Berkeley and Los Angeles: University of California Press.

Brown, Michael F. 1986. *Tsewa's Gift: Magic and Meaning in an Amazonian Society.* Washington: Smithsonian Institution Press.

Bukurura, Sufian. 1994. Sungusungu and the Banishment of Suspected Witches in Kahama. In *Witchcraft in Contemporary Tanzania,* edited by R. G. Abrahams. Cambridge: African Studies Centre, University of Cambridge.

Buur, Lars, and Helene Maria Kyed. 2003. *Implementation of Decree 15/2000 in Mozambique: The Consequences of State Recognition of Traditional Authority in Sussundenga.* Copenhagen: Centre for Development Research.

Calvert, Michael. 1973. Counter-Insurgency in Mozambique. *Journal of the Royal United Services Institute* 118 (1): 81–85.

Carvalho, Sol. 1981. Reeducação: Uma Realidade Complexa. *Tempo,* 11 October, 22–27.

Casal, Adolfo Y. 1991. Discurso Socialista e Camponeses Africanos: Legitimação Política-ideológica da Socialização Rural em Moçambique (FRELIMO, 1965–1984). *Revista Internacional de Estudos Africanos,* nos. 14–15:35–76.

Cassirer, Ernst. 1946. *Language and Myth:* Dover Publications.

Castenada, Carlos. 1968. *The Teachings of Don Juan: A Yaqui Way of Knowledge:* Penguin Arkana.

Cazzaninga, Rosa Carla. 1994. *Missão de Nang'ololo: Actos dos Apóstolos do Século XX.* Maputo, Mozambique: EdiBosco.

Chabal, Patrick, and Jean-Pascal Daloz. 1999. *Africa Works: Disorder as Political Instrument.* Oxford: International African Institute.

Chavunduka, Gordon L. 1978. *Traditional Healers and the Shona Patient.* Gwelo, Rhodesia: Mambo Press.

Chavunduka, Gordon L., and Murray Last. 1986. African Medical Professions Today. In *The Professionalisation of African Medicine,* edited by M. Last and G. L. Chavunduka. Manchester, UK: International African Institute.

Chernoff, John Miller. 1979. *African Rhythm and African Sensibility: Aesthetics and Social Action in African Musical Idioms.* Chicago: University of Chicago Press.

Chicuque, Stélio. 1996. Não se Pode Raciocinar como Ontem, num Estado de Hoje. *Domingo,* 6 October.

Chilcote, Ronald H., ed. 1972. *Emerging Nationalism in Portuguese Africa: Documents.* Stanford, CA: Hoover Institution Press.

Chipande, Alberto. 1970. 16 June 1960–1970: The Massacre of Meuda. *Mozambique Revolution,* April–June, 12–14.

Chowning, Ann. 1987. Sorcery and the Social Order in Kove. In *Sorcerer and Witch in Melanesia,* edited by M. Stephen. New Brunswick, NJ: Rutgers University Press.

Ciekawy, Diane M. 1998. Witchcraft in Statecraft: Five Technologies of Power in Colonial and Postcolonial Kenya. *African Studies Review* 41 (3): 119–141.

———. 2001. Utasi as Ethical Discourse: A Critique of Power from Mijikenda in Coastal Kenya. In *Witchcraft Dialogues: Anthropological and Philosophical Exchanges,* edited by G. C. Bond and D. M. Ciekawy. Athens: Ohio University Center for International Studies.

Ciekawy, Diane, and Peter Geschiere. 1998. Containing Witchcraft: Conflicting Scenarios in Postcolonial Africa. *African Studies Review* 41 (3): 1–14.

Cliff, Julie, and Abdul Razak Noormahomed. 1988. Health as a Target: South Africa's Destabilization of Mozambique. *Social Science and Medicine* 27 (7): 717–722.

Clifford, James. 1988. *The Predicament of Culture: Twentieth-Century Ethnography, Literature, and Art.* Cambridge, MA: Harvard University Press.

Cobbing, Julian. 1988. The Mfecane as Alibi: Thoughts on Dithakong and Mbolompo. *Journal of African History* 29 (3): 487–519.

Comaroff, Jean, and John L. Comaroff. 1991. *Of Revelation and Revolution: Christianity, Colonialism, and Consciousness in South Africa.* Chicago: University of Chicago Press.

———. 1993. Introduction to *Modernity and Its Malcontents: Ritual and Power in Postcolonial Africa,* edited by J. Comaroff and J. L. Comaroff. Chicago: University of Chicago Press.

———. 1999. Alien-Nation: Zombies, Immigrants, and Millennial Capitalism. *CODESRIA Bulletin,* nos. 3–4:17–28.

Comaroff, John L., and Jean Comaroff. 1997. *Of Revelation and Revolution: The Dialectics of Modernity on a South African Frontier.* Chicago: University of Chicago Press.

Cooperação Suíça. 1992. *Os Custos de Operação e Manutenção dos Sistemas de Abastecimento de Água ao Planalto de Mueda.* Maputo, Mozambique: Programa Nacional de Água Rural.

Costa, Mário. 1932. *É o Inimigo que Fala: Subsídios inéditos para o Estudo da Campanha da Africa Oriental 1914–1918.* Lourenço Marques [Maputo], Mozambique: Imprensa Nacional.

Crais, Clifton. 1998. Of Men, Magic, and the Law: Popular Justice and the Political Imagination in South Africa. *Journal of Social History* 32 (1): 49–72.

Cuehela, Ambrósio. 1996. *Autoridade Tradicional em Moçambique.* Brochura 1, *Autoridade Tradicional.* Maputo, Mozambique: Ministério da Administração Estatal/ Núcleo de Desenvolvimento Administrativo.

Danfulani, Umar Habila Dadem. 1999. Exorcising Witchcraft: The Return of the Gods in the New Religious Movements on the Jos Plateau and the Benue Regions of Nigeria. *African Affairs* 98 (391): 167–193.

da Ponte, Brigadeiro Nunes. 1940–1941. Notas da Campanha de Moçambique. *Revista Militar* 92 (7): 437–445; 92 (8): 515–525; 92 (11): 706–719; 93 (1): 23–28; 93 (2): 84–90.

Darnton, John. 1979. Mozambique, with Cuban Help, Is Shoring Up Its Internal Security. *New York Times,* 24 June, 24.

Davis, Wade. 1988. *Passage of Darkness: The Ethnobiology of the Haitian Zombie.* Chapel Hill: University of North Carolina Press.

Davis-Roberts, Christopher. 1992. Kutambuwa Ugonjuwa: Concepts of Illness and Transformation among the Tabwa of Zaire. In *The Social Basis of Health and Healing in Africa,* edited by S. Feierman and J. M. Janzen. Berkeley and Los Angeles: University of California Press.

de Brito, Luis. 1988. Une Relecture Nécessaire: La Genèse du Parti-État FRELIMO. *Politique Africaine*, no. 29:15–27.

de Heusch, Luc. 1985. *Sacrifice in Africa: A Structuralist Approach*. Manchester, UK: Manchester University Press.

Deren, Maya. 1953. *Divine Horsemen: The Living Gods of Haiti*. New Paltz, NY: Documentext, McPherson and Co.

de Sousa Santos, Boaventura. 2003. O Estado Heterogéneo e o Pluralismo Jurídico. In *Conflito e Transformação Social: Uma Paisagem das Justiças em Moçambique*, edited by B. de Sousa Santos and J. C. Trindade. Oporto, Portugal: Edições Afrontamento.

Devisch, René. 1990. The Therapist and the Source of Healing among the Yaka of Zaire. *Culture, Medicine and Psychiatry* 14:213–236.

———. 2001. Sorcery Forces of Life and Death among the Yaka of Congo. In *Witchcraft Dialogues: Anthropological and Philosophical Exchanges*, edited by G. C. Bond and D. M. Ciekawy. Athens: Ohio University Center for International Studies.

Diário de Moçambique. 1995. Para Breve Pronunciamento do Governo. 12 December.

———. 1996. Interacção Estado/Autoridade Tradicional: Dispositivo Legal Está numa Fase Avançada. 4 July.

Dias, António Jorge. 1964. *Os Macondes de Moçambique*. Vol. 1, *Aspectos Históricos e Económicos*. Lisbon: Centro de Estudos de Antropologia Cultural, Junta de Investigações do Ultramar.

Dias, António Jorge, and Margot Schmidt Dias. 1970. *Os Macondes de Moçambique*. Vol. 3, *Vida Social e Ritual*. Lisbon: Centro de Estudos de Antropologia Cultural, Junta de Investigações do Ultramar.

Dillon-Malone, Clive. 1988. Mutumwa Nchimi Healers and Wizardry Beliefs in Zambia. *Social Science and Medicine* 26 (11): 1159–1172.

Dinerman, Alice. 2001. From "Abaixo" to "Chiefs of Production": Agrarian Change in Nampula Province, Mozambique, 1975–87. *Journal of Peasant Studies* 28 (2): 1–82.

Diocese de Porto Amélia. 1957. *Relatório Referente ao Ano 1957*.

Domingo. 1996. Governo Não Vai Legislar Sobre Autoridade Tradicional. 12 December.

Donham, Donald L. 1999. *Marxist Modern: An Ethnographic History of the Ethiopian Revolution*. Berkeley and Los Angeles: University of California Press.

Douglas, Mary. 1963. Techniques of Sorcery Control in Central Africa. In *Witchcraft and Sorcery in East Africa*, edited by J. Middleton and E. H. Winter. London: Routledge and Kegan Paul.

Durham, Deborah. 1999. Civil Lives: Leadership and Accomplishment in Botswana. In *Civil Society and the Political Imagination in Africa: Critical Perspectives*, edited by J. L. Comaroff and J. Comaroff. Chicago: University of Chicago Press.

Egerö, Bertil. 1974. *Population Movement and the Colonial Economy of Tanzania*. Dar es Salaam: Bureau of Resource Assessment and Land Use Planning, University of Dar es Salaam.

———. 1987. *Mozambique, a Dream Undone: The Political Economy of Democracy, 1975–84*. Uppsala: Scandinavian Institute of African Studies.

Eliade, Mircea. 1964. *Shamanism: Archaic Techniques of Ecstasy*. New York: Bollingen Foundation.

Elias, António, and Celestino Jorge. 1988. Criada Associação dos Combatentes da Luta de Libertação Nacional: A Luta Hoje é Proteger e Fazer Crescer a Árvore. *Tempo*, 18 September, 11–15.

Ellen, Roy. 1993a. Anger, Anxiety, and Sorcery: An Analysis of Some Nuaulu Case Material from Seram, Eastern Indonesia. In *Understanding Witchcraft and Sorcery in Southeast Asia*, edited by C. W. Watson and R. Ellen. Honolulu: University of Hawaii Press.

———. 1993b. Introduction to *Understanding Witchcraft and Sorcery in Southeast Asia*, edited by C. W. Watson and R. Ellen. Honolulu: University of Hawaii Press.

Ellis, Stephen. 1999a. *The Mask of Anarchy: The Destruction of Liberia and the Religious Dimension of an African Civil War*. New York: New York University Press.

———. 1999b. The New Frontiers of Crime in South Africa. In *The Criminalization of the State in Africa*, edited by J.-F. Bayart, S. Ellis, and B. Hibou. Oxford: International African Institute.

Ellis, Stephen, and Gerrie ter Haar. 1998. Religion and Politics in Sub-Saharan Africa. *Journal of Modern African Studies* 36 (2): 175–201.

Engelke, Matthew. 2004. Text and Performance in an African Church: The Book, "Live and Direct." *American Ethnologist* 31 (1): 76–91.

Englund, Harri. 2002. *From War to Peace on the Mozambique-Malawi Borderland*. International African Library 26. Edinburgh: Edinburgh University Press for the International African Institute, London.

Englund, Harri, and James Leach. 2000. Ethnography and the Meta-narratives of Modernity. *Current Anthropology* 41 (2): 225–248.

Evans-Pritchard, Edward E. [1929] 1967. The Morphology and Function of Magic: A Comparative Study of Trobriand and Zande Rituals and Spells. In *Magic, Witchcraft, and Curing*, edited by J. Middleton. Garden City, NY: Published for the American Museum of Natural History, New York, by the Natural History Press.

———. [1929] 1970. Witchcraft amongst the Azande. In *Witchcraft and Sorcery*, edited by M. G. Marwick. Harmondsworth, UK: Penguin.

———. [1931] 1970. Sorcery and Native Opinion. In *Witchcraft and Sorcery*, edited by M. G. Marwick. Harmondsworth, UK: Penguin.

———. [1937] 1976. *Witchcraft, Oracles and Magic among the Azande*. Abridged ed. Oxford: Clarendon Press.

Fabian, Johannes. 1990. *Power and Performance: Ethnographic Explorations through Proverbial Wisdom and Theater in Shaba, Zaire*. Madison: University of Wisconsin Press.

Fadiman, Jeffrey. 1993. *When We Began There Were Witchmen: An Oral History from Mount Kenya*. Berkeley and Los Angeles: University of California Press.

Favret-Saada, Jeanne. 1980. *Deadly Words: Witchcraft in the Bocage*. Cambridge: Cambridge University Press.

Feierman, Steven. 1986. Popular Control over the Institutions of Health: A Historical Study. In *The Professionalisation of African Medicine*, edited by M. Last and G. L. Chavunduka. Manchester, UK: International African Institute.

Feld, Steven. 1987. Dialogical Editing: Interpreting How Kaluli Read *Sound and Sentiment*. *Cultural Anthropology* 2 (2): 190–210.

Ferguson, James. 1995. From African Socialism to Scientific Capitalism: Reflections on the Legitimation Crisis in IMF-Ruled Africa. In *Debating Development Discourse: Institutional and Popular Perspectives*, edited by D. B. Moore and G. J. Schmitz. New York: St. Martin's Press.

———. 1999. *Expectations of Modernity: Myths and Meanings of Urban Life on the Zambian Copperbelt*. Berkeley and Los Angeles: University of California Press.

Ferguson, James, and Akhil Gupta. 2002. Spatializing States: Toward an Ethnography of Neoliberal Governmentality. *American Ethnologist* 29 (4): 981–1002.

Ferme, Mariane C. 1999. Staging Politisi: The Logics of Publicity and Secrecy in Sierra Leone. In *Civil Society and the Political Imagination in Africa: Critical Perspectives*, edited by J. L. Comaroff and J. Comaroff. Chicago: University of Chicago Press.

———. 2001. *The Underneath of Things: Violence, History, and the Everyday in Sierra Leone*. Berkeley and Los Angeles: University of California Press.

Fernandez, James W. 1991. Afterword to *African Divination Systems: Ways of Knowing*, by Philip M. Peek. African Systems of Thought. Bloomington: Indiana University Press

Fernando, Domingos. 1996. *Autoridade Tradicional em Moçambique*. Brochura 2, *A Organização Social na Sociedade Tradicional*. Maputo, Mozambique: Ministério da Administração Estatal/Núcleo de Desenvolvimento Administrativo.

Ferreira, Manuel. 1946. *Neutel de Abreu*. Colecção pelo Império, vol. 116. Lisbon: Agência Geral das Colónias.

Fields, Karen E. 1982. Political Contingencies of Witchcraft in Colonial Central Africa: Culture and the State in Marxist Theory. *Canadian Journal of African Studies* 16 (3): 567–593.

———. 1997. *Revival and Rebellion in Colonial Central Africa*. Portsmouth, NH: Heinemann.

Fisiy, Cyprian F. 1998. Containing Occult Practices: Witchcraft Trials in Cameroon. *African Studies Review* 41 (3): 143–163.

Fisiy, Cyprian F., and Peter Geschiere. 1990. Judges and Witches, or How Is the State to Deal with Witchcraft? *Cahiers d'Études Africaines* 30 (2): 135–156.

———. 1996. Witchcraft, Violence and Identity: Different Trajectories in Postcolonial Cameroon. In *Postcolonial Identities in Africa*, edited by R. Werbner and T. O. Ranger. London: Zed Books.

———. 2001. Witchcraft, Development and Paranoia in Cameroon: Interactions between Popular, Academic and State Discourse. In *Magical Interpretations, Material*

Realities: Modernity, Witchcraft, and the Occult in Postcolonial Africa, edited by H. L. Moore and T. Sanders. London and New York: Routledge.

Fisiy, Cyprian F., and Michael J. Rowlands. 1989. Sorcery and Law in Modern Cameroon. *Culture and History* 6:63–84.

Fitzpatrick, Sheila. 1994. *Stalin's Peasants: Resistance and Survival in the Russian Village after Collectivization.* New York: Oxford University Press.

Forde, Daryl. 1958. Witches and Sorcerers in the Supernatural Economy of the Yako. *Journal of the Royal Anthropological Institute* 88 (2): 165–178.

Forster, Peter Glover. 1998. Religion, Magic, Witchcraft, and AIDS in Malawi. *Anthropos* 93 (4–6): 537–544.

Forth, Gregory. 1993. Social and Symbolic Aspects of the Witch among the Mage of Eastern Indonesia. In *Understanding Witchcraft and Sorcery in Southeast Asia,* edited by C. W. Watson and R. Ellen. Honolulu: University of Hawaii Press.

Foucault, Michel. 1977. *Discipline and Punish: The Birth of the Prison.* 1st American ed. New York: Pantheon Books.

FRELIMO. 1964. From Mozambique. *Mozambique Revolution,* June, 6–7.

———. 1970. Portuguese Atrocities in Mozambique. *Mozambique Revolution,* October–December, 8–12.

———. 1972. War Review. *Mozambique Revolution,* July–September, 4–6.

———. 1973. The Enemy's New Methods. *Mozambique Revolution,* October–December, 3–5.

———. 1976. Resolução sobre Aldeias Comunais. In *Extracto dos Documentos da Oitava Sessão do Comité Central da FRELIMO.* Maputo, Mozambique: FRELIMO.

———. 1977. *O Processo Revolucionário da Guerra Popular de Libertação.* Edited by Departamento do Trabalho Ideológico da FRELIMO. Textos e Documentos da FRELIMO, vol. 1. Maputo, Mozambique: n.p.

Fry, Peter. 1976. *Spirits of Protest: Spirit-Mediums and the Articulation of Consensus among the Zezuru of Southern Rhodesia (Zimbabwe).* Cambridge: Cambridge University Press.

———. 1977. *Umbanda: The Problem Solver.* Video. Disappearing World, edited by J. Harvey. Chicago: Films Inc.

———. 1997. *Final Evaluation of the Decentralization/Traditional Authority Component of the Africa-America Institute's Project "Democratic Development in Mozambique" (Cooperative Agreement #656-A-00-4029-00).* Maputo, Mozambique: USAID.

———. 2000. Cultures of Difference: The Aftermath of Portuguese and British Colonial Policies in Southern Africa. *Social Anthropology* 8 (2): 117–143.

Gable, Eric. 1997. A Secret Shared: Fieldwork and the Sinister in a West African Village. *Cultural Anthropology* 12 (2): 213–233.

Gabriel, Phyllis Safiya, and Susan M. Stuart. 1978. The Role of Health Care in Socialist Revolutions: Mozambique and Cuba. *Ufahamu* 8 (2): 35–64.

Garro, Linda C., and Cheryl Mattingly. 2000. Narrative as Construct and Construction.

In *Narrative and the Cultural Construction of Illness and Healing*, edited by C. Mattingly and L. C. Garro. Berkeley and Los Angeles: University of California Press.

Gaspar, Felisbela, and Armando Djedje. 1994. *Crenças e Práticas Tradicionais Relativas à Diarreia Infantil e às Doenças de Transmissão Sexual em Milange, Província da Zambézia: Relatório de Pesquisa e Comunicação*. Maputo, Mozambique: Gabinete de Estudos de Medicina Tradicional, Ministério da Saúde.

Gauth, Gonçalves. 1996. Regulamento Vai ser Aprovado Brevemente—Revela Alfredo Gamito. *Notícias*, 5 June.

Geffray, Christian. 1990. *La Cause des Armes au Mozambique: Anthropologie d'une Guerre Civile*. Paris: Karthala.

Geffray, Christian, and Mögens Pedersen. 1988. Nampula en Guerre. *Politique Africaine*, no. 29:28–40.

Gengenbach, Heidi. 2000. Naming the Past in a "Scattered" Land: Memory and the Powers of Women's Naming Practices in Southern Mozambique. *International Journal of African Historical Studies* 33 (3): 523–542.

Geschiere, Peter. 1988. Sorcery and the State: Popular Modes of Action among the Maka of Southeast Cameroon. *Critique of Anthropology* 8 (1): 35–63.

———. 1992. Kinship, Witchcraft and "the Market": Hybrid Patterns in Cameroonian Societies. In *Contesting Markets: Analyses of Ideology, Discourse and Practice*, edited by R. Dilley. Edinburgh: University Press.

———. 1996. Chiefs and the Problem of Witchcraft: Varying Patterns in South and West Cameroon. *Journal of Legal Pluralism and Unofficial Law* 37–38:307–327.

———. 1997. *The Modernity of Witchcraft: Politics and the Occult in Postcolonial Africa*. Charlottesville: University Press of Virginia.

———. 1998. Globalization and the Power of Indeterminate Meaning: Witchcraft and Spirit Cults in Africa and East Asia. *Development and Change* 29 (4): 811–837.

Geschiere, Peter, and Cyprian F. Fisiy. 1994. Domesticating Personal Violence: Witchcraft, Courts and Confessions in Cameroon. *Africa* 64 (3): 323–341.

Geschiere, Peter, and Francis Nyamnjoh. 1998. Witchcraft as an Issue in the "Politics of Belonging": Democratization and Urban Migrants' Involvement with the Home Village. *African Studies Review* 41 (3): 69–91.

Gibson, Richard. 1972. *African Liberation Movements: Contemporary Struggles against White Minority Rule*. New York: Oxford University Press.

Gilbert, Michelle. 1989. Sources of Power in Akuropon-Akupem: Ambiguity in Classification. In *Creativity of Power*, edited by W. Arens and I. Karp. Washington: Smithsonian Institution Press.

Ginzburg, Carlo. [1966] 1992. *The Night Battles: Witchcraft and Agrarian Cults in the 16th and 17th Centuries*. Translated by J. Tedeschi and A. Tedeschi. Baltimore, MD: Johns Hopkins University Press.

Gluckman, Max, J. Clyde Mitchell, and J. A. Barnes. 1949. The Village Headman in British Central Africa. *Africa* 19 (2): 89–106.

Goheen, Miriam. 1996. *Men Own the Fields, Women Own the Crops: Gender and Power in the Cameroon Grassfields*. Madison: University of Wisconsin Press.

Gomes, Conceição, Joaquim Fumo, Guilherme Mbilana, and Boaventura de Sousa Santos. 2003. Os Tribunais Comunitários. In *Conflito e Transformação Social: Uma Paisagem das Justiças em Moçambique,* edited by B. de Sousa Santos and J. C. Trindade. Oporto: Edições Afrontamento.

Good, Byron. 1994. *Medicine, Rationality, and Experience: An Anthropological Perspective, The Lewis Henry Morgan Lectures, 1990.* Cambridge: Cambridge University Press.

Goody, Esther. 1970. Legitimate and Illegitimate Aggression in a West African State. In *Witchcraft Confessions and Accusations,* edited by M. Douglas. London: Tavistock.

Gottlieb, Alma. 1989. Witches, Kings, and the Sacrifice of Identity, or The Power of Paradox and the Paradox of Power among the Beng of Ivory Coast. In *Creativity of Power,* edited by W. Arens and I. Karp. Washington: Smithsonian Institution Press.

———. 1992. *Under the Kapok Tree: Identity and Difference in Beng Thought.* African Systems of Thought. Bloomington: Indiana University Press.

Gow, Peter. 1996. River People: Shamanism and History in Western Amazonia. In *Shamanism, History, and the State,* edited by N. Thomas and C. Humphrey. Ann Arbor: University of Michigan Press.

Gray, Robert F. 1963. Some Structural Aspects of Mbugwe Witchcraft. In *Witchcraft and Sorcery in East Africa,* edited by J. Middleton and E. H. Winter. London: Routledge and Kegan Paul.

———. 1969. The Shetani Cult among the Segeju of Tanzania. In *Spirit Mediumship and Society in Africa,* edited by J. Beattie and J. Middleton. London: Routledge and Kegan Paul.

Green, Edward C. 1994. *AIDS and STDS in Africa: Bridging the Gap between Traditional Healing and Modern Medicine.* Edited by E. C. Green. Boulder: Westview Press.

———. 1996. *Indigenous Healers and the African State: Policy Issues concerning African Indigenous Healers in Mozambique and Southern Africa.* New York: Pact Publications.

———. 1997. Purity, Pollution and the Invisible Snake in Southern Africa. *Medical Anthropology* 17:83–100.

———. 1999. *Indigenous Theories of Contagious Disease.* Walnut Creek, CA: AltaMira Press.

Green, Edward C., Annemarie Jurg, and Armando Dgedge [Djedje]. 1993. Sexually-Transmitted Diseases, AIDS and Traditional Healers in Mozambique. *Medical Anthropology* 15:261–281.

———. 1994. The Snake in the Stomach: Child Diarrhea in Central Mozambique. *Medical Anthropology Quarterly* 8 (1): 4–24.

Green, Edward C., Josefa Marrato, and Manuel Wilsonne. 1995. Ethnomedical Study of Diarrheal Disease, AIDS, STDS and Mental Health in Nampula, Mozambique. Maputo, Mozambique: Department of Traditional Medicine, Mozambique Ministry of Health.

Green, Maia. 1994. Shaving Witchcraft in Ulanga. In *Witchcraft in Contemporary Tan-*

zania, edited by R. G. Abrahams. Cambridge: African Studies Centre, University of Cambridge.

———. 1997. Witchcraft Suppression Practices and Movements: Public Politics and the Logic of Purification. *Comparative Studies in Society and History* 39 (2): 319–345.

Greene, Shane. 1998. The Shaman's Needle: Development, Shamanic Agency, and Intermediality in Aguaruna Lands, Peru. *American Ethnologist* 25 (4): 634–658.

———. n.d. A Battle of Bad Odds and Big Expectations: Pharmaceutical Bioprospection, Traditional Knowledge and Intellectual Properties in Peru. Computer printout, University of Chicago.

Gufler, Hermann. 1999. Witchcraft Beliefs among the Yamba (Cameroon). *Anthropos* 94 (1–3): 181–198.

Gulube, Lucas Langue. 2003. *Organização da Rede Sanitária Colonial no Sul do Save (1960–1974)*. Maputo, Mozambique: Promédia.

Hall, Margaret. 1990. The Mozambican National Resistance Movement (RENAMO): A Study in the Destruction of an African Country. *Africa* 60 (1): 39–68.

Hamilton, Carolyn. 1997. Mfecane: Historiography. In *The Encyclopedia of Africa South of the Sahara*, edited by J. Middleton. New York: Charles Scribner's Sons.

Hammond-Tooke, W. D. 1970. The Witch Familiar as a Mediatory Construct. In *Witchcraft and Sorcery*, edited by M. G. Marwick. Harmondsworth, UK: Penguin.

Hanlon, Joseph. 1990. *Mozambique: The Revolution under Fire*. London: Zed Books.

———. 1991. *Mozambique: Who Calls the Shots?* London: James Currey.

———. 2000. New Decree Recognises "Traditional Chiefs": AWEPA. Computer printout, Open University.

Hansen, Thomas Blom, and Finn Stepputat. 2001. *States of Imagination: Ethnographic Explorations of the Postcolonial State*. Durham, NC: Duke University Press.

Harries, Patrick. 1993. *Work, Culture, and Identity: Migrant Laborers in Mozambique and South Africa, c. 1860–1910*. Social History of Africa. Portsmouth, NH: Heinemann.

———. 2001. Missionaries, Marxists and Magic: Power and the Politics of Literacy in South-East Africa. *Journal of Southern African Studies* 27 (3): 405–427.

Harrison, Graham. 1999. Corruption as "Boundary Politics": The State, Democratisation, and Mozambique's Unstable Liberalisation. *Third World Quarterly* 20 (3): 537–550.

Hartwig, Gerald W. 1971. Long-Distance Trade and the Evolution of Sorcery among the Kerebe. *African Historical Studies* 4 (3): 505–524.

Harwood, Alan. 1970. *Witchcraft, Sorcery, and Social Categories among the Safwa*. London: International African Institute.

Hedges, David. 1985. Educação, Missões e a Ideologia Política de Assimilação, 1930–60. *Cadernos de História*, no. 1:7–17.

Henriksen, Thomas H. 1978. *Mozambique: A History*. London: Rex Collings.

———. 1983. *Revolution and Counter-Revolution: Mozambique's War of Independence, 1964–1974*. Westport, CT: Greenwood Press.

Henrique, Arnaldo. 1988. Associação dos Combatentes da Luta de Libertação Nacional: Um Sonho Quase Realidade. *Tempo,* 24 January, 6–9.

Hibou, Beatrice. 1999. The "Social Capital" of the State as an Agent of Deception; or, The Ruses of Economic Intelligence. In *The Criminalization of the State in Africa,* edited by J.-F. Bayart, S. Ellis, and B. Hibou. Oxford: International African Institute.

Honwana, Alcinda Manuel. 2002. *Espíritos Vivos, Tradições Modernas: Possessão de Espíritos e Reintegração Social Pós-Guerra no Sul de Moçambique.* Maputo, Mozambique: Promédia.

Hopa, M., L. C. Simbayi, and C. D. du Toit. 1998. Perceptions on Integration of Traditional and Western Healing in the New South Africa. *South African Journal of Psychology* 28 (1): 8–14.

Horton, Robin. [1967] 1970. African Traditional Thought and Western Science. In *Rationality,* edited by B. R. Wilson. Oxford: Basil Blackwell.

———. 1993. *Patterns of Thought in Africa and the West.* Cambridge: Cambridge University Press.

Hountondji, Paulin. 1983. *African Philosophy: Myth and Reality.* Bloomington: Indiana University Press.

Howes, Michael, and Robert Chambers. 1980. Indigenous Technical Knowledge: Analysis, Implications and Issues. In *Indigenous Knowledge Systems and Development,* edited by D. Brokensha, D. M. Warren, and O. Werner. Washington, DC: University Press of America.

Humphrey, Caroline. 2003. Stalin and the Blue Elephant: Paranoia and Complicity in Post-Communist Metahistories. In *Transparency and Conspiracy: Ethnographies of Suspicion in the New World Order,* edited by H. G. West and T. Sanders. Durham, NC: Duke University Press.

Humphrey, Caroline, and Urgunge Onon. 1996. *Shamans and Elders: Experience, Knowledge and Power among the Daur Mongols.* Oxford Studies in Social and Cultural Anthropology. Oxford: Clarendon Press.

Iliffe, John. 1969. The Age of Improvement and Differentiation (1907–1945). In *A History of Tanzania,* edited by I. N. Kimambo and A. J. Temu. Nairobi: East African Publishing House.

Institutions for Natural Resource Management. n.d. *Implementing CBNRM in M'punga.* Brighton: University of Sussex.

Isaacman, Allen. 1982. The Mozambique Cotton Cooperative: The Creation of a Grassroots Alternative to Forced Commodity Relations. *African Studies Review* 25 (2–3): 5–25.

———. 1996. *Cotton Is the Mother of Poverty: Peasants, Work, and Rural Struggle in Colonial Mozambique, 1938–1961.* Edited by A. Isaacman and J. Hay. Social History of Africa. Portsmouth, NH: Heinemann.

Isaacman, Allen, and Barbara Isaacman. 1984. The Role of Women in the Liberation of Mozambique. *Ufahamu* 13 (2–3): 128–185.

Jackson, Michael. 1989. *Paths toward a Clearing: Radical Empiricism and Ethnographic Inquiry.* Bloomington: Indiana University Press.

Jansen, P. C. M., and Orlando Mendes. 1983–1984. *Plantas Medicinais: Seu Uso Tradicional em Moçambique.* 4 vols. Maputo, Mozambique: Gabinete de Estudos de Medicina Tradicional, Ministério da Saúde, República Popular de Moçambique.

Janzen, John M. 1978. *The Quest for Therapy: Medical Pluralism in Lower Zaire.* Berkeley and Los Angeles: University of California Press.

———. 1989. Health, Religion, and Medicine in Central and Southern African Traditions. In *Healing and Restoring: Health and Medicine in the World's Religious Traditions,* edited by L. E. Sullivan. New York: Macmillan.

———. 1992. *Ngoma: Discourses of Healing in Central and Southern Africa.* Comparative Studies of Health Systems and Medical Care 34. Berkeley and Los Angeles: University of California Press.

Johnston, Anton. 1984. *Education in Moçambique, 1975–84.* Stockholm: Swedish International Development Authority.

———. 1989. *Study, Produce, and Combat: Education and the Mozambican State, 1962–1984.* Studies in Comparative and International Education 14. Stockholm: Institute of International Education, University of Stockholm.

———. 1990a. Adult Literacy for Development in Mozambique. *African Studies Review* 33 (3): 83–96.

———. 1990b. The Mozambican State and Education. In *Education and Social Transition in the Third World,* edited by M. Carnoy, J. Samoff, M. A. Burris, A. Johnston, and C. A. Torres. Princeton: Princeton University Press.

Jones, G. I. 1970. A Boundary to Accusations. In *Witchcraft Confessions and Accusations,* edited by M. Douglas. London: Tavistock.

Joralemon, Donald, and Douglas Sharon. 1993. *Sorcery and Shamanism:* Curanderos *and Clients in Northern Peru.* Salt Lake City: University of Utah Press.

Kapferer, Bruce. 1997. *The Feast of the Sorcerer: Practices of Consciousness and Power.* Chicago: University of Chicago Press.

Kappel, Rolf. 1994. Monitoring Adjustment and Rural Poverty: Concept and Major Results of the Swiss Monitoring Programme in Cabo Delgado, Mozambique. *Journal für Entwicklungspolitik* 10 (4): 473–490.

Karlström, Mikael. 1999. Political Society and Its Presuppositions: Lessons from Uganda. In *Civil Society and the Political Imagination in Africa: Critical Perspectives,* edited by J. L. Comaroff and J. Comaroff. Chicago: University of Chicago Press.

Karlyn, Andrew S. 2001. The Impact of a Targeted Radio Campaign to Prevent STIs and HIV/AIDS in Mozambique. *AIDS Education and Prevention* 13 (5): 438–451.

Kaspin, Deborah. 1993. Chewa Visions and Revisions of Power. In *Modernity and Its Malcontents: Ritual and Power in Postcolonial Africa,* edited by J. Comaroff and J. L. Comaroff. Chicago: University of Chicago Press.

Kendall, Laurel. 2003. Gods, Markets, and the IMF in the Korean Spirit World. In *Transparency and Conspiracy: Ethnographies of Suspicion in the New World Order,* edited by H. G. West and T. Sanders. Durham, NC: Duke University Press.

Kingdon, Zachary. 2002. *A Host of Devils: The History and Context of the Making of Makonde Spirit Sculpture.* London: Routledge.

Kluckhohn, Clyde. 1944. *Navaho Witchcraft.* Boston: Beacon Press.

Knipe, David. 1989. Hinduism and the Tradition of Ayurveda. In *Healing and Restoring: Health and Medicine in the World's Religious Traditions,* edited by L. E. Sullivan. New York: Macmillan.

Kohnert, Dirk. 1996. Magic and Witchcraft: Implications for Democratization and Poverty-Alleviating Aid in Africa. *World Development* 24 (8): 1347–1355.

Krige, J. D. [1947] 1970. The Social Function of Witchcraft. In *Witchcraft and Sorcery,* edited by M. G. Marwick. Harmondsworth, UK: Penguin.

Kriger, Norma J. 1992. *Zimbabwe's Guerrilla War: Peasant Voices.* African Studies Series 70. Cambridge: Cambridge University Press.

Laderman, Carol. 1991. *Taming the Wind of Desire: Psychology, Medicine, and Aesthetics in Malay Shamanistic Performance.* Berkeley and Los Angeles: University of California Press.

La Fontaine, Jean. 1963. Witchcraft in Bugisu. In *Witchcraft and Sorcery in East Africa,* edited by J. Middleton and E. H. Winter. London: Routledge and Kegan Paul.

Lambek, Michael. 1993. *Knowledge and Practice in Mayotte: Local Discourses of Islam, Sorcery, and Spirit Possession.* Anthropological Horizons. Toronto: University of Toronto Press.

Lan, David. 1985. *Guns and Rain: Guerrillas and Spirit Mediums in Zimbabwe.* London: James Currey.

Landau, Paul Stuart. 1995. *The Realm of the Word: Language, Gender, and Christianity in a Southern African Kingdom.* Social History of Africa. Portsmouth, NH: Heinemann; Cape Town: D. Philip; London: J. Currey.

Langford, Jean M. 2002. *Fluent Bodies: Ayurvedic Remedies for Postcolonial Imbalance.* Durham, NC: Duke University Press.

Last, Murray. 1992. The Importance of Knowing about Not Knowing: Observations from Hausaland. In *The Social Basis of Health and Healing in Africa,* edited by S. Feierman and J. M. Janzen. Berkeley and Los Angeles: University of California Press.

Last, Murray, and Gordon L. Chavunduka. 1986. The Professionalisation of African Medicine: Ambiguities and Definitions. In *The Professionalisation of African Medicine,* edited by M. Last and Gordon L. Chavunduka. Manchester, UK: International African Institute.

Lattas, Andrew. 1993. Sorcery and Colonialism: Illness, Dreams and Death as Political Languages in West New Britain. *Man* 28 (1): 51–77.

Leach, Edmund Ronald. 1954. *Political Systems of Highland Burma: A Study of Kachin Social Structure.* Cambridge, MA: Harvard University Press.

Lebreton, Padre Alain, and Padre Theodoor Vloet. n.d. Chronique de Nang'ololo. n.p.

LeVine, Robert A. 1963. Witchcraft and Sorcery in a Gusii Community. In *Witchcraft and Sorcery in East Africa,* edited by J. Middleton and E. H. Winter. London: Routledge and Kegan Paul.

Lévi-Strauss, Claude. 1963. The Sorcerer and His Magic. In *Structural Anthropology,* by C. Lévi-Strauss, translated by C. Jacobson and B. G. Schoepf. New York: Basic Books.

Lewis, Gilbert. 1994. Magic, Religion and the Rationality of Belief. In *Companion Encyclopedia of Anthropology*, edited by T. Ingold. London and New York: Routledge.

Liebenow, J. Gus. 1971. *Colonial Rule and Political Development in Tanzania: The Case of the Makonde*. Evanston, IL: Northwestern University Press.

Lienhardt, Godfrey. 1951. Some Notions of Witchcraft among the Dinka. *Africa* 21 (4): 303–318.

Limbombo, Óscar. 2003. Leões de Muidumbe. *Questão de Fundo*, Rádio Moçambique, Pemba.

Limón, José Eduardo. 1994. *Dancing with the Devil: Society and Cultural Poetics in Mexican-American South Texas*. New Directions in Anthropological Writing. Madison: University of Wisconsin Press.

Lindenbaum, Shirley. 1979. *Kuru Sorcery: Disease and Danger in the New Guinea Highlands*. Palo Alto, CA: Mayfield.

Littlejohn, Gary. 1988. Rural Development in Mueda District, Mozambique. *Leeds Southern African Studies*, no. 9:1–18.

Lopes, Armando Jorge, Salvador Júlio Sitoe, and Paulino José Nhamuende. 2002. *Moçambicanismos: Para um Léxico de Uso do Português Moçambicano*. Maputo, Mozambique: Livraria Universitária, Universidade Eduardo Mondlane.

Lubkemann, Stephen. 2001. Rebuilding Local Capacities in Mozambique: The National Health System and Civil Society. In *Patronage or Partnership: Local Capacity Building in Humanitarian Crises*, edited by I. Smillie. Bloomfield, CT.: Kumarian Press.

Luedke, Tracy J. n.d. Presidents, Bishops, and Mothers: The Construction of Authority in Mozambican Healing. In *Borders and Healers: Brokering Therapeutic Resources in Southeast Africa*, edited by T. J. Luedke and H. G. West. Bloomington: Indiana University Press. Forthcoming.

Lundin, Iraê Baptista. 1995. A Pesquisa Piloto Sobre a Autoridade/Poder Tradicional em Moçambique—Um Somatório Comentado e Analisado. In *Autoridade e Poder Tradicional*, vol. 1, edited by I. B. Lundin and F. J. Machava. Maputo, Mozambique: Ministério da Administração Estatal/Núcleo de Desenvolvimento Administrativo.

———. 1996. Traditional Authorities in Mozambique. Paper presented at "The Role of Traditional Leaders in the New South Africa" conference, Umtata, South Africa, 4–5 July.

Luomala, Katherine. 1989. Polynesian Religious Foundations of Hawaiian Concepts regarding Wellness and Illness. In *Healing and Restoring: Health and Medicine in the World's Religious Traditions*, edited by L. E. Sullivan. New York: Macmillan.

MacCormick, Carol P. 1983. Human Leopards and Crocodiles: Political Meanings of Categorical Anomalies. In *The Ethnography of Cannibalism*, edited by P. Brown and D. Tuzin. Washington, DC: Society for Psychological Anthropology.

———. 1986. The Articulation of Western and Traditional Systems of Health Care. In *The Professionalisation of African Medicine*, edited by M. Last and G. L. Chavunduka. Manchester, UK: International African Institute.

MacGaffey, Wyatt. 1980. African Religions: Types and Generalizations. In *Explorations in African Systems of Thought*, edited by I. Karp and C. S. Bird. Washington, DC: Smithsonian Institution Press.

Machel, Samora. 1978. *Produzir é Aprender: Aprender para Produzir e Lutar Melhor.* Maputo, Mozambique: FRELIMO.

———. 1985. *Samora Machel, An African Revolutionary: Selected Speeches and Writings.* Edited by Barry Munslow. London: Zed Books.

Mackintosh, Maureen, and Marc Wuyts. 1988. Accumulation, Social Services and Socialist Transition in the Third World: Reflections on Decentralised Planning Based on the Mozambican Experience. *Journal of Development Studies,* no. 24:136–173.

Mair, Lucy Philip. 1969. *Witchcraft.* New York: McGraw-Hill.

Mamdani, Mahmood. 1996. *Citizen and Subject: Contemporary Africa and the Legacy of Late Colonialism.* London: Currey.

Manning, Carrie. 2001. Competition and Accommodation in Post-conflict Democracy: The Case of Mozambique. *Democratization* 8 (2): 140–168.

Marshall, Judith. 1990. Structural Adjustment and Social Policy in Mozambique. *Review of African Political Economy,* no. 47:28–43.

———. 1993. *Literacy, Power, and Democracy in Mozambique: The Governance of Learning from Colonization to the Present.* Boulder: Westview Press.

Martinez, Francisco Lerma. 1989. *O Povo Macua e a sua Cultura.* Lisbon: Ministério da Educação, Instituto de Investigação Científica Tropical.

Marwick, Max G. 1950. Another Modern Anti-witchcraft Movement. *Africa* 20 (1): 100–112.

———. 1965. *Sorcery in Its Social Setting: A Study of the Northern Rhodesian Ceŵa.* Manchester, UK: Manchester University Press.

———. 1967. The Sociology of Sorcery in a Central African Tribe. In *Magic, Witchcraft, and Curing,* edited by J. Middleton. Austin: University of Texas Press.

———. 1970. Witchcraft and the Epistemology of Science. In *Witchcraft and Sorcery,* edited by M. G. Marwick. Harmondsworth, UK: Penguin.

Masquelier, Adeline. 1987. Cooking the Bori Way: The Logic of Healing in the Hausa Cult of Possession. *Chicago Anthropology Exchange* 16:96–103.

———. 1997. Vectors of Witchcraft: Object Transactions and the Materialization of Memory in Niger. *Anthropological Quarterly* 70 (4): 187–198.

———. 2000. Of Headhunters and Cannibals: Migrancy, Labor, and Consumption in the Mawri Imagination. *Cultural Anthropology* 15 (1): 84–126.

———. 2001. *Prayer Has Spoiled Everything: Possession, Power, and Identity in an Islamic Town of Niger.* Durham, NC: Duke University Press.

Maxwell, David. 1999. *Christians and Chiefs in Zimbabwe: A Social History of the Hwesa People.* Westport, CT: Praeger.

Mayer, Phillip. 1970. Witches. In *Witchcraft and Sorcery,* edited by M. G. Marwick. Harmondsworth, UK: Penguin.

Mbembe, Achille. 2001. *On the Postcolony.* Studies on the History of Society and Culture 41. Berkeley and Los Angeles: University of California Press.

McBrien, Richard P., and Harold W. Attridge. 1995. *The HarperCollins Encyclopedia of Catholicism*. 1st ed. New York: HarperCollins.

Melo, António, José Capela, Luís Moita, and Nuno Teotónio Pereira, eds. 1974. *Colonialismo e Lutas de Libertação: 7 Cadernos sobre a Guerra Colonial*. Oporto: Afrontamento.

Membe, Remígio. 1995. Fenómeno "Ningore" Renasce em Cabo Delgado: "Perseguido" é Agora o Mais Famoso Curandeiro daquela Província. *Savana*, 18 August, 12.

Meneses, M. Paula G. 2000. *Medicina Tradicional, Biodiversidade e Conhecimentos Rivais em Moçambique*. Coimbra: Centro de Estudos Sociais, Universidade de Coimbra.

———. n.d. *"When There Are No Problems, We Are Healthy, No Bad Luck, Nothing": Towards an Emancipatory Understanding of Health and Medicine*. Coimbra: Centro de Estudos Sociais, Universidade de Coimbra.

Meneses, Maria Paula, Joaquim Fumo, Guilherme Mbilana, and Conceição Gomes. 2003. As Autoridades Tradicionais no Contexto do Pluralismo Jurídico. In *Conflito e Transformação Social: Uma Paisagem das Justiças em Moçambique*, edited by B. de Sousa Santos and J. C. Trindade. Oporto: Edições Afrontamento.

Mesaki, Simeon. 1994. Witch-Killing in Sukumaland. In *Witchcraft in Contemporary Tanzania*, edited by R. G. Abrahams. Cambridge: African Studies Centre, University of Cambridge.

Métraux, Alfred. [1959] 1972. *Voodoo in Haiti*. New York: Schocken Books.

Meyer, Birgit. 1992. "If You Are a Devil, You Are a Witch and, If You Are a Witch, You Are a Devil": The Integration of "Pagan" Ideas into the Conceptual Universe of Ewe Christians in Southeastern Ghana. *Journal of Religion in Africa* 22 (2): 98–132.

———. 1995. Delivered from the Powers of Darkness: Confessions of Satanic Riches in Christian Ghana. *Africa* 65:236–255.

———. 1998. The Power of Money: Politics, Occult Forces, and Pentecostalism in Ghana. *African Studies Review* 41 (3): 15–37.

———. 1999. *Translating the Devil: Religion and Modernity among the Ewe in Ghana*. Trenton, NJ: Africa World Press.

Middleton, John. 1963. Witchcraft and Sorcery in Lugbara. In *Witchcraft and Sorcery in East Africa*, edited by J. Middleton and E. H. Winter. London: Routledge and Kegan Paul.

———. 1967. The Concept of "Bewitching" in Lugbara. In *Magic, Witchcraft, and Curing*, edited by J. Middleton. Austin: University of Texas Press.

Mignolo, Walter. 2000. *Local Histories/Global Designs: Coloniality, Subaltern Knowledges, and Border Thinking*. Princeton Studies in Culture/Power/History. Princeton, NJ: Princeton University Press.

Ministério da Administração Estatal/Núcleo de Desenvolvimento Administrativo. 1997. *Projecto "Descentralização e Autoridade Tradicional—DAT": CTD Nacional, Documento Somatório das Conclusões dos CTDs*. Maputo, Mozambique: Ministério da Administração Estatal/Núcleo de Desenvolvimento Administrativo.

Minter, William. 1994. *Apartheid's Contras*. London: Zed Books.

Mitchell, J. Clyde. 1956. *The Yao Village: A Study in the Social Structure of a Malawian People.* Manchester, UK: Manchester University Press.

Mohomed, Mussá. 1995a. Administração Conjun Vai Vigorar no País. *Notícias,* 21 June.

———. 1995b. Chefes Tradicionais Devem Colaborar com o Governo. *Notícias,* 22 June.

———. 1996. Régulos Não Querem Ser Eleitos para Cargos Públicos—Revelam Estudos sobre a Autoridade Tradicional no País. *Notícias,* 13 July.

Mombeshora, Solomon. 1994. Witches, Witchcraft and the Question of Order: A View from a Bena Village in the Southern Highlands. In *Witchcraft in Contemporary Tanzania,* edited by R. G. Abrahams. Cambridge: African Studies Centre, University of Cambridge.

Mondlane, Eduardo. 1969. *The Struggle for Mozambique.* Edited by R. Segal. Penguin African Library. Middlesex, UK: Penguin.

Monks, Giles Edward. 1990. Operation Gordian Knot: A Survey of Portuguese Counter-Insurgency: Mozambique. M.A. thesis, University of York.

Monteiro, José Óscar. 1989. *Power and Democracy.* Maputo, Mozambique: People's Assembly.

Morgan, Glenda. 1990. Violence in Mozambique: Towards and Understanding of RENAMO. *Journal of Modern African Studies* 28 (4): 603–619.

Morris, Rosalind C. 2000. Modernity's Media and the End of Mediumship? On the Aesthetic Economy of Transparency in Thailand. *Public Culture* 12 (2): 457–475.

Mpalume, Estêvão Jaime, and Marcos Agostinho Mandumbwe. 1991. *Nashilangola wa Shitangodi sha Shimakonde.* Pemba: Núcleo da Associação dos Escritores Moçambicanos de Cabo Delgado.

Mucussete, Hamido. 1996. *Autoridade Tradicional em Moçambique.* Brochura 4, *Terra e Meio Ambiente.* Maputo, Mozambique: Ministério da Administração Estatal/ Núcleo de Desenvolvimento Administrativo.

Mueggler, Erik. 2001. *The Age of Wild Ghosts: Memory, Violence, and Place in Southwest China.* Berkeley and Los Angeles: University of California Press.

Munslow, Barry. 1983. *Mozambique: The Revolution and Its Origins.* London: Longman.

Murphy, Joseph M. 1988. *African Spirits in America.* Boston: Beacon Press.

Myers, Gregory W. 1994. Competitive Rights, Competitive Claims: Land Access in Postwar Mozambique. *Journal of Southern African Studies* 20 (4): 603–632.

Myers, Gregory W., and Harry G. West. 1993. Land Tenure Security and State Farm Divestiture in Mozambique: Case Studies in Nhamatanda, Manica and Montepuez Districts. Madison, WI: Land Tenure Center.

Nadel, S. F. 1970. Witchcraft in Four African Societies. In *Witchcraft and Sorcery,* edited by M. G. Marwick. Harmondsworth, UK: Penguin.

Nash, June. [1979] 1993. *We Eat the Mines and the Mines Eat Us: Dependency and Exploitation in Bolivian Tin Mines.* New York: Columbia University Press.

Nash, Manning. 1967. Witchcraft as Social Process in a Tzeltal Community. In *Magic,*

Witchcraft, and Curing, edited by J. Middleton. Garden City, NY: Published for the American Museum of Natural History, New York, by the Natural History Press.

Needham, Rodney. 1972. *Belief, Language, and Experience.* Oxford: Blackwell.

Negrão, José Guilherme. 1984. *A Produção e o Comércio nas Antigas Zonas Libertadas.* Maputo, Mozambique: Arquivo Histórico de Moçambique.

Neil-Tomlinson, Barry. 1977. The Nyassa Chartered Company: 1891–1929. *Journal of African History* 18 (1): 109–128.

Newitt, Malyn. 1995. *A History of Mozambique.* Bloomington: Indiana University Press.

Ngcongco, L. D. 1989. The Mfecane and the Rise of New African States. In *Africa in the Nineteenth Century until the 1880s,* edited by UNESCO International Scientific Committee for the Drafting of a General History of Africa. Oxford: Jordin Hill.

Nhancale, Orlando. 1996. *Autoridade Tradicional em Moçambique.* Brochura 5, *Normas, Regras e Justiça Tradicional: Como Evitar e Resolver Conflitos?* Maputo, Mozambique: Ministério da Administração Estatal/Núcleo de Desenvolvimento Administrativo.

Niehaus, Isak A. 1998. The ANC's Dilemma: The Symbolic Politics of Three Witch-Hunts in the South African Lowveld, 1990–1995. *African Studies Review* 41 (3): 93–118.

———. 2001. Witchcraft in the New South Africa: From Colonial Superstition to Post Colonial Reality? In *Magical Interpretations, Material Realities: Modernity, Witchcraft, and the Occult in Postcolonial Africa,* edited by H. L. Moore and T. Sanders. London and New York: Routledge.

Niehaus, Isak A., Eliazaar Mohlala, and Kally Shokane. 2001. *Witchcraft, Power and Politics.* London: Pluto Press.

Nitibaskara, Ronny. 1993. Observations on the Practice of Sorcery in Java. In *Understanding Witchcraft and Sorcery in Southeast Asia,* edited by C. W. Watson and R. Ellen. Honolulu: University of Hawaii Press.

Noormahomed, Abdul Razak. 1991. Evolution and Future of Health Care Policies and Systems in Mozambique since Independence. N.p.

Noormahomed, Abdul Razak, Antónia C. Cunha, António V. Sitoi, Herculano Bata, and Lucas Chomera Jeremias. 1990. *Evaluation of the Health System in Mozambique.* Maputo, Mozambique: Ministério de Saude.

Nordstrom, Carolyn. 1998. Terror Warfare and the Medicine of Peace. *Medical Anthropology Quarterly* 12 (1): 103–121.

Notícias. 1995a. Autoridade Tradicional Deve Participar na Gestão de Municípios. 24 April.

———. 1995b. Autoridade Tradicional Quer Cooperar com o Governo. 23 December.

———. 1995c. Envolver Autoridades Tradicionais na Resolução dos Problemas Locais. 22 March, 4.

———. 1995d. Poder Tradicional Constitui Matéria Bastante Delicada. 8 November.

———. 1996a. Administradores e Autoridade Tradicional em Inhambane Têm Bom Relacionamento. 5 September.

———. 1996b. Alguns Cidadãos Contestam Métodos do Régulo Local. 23 October.

———. 1996c. Governo Deve Repor a Autoridade Tradicional—Segundo Régulos Reunidos em Manica. 24 April.

———. 1996d. Governo Estuda Formas de Reinserção dos Regulados—Segundo o Ministro Gamito. 25 March.

———. 1996e. Pai de Dhlakama Dispõe-se a Colaborar com o Governo—Felisberto Tomás Acaba de Efectuar a sua Primeira Visita ao Regulado Deste. 2 December.

———. 1996f. População Pede Restituição da Autoridade Tradicional. 10 June.

———. 1996g. Régulos de Gorongosa Manifestam Desejo de Cooperar com Governo. 27 June.

———. 1996h. Régulos Poderão ser Subsidiados pelo Seu Trabalho—Projecto Vai Ser Canalizado ao Conselho de Ministros para Aprovação. 16 May.

———. 1996i. Sofala Vai Debater Funcionamento dos Régulos e GD's. 1 April.

———. 1997a. Autoridades Tradicionais Lutam pelo Poder na Província de Nampula. 2 June.

———. 1997b. Poder Tradicional Assume Justiça no Niassa. 22 January.

———. 1997c. Régulos Acusados de Molestar Populações. 16 July.

———. 1997d. Régulos Colaboram com Governo. 17 July.

———. 1997e. Régulos em Homoíne Acusados de Desobedecerem Autoridades. 18 July.

———. 1997f. Régulos Reclamam Fardamento, Bandeira e Outros Símbolos. 21 May.

Nyamnjoh, Francis. 2001. Delusions of Development and the Enrichment of Witchcraft Discourses in Cameroon. In *Magical Interpretations, Material Realities: Modernity, Witchcraft, and the Occult in Postcolonial Africa,* edited by H. L. Moore and T. Sanders. London and New York: Routledge.

Obbo, Christine. 1996. Healing, Cultural Fundamentalism and Syncretism in Buganda. *Africa* 66 (2): 183–201.

Oficina de História. 1984. *Situação Actual em Mueda.* Maputo, Mozambique: Centro de Estudos Africanos, Universidade Eduardo Mondlane.

———. 1986. *Poder Popular e Desagregação nas Aldeias Comunais do Planalto de Mueda.* Maputo, Mozambique: Centro de Estudos Africanos, Universidade Eduardo Mondlane.

Olivier de Sardan, Jean-Pierre. 1992. Occultism and the Ethnographic "I": The Exoticizing of Magic from Durkheim to "Postmodern" Anthropology. *Critique of Anthropology* 12 (1): 5–25.

Omer-Cooper, John D. 1966. *The Zulu Aftermath: A Nineteenth-Century Revolution in Bantu Africa.* London: Longmans.

O'Neil, R. J. 1991. Authority, Witchcraft, and Change in Old Moghamo. *Anthropos* 86:33–43.

O'Neill, Henry E. 1883. Journey in the District West of Cape Delgado Bay. *Proceedings of the Royal Geographical Society,* n.s., 5:393–404.

Opello, Walter C. 1974. Guerrilla War in Portuguese Africa: An Assessment of the Balance of Force in Mozambique. *Issue* 4 (2): 29–37.

———. 1975. Pluralism and Elite Conflict in an Independence Movement: FRELIMO in the 1960s. *Journal of Southern African Studies* 2 (1): 66–82.

Ortner, Sherry B. 1990. Patterns of History: Cultural Schemas in the Foundings of Sherpa Religious Institutions. In *Culture through Time: Anthropological Approaches*, edited by E. Ohnuki-Tierney. Stanford, CA: Stanford University Press.

Oyebola, D. D. O. 1986. National Medical Policies in Nigeria. In *The Professionalisation of African Medicine*, edited by M. Last and G. L. Chavunduka. Manchester, UK: International African Institute.

Palmié, Stephan. 2002. *Wizards and Scientists: Explorations in Afro-Cuban Modernity and Tradition*. Durham, NC: Duke University Press.

Parkin, David. 1982. *Semantic Anthropology*. New York: Academic Press.

Parsons, Elsie Clews. [1927] 1970. Witchcraft among the Pueblos: Indian or Spanish? In *Witchcraft and Sorcery*, edited by M. G. Marwick. Harmondsworth, UK: Penguin.

Pearce, Tola. 1986. Professional Interests and the Creation of Medical Knowledge in Nigeria. In *The Professionalisation of African Medicine*, edited by M. Last and G. L. Chavunduka. Manchester, UK: International African Institute.

Peek, Philip M. 1991. *African Divination Systems: Ways of Knowing*. African Systems of Thought. Bloomington: Indiana University Press.

Peel, John D. Y. 2000. *Religious Encounter and the Making of the Yoruba*. African Systems of Thought. Bloomington: Indiana University Press.

Peletz, Michael G. 1993. Knowledge, Power, and Personal Misfortune in a Malay Context. In *Understanding Witchcraft and Sorcery in Southeast Asia*, edited by C. W. Watson and R. Ellen. Honolulu: University of Hawaii Press.

Pélissier, René. 1994. *História de Moçambique: Formação e Oposição 1854–1918*. Vol. 2, *História de Portugal*. Lisbon: Editorial Estampa.

Pels, Peter. 1998. The Magic of Africa: Reflections on a Western Commonplace. *African Studies Review* 41 (3): 193–209.

———. 1999. *A Politics of Presence: Contacts between Missionaries and Waluguru in Late Colonial Tanganyika*. Studies in Anthropology and History 24. Amsterdam, Netherlands: Harwood Academic Publishers.

Penvenne, Jeanne. 1991. "We Are All Portuguese!": Challenging the Political Economy of Assimilation: Lourenço Marques, 1870–1933. In *The Creation of Tribalism in Southern Africa*, edited by L. Vail. Berkeley and Los Angeles: University of California Press.

People's Republic of Mozambique. [1975] 1990. The Constitution of the People's Republic of Mozambique. In *Constitutions of the Countries of the World*, edited by A. P. Blaustein and G. H. Flanz. Dobbs Ferry, NY: Oceana Publications.

Pereira, Edgar Nasi. 1998. *Mitos, Feitiços e Gente de Moçambique*. Lisbon: Caminho.

Pfeiffer, James. 2002. African Independent Churches in Mozambique: Healing the Afflictions of Inequality. *Medical Anthropology Quarterly* 16 (2): 176–199.

Pigg, Stacy Leigh. 1996. The Credible and the Credulous: The Question of "Villagers' Beliefs" in Nepal. *Cultural Anthropology* 11 (2): 160–201.

Piot, Charles. 1999. *Remotely Global: Village Modernity in West Africa*. Chicago: University of Chicago Press.

Pires, Capitão António J. 1924. *A Grande Guerra em Moçambique*. Oporto: Author.

Pitcher, M. Anne. 2002. *Transforming Mozambique: The Politics of Privatization, 1975–2000*. Cambridge: Cambridge University Press.

Pitt-Rivers, Julian. 1970. Spiritual Power in Central America. In *Witchcraft Confessions and Accusations*, edited by M. Douglas. London: Tavistock.

Plotkin, Mark J. 1993. *Tales of a Shaman's Apprentice: An Ethnobotanist Searches for New Medicines in the Amazon Rain Forest*. New York: Viking.

Prechtel, Martin. 1998. *Secrets of the Talking Jaguar: Memoirs from the Living Heart of a Mayan Village*. New York: Putnam.

———. 1999. *Long Life, Honey in the Heart: A Story of Initiation and Eloquence on the Shores of a Mayan Lake*. New York: Putnam.

Probst, Peter. 1999. Mchape '95; or, the Sudden Fame of Billy Goodson Chisupe: Healing, Social Memory and the Enigma of the Public Sphere in Post-Banda Malawi. *Africa* 69 (1): 108–138.

Purcell, Trevor, and Elizabeth Akinyi Onjoro. 2002. Indigenous Knowledge, Power and Parity: Models of Knowledge Integration. In *Participating in Development: Approaches to Indigenous Knowledge*, edited by P. Sillitoe, A. Bicker, and J. Pottier. London: Routledge.

Ranger, Terence O. 1969. The Movement of Ideas, 1850–1939. In *A History of Tanzania*, edited by I. N. Kimambo and A. J. Temu. Nairobi: East African Publishing House.

———. 1992. Godly Medicine: The Ambiguities of Medical Mission in Southeastern Tanzania, 1900–1945. In *The Social Basis of Health and Healing in Africa*, edited by S. Feierman and J. M. Janzen. Berkeley and Los Angeles: University of California Press.

Rasmussen, Susan. 2001a. Betrayal or Affirmation? Transformations in Witchcraft Technologies of Power, Danger and Agency among the Tuareg of Niger. In *Magical Interpretations, Material Realities: Modernity, Witchcraft, and the Occult in Postcolonial Africa*, edited by H. L. Moore and T. Sanders. London and New York: Routledge.

———. 2001b. *Healing in Community*. Westport, CT: Bergin and Garvey.

Redding, Sean. 1996. Government Witchcraft: Taxation, the Supernatural, and the Mpondo Revolt in the Transkei, South Africa, 1955–1963. *African Affairs* 95:555–579.

Redmayne, Alison. 1970. Chikanga: An African Diviner with an International Reputation. In *Witchcraft Confessions and Accusations*, edited by M. Douglas. London: Tavistock.

Reichel-Dolmatoff, Gerardo. 1975. *The Shaman and the Jaguar: A Study of Narcotic Drugs among the Indians of Colombia*. Philadelphia: Temple University Press.

Rekdal, Ole Bjørn. 1999. Cross-Cultural Healing in East African Ethnography. *Medical Anthropology Quarterly* 13 (4): 458–482.

Reynolds, Pamela. 1996. *Traditional Healers and Childhood in Zimbabwe*. Athens: Ohio University Press.

Richards, Audrey. [1935] 1970. A Modern Movement of Witch-Finders. In *Witchcraft and Sorcery*, edited by M. G. Marwick. Harmondsworth, UK: Penguin.

Rodman, William. 1993. Sorcery and the Silencing of Chiefs: "Words of the Wind" in Postindependence Ambae. *Journal of Anthropological Research* 49:217–235.

Roesch, Otto. 1992. RENAMO and the Peasantry in Southern Mozambique: A View from Gaza Province. *Canadian Journal of African Studies* 26 (3): 462–484.

Rosaldo, Michelle Z. 1980. *Knowledge and Passion: Ilongot Notions of Self and Social Life*. Cambridge: Cambridge University Press.

Rosenthal, Judy. 1998. *Possession, Ecstasy, and Law in Ewe Voodoo*. Charlottesville: University Press of Virginia.

Rouch, Jean. 1989. *La Religion et la Magie Songhay*. 2d ed. Brussels: Editions de l'Université de Bruxelles.

Ruel, Malcolm. 1969. *Leopards and Leaders*. London: Tavistock.

———. 1970a. Lions, Leopards and Rulers. *New Society* 15 (380): 54–56.

———. 1970b. Were-animals and the Introverted Witch. In *Witchcraft Confessions and Accusations*, edited by M. Douglas. London: Tavistock.

Sachs, Albie, and Gita Honwana Welch. 1990. *Liberating the Law: Creating Popular Justice in Mozambique*. London: Zed Books.

Sahlins, Marshall. 1993. Goodbye to *Tristes Tropes:* Ethnography in the Context of Modern World History. *Journal of Modern History*, no. 65:1–25.

Saler, Benson. 1967. Nagual, Witch, and Sorcerer in a Quiché Village. In *Magic, Witchcraft, and Curing*, edited by J. Middleton. Austin: University of Texas Press.

Sanders, Todd. 1999. Modernity, Wealth, and Witchcraft in Tanzania. *Research in Economic Anthropology* 20:117–131.

———. 2001. Save Our Skins: Structural Adjustment, Morality and the Occult in Tanzania. In *Magical Interpretations, Material Realities: Modernity, Witchcraft, and the Occult in Postcolonial Africa*, edited by H. L. Moore and T. Sanders. London and New York: Routledge.

———. 2003. Invisible Hands and Visible Goods: Revealed and Concealed Economies in Millennial Tanzania. In *Transparency and Conspiracy: Ethnographies of Suspicion in the New World Order*, edited by H. G. West and T. Sanders. Durham, NC: Duke University Press.

Sanders, Todd, and Harry G. West. 2003. Power Revealed and Concealed in the New World Order. In *Transparency and Conspiracy: Ethnographies of Suspicion in the New World Order*, edited by H. G. West and T. Sanders. Durham, NC: Duke University Press.

Saul, John S., ed. 1985. *A Difficult Road: The Transition to Socialism in Mozambique*. New York: Monthly Review Press.

———. 1993. *Recolonization and Resistance in Southern Africa in the 1990s.* Trenton: Africa World Press.

Savana. 1994. O "Imperador" Chissano em Campanha. 7 October, 1.

Schapera, Isaac. 1970. Sorcery and Witchcraft in Bechuanaland. In *Witchcraft and Sorcery,* edited by M. G. Marwick. Harmondsworth, UK: Penguin.

Schatzberg, Michael G. 1993. Power, Legitimacy and "Democratisation" in Africa. *Africa* 63 (4): 445–461.

Schmoll, Pamela G. 1993. Black Stomachs, Beautiful Stones: Soul-Eating among Hausa in Niger. In *Modernity and Its Malcontents: Ritual and Power in Postcolonial Africa,* edited by J. Comaroff and J. L. Comaroff. Chicago: University of Chicago Press.

Scott, James C. 1985. *Weapons of the Weak: Everyday Forms of Peasant Resistance.* New Haven, CT: Yale University Press.

———. 1998. *Seeing Like a State: How Certain Schemes to Improve the Human Condition Have Failed.* Yale Agrarian Studies. New Haven, CT: Yale University Press.

Semali, I. A. J. 1986. Associations and Healers: Attitudes towards Collaboration in Tanzania. In *The Professionalisation of African Medicine,* edited by M. Last and G. L. Chavunduka. Manchester, UK: International African Institute.

Serra, Carlos, ed. 1983. *História de Moçambique.* Vol. 2, *Agressão Imperialista (1886/1930).* Maputo, Mozambique: Departamento de História, Universidade Eduardo Mondlane.

———. 2003. *Cólera e Catarse.* Maputo, Mozambique: Imprensa Universitária, Universidade Eduardo Mondlane.

Shaw, Rosalind. 1996. The Politician and the Diviner: Divination and the Consumption of Power in Sierra Leone. *Journal of Religion in Africa* 26 (1): 30–55.

———. 1997. The Production of Witchcraft/Witchcraft as Production: Memory, Modernity, and the Slave Trade in Sierra Leone. *American Ethnologist* 24 (4): 856–876.

———. 2001. Cannibal Transformations: Colonialism and Commodification in the Sierra Leone Hinterland. In *Magical Interpretations, Material Realities: Modernity, Witchcraft, and the Occult in Postcolonial Africa,* edited by H. L. Moore and T. Sanders. London and New York: Routledge.

———. 2002. *Memories of the Slave Trade: Ritual and the Historical Imagination in Sierra Leone.* Chicago: University of Chicago Press.

Sheldon, Kathleen. 1998. "I Studied with the Nuns, Learning to Make Blouses": Gender Ideology and Colonial Education in Mozambique. *International Journal of African Historical Studies* 31 (3): 595–625.

Simmons, William Scranton. 1980. Powerlessness, Exploitation and the Soul-Eating Witch: An Analysis of Badyaranke Witchcraft. *American Ethnologist* 7 (3): 447–465.

Slaats, Herman, and Karen Portier. 1993. Sorcery and the Law in Modern Indonesia. In *Understanding Witchcraft and Sorcery in Southeast Asia,* edited by C. W. Watson and R. Ellen. Honolulu: University of Hawaii Press.

Smith, Wilfred Cantwell. 1977. *Belief and History.* Charlottesville: University Press of Virginia.

Stadler, Jonathan. 1996. Witches and Witch-Hunters: Witchcraft, Generational Relations and the Life Cycle in a Lowveld Village. *African Studies* 55 (1): 87–110.

Stephen, Michele. 1996. The Mekeo "Man of Sorrow": Sorcery and the Individuation of the Self. *American Ethnologist* 23 (1): 83–101.

Stewart, Pamela J., and Andrew Strathern. 2003. *Witchcraft, Sorcery, Rumors and Gossip.* Cambridge: Cambridge University Press.

Stoll, David. 1993. *Between Two Armies in the Ixil Towns of Guatemala.* New York: Columbia University Press.

Stoller, Paul. 1989. *Fusion of the Worlds: An Ethnography of Possession among the Songhay of Niger.* Chicago: University of Chicago Press.

———. 1995. *Embodying Colonial Memories: Spirit Possession, Power, and the Hauka in West Africa.* London: Routledge.

Stoller, Paul, and Cheryl Olkes. 1987. *In Sorcery's Shadow: A Memoir of Apprenticeship among the Songhay of Niger.* Chicago: University of Chicago Press.

Tait, D. 1963. A Sorcery Hunt in Dagomba. *Africa* 33 (2): 136–147.

Taussig, Michael. 1987. *Shaminism, Colonialism, and the Wildman: A Study in Terror and Healing.* Chicago: University of Chicago Press.

———. 1997. *The Magic of the State.* London: Routledge.

Técnica Engenheiros Consultores Lda. 1994. *Estudo de Combate à Erosão no Planalto de Mueda.* Maputo, Mozambique: Programa Nacional de Água Rural.

Thomson, Joseph. 1882. Notes on the Basin of the River Rovuma, East Africa. *Proceedings of the Royal Geographical Society and Monthly Record of Geography,* n.s., 4:65–79.

Todorov, Tzvetan. 1984. *Mikhail Bakhtin: The Dialogical Principle.* Translated by Wlad Godzich. Minneapolis: University of Minnesota Press.

Trindade, João Carlos. 2003. Rupturas e Continuidades nos Processos Políticos e Jurídicos. In *Conflito e Transformação Social: Uma Paisagem das Justiças em Moçambique,* edited by B. de Sousa Santos and J. C. Trindade. Oporto: Edições Afrontamento.

Turner, Victor Witter. [1957] 1996. *Schism and Continuity in an African Society: A Study of Ndembu Village Life.* Oxford: Berg.

———. 1964. Witchcraft and Sorcery: Taxonomy versus Dynamics. *Africa* 34 (4): 314–325.

———. 1968. *The Drums of Affliction: A Study of Religious Processes among the Ndembu of Zambia.* Oxford: Clarendon Press; London: International African Institute.

Twumasi, Patrick A., and Dennis Michael Warren. 1986. The Professionalisation of Indigenous Medicine: A Comparative Study of Ghana and Zambia. In *The Professionalisation of African Medicine,* edited by M. Last and G. L. Chavunduka. Manchester, UK: International African Institute.

UNICEF. 1981. *Mueda Plateau Water Project.* Maputo, Mozambique.

———. 1993. *Despite the Odds: A Collection of Case Studies on Development Projects in Mozambique.* Maputo, Mozambique: UNICEF.

US Department of State. 1984. *Country Report on Human Rights Practices.* Washington, DC: Government Printing Office.

Vail, Leroy. 1976. Mozambique's Chartered Companies: The Rule of the Feeble. *Journal of African History* 17 (3): 389–416.

Van Binsbergen, Wim. 1991. Becoming a Sangoma: Religious Anthropological Field-Work in Francistown, Botswana. *Journal of Religion in Africa* 21 (4): 309–344.

———. 2001. Witchcraft in Modern Africa as Virtualized Boundary Conditions of the Kinship Order. In *Witchcraft Dialogues: Anthropological and Philosophical Exchanges,* edited by G. C. Bond and D. M. Ciekawy. Athens: Ohio University Center for International Studies.

van der Geest, Sjaak. 1988. The Articulation of Formal and Informal Medicine Disattribution in South Cameroon. In *The Context of Medicines in Developing Countries,* edited by S. van der Geest and S. R. Whyte. Dordrecht: Kluwer Academic Publishers.

———. 1997. Is There a Role for Traditional Medicine in Basic Health Services in Africa? A Plea for a Community Perspective. *Tropical Medicine and International Health* 2 (9): 903–911.

van Dijk, Rijk. 1992. *Young Malawian Puritans: Young Born-Again Preachers in a Present-Day African Urban Environment.* Utrecht: ISOR.

———. 2001. Witchcraft and Scepticism by Proxy: Pentecostalism and Laughter in Urban Malawi. In *Magical Interpretations, Material Realities: Modernity, Witchcraft, and the Occult in Postcolonial Africa,* edited by H. L. Moore and T. Sanders. London and New York: Routledge.

van Dijk, Rijk, Ria Reis, and Marja Spierenburg. 2000. *The Quest for Fruition through Ngoma: The Political Aspects of Healing in Southern Africa.* Athens: Ohio University Press.

Vaughan, Megan. 1991. *Curing Their Ills: Colonial Power and African Illness.* Stanford, CA: Stanford University Press.

VeneKlasen, Lisa, and Harry G. West. 1996. *Mid-term Evaluation Report of the Africa-America Institute's Project for Democratic Development in Mozambique.* Maputo, Mozambique: USAID.

Verran, Helen. 2001. *Science and an African Logic.* Chicago: University of Chicago Press.

Vines, Alex. 1991. *RENAMO: Terrorism in Mozambique.* London: James Currey.

Voeks, Robert A. 1997. *Sacred Leaves of Candomblé: African Magic, Medicine, and Religion in Brazil.* 1st ed. Austin: University of Texas Press.

Wafer, James William. 1991. *The Taste of Blood: Spirit Possession in Brazilian Candomblé.* Contemporary Ethnography Series. Philadelphia: University of Pennsylvania Press.

Wagner, Roy. 1975. *The Invention of Culture.* Englewood Cliffs, NJ: Prentice-Hall.

Weinstein, Jeremy. 2002. Mozambique: A Fading Success Story. *Journal of Democracy* 13 (1): 141–156.

Werbner, Richard. 2001. Truth-on-Balance: Knowing the Opaque Other in Tswapong Wisdom Divination. In *Witchcraft Dialogues: Anthropological and Philosophical Exchanges*, edited by G. C. Bond and D. M. Ciekawy. Athens: Ohio University Center for International Studies.

West, Harry G. 1997a. Creative Destruction and Sorcery of Construction: Power, Hope, and Suspicion in Post-war Mozambique. *Cahiers d'Études Africaines* 37 (147): 675–698.

———. 1997b. Sorcery of Construction and Sorcery of Ruin: Power and Ambivalence on the Mueda Plateau, Mozambique (1882–1994). Ph.D. diss., University of Wisconsin.

———. 1998. "This Neighbor Is Not My Uncle!" Changing Relations of Power and Authority on the Mueda Plateau. *Journal of Southern African Studies* 24 (1): 141–160.

———. 2000. Girls with Guns: Narrating the Experience of War of FRELIMO's "Female Detachment." *Anthropological Quarterly* 73 (4): 180–194.

———. 2001. Sorcery of Construction and Socialist Modernization: Ways of Understanding Power in Post-colonial Mozambique. *American Ethnologist* 28 (1): 119–150.

———. 2003a. Voices Twice Silenced: Betrayal and Mourning at Colonialism's End in Mozambique. *Anthropological Theory* 3 (3): 339–361.

———. 2003b. "Who Rules Us Now?" Identity Tokens, Sorcery, and Other Metaphors in the 1994 Mozambican Elections. In *Transparency and Conspiracy: Ethnographies of Suspicion in the New World Order*, edited by H. G. West and T. Sanders. Durham, NC: Duke University Press.

———. 2004a. Inverting the Camel's Hump: Jorge Dias, His Wife, Their Interpreter, and I. In *Significant Others: Interpersonal and Professional Commitments in Anthropology*, edited by R. Handler. Madison: University of Wisconsin Press.

———. 2004b. Villains, Victims, or Makonde in the Making? Reading the Explorer, Henry O'Neill, and Listening to the Headman, Lishehe. *Ethnohistory* 51 (1): 1–43.

West, Harry G., and Scott Kloeck-Jenson. 1999. Betwixt and Between: "Traditional Authority" and Democratic Decentralization in Post-war Mozambique. *African Affairs* 98 (393): 455–484.

West, Harry G., and Gregory W. Myers. 1996. A Piece of Land in a Land of Peace? State Farm Divestiture in Mozambique. *Journal of Modern African Studies* 34 (1): 27–51.

West, Harry G., and Todd Sanders. 2003. *Transparency and Conspiracy: Ethnographies of Suspicion in the New World Order*. Durham, NC: Duke University Press.

West, Harry G., and Stacy Sharpes. 2002. Dealing with the Devil: Meaning and the Marketplace in Makonde Sculpture. *African Arts* 35 (3): 32–39, 90–91.

Wheeler, Douglas L. 1976. African Elements in Portugal's Armies in Africa (1961–1974). *Armed Forces and Society* 2 (2): 233–250.

White, Luise. 1994. Blood Brotherhood Revisited: Kinship, Relationship, and the Body in East and Central Africa. *Africa* 64 (3): 359–372.

———. 2000. *Speaking with Vampires: Rumor and History in Colonial Africa*. Berkeley and Los Angeles: University of California Press.

Whitehead, Neil L. 2002. *Dark Shamans: Kanaimà and the Poetics of Violent Death.* Durham, NC: Duke University Press.

Whyte, Susan Reynolds. 1982. Penicillin, Battery Acid, and Sacrifice: Cures and Causes in Nyole Medicine. *Social Science and Medicine* 16:2055–2064.

———. 1988. The Power of Medicines in East Africa. In *The Context of Medicines in Developing Countries: Studies in Pharmaceutical Anthropology,* edited by S. van der Geest and S. R. Whyte. Dordrecht: Kluwer Academic Publishers.

———. 1997. *Questioning Misfortune: The Pragmatics of Uncertainty in Eastern Uganda.* Cambridge: Cambridge University Press.

Whyte, Susan Reynolds, Sjaak van der Geest, and Anita Hardon. 2002. *Social Lives of Medicines.* Cambridge: Cambridge University Press.

Wild, Emma. 1998. "Is It Witchcraft? Is It Satan? It Is a Miracle": Mai-Mai Soldiers and Christian Concepts of Evil in North-East Congo. *Journal of Religion in Africa* 28 (4): 450–467.

Willis, Roy G. 1968. Kamcape: An Anti-sorcery Movement in South-West Tanzania. *Africa* 38:1–15.

———. 1970. The Kamcape Movement. In *Witchcraft and Sorcery,* edited by M. G. Marwick. Harmondsworth, UK: Penguin.

Willis, Roy G., and K. B. S. Chisanga. 1999. *Some Spirits Heal, Others Only Dance: A Journey into Human Selfhood in an African Village.* Oxford and New York: Berg.

Wilson, Ken B. 1992. Cults of Violence and Counter-Violence in Mozambique. *Journal of Southern African Studies* 18 (3): 527–582.

Wilson, Monica. [1951] 1970. Witch-Beliefs and Social Structure. In *Witchcraft and Sorcery,* edited by M. G. Marwick. Harmondsworth, UK: Penguin.

World Health Organization. 1978. *The Promotion and Development of Traditional Medicine: Report of a WHO Meeting.* Geneva: World Health Organization.

———. 1995. *Traditional Practitioners as Primary Health Care Workers.* Geneva: World Health Organization.

Worsley, Peter. 1968. *The Trumpet Shall Sound: A Study of "Cargo" Cults in Melanesia.* New York: Schocken Books.

Wyatt, A. W. 1950. The Lion Men of Singida. *Tanganyika Notes and Records* 28:3–9.

Wyllie, R. W. 1970. Introspective Witchcraft among the Effutu. In *Witchcraft and Sorcery,* edited by M. G. Marwick. Harmondsworth, UK: Penguin.

Yamba, C. B. 1997. Cosmologies in Turmoil: Witchfinding and AIDS in Chiawa, Zambia. *Africa* 67 (2): 200–223.

Young, Eric T. 1997. *N'angas, Varoyi,* and *Midzimu:* The Institutionalization of Traditional Beliefs in the Zimbabwe National Army. *Armed Forces and Society* 24 (2): 245–268.

Young, Tom. 1990. The MNR/RENAMO: External and Internal Dynamics. *African Affairs,* November, 491–509.

Index